Romantic Egypt

Romantic Egypt

Abyssal Ground of British Romanticism

Elizabeth A. Fay

LEXINGTON BOOKS
Lanham • Boulder • New York • London

Published by Lexington Books
An imprint of The Rowman & Littlefield Publishing Group, Inc.
4501 Forbes Boulevard, Suite 200, Lanham, Maryland 20706
www.rowman.com

6 Tinworth Street, London SE11 5AL, United Kingdom

Copyright © 2021 The Rowman & Littlefield Publishing Group, Inc.

All rights reserved. No part of this book may be reproduced in any form or by any electronic or mechanical means, including information storage and retrieval systems, without written permission from the publisher, except by a reviewer who may quote passages in a review.

British Library Cataloguing in Publication Information Available

Library of Congress Cataloging-in-Publication Data

Names: Fay, Elizabeth A., 1957- author.
Title: Romantic Egypt : abyssal ground of British romanticism / Elizabeth Fay.
Description: Lanham : Lexington Books, [2021] | Includes bibliographical references and index.
Identifiers: LCCN 2021002281 (print) | LCCN 2021002282 (ebook) |
  ISBN 9781793635679 (cloth) | ISBN 9781793635686 (epub)
  ISBN 9781793635693 (pbk)
Subjects: LCSH: Romanticism—Great Britain. | English literature—18th century—History and criticism. | English literature—19th century—History and criticism. | English literature—Egyptian influences. | Romanticism—Germany. | German literature—18th century—History and criticism. | German literature—19th century—History and criticism. | German literature—Egyptian influences. | Civilization, Ancient, in literature. | Egypt—In literature.
Classification: LCC PR447 .F39 2021 (print) | LCC PR447 (ebook) |
  DDC 820.9/145—dc23
LC record available at https://lccn.loc.gov/2021002281
LC ebook record available at https://lccn.loc.gov/2021002282

Romantic Egypt *is dedicated to my mother, Eleanor Marie Fox Fay, who realized a lifelong dream when she traveled with me to Egypt in January 2011, which was to be one of the last months of her life. Her greatest joy as an artist on that trip was to descend, however painfully, into a tomb in the Valley of the Kings and see for herself the vivid colors of tomb paintings whose hues seemed untouched by time.*

Contents

Introduction		ix
1	Prior Time	1
2	Geographica	41
3	Ruins: Monumentality, Rubble, and Cities of the Dead	87
4	Spirit Magic	131
5	Hieroglyphica	173
Appendix: Further Reading		215
Works Cited		219
Index		229
About the Author		237

Introduction

Ever since we have learned to gesticulate we have forgotten the art of pantomime, for the same reason that, with all of our fancy grammars, we no longer understand the symbols of the Egyptians. What the ancients said most forcefully they expressed not in words, but in signs; they did not say it, they showed it.[1]

Jean-Jacques Rousseau's nostalgia for the immediacy of Egyptian knowledge, the potency of its wisdom ("But the most vigorous speech is that in which the Sign has said everything before a single word is spoken"[2]) resonates with the longing of the western imagination to regain an intimacy with the enigma that is Ancient Egypt, "knowable" only through its signs. The lost culture and wisdom of this early empire held a fascination for the west because it represented a fruitful not-knowing, an imaginative and philosophically speculative space in which to hold what can be empirically known in balance with what can be thought. Egypt as a conceived space represents the possibility that all that can be thought is also real; in this sense it is the ground of thought for the west. But ground in a peculiar way, ground as the ungrounded, the subterranean or buried, ground as potentiation. Egypt before the west existed as such served, then, as both an abyssal time and a fulcrum between historically grounded knowing and the archaic or abyssal ground of not-knowing. And it is this movement back and forth between the unknowable and "knowledge," present in relation to Egypt on and off throughout western intellectual history, resurfacing during the Enlightenment, and fully embraced in the Romantic period even in material culture and architectural style, that solidified Romanticism's restless querying of the power of the imagination to influence both the present and the future. My argument, then, includes the claim that imagining Ancient Egypt was fundamental to the development of Romanticism as a major intellectual and artistic movement.

My project did not start with that premise: it was initiated the moment I read with wonder that Princess Charlotte Augusta's funerary procession included the ritual carrying of discrete, covered vessels (like Egyptian canopic jars) after the hearse carriage; each vessel contained a different bodily organ, as if the royal family were enacting Ancient Egyptian burial rites performed for a king. If the description of the procession of vessels is apocryphal, the fact that the whole nation mourned Charlotte—resulting in linen-drapers running out of black cloth for mourning armbands, the shops all being closed for two weeks, business and trade in general shut down (from the Royal Exchange to the docks, and including the courts of law and even gambling dens)—certainly invites comparison with Ancient Egyptian practices surrounding the death of the pharaoh. It seems to me that despite the usual claim that Britain's interest in Ancient Egypt stemmed from Napoleon's Egyptian Campaign, the foundations of this interest were both more historically laid, and more integral to British polity and its imagining. The sudden acquisition of both factual knowledge about, and artifacts of the remains of this ancient culture—held during the Classical Age to be foundational to western culture—only supported and reified traditional reliance on Ancient Egypt as a holding place for where western culture and state religion came together. As if to embody this holding place, an obelisk was erected by a Liberal MP on his estate grounds to commemorate Charlotte's death. Despite political difference, and the loss of the royal heir, the foundation stands firm.

We can look farther back than Plato for how long the west has considered Egypt a foundational ground, as well as progenitor of thought and art. But his Grecian desire to reconstitute Egyptian as predecessor cultural spirit makes him a key figure in this heritage; his inclusion of Egypt's antecedence in the *Timaeus*, which spells out the Platonic origin myth and which was essential reading for some of the most influential Romantic thinkers, solidified the association of priority and Egypt in Romantic thought. Plato is rehearsing Greek admiration for Ancient Egypt in the *Timaeus*, which was echoed in works by Plutarch, Herodotus, and Aeschylus; it is this valorization that spurred Martin Bernal's theory of Greece in his 1987 *Black Athena* as colonized by Egyptians and Phoenicians, and those cultures as the true predecessors of western civilization. *Black Athena* is a polemical work that caused controversy for a number of years and is worth mentioning for its recent revival of the Romantic fervor for Ancient Egypt as archaic ground. The sixteenth-century Dominican philosopher and astronomer Giordano Bruno, another important philosopher for the Romantic reception of Egypt, created a Christian cosmogony overlain with what he termed "Egyptianism," which arose from his adherence to the westernized understanding of the Egyptian god Thoth. His "Egyptianism," pantheism, belief in the transmigration of souls and other anti-Vatican theories were heresies that ended in his Vatican trial and execution in 1600. But before that he taught and spread his theories in Paris, Lyons, and London, where he was celebrated. Both a scientist and a Renaissance Hermetic occultist, Bruno fascinated Romantic-period thinkers like F. W. J. Schelling. But less obvious adherents to Egypt's allure populate western intellectual history; Gottfried Leibniz's theory of the monad, for instance, expresses the potential at the convergence of limits; pyramids and obelisks embody this mathematical concept. Curiously, Leibniz's first salaried position was in Nuremberg was as secretary to an alchemical society; alchemical symbols were drawn from Egyptian symbols and associated with Hermetic beliefs, both resonating in Leibniz's monist views of the cosmos; as with alchemists, Leibniz's rationalist mathematics had symbolic alliance with Egyptiana. No less does the Jewish intellectual heritage of dislocation as represented by Moses' Egyptianism represent the status of Ancient Egypt as simultaneously alienating and grounding.[3] Even Cook's Victorian steamer tours of the Nile and Wallis Budge's popular histories of Ancient Egypt in the nineteenth century, no less than Rider Haggard's *She*, respond to the same longing to recoup Egyptianism as *the* kernel in which to locate an embalmed essence, an absent presence whose access has been lost but whose vital spirit survives even yet.

The idea of a kernel evokes the great pyramids at Giza, most obviously in the grain thought in medieval times to be stored there. But the kernel was thought by G. W. Hegel to be a crystal of becoming-spirit that he associates with the Giza pyramids in his aesthetic theory; a centuries-long belief that the pyramids sit over subterranean labyrinths was revived by the Freemasons and encrypted into their initiation rites in a variation on the kernel as essence. The great pyramids do not, however, sit over labyrinths, although some of the cult temples do have underground labyrinths where ritually sacrificed and mummified sacred animals were buried, or where, as in the Serapeum at Saqqara, the apis bulls as embodiments of the god were buried. Pyramid interiors do have a labyrinth-like system of actual and false passages, but it is the architecture of the lesser burial sites either with mastabas or small pyramids that have labyrinthine substructures of hallways, ceremonial rooms, and storage and burial rooms. All of these determined forms with their precise meanings and functions operate as signs resembling each other, however, so that the great pyramids sitting over labyrinths became the Renaissance image of Egyptian mystery. The magically induced afterlife, and the labyrinth in which such miracles occurred, were both symbolized by the pyramid.

Hegel's crystal, with its evocation of the king's mummy, provides a Romantic conception of that sign. Hegel had the advantage of Richard Pococke's 1754 rendering of the interior of the Great Pyramid of Cheops (or Khufu), and so knew that most of the labyrinth was housed in the pyramid itself, and led inexorably upward until the sarcophagus chamber could be understood from Pococke's drawing to sit directly under the pyramid's triangulated top point. Like everyone else, Hegel would have understood that this was a celestial triangulation (pyramids were, with some exceptions, built on an east-west axis), not for the reasons archaeologists hold today, but because it was known that Ancient Egyptian priests had conducted their astronomical and astrological research atop the main temples, and it was believed the pyramids had a similar scientific and religious purpose. Hegel would not have known of the archaeological interior of earlier royal pyramids at Saqqara (known for its Step Pyramid of Djoser, not excavated until the twentieth century), also located near present-day Cairo; both Saqqara and then Giza served as the royal cemeteries or necropolises of ancient Memphis (and just as for the necropolis for ancient Thebes—now modern Luxor—were located across the Nile on the west bank). But none of this would have mattered to either a Romantic-period philosopher or to Europe in general during the late eighteenth and early nineteenth century. As for British Romantic literary artists fascinated by Ancient Egypt, the pyramids and necropolises represented a way to figure the sublime, life-in-death, prophetic visions, and a relation to death that was fascinatingly alien to Judeo-Christian orthodoxies. Its hieroglyphic script figured powerfully mystical symbols, illegibility, and hidden knowledge. Romantic-period material culture was much given to inventing hieroglyphs in the decorative arts, or inventing translations from actual hieroglyphs copied from obelisks, in a kind of making real what can't be known. Largely speaking then, the west had long been concerned not with Ancient Egypt's history but with its representativeness as the spiritual kernel of western culture.

Yet Ancient Egypt was also eastern, and not just in its overlay of influences even in ancient times from Mesopotamia, Persia, and what is now northern Turkey. It was eastern in its obscurity, its incomprehensibility, even as it was western in providing an origin story for Greek culture (resumed in Shakespeare's Cleopatra), as well as for a Jewish self-identity in diaspora. The spiritual—and cultural—kernel that Ancient Egypt symbolized resulted from this hybrid east-west identity in its straddling of the divide traditionally conceived after the fall of the Roman Empire as what set off the Orient from the Occident. If neither Ancient Greece nor Rome thought in these terms, Egypt was considered by them to at least hover over the entrance to the east; certainly Alexander thought conquering Egypt was an essential step to his progress toward India, and Greek traders in Alexandria after Alexander's death treated the Egyptian Delta as an east-west meeting ground. Egypt's importance throughout the Middle Ages was for its strategic positioning at the entrance to the Silk Route, and the fact that Ancient Egypt itself had looked no further east than its immediate neighbors—gold, gems, and luxury goods were easily enough obtained from African traders as well as those cultures encircling the Asiatic Sea—was erased in favor of a more potent story of imperial reach. Yes, what was preserved in the Romantic period was little more than the ruins of monumental stone forms, the biblical account of Moses in Egypt, and the occasional mummy brought back to Europe to be put on display. Mummies were easily uncovered in the late-period Greco-Roman cemeteries with their shallow graves, mummification being a Hellenic borrowing of Egyptian practices for those residing there. Thus, even the mummies circulating Europe were mere ruins, as nonrepresentative of actual Ancient Egyptian culture as were the monumental ruins and biblical histories.

It is this westernized version of Egypt that fueled the Romantic imagination. Archaeology was beginning its transformation into a science during the last years of the period, enough so that artifacts could be accurately measured and depicted in exquisitely rendered drawings such as those produced by Napoleon's Commission des Sciences et Arts d'Égypte in the famous *Descriptions de l'Égypte*, published between 1809 and 1829.[4] Even so, it was the mythical import of Ancient Egypt rather than its anthropological facts that attracted the west. Hegel is symptomatic in locating an origin point in Egypt for his lectures on aesthetic philosophy; symptomatic, too, was his restriction of aesthetic concerns to Egyptian architecture and other monumental stone objects such as colossal statues, reserving any real discussion of sculptural excellence for Ancient Greek art, since neither architecture nor colossi displayed what he viewed as the appropriate aesthetic elements. Their status for him was as antecedent rather than as achievement in and of itself. But it is Hegel's understanding of Egyptianness as entombed spirit, as walled off and inaccessible rather than buried, that is representative of his age. Unlike Leibniz, whose classical theory of a world replete with monads harmoniously rising and falling cannot account for the rise and fall of cultures, Hegel's teleological aesthetics is utterly Romantic in its treatment of art as a history of spirit. The Romantics, perhaps searching for a ground for thought other than the empiricism of the Enlightenment, resuscitated Egypt's emblematic otherness for the western imaginary in a way that we still feel today. Ancient Egypt is more than the fabulous museum displays of artifacts through which most of the west has come to know it; the Romantics knew this and sought to represent its importance as a kind of grounding obscurity for the production of philosophical ideas and artistic creation.

I. ENCOUNTERING EGYPT

The decoding of hieroglyphic inscriptions and papyrus remnants had occupied scholars such as the brilliant Athanasius Kircher well before Romantic interest in ancient scripts took hold of the popular imagination. Many historical periods, eastern and western, were interested in Egypt, from Cambyses II and Alexander the Great, to the Ottoman sultanate and Napoleon Bonaparte, and in this sense the Romantic period's interest in Egypt was not just speculative history but also mercantile, and therefore political since trade was the main business of British ambassadors abroad. Europeans were in Egypt because it was the fastest land route to India as well as to the Silk Route, and Ancient Egyptian artifacts were a by-product of British, French, and German interests in exploiting Ottoman disregard for a relatively unimportant part of their empire. Napoleon started the Egyptian Campaign for two reasons: the more important was to disrupt British colonial communication and trade with South Asia through the East India Company; of lesser importance was wresting Egypt from Ottoman control. But European diplomats such as Henry Salt were in Egypt well before Napoleon set his sights on it, unearthing archaeological treasures as a pastime and self-enrichment scheme while conducting his ambassadorial duties of encouraging trade and protecting British subjects on Egyptian soil.

Romantic travelers and Romantic readers, then, encountered two Egypts: the contemporary, Islamic protectorate of the Ottoman Empire, and the buried, ruinous, but sometimes vicariously exposed and always mysterious remains of Ancient Egypt. Although the figures that walk through the following chapters either encountered Ottoman Egypt on the ground or contemporary accounts and visual representations of it, what is underground intruded on and organized their experience. The labyrinth as a sign of Egyptian mystery continued to function as a trope for all half-buried ruins; each one read as a remnant of the culture's supposed highest goal of ensuring life after death. As such, Ancient Egypt represented an entirety, not a fragmented past where parts could be at least known. Its remains were both physical—in the sense of stone ruins and bodily ruins, monuments and mummies, hieroglyphs and burial items—and figurative—in the sense of highly biased historical records left by other cultures such as Greece and Persia, biblical accounts, and literary and artistic references to the Hellenistic worship of the Egyptian goddess Isis through the known world. Freemason rituals only encouraged occultist interpretations of these remains, as did the artistic assimilation of Egyptianism in interior décor and material objects, encouraged by the associated revivalisms of ancient cultures such as Ancient Greece as Hellenism, the French Republic's revival of Roman Republican values and ideals, and the Chinoiserie movement.

Egyptian remains, ruinous and partial as they are, suggested to those interested in real and imagined borders between west and east that Ancient Egypt was holistically recoverable as a conceptual entity that embodied their meeting point as both east and west. Unlike more forgotten cultures such as those of Asia Minor, whose frustratingly fragmentary and unrecognizable remains sometimes surfaced (the discovery of cuneiform tablets at Nineveh in 1849, for instance), Ancient Egypt culture was imagined as a discoverable whole. That whole, shrouded in mystery, might ultimately be irrecoverable but at its core it was imaginable.

II. TRANSLATION AND THE PROBLEM OF EGYPT

Understanding Egypt, both as a contemporaneous phenomenon and as an incomprehensibly ancient one, required translation into western cultural and religious belief systems, conceptual apparatus, intellectual traditions, and historical schema. The same requirement was applied to Ancient India, Ancient China, and a need driven by new geological discoveries to scientifically justify biblical accounts of the age of the earth. Translation in this period, with its faltering understanding of colonial rule and the translation, mitigation, and transplantation of cultures, and with its continued engagement with the Enlightenment project of translating ancient languages and thus ancient mentalities, essentially took on the character of ethnography. Languages were the key to understanding cultures, while even contemporary ethnographic observation could provide translative clues to ancient practices; the land's topography itself was translational, bringing to ground the antique culture and kind of people now interred in it. In some sense *Romantic Egypt* is a study of translation, or rather of translation effects, which is to say, it is a study of the quest for the beforeness that is before the origin of history and culture in western terms. Ancient Egypt is the ground of that beforeness, already lost in the time before dynastic Egypt began. Poets were particularly keen to contemplate ancient cultures in the vein of Volney's introductory dream vision in *Ruins of Empires*, with Egypt as emblematic of the human inability to overcome mortality, even when monumental structures and elaborate ceremonies are used to fend off the inevitability of dust and rubble. If Volney's vision concerns human vanity, Hegel takes Egypt to represent historical man as a work in progress, a step along the way in the history of spirit. But others, such as William Wordsworth, Hegel's exact contemporary, took Egypt in its biblical dimension, viewing it as apocalyptic and therefore both a vain ruinousness and a spiritual embodiment at once: a spiritual ruin. This, too, is a translation of Egypt into western terms.

Wordsworth's engagement with Egypt, slight though it is, can be found in his treatment of the apocalypse in Book VI of *The Prelude* (1805), but a less obvious yet more powerful locus in this epical work is a site of translation in which vestigial echoes of inspirited inscription and transcription appear: the "Dream of the Arab" section of Book V of *The Prelude*, in which the narrative shifts to a dream vision not dissimilar to that initiating Volney's *Ruins of Empire*. Wordsworth's poet-dreamer, however, is envisioning the ruins of prior epistemes, specifically that of the Greco-Alexandrian epistemology represented by Ptolemy, Aristotle, and Euclid; that of the Medieval episteme represented by the Arabian reclamation of Greco-Alexandrian learning; the Renaissance episteme, with its conservation of Alexandrian learning as Hermetic, occulted, symbolic, apocalyptic, with perhaps Spinoza's philosophical use of Euclid in his metaphysics lurking there as well. Suggestively, the Enlightenment episteme is also possibly threatened by the sands (or waters) of time by virtue of an engulfing tide of erasure that menaces not just Enlightenment thought but all that it conserves of the past, including Aristotelian and Euclidian thought. Doubling back on this bifocal reading—that of ruinous erasure and that of liberatory poetic knowledge the past still holds—is a fear haunting the dream as a whole, which is the problem of a origin, which is the problem of Egypt. Romanticism characteristically looks back in order to look forward: Hölderlin looked to Greek myth and culture, Novalis looked to Egyptian culture and ritual as well; Freemasons incorporated Egyptian symbols and what they believed to be Egyptian religious rituals into their initiation rites in order to promulgate democratic political thought; Percy Shelley looked to Greek literature for his epic on a future liberatory politics, *Prometheus Unbound*. Examples are endless, and the more typical resort to a Greco-Roman heritage in literary, philosophical, and political works cannot disguise the presence of an enduring interest in an even earlier Egyptian origination point, as Keats's *Hyperion* fragments make clear. And as Wordsworth's dream vision indicates, to think Egypt is to consider the shifting sands of erasure and possibility, of an archaic and unreconstructable past *and* a futurity yet to be imagined.

Romantic Egypt explores the shifting sands of an Egypt that had already been made Romantic even before the Enlightenment was properly conceived. My overarching metaphor for coming at this shifting terrain is what I am calling "The Alexandrian Dream," based on Ptolemy I's dream of matching Alexander the Great's terrestrial empire with an empire of knowledge, a cosmic empire based in Egypt's new capital, Alexandria. To consider this unorthodox history I require multiple ways into that history and its cosmology as it influenced Romanticism in Britain and Germany; the first and foremost is to use the term "metaphysical Egypt" to denominate an Egypt that is otherwise and elsewhere: that which is always prior and serves as an originary vortex, an abyss that is yet a starting point.

In the way I have been describing it so far, Romantic translation is a suturing of fragments within a larger recursive project, the philological effort to restore lost languages, cultures, knowledges, and histories to life. The key to all ancient writing systems was thought to be a common root;[5] the unlocking of one mystery would sever the knot. The Romantic act of translation, most particularly in the writing systems of Ancient Egypt, rehearses a similar logic, that is, to recursively align origin with afterness, and memory with futurity,[6] employing the scientificism inherent in world-enabling or systematizing projects (aligned as they necessarily are with imperial aims) which always serves to cover over what was different, unassimilable, and only metaphysically available. Unsurprisingly, perhaps because such a project is always escaping from the historical, it is unable to leave an Egypt that is elsewhere. Alexandrian, Renaissance, Enlightenment, and Romantic projects cannot displace a "metaphysical" Egypt precisely because an Egypt that is always otherwise resists the geopolitics of empire by inhabiting its monumentality rather than its physical placement, figuring itself through its pyramids, obelisks, colossi, and very antiquity, as an opaque and predetermined ruin.

The tropes I am using to make sense of historical and conceptual connections, always contingent despite their different registers, include metaphysical Egypt as the Egypt that is prior and elsewhere, and so an Egypt that figures beforeness by necessity connected to "afterness"; Romantic Egypt as a specific version of Ancient Egypt in the western imaginary; "spirit" or presence as grounded in Nature as Isis or the-all-in-one, and as related to a certain kind of magic associated with phenomenological nature supposed to have been invented by Isis, the great magician;[7] and finally translation as self-reorganization and the compulsion of translative effects.

In Romantic Egypt, which is textured by this set of figures, a dual understanding of knowledges, one celestial and the other terrestrial, was always at work, its seeds being sown even before the demise of dynastic Egypt, and strongly influencing Romantic-period reception of that ancient culture. This conception is not at odds with contemporary comprehensions of an orientalized, Ottoman Egypt as a focal point for the period's geopolitical desire among competing western nations to gain a faster route to the east; instead, it functions as its other, an alternative understanding that underlies, abuts, and jostles with the Egypt on the ground. The speculative, imaginative Egypt has several sources that derive from three early points of contact important to western culture's understanding of itself, all of which overwrote a culture so prior to Greco-Roman control of the Mediterranean and Levant as to be already a ghost culture by the time Alexander set foot on the Nile delta: these are (1) the biblical account of Egypt's own empire as experienced by both Moses and Joseph; (2) the monumental remains of dynastic regimes stretching from well before the height of Egypt's power up to Alexander the Great's conquest of Egypt; and (3) the legacy of the Alexandrian Museum, best known now for its great Library and for the intellectual empire this continues to represent. All of these main points of western contact involve memory, forgetting, pastness, and translation, and are how the western philosophical and literary imagination understood—and why it so incompletely metabolized—the symbolic value of Egyptian monumentality as both monumental ruins and its ancient civilization as a totality. These ancient forms generated a productive belief in a mysterious wisdom that encodes presence, voice, and Being coincident with the monumental ruins and their hieroglyphic inscriptions. There is therefore a necessary relation between monumentality as an entombment of spirit that is also spirit's promissory note, and the quest for that which resides in the hieroglyph's invocative power as resonant, magical symbol—the writing of which produced a symbolic field used by Egyptian priests to call down the gods into their representative statues, to *inspirit*. The relation between monumentality and hieroglyphics, then, lies in an archaic and naturalized relation of inscription being understood as an algebraic medium, a translation of the relation that encrypts it. Therefore, it is not the case that either the monumental or the hieroglyph functions as an incomprehensibility in and of itself, that is, as a residue that blocks or closes down meaning, but rather, the reverse. Hermeticism reinstantiates the hieroglyph's powerful symbolic force that it had held during the Egyptian dynasties by revising and restoring the Alexandrian god Hermes Trismegistus as magician-author of the Hermetic Corpus. Rediscovered during the Renaissance, these texts were used to create theological histories that translated past ages into the stages of the revealed world of God. The hieroglyphs, used to represent Hermetic knowledge, are thus reocculted, and it is this Hermetic occultation that is the precedence for Romantic Egypt.

III. NOT-KNOWING

Not-knowing Egypt is a contested territory. Traditionally the earliest information about Egypt was from Classical-period travel accounts such as those by Herodotus. A Romantic-period contemporary, the historian and scholar Al-Jabartai offers a similarly alien view in the sense that to be Muslim in Egypt, albeit Ottoman Egypt, is to still not be native to the land, for those with lineages back to antiquity occupied the very lowest ranks of society during Ottoman occupation. Herodotus traveled little beyond Alexandria, and gathered his information from priests who could no longer read hieroglyphic script, and therefore had no knowledge of the Kings' Lists, the battles recorded on temple and tomb walls, and other records of dynastic Egypt. Even the history by Ptolemaic-period Egyptian priest and scholar Manetho was not consulted; Herodotus preferred oral histories by different cult priests that he could compare for his information. The myths Herodotus was told in lieu of veritable practices and histories were what he in turn reported as verities. Al-Jabartai, by contrast, is uninterested in the Egypt before Ottoman rule, and his multivolume tome on Egyptian history concerns the four centuries of Ottoman rule but nothing prior.[8] Egyptian history as such is an alien one, fictionalized or repressed by historians unable to access historical documentation or uninterested in it. But both Herodotus's and Al-Jabartai's histories are all that was available, and in Al-Jabartai's case still is, of the periods in questions: Alexandrian knowledge of Ancient Egypt and Romantic-period knowledge of Ottoman Egypt. In this way, by focusing on Egypt itself, Al-Jabartai avoids joining the ranks of works such as *The Travels of Mirza Abu Taleb Khan*, works that focus an outsider's critical eye on western practices, foibles, and prejudices (in this case, that of Georgian England). And precisely by ignoring Egypt's past, he provides a contemporary ethnography of Romantic-period Egypt that thereby escapes Egyptian Romanticism.[9]

Herodotus documented the myths and legends told to him by priests, often presenting anecdotes as history; likewise, he traveled to few important monuments that even in his day were in ruins, but he rendered those visited by a mixture of fact and fiction. For instance, at Memphis the priests of "Vulcan" told him "that the first man who ruled over Egypt was Min, and that in his time all Egypt, except the Thebaic canton, was a marsh, none of the land below Lake Moeris then showing itself above the surface of the water. This is a distance of seven days' sail from the sea up the river." Likewise, Egyptians are "religious to excess, far beyond any other race of men."[10] Al-Jabartai similarly provides an ethnographic overview of Egypt and Cairene society, both historians rendering fact and hearsay much in the same style as Romantic-era British travelers to Egypt who also write ethnographically and, like these historians, include information concerning the political structure, caste structure, social patterns of engagement, military preparedness, culturally enforced gender distinctions, food supply, and trade. Both historians were also biased: Herodotus, born in Halicarnassus in the Persian Empire, treats the older Egyptian culture as superstitious and less sophisticated than the Greeks; Al-Jabartai is proudly Cairene but under Ottoman rule. For instance, he writes that during his childhood, "the people of Cairo had customs and habits pertaining to generosity not to be found anywhere else.... They had various customs and expressions of charity connected with such religious festivals," so that "At every (amir's) house many poor people would gather, and they would receive bread and eat until satisfied with milk and sweet puddings. Afterwards, money would be distributed."[11] In both accounts Ancient Egypt is buried, overwritten by the colonizing cultures of Alexandrian Greeks and Ottoman Turks, and its ancient culture revised by Hellenistic and Persian ones. In considering how Egypt's antiquity prior to Alexandrian conquest has been told by those unfamiliar with that pastness, it becomes clear that the role Egypt has held in the western imaginary as a speculative space and a room for imaginative thought—a *chora* of becoming—has been in place since Alexandria's displacement of Thebes and Memphis as the cities from which Egypt was ruled.

In the chapters that follow, the first chapter, "Prior Time," explores Egypt as archaic ground, as the emanating site of ancient wisdom later to be encrypted by Hermeticism. The Alexandrian Library weds Egyptian learning and wisdom with Greek philosophical endeavor to produce the doubled strain of western linguistic decipherment of ancient scripts with theological speculation. I discuss the material effects of Egyptian ruins in terms of the monumental but also the artifacts brought back to Europe, and especially to England; these are cultural remains that reinforced the west's perception of Ancient Egypt as the burial ground of an originary moment in the history of civilization, a perception that realized materially the conceptual understanding of Ancient Egypt as originary in terms of the history of spirit and of language. Kant's *Critique of Judgment*, Schelling's *Bruno*, Volney's *Ruins*, and a brief survey of British writers demonstrate that these attitudes toward Ancient Egypt were still firmly in place in the Romantic period.

Chapter 2, "Geographica" focuses on the phenomenon of the Alexandrian Library and its place in the intellectual history of the west, as well as its role in the west's belief in the power of a depository of knowledge and of the archive as the grounding of knowledge. This belief, fueled by the bibliomania of the early Ptolemaic pharaohs following Alexander's conquest and by similar archival accumulation elsewhere in the Hellenic Mediterranean, has made the Alexandrian Library a ghost memory or trace of the heritage, both philosophical and occulted, of western metaphysics. The Alexandrian Library tropes the human desire for an encyclopedic account of the ways in which the celestial and terrestrial map onto each other both phenomenally and spiritually. I explore the encyclopedic imagination or "geographica" that this trace and trope reinforces, producing such different accounts as Volney's vision of ancient civilizations in *Ruins; or, Meditations on the Ruins of Empire* and Schelling's *Ages of the World*. I also discuss Ali Ibn Yusuf al-Qifti's *Ta'rikh al-hukama'* (*History of Learned Men*) in order to understand Egyptian Ottoman scholars' attitudes toward the Alexandrian Library, and the great loss the library's final destruction caused them. Key sections of the chapter are devoted to Mary Shelley's Egyptian imagining in *The Last Man*, William Blake's illuminated books, the development of art history and Hegel's treatment in the *Aesthetics* of an Egyptian beginning to that encyclopedic imagining, and John Keats's aestheticized poetic treatment of the Egyptianism hovering behind the Grecian world in the *Hyperion* fragments.

Chapter 3, "Ruins," treats the Ancient Egyptian remainder. If ruins are what is left of that lost civilization, they nevertheless embody spirit and, particularly in the necropolises and pyramids, locate the places of the dead. This is the site, literally, of Hegel's negative, which can be read into the west's contemplation of Egyptian ruins. The Ancient Egyptian belief in a material afterlife and the western conception of soul sleep come together in the contemplation of ruins. This is the force of a section on Wordsworth's Lucy poems, as well as Percy Bysshe Shelley's *Alastor*. Shelley's Egyptian sonnet "Ozymandias," however, follows the tradition popularized by Volney's *Ruins* of ruins as a meditation on empire. The sonnet provokes a confrontation between Romantic critiques of empire and historical confusion as to the identity and monumental remains of the colossi of Shelley's imagined Egypt. The chapter ends with the treatment of the necropolis as a site of necropolitics as read through a contemporary travelogue by C. Rochefort Scott, *Rambles in Egypt and Candia* (providing a contrary perspective to that offered by Al-Jabartai's *Chronicle of the French Occupation 1798*, discussed above).

The first three chapters are largely focused on history and Romantic-era literary interpolations of the historical imaginary attached to it. The last two chapters are organized by a concern with language and its correlation to things on the ground, and the contemplation of them as both phenomenal and as inspirited. Chapter 4, "Spirit Magic," therefore focuses on the occultation of Ancient Egypt beginning with Plato's *Timaeus*. That work provides the concept of the *chora*, which when Egyptianized and Hermeticized becomes a dark center that generates philosophical unease as well as conceptual innovation. I return to Schelling's *Ages of the World* briefly in order to investigate the different accounts of origination in his *Treatise on the Essence of Human Freedom*, and then move to a work of his earlier nature philosophy, *Bruno, or On the Natural and Divine Principle of Things*. This work provides a lens for understanding Schelling's occultation via Bruno's "Egyptianism" of creative space as the dark center of Ancient Egyptian magic, with its ability to restore life and light to the dead. I explore this element in Novalis's *Novices of Saïs* and Keats's *Lamia* as well.

Chapter 5, "Hieroglyphica," examines the prevalent conception of language as a writing system originating in hieroglyphics. I begin with the mind-language associations in western philosophy that accrued both a kind of magical thinking associated with Egyptian hieroglyphs, and a scientific approach to their decryption that eventuated in Champollion's deciphering of the Egyptian writing system. The mainstay of the chapter is devoted to the case study of an amateur Orientalist and linguist, William Hook Morley, who at the end of his life was also the first librarian of the Royal Asiatic Society. Morley's interest in the three Egyptian writing systems, and his attempt to decipher the everyday demotic system, in combination with his romanticized Orientalism makes him a model of late-Romantic Alexandrianism.

NOTES

1. Rousseau, *The First and Second Discourses together with the Replies to Critics and Essay on the Origin of Language*, 241.
2. Ibid.
3. See Yates, *Giordano Bruno and the Hermetic Tradition*; Deleuze, *The Fold: Leibniz and the Baroque*, translated by Tom Conley; Assmann, *Moses the Egyptian*; Sloterdjik, *Derrida, An Egyptian*. Plato describes the role of Egyptianism in the Greek imaginary in the *Timaeus*.
4. Néret, ed., *Description de l'Egypte*. See also Strathern's account of the Egyptian Campaign in *Napoleon in Egypt*.
5. Derrida, *Of Grammatology*, 93. "Indeed, one must understand this *incompetence* of science which is also the incompetence of philosophy, the *closure* of the *epistémè*. Above all it does not invoke a return to a prescientific or infra-philosophic form of discourse. Quite the contrary. This common root, which is not a root but the concealment of the origin . . . this unnameable movement of *difference-itself*, that I have strategically nicknamed *trace, reserve,* or *difference*, could be called writing only within the *historical* closure, that is to say within the limits of science and philosophy."
6. Both Gerhard Richter and David Clark have argued this point: see Richter, *Afterness: Figures of Following in Modern Thought and Aesthetics*; Clark, "Lost and Found in Translation: Romanticism and the Legacies of Jacques Derrida."
7. Witt, *Isis in the Ancient World*, 32.
8. A similarly Eurocentric-disruptive text is Ibn Fadlan's compendium of Arab travel narratives, *Ibn Fadlan and the Land of Darkness: Arab Travellers in the Far North*.
9. For more comparative analysis of eastern and western understandings of Egypt, see Colla, *Conflicted Antiquities: Egyptology, Egyptomania, Egyptian Modernity*. This book came to my attention too late to integrate it into my own historical research; Colla's project is entirely historical, however, whereas my interest is in the history of ideas as these play out in the Romantic imaginary. For another alternative history of Egypt, see Charles Bonnet's recent *The Black Kingdom of the Nile*. Bonnet's archaeological research, like Assmann's alternative treatment of Egypt's monotheism, effectively reroute our received understanding of Ancient Egyptian history.
10. Herodotus, *The Histories*, Chapter II.
11. *Al-Jabarti's History of Egypt*, 82–83.

Chapter 1

Prior Time

History and language are two of the main concepts that the west has used to try to understand Ancient Egypt in its imponderability and inaccessibility. Novalis opines that "Formerly all things were spirit appearances. Now we can see nothing but dead repetition, which we do not understand. The meaning of the hieroglyph is missing. We are still living on the fruit of better times."[1] Those better times are the gold that is the mystical wisdom and appearing of spirit encoded in the hieroglyphs, in the pyramids and obelisks and colossi. Where reason breaks down, the imagination takes over, but so do analogic formations such as medieval alchemy and esoteric religious systems in which Egypt's archaic pastness is employed as a liminal space where associative, magical thinking can do its work. This is the case in Giordano Bruno's cosmological system, which married Copernican cosmology, Chaldean astrology, Hermeticism, and Neoplatonism with Egyptian deities. It is also the case in Paracelsus's theory of sympathies, which he derived from astrology, esoteric beliefs, the Kabbalah, Hermetic beliefs, and the medical training he received at the University of Bael and the University of Ferrara. He believed in the mirroring of the celestial and terrestrial, a belief common to esoteric sects and Hermeticism, and theorized that since the seven organs of the human body mirrored the seven planets, the body can be medically treated by way of this sympathetic reflection; moreover, ancient wisdom and the precise timing of ritual wording are required for cures to be effective. In the *Archidoxis Magica* (c. 1570) the Paracelsian Gerhard Dorn describes the cure for epilepsy as including creating a triangular form of silver and gold filled with characters, a form that looks very like a hieroglyph-covered pyramid. It thereby concentrates the multiple knowledges of ancient histories and languages as they were sedimented in forms known to hold Egyptian magic and wisdom, the pyramid and the hieroglyph. If the ancient histories as well as the secret knowledge of ancient languages that can speak mystical wisdom are the purview of scientists, philosophers, and heterodox religionists, their findings (as with Paracelsus's texts) were often published and widely disseminated, greatly influencing the western imaginary over the centuries.

I. EGYPTIANISM

The first several chapters of *Romantic Egypt* will treat history foremost but not exclusively, and the last several chapters will focus increasingly on language, but again, not exclusively; for any culture the two are entwined, but because both were for so long enigmas they were also mythical, imagined rather than known. They belonged to the territory of generative no-knowing. To begin: What *is* Egypt's history, and what can be known of it? Egyptian priests during the Predynastic and Dynastic periods were responsible for keeping its history, but in oral form, and each priesthood tended a different cult deity, recording different historical events and therefore differentiated histories. Moreover, when Ancient Egypt was not united under one pharaoh, the histories of Lower Egypt, centered around Memphis, and Upper Egypt, controlled from Thebes, were distinctly different histories tended by different or variant gods. Of necessity there could be no one uniform history of Egypt, and in addition internecine wars and dynastic battles insured that some pharaohs would be erased from the kings' list (such as Hatshepsut) while others (such as Akhenaten) would be eradicated for all time, at least until he and his famous queen Nefertiti were rediscovered in the Modern period.

It was the Greek scholar Hecataeus of Abdera who wrote the *Aegyptiaca* (*History of Egypt*) after his visit on the invitation of Ptolemy I, a lost account for which we have only a partial transcription that Diodorus Siculus made two and a half centuries later. Hecataeus's account is therefore Grecian, biased and imperfect. He could be considered the first Neo-Egyptian in treating Ancient Egypt and its forgotten history as already otherwise and elsewhere. It is a term I borrow from Peter Sloterdijk's *Derrida the Egyptian*, where he uses it to refer to the self-othering of Jews based on the Mosaic story of exile in Egypt. But I am using it somewhat inversely to refer to the othering and lost ground of Ancient Egypt itself, along with the sense of a recoverable spiritual identity adhering to it for the west despite the Judaic account. It is an account that layers onto Greek and early Christian Hermetic accounts of Egypt as spiritual self-recognition. I will push this further to associate that spiritual self-recognition with what Hegel terms "*Pure* self-recognition in absolute otherness, this Aether *as such*, [which] is the ground and soil of Science [that is, philosophy] or *knowledge in general*."[2] Hegel is describing the movement and medium of conscious thought in its attempt to know something of the world and therefore the self. In this Romantic formulation, pure self-recognition in the absolutely alien other is the foundation of knowledge. I am taking that claim as summarizing Ancient Egypt as the fulcrum where not-knowing and knowing meet, where speculative thought and factual knowledge produced spiritual self-recognition, but also an imaginable future predicated on a way to newly understand the past. This Egyptian fulcrum provides a point of departure for understanding the achievements of the Alexandrian scholars who worked in its Museum and Library.

Following the teachings of Aristotle, the work of Library scholars and Museum scientists pushed the boundaries of what could be known about the material world, but they also produced the historical basis for a form of philosophy that combined the systems of Pythagoras, Plato, and other Greek philosophers, with Egyptian thought, medicine, and astronomy, *and* with Aristotelian science. These three ways of understanding what can be known and how the world might be experienced were perhaps best posited by Plato's *Symposium*, Aristotle's categories, and Egyptian sacred texts. Plato's dialogue explains ideal forms in terms of truth and beauty. Aristotle's categories not only sharply contrast with Plato's Idealist view but also construct the very bones of Alexandrian scientific endeavor in distinguishing "species of knowledge," categories that rely on predication: "When one thing is predicated of another, all that which is predicable of the predicate will be predicable also of the subject."[3] This is the line of thinking Kant uses to differentiate pure logic from cosmological or magical thinking. But it is also how speculative thought and knowable fact meet to produce something knowably new about the unknown or illegible. Moreover, in the *Metaphysics* Aristotle notes that "all men suppose what is called Wisdom to deal with the first causes and the principles of things. . . . Wisdom is knowledge about certain principles and causes."[4] His point is that wisdom is inductive and not esoteric; it is based on commonly held, reputable beliefs (*endoxa*) as these concur with phenomena (*phainomena* or appearances). Somewhat sternly he notes, "it is fatal to make Ideas substances and yet hold that they are composed of other Ideas."[5] For Alexandrian scientists and intellectuals trained in Aristotelian thought, mystical speculation should have been anathema, or "fatal"; indeed, this proved to be the case when Christian mobs finally wrested control of Alexandrian thought regimes from the pagan intellects. But mystical speculation had its place in the scholars' work, as did the literary productions of those very scholars. Rational thought was not the only thought regime employed at the Museum.

Alexandrian scholars schooled in Aristotelian distinctions were in fact eager to explore the mysteries of Egyptian medicine and ritualistic magic, to learn the wisdom of the mystery cults, and to study the secrets of Chaldean astronomy and astrology (with works accumulated by Alexander from the conquest of Babylon, and added to by the huge donation of books to Cleopatra by Marc Antony). This combined heritage, then, is the basis for "the ground and soil of Science" as the highest form of philosophy for Hegel, and for "knowledge in general," and it represents the "Aether *as such*" in seeking a correlation between celestial knowledge *and* terrestrial knowledge, *cosmos* and *mundus*. It was the Alexandrian scholars, in my view, along with the occultation of Egypt that continued in Hermeticism and Freemasonry, who made possible the conditions for Romantic-era philosophy to produce accounts of self-consciousness so necessary for thinking about the individual as a self-aware and imaginative being. These traditions also provided the ground for a Romantic-period conception of history as world history and even spiritual history.[6]

Despite its inaccuracies, then, Hecataeus's *History of Egypt* is important because it represents the first real treatment of Egypt as alienated from itself (unlike Plato's references to Egypt in the *Timaeus*, which treats it as merely a forerunner culture, and or Herodotus's reliance on priests' incomplete or fabricated knowledge). It also contains the only known description of the Ramesseum, the mausoleum of Ramesses II (known later by his Greek name, Ozymandias); even so, the account only goes as far as the sacred library. This library is extremely important for it not only held the sacred texts important to Egyptian science and spirit but also provided the blueprint for the Alexandrian Library and its astronomical observatory, and so also the model for both occulted and scientific thought. The inner sanctum of the complex, containing the sarcophagus chamber and the rooftop astronomical observatory above it, is described third hand, Hecataeus relying on the priest-guides' description of the prohibited area.[7] Although he also succumbed to priestly prejudice in relating some of his material, we can thank him as well as the much earlier Persian sovereign Cambyses—remembered for having killed the sacred Apis bull—for not having desecrated the Ramesseum during his general plunder of Thebes and the Nile Valley, allowing Hecataeus to document it. Hecataeus's description preserved the memory of the Ramesseum in itself and as the model for the Alexandrian Museum and Library. Much of the later Romantic project was not so much to rediscover blueprints such as these, even though floor plans and elevations of pyramids and temple complex were painstakingly drawn, but to translate these ruins and the spirit they embalmed. Novalis's statement, "The meaning of the hieroglyph is missing" in his *Logical Fragments* sums up the thing sought in Egyptian artifacts: the "spirit appearances" that "formerly" had been in all things. If resuscitating the Ramesseum could restore in some way the Library of Alexandria, the archaic ground of western spirit could also be brought back. This lost ground, this buried past, is the reclamation project that was Ancient Egypt.

Because the Greek legends of Memnon provided not a little of Romantic familiarity with a nonbiblical Egypt, though Ramesses II was equated with the biblical Pharaoh, it is worth noting Romantic period devotion to all things Ramesside. The Ramesseum, also known as the Memnonium, had completely disappeared well before the eighteenth century, but its outer court and peristyle hall remained. The outer court is where Giovanni Belzoni discovered the colossus of Ramesses II, whose head and torso now reside in the British Museum due to his efforts. Hecataeus had described the pharaoh's colossus along with its inscription; both later became confused with the "Memnon" colossus of Amenhotep III near the Valley of the Kings that Percy Shelley's "Ozymandias" reflects on. This composite confusion, and others like it, informs much of Ancient Egypt's Romantic-era mythopoetics; the resulting fabrications resulted in works such as Percy Shelley's famous sonnet or in the centuries-long belief in the Memnon colossus's ability to "sing" at dawn (the exact scientific reasons for which not being understood until later). The great statue's phenomenal speaking out—its expression of spirit—was recorded as early as Herodotus. When the Ramesseum was visited by Napoleon's team of scientists and later by Champollion, both teams used Hecataeus's description to decipher any further remains. With Hecataeus's detailed notes, Champollion succeeded in locating two bas-reliefs in the Ramesseum representing Thoth, god of knowledge and writing, and his sister Seshat, goddess of archives. Near these reliefs were representations of deities signifying sight and hearing, the last carrying scribal tools; but despite Champollion's belief that these were indications of the library or archive's location, later archaeologists determined that the Ramesseum's library was quite small, a matter of book shelves, and was located further back toward the burial chamber. Nevertheless, Champollion's translation of these remains was an attempt to restore the spirit of the place, and to reinstate Thoth's archaic power to endow man with knowledge and inscription. Libraries in Ancient Egypt, and not temples, were known as "the double house of life," for they were always libraries of magical books, and magical books were believed to have been written by Thoth himself.[8] Egyptian magic is the formulation of supernatural intervention; here writing does indeed come before speech, the trace before the inscription.

The Ramesseum thus provides the primal archive: not just the Egyptian "Double House of Life" of priestly magic books, but the books Ramesses would need in the afterlife, books of eternity. If these have been forgotten, the dream of them has not: the Book of the Dead understood *post facto* as tomes of eternal life, sacred wisdom from before the ruin of empires, have left a trace discernible in the books resurrected from the Alexandrian Library, even if these few scattered and fragmented texts—only a tiny fraction of which were recovered during the Renaissance retrieval and translation of Classical texts—represented for the most part Greco-Alexandrian knowledge and not that of Ancient Egypt. The significance for Romanticism was of a primal archive, a trace of forgotten knowledge concerning the nature of eternity and cosmic origin, with Greek and Egyptian wisdom conflated into an ur-archive. This was the forgotten, lost heritage of Ancient Egypt before the archaeology of the nineteenth century began to untangle the translative contortions of the previous period. That primal trace—identified with the crumbling pyramids, relocated obelisks, disfigured colossi—was hauntingly believed to reside in secret, Hermetic knowledge, in alchemical science, and in the science of linguistics. The key to all languages *was* the key to all knowledge, which was the key to cosmic origin, which was the key to the prior. The Greeks thought that history began in Egypt; the Egyptians thought that they had invented writing; for the Romantics Ancient Egypt was the ground of the primal archive.

The identity of Ramesses's archive with both occulted and scientific knowledge made it an exemplary trope for Ancient Egypt as the ground of origin, primordial wisdom, and originary magic well before the Alexandrian period; magic was the gift of Thoth's knowledge to Isis, allowing her to become "the Great Magician" according to Wallis Budge, late nineteenth-century Keeper of Egyptian and Assyrian Antiquities in the British Museum. Magic is knowledge, a fact understood by Hermeticists and alchemists alike; both are kept powerful only through writing, only through textuality itself. In arguing for the importance of Romanticism's engagement with a mystical and mystified Egypt through textual magic, one need only point to Napoleon's *Oraculum* or *Book of Fate*, his oracle recovered from an Egyptian tomb in 1802 and consulted daily by him until 1813. The *Oraculum*, used by one of the premiere logicians of the Romantic period, indicates the importance of mystical wisdom for sustaining that logic. It also signals the necessity of a grounding *beforeness* for Romantic revolution and Romantic revelation. The history of spirit, told both as a national tale (Volney's *Ruins* for instance, or Napoleon's cartographic missions) and as an unfolding of Romanticism's zeitgeist, traces itself back to Ancient Egypt, to its essential encryption, to its tomb/womb signifiers. The Ramesses's archive also stands in for the prior existence in Egypt of what I refer to as the "Alexandrian Dream," the dream of terrestrial and celestial empire held first by Alexander the Great and then by Ptolemy Soter. (Ptolemy I or Ptolemy Soter was Alexander's general and then self-proclaimed pharaoh of Egypt.) Ramesses's entanglement in the biblical Mosaic story and his defeat by Moses the Magician (as he was known according to Wallis Budge) initiates a pattern in the struggle for cosmological mastery—a struggle epitomized in the Romantic period by, among other things, the race to decipher the hieroglyphs, the key to which would decode all oriental and orienting or divine wisdom.

Of the major points of contact for the west with Ancient Egypt, that of Moses's experience under the biblical Pharaoh was so potent that it overshadowed all others; there is, however, another Judaic presence in the Egyptian history that stems from the translation of the Old Testament for the Alexandrian Library by Ptolemy I's order. It was this Hellenic Judaism that became important in the Italian Renaissance's resuscitation of Greco-Roman culture, as did two other major points of contact: those of Alexandria's legacy in the Macedonian and Roman empires; and of the symbolic value of monumental remains and hieroglyphics so important later to Romantic literature and philosophy. The texts re-collected and translated in Renaissance Florence were largely from the period of Alexandria's ascendency in the Mediterranean and Levantine world of terrestrial and intellectual empire. I take the act of translation, exemplified in a foundational or scribal moment by the scholarly translations performed at the Library of Alexandria, to be emblematic of the west's need for an Egypt that resides beyond comprehension, always buried in its own illegibility but never out of sight. At once entombed yet accessible, Ancient Egypt is itself the tomb that marks the place of the dead and of loss, serving as placeholder for the dead when they are no longer in place. Because translation can only reconfigure what it seeks to re-present, it necessarily recodes what was already an opaque cipher. Renaissance translators attempted to recreate the scribal moment of Alexandrian genius, when Hellenic scholars parsed the known world by observational logic but scoped the unknown world via stunningly precise mathematical thought at the same time that they collected the mystical wisdoms of other cultures. However, in their resuscitative efforts, Renaissance-era translators neglected to imitate the scholarly and scientific conditions of such thought. Instead, they misconstrued Egypt by exaggerating what Herodotus or Clement of Alexandria had already written of it, just as Alexandrian histories of Egypt necessarily translated what contemporaneous Egyptian priests could remember or misremember of an already forgotten past.[9]

Indeed, Renaissance translations were predicated on serious errors in historical dating. There is some defense for this: most of the Alexandrian Library's holdings had been lost through a variety of political and ideological misfortunes, and Classical authors and fathers of the church retained their medieval authority for the early Renaissance, so that patristic descriptions of Egypt were taken as self-contained truth, a remembering, rather than a partial truth, a forgetting and translation. But there was another layer of desire in early Renaissance recoveries, particularly those carried out by Marsilio Ficino (1433–1499) in Medici-controlled Florence (whose job was to recreate Plato's Academy as the Florentine Academy, in the process reviving Neoplatonism). Ficino was the scholar tasked in particular by Cosimo de' Medici to translate the recently recovered and collated works of

Plato, making him Plato's first modern translator, but he was also ordered to translate the newly discovered Hermetic corpus, which Cosimo wanted attended to first, prior to Plato, as Ficino's reconstruction had placed Hermes Trismegistus prior to Moses, Zoroaster, and the Greeks. Ficino was especially eager to pinpoint the moment of revelatory origin and a chronology of spirit, supposed to be traceable in the *Corpus Hermetica*, and he did so in a fashion that allowed complex correlations to be made between Egyptian, Judaic, and Christian genesis, world systems, and mythologies. Thus, Hermes Trismegistus, through a complex calculus, was the Egyptian Moses whose revelatory teachings relayed the originary moment of God's intervention on earth.[10]

The force of desire on Ficino's translative acts was not idiosyncratic, but was instead fed by a current of mystical thought preexisting the Alexandrian Library, and traceable certainly as far back as Pythagoras and his cult focused on the secret knowledge encoded in the interplay of numbers, music, and cosmology.[11] Neoplatonism kept this current alive, as did alchemy. The magus Cornelius Agrippa (1486–1535), for instance, was both a Neoplatonist and kabbalist, combining both western and eastern mysticisms in a Renaissance setting of medico-scientific "knowledge." That Cosimo ordered Ficino to translate the Hermetic texts before Plato's works ensured that for Renaissance readers Plato comes *after* Hermetic knowledge based on the Egyptian Thoth: this purposive sheltering of a *prior* archival and conceptual space provides something like the recessiveness that for Heideggerians resides in the sense of "afterness." The extant Hermetica consists of two separate manuscripts: first is the *Asclepius*, known to the Romantics as *The Golden Ass*, by the Libyan Apuleïus (Lucius Apuleïus of Madaura).[12] Apuleïus was a second-century Greek who traveled to Egypt where he was supposedly initiated into the holy rites of Isis, and after its translation the work was understood to describe Egyptian religious magic whereby the gods are installed in their statues as presence. The second work, called *The Pimander* by Ficino, is actually a pastiche of fifteen dialogues by different authors, but was thought to be by Hermes Trismegistus himself.[13] These works reflect a Greco-Roman world highly inflected by a resurgent interest in the Pythagorean cult, and a concomitant popularity of mystery cults throughout the empire including that of the Ancient Egyptian cult of the Apis bull which, like the cult of Isis, gained in widespread popularity through the specifically Alexandrian cult of Serapis. Apis is the Ka or spirit of Osiris, god of the dead.[14] Ficino believed the occulted Hermetic texts to be from dynastic Egypt rather than Greco-Egyptian Alexandria where mystery cults and gnosticism intermingled. What he discovered in them were teachings about "the Father," the "*Logos*," and the demiurge or the "Son of God."[15] What excited Ficino and his colleagues in particular was the relevance of Hermes's teachings to Christian conceptions of presence, Being, and the divine power of the word. Ficino would extend his interpretation of the long tradition of Hermes-Thoth as the god of writing and wisdom, dialectically transformed by early gnostics, into license for a renewed science of the universe.

The Corpus Hermeticum is probably an early Christian text focused heavily on the word and the son. Volney's dream vision opening for the *Ruins* appears to be modeled on this text, which begins with a dialogue between the speaker and Poimandres, "The Shepherd of Men":

1. It chanced once on a time my mind was meditating on the things that are, my thought was raised to a great height, the senses of my body being held back—just as men who are weighed down with sleep after a fill of food, or from fatigue of body.

    Methought a Being more than vast, in size beyond all bounds, called out my name and saith: What wouldst thou hear and see, and what hast thou in mind to learn and know?
2. And I do say: What art thou?

    He saith: I am Man-Shepherd (Poimandres), Mind of all-masterhood; I know what thou desirest and I'm with thee everywhere.
3. [And] I reply: I long to learn the things that are, and comprehend their nature, and know God. This is, I said, what I desire to hear.

    He answered back to me: Hold in thy mind all thou wouldst know, and I will teach thee.
4. E'en with these words His aspect changed, and straightway, in the twinkling of an eye, all things were opened to me, and I see a Vision limitless, all things turned into Light—sweet, joyous [Light]. And I became transported as I gazed. (Copenhaver, *Hermetica*, 1)

In this excerpt we see evident the two strains of Alexandrian scholarship—of the history of spirit and the scientific basis for the mysteries of the universe—which were hereby transposed onto the Florentine intellectual community. It was to answer certain questions about both puzzles—the mystical and the scientific—that Ficino approached his translative tasks and continued his revisions of both history and the original texts through his own speculative writing. Ficino's contributions to the new mystical Christian strain of Renaissance humanism then influenced Giordano Bruno's cosmological thought, his "Egyptianism," which he disseminated while in London. Athanasius Kircher, an equally brilliant polymath of the seventeenth century, carried on Ficino's and Bruno's "Egyptian" work by replicating Alexandrian science and scholarship in his attempts to map the universe, analyze the mundane world, and recover lost mystical wisdom, while adding to the overlay of mistranslation, misconception, and forced interpretations so essential to

Ficino's and Bruno's work.[16] Bruno's and Ficino's quest for a precise history of spirit—a chronology of divine Christian revelation originating in Egypt (for the historicity of God's first appearance was important to track down)—can be seen recapitulated in broadstroke outlines in Hegel's oeuvre whereby absolute knowledge performs a spiritual work aesthetically reproduced in the dialectical revelation of spirit through the ages. Indeed, German Idealism was much taken with certain issues raised by Ficino's foundational misreadings, and not just Hegel but Goethe, Schelling, and Novalis also contemplated their originary force.

It is significant that Romantic-era engagements with contemporary Egypt, in which the engineering and proto-archaeological, as well as linguistic sciences were ascendant, nevertheless retranslated the antique without ever disengaging from the "unground" of the lost, opaque, or illegible past. The race to decipher the hieroglyphs, made possible by the discovery of the Rosetta Stone, stands in relation to prior translations that sought to identify the hieroglyphic cyphers with magical power and secret wisdom. It was a demystifying effort; in seeking to demystify Egypt, however, such translations, like Ficino's, only produced their own alchemy and thus their own revisionism of the unrecoverable abyssal ground. The alchemical imagination, the combining of scientific with esoteric thought, continued with Kircher in seventeenth-century Rome, and reappeared in the eighteenth century in the opening made by the power struggle between empirical and rational philosophical schools for other interventions. A particular thread of German Idealism, it seems to me, participates in this intervention by paying serious attention to the chemistry of logic, and to a more secretive divination; the desire for a history of spirit that can point to a more comprehensive knowing. By mapping the terrestrial and celestial worlds onto each other, so that scientific and mystical knowledges mirror each other much in the manner of Pythagoras's numerology, German Idealism reenacts Egyptianism as a form of translation, a recovery-recoding-rewriting that performs a particular rite. This is the rite of Egyptian magic, in which Being is brought into presence, in which gods are installed in their idols,[17] in which death is merely a transmutation into a different life. And Egyptian magic was why, through the ages, the hieroglyphs have needed to be translated, for they spelled the mystery that could be revealed.

II. THE ALEXANDRIAN DREAM

My aim here is to approach the problem of Egypt as one of archaeological strata that have been disrupted, so as to become confusingly mixed in with the leavings of other cultures and other times, a kind of dis-assemblage. Such a dis-assemblage also allows for a reweaving (not a fabrication but a way to make connections) of the unraveled and separated strands of Egyptianeity, or all the Egyptianisms that became such an object of fascination for the Romantics. Egypt compelled occidental interest not just for its geopolitical importance as a gateway to the east, but also by virtue of its elsewhereness, its lost intellectual and cosmological empire. To think about a genealogy of intellects in the Egyptianist vein is to consider a particular combination of imperial archival desire and an unbounded will to know. I would include in such a genealogy any systematizing thinkers focused on mapping what can be known as well as what can be ideated, such as the Alexandrian scholar Eratosthenes, who in addition to proving the earth's curvature also accurately measured its circumference and theorized its tilt toward the sun; created the first armillary sphere or celestial model; wrote on mathematics; and composed poetry—all of which resulted from his project to elaborate the mathematical system he believed to be embedded in Plato's philosophy. Before him of course were the systematizing philosophers Plato and Aristotle, whose combined works aimed to cover the terrain of human and ideal knowledge; after him and his fellow Alexandrians were the great alchemists such as Cornelius Agrippa and Paracelsus (both of whom William Godwin commentated on in his 1834 *Lives of the Necromancers*), and Renaissance scholars such as Ficino, Bruno, and Kircher. Romantic-period thinkers were drawn to such intellectual restlessness, and the collection and assimilation of human knowledge. What connected the Renaissance scholar to the Alexandrian one was his desire for a key, a philosopher's stone, that would reduce all knowledge to a system of symbols, an algebra of truth.

This hoarding of knowledge was pursued in tandem with its seeming adversarial epistemological form of occult wisdom, springing from the western and eastern arms of Alexander's territorial grasp. Although each form of knowledge suffered tremendous losses during the suppressive reign of Christian orthodoxy, the Italian Renaissance did not resuscitate the epistemological dialectic that had emerged during the Alexandrian period so much as reendow the natural sciences/occult dialectic with authoritative weight. Poggio Bracciolini, who recovered Lucretius's *De Rerum Natura*, did so because he had embarked, following Petrarch's example and in line with Ficino, on a collective endeavor to resurrect the ruins of this apparently lost empire. Following this decisive return to the Alexandrian vision, with its dialectic of scientific predication and esoteric wisdom, Enlightenment and Romantic-era intellectuals provoked an historical restatement, recurring to the fragments, ruin, and rubble of the past in the effort to know what reinspirited the "pastness of the past" with its "already-thereness and eternal return," as David Clark puts it.[18] Such a history of spirit, the story of divine originary or founding revelation, however variously pursued, always came down to a nature fecund with the spirit's potentiality: it is the foundational concept of Hermeticism, alchemy and the "veil of Isis," and indeed of Romanticism. Enlightenment and Romantic scholars investigated encyclopedically a world that is both empirical and spirit-inhabited,[19] one in which a translation of an unknowable past into a world system could mightily extend knowledge's reach. Novalis calls this "encyclopedistics." Thus, the work of alchemical and Hermetic scholars such as Kircher was not entirely sideswiped by the racing engine of the Enlightenment; this might be seen by Godwin's account in *Lives of the Necromancers* in which Pythagoras, Albertus Magnus, and Paracelsus are discussed along with Egyptian magic, Zoroaster, Apuleïus, and Raymond Llull, the mystic who inspired Bruno. And when Victor Frankenstein is able to construct a body of work, as it were, and translate death into life, it is perhaps because he has studied his Cornelius Agrippa and Paracelsus rather than because he has not. The goal in both Renaissance and Romantic world-inscription was more than a terrestrial mapping of cosmological possibilities; now it was to attain surer footing in cosmology's seductively analogic regimes.

Bruno, who had read his Lucretius, and, born just after Paracelsus died, had inherited his teachings as well, was a Dominican friar, philosopher, mathematician, poet, and astrologer who used the Hermetic tradition to expand his heretical embrace of a Copernican cosmology and an atomistic world system. The heliocentric cosmos was, in Bruno's view, now unlinked from the armillary spheres, so that nothing, especially man, was moored in its place any longer; the Lucretian universe was similarly unmoored, but from death, since the atomistic universe is infinite. Bruno's oeuvre conceives the restored and revitalized natural and psychic dynamic interlacing terrestrial and celestial worlds as chartable, reducible to algorithms that yield the key to escaping the limits of temporality and death, a key founded on the wisdom of Ancient Egypt and the art of memory, which was thought to originate in Egyptian rituals.[20] The Hermetic rites of memory were developed to install a celestial map in the mystic's mind, a mirroring that facilitates revelation; Bruno believed that if the art of memory is correlated to a systematic charting of astronomical, or Egyptian and Hebrew symbols that channel divine power, the practitioner can transcend to the ultimate gnosis, an understanding of the nature of the many as an understanding of the One. He devised memory wheels that are complex combinations of his understanding of cosmic and terrestrial knowledge systems; these were "Egyptianized" through the inclusion of Egyptian symbols and deities (translated through Classical lenses). What Bruno called his "Egyptian" religion, which he believed to be more true than orthodox Christianity, depended on Ficino and Pico della Mirandola's interweaving of Kabbalistic and Zoroastrian mysticisms in their genealogies of a true Christianity.[21] That F. W. J. Schelling was fascinated by Bruno's work, using the heretical thinker iconically to argue the nature of origin and truth in his 1802 *Bruno, or On the Natural and the Divine Principle of Things*, reveals the potentiality of such world-inscription as a project that enables free thought rather than restricting it. As Bruno's multivolume works on cosmology and morality, and Schelling's work here and in *The Ages of the World* demonstrate, a systematizing cogito combined with mystical wisdom as a resurgent Egyptianism can expansively rethink what terrestrial regimes had barred. The point of both Bruno's *Heroic Frenzies* and Schelling's recovery and translation of these Hermetic dialogues in his account of Bruno's "natural and divine principle of things" is that both rely on the moment of illumination that is a worldly and celestial intersection, so that the *beyond-thought* can be realized.

It is with this recognition that it becomes clear that world-mapping in the Alexandrian sense is coincident with translative thinking. The empirical and organic stretch of the systematizing project requires in the Egyptian case a coordinate grasp of esoteric knowledge. We might call this dialectic of scientific predication and esoteric wisdom the Neo-Egyptian mandate following Freud's *Moses and Monotheism* (1937) in which Moses's Egypt is the origin for the place that is always elsewhere.[22] This other Egypt, which the west perpetually carried with it in order to find itself there, attributes to the remains of Ancient Egypt an *Ungrund*, an "unground" that is the place of the abyssal pastness of a forgotten past. One aspect of a speculative history of Egypt that intrigued Renaissance scholars is the Essene mysticism that developed in Alexandria from a Judaic Hellenism reemerging as a medieval Kabbalism. Intriguingly this mystical strain was then revived in Spinoza's philosophy.[23] Freud shifted the debate on the Egypto-Judaic relation by hewing to a different esoteric tradition belonging to biblical testimony, using *Moses and Monotheism* to work through his theory of the Mosaic inheritance.

In fact, it is *alchemy* that sits so precisely on that fulcrum between speculative thought and rationalism, between the desire for the infinite and the failure of any system to contain it. Alchemy also indulges in the Gordian knot of metaphor and occultation that so often resolves into hieroglyphics.[24] Like the Alexandrian scholars, alchemy quests for the founding moment and its fundamental materials, and for the world's contradictory presentation and withdrawal. In essence, alchemy presumes to get at the vehicle of spirit that monumentality appears to be; it does so using a combination of laboratory science and mystical, Hermetic knowledge, with the rhythms of poetry contained in ritual spells and incantations. The predecessor text of such incantation was supposed to have been the Egyptian Book of the Dead, whose magic words would ensure eternal life.[25] The best examples for my purposes of alchemical world-inscription are Kircher and Bruno. The complete works of these Catholic-trained (Dominican and Jesuit) scholars trace the known world just as the Alexandrian scholars' systematizing works did, and in Kircher's case, with similarly exacting, even spectacular results. But the works of both scholars also transgressed into the unlimited world of speculative knowledge, with Bruno extending his embrace of a Copernican cosmology into Hermetic charts that map the interlacing lines of spheres of knowledge, Aristotle's categorical "species of knowledge," the art of memory, and the intercession of esoteric or "Egyptian" wisdom. He pushed Ficino's interpretation of the *Corpus Hermetica* to the limits when he "maintain[ed] that the magical Egyptian religion . . . was not only the most ancient but also the only true religion, which both Judaism and Christianity had obscured and corrupted,"[26] and intriguingly he gained a wide audience for his ideas. His publications ran to thirty-five books; Kircher, living later but still embodying the alchemical spirit of encyclopedic endeavor, also wrote thirty-five treatises. Kircher theorized the physical sciences with amazing exactitude, but he also believed he had decoded Ancient Egyptian hieroglyphics and other ancient scripts supposed to hold lost wisdom. Indeed, it was Kircher who drew attention to the importance of the veil of Isis, sparking a revival of interest in Ancient Egypt that fed into Masonic rituals, making him what might be considered the first Egyptologist.[27]

However, for the Romantics, it was Bruno's poetic approach to Egyptianism that conjured the imagination, not Kircher's scientific one. Bruno far better exemplified the sublime thinker, the mystic who could parse the external. Thoth the Egyptian god of writing, who the Greeks collapsed into Hermes-Mercury, was his particular inspiration. In using the newly rediscovered Hermetic texts in conjunction with his reading of Epicurus, the *Asclepius*, and the newly available *De Rerum Natura*, along with Cartari's charts of Greek and Egyptian deities to conduct his "Egyptian" reform of the heavens—his "Egyptianism" as he called it—Bruno returned Egypt and the lost texts of the Alexandrian Library to their central place in western thought. The acknowledged magus' central Egyptian or Hermetic tenets are laid out in the work written in dialogue form dedicated in part to Sir Philip Sidney, the 1584 *Spaccio della bestia trionfante* (printed the same year in English as *The Expulsion of the Triumphant Beast*). Sidney belonged to the Hermetic circle led by John Dee, and during his London period Bruno became acquainted with its members through the poet, lecturing on his own reinterpretation of the Alexandrian Dream. His restoration of Egyptianism is acknowledged in Schelling's *Bruno or On the Natural and Divine Principle of Things* (1802), whose title does homage to the cosmological systematizing and essentializing Bruno achieves. Schelling's choice of the dialogue genre is a more subtle homage, imitating both Bruno's genre choice—few of Schelling's readers may have known Bruno's treatise, though they would have recognized the genre of philosophical dialogue—and perhaps alluding to Sidney's coterie and their conversational philosophic exchanges. Schelling's characters, or embodied philosophical positions, are counterbalanced in the dialogue to elucidate the nature of beauty and truth: he names these characters "Alexander," "Lucian," and "Anselm." The eleventh-century Anselm of Canterbury was best known for his "ontological argument" for the existence of God, whereas Lucian the Assyrian, admirer of Epicurus, wrote *Dialogues of the Dead*, and *Dialogues of the Gods*, and attacked Alexander of Abonoteichus for his burning of Epicurus's work.

Lucian's other writings include a narrative that provides the original of "The Sorcerer's Apprentice," proving his familiarity with Hermetic teachings. Schelling uses Lucian along with his rival Alexander in the *Bruno* to articulate the Alexandrian position for the benefit of the fourth character, named Bruno, who applies the analogy of chemistry to approach relative oppositions that are in fact dialectical.[28] Anslem begins the dialogic debate by saying "Lucian, would you repeat what you said yesterday about the relation of truth and beauty, when we discussed the mystery rites?" (The mystery rites of the late Hellenic and the Roman period were associated with the Aegean islands where the shrines associated with those rites were located, an association woven into Hermetic texts, which provide the source for Masonic rites, as well as other secretive groups.) Lucian responds, "It was my opinion that many works of art could embody the highest sort of truth and yet not, for that reason, deserve the prized title 'beauty' too," while Alexander posits the view that "truth itself satisfies all the demands of art, and that solely through its truth does a work of art become truly beautiful."[29] For my purposes at least, this declaration describes what Hegel terms the highest art, philosophy: as Alexander notes, "Through the rivalry of shared discussion, we penetrate ever more deeply into the heart of the matter; though dialogue begins on a gentle tone and proceeds slowly, finally it swells up like a tidal wave and carries away its participants, filling them all with joy!" Here joy is sublime ecstasy in the Hermetic sense. Such *ekstasis* is suggestively spelled out in the title of Bruno's own poetico-philosophical work of 1585 *On the Heroic Frenzies*. From this conception of the cosmic reformulation of the limits of thought, Schelling formulates Romantic-period Egyptianism in the Brunonian sense. Isis's comment in Bruno's dialogue *Spaccio* helps make this connection between the hidden depths or "heart of the matter" and philosophical wisdom: "'Let not this trouble you, Momus, ... since fate has ordained a vicissitude of darkness and light.' 'But the worst of it is, said Momus, that they hold it for certain that they are in the light.' 'And Isis replied that darkness would not be darkness to them, if they knew it.'"[30]

III. ARCHAIC EGYPT

Horus, a Predynastic Egyptian falcon-headed deity and son of Osiris and Isis (god of the dead and his consort), and the Comte de Volney, whose 1802 dream vision of the ruin of civilizations focused on Ancient Egypt as a land corrupted by its own drive to power, have in common their bird's-eye or god's-eye perspective. As the son of Osiris and Isis, Horus was a major deity, and as for his father the dismembered Osiris, subjected to much mutilation. One signal body part whose repeated loss and restoration came to represent Horus was his all-seeing eye, which was also associated with the sun god Ra's eye. Ra, known as the Elder Horus, was he from whose tears sprang the human race. Volney's *The Ruins of Empires* begins by situating the reader in the middle zone between east and west: "In the eleventh year of the reign of Abd-ul-Hamid, son of Ahmid, emperor of the Turks; when the Nogais-Tartars were driven from the Crimea, and a Mussulman prince of the blood of Gengis-Kahn became the vassal and guard of a Christian woman and queen, I was travelling in the Ottoman dominions, and through those provinces which were anciently the kingdoms of Egypt and Syria."[31] Very quickly this traveler assumes the Horus position: "I sat on the shaft of a column; and there, my elbow reposing on my knee, and head reclining on my hand, my eyes fixed, sometimes on the desert, sometimes on the ruins."[32] Straddling these two domains of ruined nature and ruined city, the narrator is also within the ruins on his marble column, which could only be from a temple and therefore the broken remains of ruined spirit. In his meditation the narrator contemplates the lost history the remains represent: "And now a mournful skeleton is all that subsists of this powerful city: naught remains of its vast domination, but a doubtful and empty remembrance!"[33] The spirit itself, ruined and lost, must now be doubted for it is merely an empty shell, a judgment Hegel will in a few years also cast on Egypt's ruins. Just a few pages later a dream vision translates the narrator to a celestial standpoint from which he surveys the globe through a more truly Horus-eye perspective, enabling him to continue his assessment of imperial ruin as the necessary consequence of a doubtful and empty possession. "Thus perish the works of men, and thus do empires and nations disappear!";[34] the judgment of Egypt rendered here is universalized. What cannot be known can, through the Horus eye, be known in its universalized form of human endeavor and its disappearance.

Volney was not unique in seeking an Egyptian-like bird's-eye or cosmic perspective from which to survey universal history. While the Renaissance produced many who embarked on universal histories, such as the startlingly erudite Athanasius Kircher, the eighteenth century produced those eager to imagine a perspective located at the far reaches of the telescope or even the lower heights of the hot air balloon. The anonymous *The Golden Age, or*

The Future Glory of North America, Discovered by an Angel to Celadon in Several Entertaining Visions (attributed to "Celadon," 1785), for instance, predates Volney's *Ruins of Empires* by several years. (*Ruins* was not published in its final form until 1791, soon translated for London readers but not until 1804 for America; Volney had been working on it since the mid-1780s, however, and so the two texts are contemporary in composition.) Although Celadon is an American terrestrial, the visions are from the angel's perspective, that is, the point of cosmogony's beginning. Like Volney's narrator, Celadon has a dream vision, a conceit recurrent throughout literary history but particularly appealing to Romantic contemporaries such as Blake, and soon thereafter becoming part of the repertoire of Wordsworth, Shelley, Keats, and Mary Shelley. The essential message the angel has to deliver, confirming American's right to revolt against British Empire, is that "All sublunary things are subject to mutation. The greatest empires have had their birth, their growth, their maturity, their fall. Nor can America, should the world stand long enough, expect an exemption from the usual vicissitudes of fortune."[35] In the end, the angel warns that America, which the angel's language suggests here is already an empire, with its colonization of Indian-held lands and its treatment of blacks, may be divided up through racial hostilities into several free nations. The alternative is to invite in Christ's transformation of America and then the world beginning with the transference of the Jewish diaspora to American shores, that is, all ethnicities will be united under Christ.

From a cosmic perspective, whether that of Horus or Volney's narrator, or even of Celadon's evangelism, Ancient Egypt was, like America, an empire even before and after it actually was. Volney's guardian spirit, sounding like Isaiah on the Babylonians, intones, "Those piles of ruins, said he, which you see in that narrow valley watered by the Nile, are the remains of opulent cities, the pride of the ancient kingdom. . . . Behold the wrecks of her metropolis, of Thebes with her hundred palaces, the parent of cities, and monument of the caprice of destiny."[36] But it is incorrect to think of this empire in terms of its own colonialism of other territories, as in Alexandrian and Napoleonic or even American Empire, until fairly late in its history. Egypt's center of power was kept firmly in Egypt and when other lands were added to the core area, as in the union of Upper and Lower Egypt, it was essentially the addition of likenesses rather than the acquisition of othernesses, similar to the union of the kingdoms of Israel and Judah. However, the concepts of both empire and colonialism are important to understanding past comprehensions of Egypt, as is the concept of translation. Volney's narratorial translation from diurnal to cosmic viewpoint, even more than Celadon's dream dialogue, represents a defamiliarizing shift. Most translative attempts by visitors to foreign lands attempt to make familiar what seems strange and unknowable. The translative dynamic is bidirectional, in other words, and is so because in cross-cultural contact old assumptions about subjectivity, identity, and difference come into question, and are renegotiated through access to the other. Self-translation is part of this mediation, but whether the translation is to a new position of power, as in the case of Volney's narrator, or toward a subjugation of formerly powerful others, as in western understandings and appropriations of ancient civilizations such as Horus's Egypt, defines the political economy of the transaction.

Within a political economy that can encompass eighteenth- and nineteenth-century conceptions of both a contemporary and an Ancient Egypt, several terms will aid in pinpointing some of its structural assumptions concerning empire, and in forming a focus for what follows. The British conception of "state building" as suggesting a top-down conception of nation, and "state formation" gesture toward a more heterogeneous activity from a variety of publics whose interactions shape the conception, structure, and functioning of the state are useful here. States achieve their mature character, whether through building or plural formative activities, once in their maturity they conceive of themselves as a built structure: planned, functionally operative or efficient, consistent in character or unified, and having permeable boundaries that can be quickly retrenched for defensive purposes. Once powerful, these states begin to consider their permeable boundaries as extendable. Whether "empire" in Ancient Egypt can be properly considered as such is questionable, since dynastic Egypt relied on consolidation rather than expansion strictly speaking to delineate its cultural identity. Empire in the west, however, beginning with the Roman Empire (Alexander's empire, including its early acquisition of Egypt, provides a basic model, but it could not sustain itself functionally) can be defined as the outgrowth of the state as a built structure, requiring state control in order to keep its borders secure even as these were expanding and constantly being redefined to include territories and peoples new to the prior definition of the state. This is certainly how Volney was interpreting Ancient Egypt, particularly in his focus on a drive to power, drawn from biblical representations of an aggressively imperial Egypt.

Because empire requires identification with the central state and its heritage, permeable boundaries can be threatening and need to be constantly policed both ideologically and militarily. Borders can be crossed but must be under vigilant surveillance. During the Romantic period in Britain, Tories were pushing for strengthening state control through censorship and strong borders. Whigs retained their preference for greater democratic representation in the government's functioning but also retained the idea of overall top-down leadership; democratically formed groups such as the Methodists were worrisome to them. The empire's boundaries, in other words, are internally policed as well as externally so. And Britain's early modern-era maritime imperialism was a natural outgrowth of this national identity.[37]

By this description, Britain was more like Assyria and Persia than Ancient Egypt. But it is not "like" that exerts magnetic appeal, it is the complementary double, the supplement that reveals alternate identity. Ancient Egypt presented that enigma, the empire that, at least until it had experienced devastating conquest by the Hyksos from western Asia, was not itself predicated on the colonization of others but rather unification of a divided self: Lower with Upper Egypt. The mythical struggles between Horus (symbolized by the falcon) and Seth (the serpent) over the right to rule can be seen as representing the repeated struggle between Lower Egypt (represented by Horus) and Upper Egypt (whose worship of Seth, strongest of the gods, was centered at Memphis). The separation of Lower from Upper was as much a disagreement over whether to give priority to Horus or to Seth as it was a bid for control by powerful political players; repeatedly unification was followed by another round of violent clashing and separation, and the relocation of the capital between Memphis and Thebes, and later Heliopolis. Unification, when finally stabilized, was represented by both the falcon and the serpent insignia appearing on the pharaoh's crown. The copula, therefore, signifies Egyptian identity, the yoking of self with other-as-self.

This mysterious form of empire, so unlike that of other ancient imperial entities, provided a seductive model of a powerful and extraordinarily long-lived civilization. Egypt in its ancient state, unlike its modern subjugated form, provided that alternative identity for Britain (and as an assemblage that worked, for a united Germany as well) which could not, because of Alexander, even be accorded to Greece. Whereas no nonimperial culture could be attractive as a precursive identity, so no empire other than Greece and Rome could be viewed by the eighteenth century as precursive either. Near Eastern empires, whether biblical, Classical, or the contemporary Ottoman Empire, were too adversarial and thus too recognizably other. Ancient Egypt, however, occupies a middle ground, not just geographically between east and west, but imaginatively; it functions for the west as a translative dream vision. Imperially it functions as archaic supplement, the alternate precursor, the what-if. What if the British had been like the Egyptians? This is not the question Volney asks, condemning Egypt in its biblical identity along with all other ancient empires. But it is a question Britain's imperial ideology, confronted with the ambivalences brought on by the slave trade and colonialism, and eighteenth-century proto-archaeological explorations of Egyptian ruins prompted.

Because colonialism creates supplementary centers beyond the borders of the state proper, and because it is a phenomenon external to the state center regardless of the traffic between nation and colonies, it exhibits a different structure as seen from the colonial perspective. Its boundaries are extremely permeable both internally and external to the colony. Within the colony the national state center is displaced to the fatherland or only symbolically present, an absent presence, while the new colonial center functions as a supplement to the original. But as with all supplements, the colonial center's difference affects the old state center's control over cultural definition, and the empire begins to acculturate to the colony just as the colony must negotiate its own processing of the colonizing culture. The entire extended structure is affected by the colonized. The same was beginning to be recognized, if only through heightened cultural anxiety, with the slave trade.[38] Because so much of Egypt's history, including that of the eighteenth and nineteenth century, was spent in subjugation (first to the Hyksos, then the Nubians, Assyrians, Persians, Greeks, Romans, and Ottomans), it had to be thought of as both an empire and a colonial state. As a colonial state its history provided a Volney-like cautionary tale, but as a self-composed ancient empire its allure was very strong.

The British Empire's policed internal and external boundaries and its colonies' permeable internal and external boundaries created two spheres of agency, each of which was functionally different. Colonial agents are influenced by colonized subjects even as the colonizers work to assert their cultural superiority over native practices, customs, institutions, and belief systems. This creates an internal permeability in which a new state system begins to be formed between colonizers and colonized, as well as a new agency in which previously underprivileged colonial agents can rise to power, while colonized subjects may remain in their old hierarchical positions but in relation to the elevated status of the colonizers, or may negotiate new places for themselves according to their usefulness and abilities. This new system undergoes the formative processes that the original state did, but with the difference of being under state surveillance from the old center.

IV. EGYPTIAN IDEALISM

In *Kant Trouble: The Obscurities of the Enlightened*, Diane Morgan identifies the "Egyptian metaphor" as what troubles eighteenth-century thought and Kant in particular. The Egyptian metaphor refers to the problem of a beginning but not an origin, a meandering vagueness of thought and concept that is without clear historiographical sequence, which nevertheless must ground a stable architectonic. That is, Egypt provides the underground roots or the archaic (that which succeeds the *Ungrund*), while the ground—the origin or founding—begins at ground level, at the foundation with Alexandria and thus Greece. (If Alexander was Macedonian, the Ptolemaic dynasty that his Macedonian general Ptolemy—as pharaoh, Ptolemy I Soter—formed after his death was certainly more Hellenic than Egyptian, and the scholars brought to Alexandria were either from Greece itself or its colonies.) Whereas the beginning is shrouded in mystery, both historical and mythical, the foundation is an originary act, a necessary fiction of origin that declaratively performs the displacement of the historical what-was with a new what-is. As the beginning before the founding of western epistemology by Greece, Egypt assumes the role of the archaic, of the mother whose body is acted upon by the mind of the father.

The Egyptian metaphor also provides Kant with the concept of the king's doubled body, Morgan points out; this is a slightly different conception than that of the Elizabethan division between a body politic and the king's individual body. In the Tudor invention of the king's two bodies, the personal body can learn to become more attuned to the needs of the state, which are acted upon by the monarch in her/his political identity or body. In Kant's Egyptian version of this concept, the two bodies are stable identities that cannot grow together, as in the Elizabethan conceit. For Kant, the mortal, empirical body is corruptible; the theoretical body politic is Law and Sovereignty. When the king acts in his political body, he is temporarily unconnected to his empirical identity; he enacts the Law rather than his own interest. Whereas his private person is susceptible to error, his political person must be obeyed as Law and Justice. The double crown of the Egyptian pharaoh, Morgan suggests, represents the king's two bodies, his "temporal and spiritual power."[39] (She does not mention its actual meaning of uniting Upper and Lower Egypt, the 'two lands.') The spiritual power, the king's "ka" in Egyptian terms, which is more potent than that ascribed to the ordinary human, must be carefully controlled; its force can be used for ill if the king is allowed to follow his own desires. Thus, his mortal identity must be disciplined, and his spiritual identity safeguarded from it. This separation, as the west views it, of the king's two bodies "confounds attempts to found the state in the person of the sovereign."[40] The Egyptian beginning without origin (Greek histories of Egypt such as Herodotus' are exemplary in documenting its murky past as a matter of myth rather than record) means that the Egyptian state had no true foundation, and thus could not adequately ground civil society. Its biblical representation of a tyrannous state supported by slavery was taken as proof against originary value; only the Greeks lived up to this standard (Greek and Roman uses of slavery were apparently taken to be more democratic). Because Kant's main reference to Egypt is to their murkiness, what he called their "groping" (*herumtappen*) after knowledge rather than a clearheaded approach such as the Greeks took, it is unclear what Kant knew of the double crown's significance or of the Egyptian 'ka.'[41] As Morgan points out, Freemasonry appreciates this groping around, this searching and always becoming aspect of individual knowledge, but Kant preferred a less open-ended, process-oriented approach.

However, Morgan's main connection between Kant and Ancient Egypt is how Egypt provides one of several tropes that destabilize Kant's masterful system. The Egyptian metaphor represents the quandary of social beginning, a quandary posed by the king's two bodies: the first is theoretical, representing moral freedom and the ideal of sovereignty to which people subject themselves; the second is that of a fallible human to which they do not. (The latter body is the basis of Kant's reading of regicide as permissible.[42]) "[T]he 'Egyptian' metaphor demonstrates the inability of a community to ever completely unite itself under the authoritative person of a sovereign founder or lawgiver."[43] Foundation itself is called into question: both the foundation of human community, and therefore also the state, as well as—and importantly—the foundation of critical thought. As Morgan repeatedly notes, Kant desires to build his system on firm ground, and she connects this desire to the west's fascination with the ancient pyramids as the prime metaphor of Egyptian beginnings. Although Kant uses the pyramid in the *Critique of Judgment* to discuss the concept of vastness in the sublime, Morgan views this architectural image as functioning more largely: standing in for the place of Egypt itself in Kant's thinking, the pyramid metaphor provides an equally firm standing. Architecturally understood, the pyramid represents the lowest or earliest art form precisely because it is so entirely joined to the ground and bound by necessity. But the pyramid also tropes Egypt in its connection between its interior dark matter, which is simultaneously the archaic past. Finally, the pyramid stands in for the Ancient Egyptians, who for Kant were weighed down with matter, unable to think their way to logical clarity and therefore only capable of groping around in the dark.

Morgan cites Hegel to support her reading of Kant's use of Egypt for his architectonic, but in fact Hegel considers the pyramid as a combination of the above-ground pyramidal structure and the underlying labyrinth. Hegel understood the subterranean structure to be precisely what is foundational; through it one travels to reach the burial chamber in which the king's mummy preserves his identity as the Law, thus preserving the state. This is a considerably more stable image of Egyptian beginnings than Morgan reads into Kant's pyramid. Another way to interpret this schema is that Hegel's underground labyrinth and grounded pyramid represent the dark and light forces of Schelling's first two potencies; they arise out of the unity of under/above ground that is Schelling's *Ungrund*. Derrida explains in *Glas* that "the abyssal absolute (Un-*grund*) is powerless *(Potenzlos)*. This im-potence is its primitive germ."[44] Or we could take the course of Hegel's meandering labyrinth recalling Freemasonry's meandering journey toward knowledge, toward becoming-spirit. In Masonic rites, the initiation ceremony involves following an imaginarily underground labyrinth symbolically represented on a temporary floor covering. Successful passage, similar to the Egyptian journey detailed in the Book of the Dead, results in spiritual release, or becoming one with one's spirit. Masonic symbols begin with those of the architect, and logically include symbols of Egypt, including the pyramid, as grounding architecture. Masonic insight, gained through initiation, results in knowledge that is essentially the king's double body as mortal reflection of divine Law. Kant would not have approved of such meditations on the pyramid's substructure because he declined such an underworld journey, as his critique of Emanuel Swedenborg's "secret philosophy" in *Dreams of a Spirit-Seer* (1766) demonstrates. Moreover, Kant's refusal to go beyond what he could rationally know—which is the very essence of Masonic, Hermetic, and Egyptian wisdom—was what Schelling and Hegel objected to in his system. Even so, his ambiguous treatment of Swedenborg's mysticism in *Dreams of a Spirit-Seer*, particularly chapters such as "A Dreamer's Ecstatic Journey through the World of Spirits," reveals perhaps a secret longing for just such a journey. Novalis would later embark on such a journey via Swedenborg in yoking the inner sensuous world to the spiritual truth of the outer world.[45]

The locus for ambivalence toward metaphysics and nonmetaphysics for Kant, which in *Spirit-Seer* he calls a "metaphysical knot," is what we associate with the aesthetic realm. And, the strong association of Egypt with pyramids puts Ancient Egypt squarely in the realm of aesthetics. In Kant's critiques, aesthetics was intended to provide the bridge between practical and pure reason, between nature and the theoretical realm of moral freedom. This was a mediation meant to be temporary, a linkage in the critical project that would allow for the more organic, synthetic philosophical system Kant projected. Kant's immanent metaphysics—in which critique both forms and deforms in a chemical action that strips away impurities from the building blocks of system—would finally depart from the purely architectonic, and build an organic system in which judgment, affinity (*Verwandtschaft*), and relations mediate practical and speculative thought. Nevertheless, Kant had to rely on mechanics as well to support his system; the aesthetic foundation was both unreliable and although meant to be a temporary helpmate, it ultimately problematizes the entire system, just as myths of originary foundation problematize by obscuring cultural heritage. Aesthetic judgment should discover the difference between beauty and mundanity, nature and artifice, while moral judgment detected innocence and guilt, sincerity and hypocrisy. Examined closely, however, acts of judgment can never be calculated so nicely, it can never be "ground[ed] . . . upon proofs."[46] Instead, judgment is complicated by affinities, a chemical metaphor referring to the union and dissolution of substances; affinities change clear-cut situations into extenuating ones. Kant's use of the chemical analogy, which he intended as an aid in creating his scientific metaphysics, rather than "uncovering reassuring and reasonable foundations" in nature as the basis for immanent sciences, "instead opens up a bewildering entanglement of faculties that do not know when they have gone too far in their imitation of the [chemical] separations and unions observed natural phenomena."[47] The entanglement of mental faculties occurs through affinities that throw off any determinate regulatory system. Hegel, too, uses the concept of affinities when discussing the Egyptian proclivity for symbolism. Everything refers to other things; nothing is separate and intact but always acted upon by its associations: "In Egypt, on the whole, almost every shape is a symbol and hieroglyph not signifying itself but hinting at another thing to which it has affinity (*Verwandtschaft*) and therefore relationship."[48] Affinity in Kant is the bond between the mechanical, or structural, and organic; in Hegel's aesthetic theory it mediates Egypt's limitations in the realm of art with its religious striving after spirit. In Kant it is a crucial chemical reaction; in Hegel it impedes the progress toward Spirit.

Kant's insistence on secure foundations meant that it is not the spirit/soul he is after, but rather science. Moreover, the natural must be synthesized with, but not take the place of or be denied by, reason. His argument with empiricists such as Edmund Burke was that they held that taste was unconditioned; on the contrary, Kant believed, taste is heavily conditional, requiring thought and judgment.[49] If his problem was to explain how aesthetic judgment could be both subjective and universal, he could at least reject both the empiricist and rationalist claim that taste is experienced subjectively simply because it is universal without any proof of such universality. That is, those schools of thought had to resort to pure metaphysics for proof of shared taste, which in Leibnizian terms would be a "monadological metaphysics of the preestablished harmony" premised on "the divinely established harmony of the monads [that] would establish a basic agreement among the views of different souls."[50] Rather than presuming a shared similarity, Kant believed that the individual could share judgments of taste because these are not in fact based on the sensory object, but on a mental function like those of practical and pure cognitions: reflection. These mental acts are specific to our species and those are shared as human functions. We recognize and can enter into rational thought and speculative thought in each other; thus, we also recognize taste and share acts of judgment. Indeed, taste is pleasurable not because the object is beautiful, but because the process of finding it beautiful—which involves an interaction of the imagination and understanding—gives us pleasure. This mental interaction—which he called a harmony or free play—demands a metacognition or reflection concerning our subjective experience, our history with such feelings and those objects yielding such feelings, which we determine empirically. Thus, the aesthetic judgment that we feel sure will be shared by others is based on an assumed essential resemblance between oneself and others, an assumption of similarity rather than difference. Importantly for considering Egypt as the precondition for western thought and aesthetics, historical and cultural difference does not intrude in our judgments. Kant's claim that "the *universal validity* of a *singular judgment*, which expresses the subjective finality of an empirical representation of the form of an object" is possible because "the estimation of an object for the sake of *a cognition* in general has universal rules, [so that] the delight of any one person may also be pronounced as a rule for every other."[51] The taste for pyramids is ahistorical.

As a temporary prop between praxis and pure reason, Kantian aesthetics should be able to move beyond Egyptian groping around and heavy matter. Yet like Hegel, Kant finds affinities impeding his progress; so, as Morgan proves, Kant changes his mind on key issues around affinities in his discussion of the laws of judgment, unable to pin judgment down as he had intended. Affinity defines the home as a dwelling place, the body as a part of the community; but the home as ruin, and the ruined individual, still have their place in the spiritual community of the place. This place is bordered by an intervening space between the habitat and external ground, the middle ground mediating the inside and outside of dwellings. What emotional ties disturb universal judgment? What mourning of the past and of the dead disrupt aesthetic judgment? To translate Enlightenment Europe into Egyptian terms, consider the place of middle ground, between foreground and background. In spatial terms that take into account affinities, the interior of the home is mediated by a garden before being confronted by the social exterior. The aestheticized garden of estates often sported landscape architecture such as Greek temples, medieval ruins, and Egyptian pyramids. Kant saw houses as symbols of uncanny familiarity; pyramids, we might say, were uncanny houses of death, and both kinds of houses are subject to ruin. Here both the foreground and the background bespeak impending ruin through their networks of filiation, their emotive affinities. The place of the middle ground or garden, the forecourt as it were, is essential then to aesthetic judgment.

The relation of intermediation of garden to home, and the resulting clarity of the (sacred) hearth to Kant's architectonic and the problem of stable foundation for human community in Kant's system might be seen in the Egyptian temple, where the pylons that provide the gate to the temple allow one to enter an outer or forecourt; only priests were admitted to the inner court and then the sanctum, the sacred space of clarity, known to Egyptians as the house of the god. Like the temple, Egyptian pyramids, obelisks, colossi, and sphinxes were sacred constructs always placed in spaces marked off as intermediary between the realm of the living and the divine. The pyramids of Giza are on the west bank, itself an intermediary location between life and death; the pyramids sit at the back of a large temple complex; the two pyramids of Khufu and Khafre flank the Great Sphinx, which faces the rising sun. Like the gardens of great estates, the Sphinx is a midway construct between the home and the external world, and it, too, was carefully sited within the space of meaning. Pyramids, obelisks, colossi, and sphinxes were typically sited in relation to a solar axis; they were built on ground deemed sacred, and the ground around a pyramid, temple, and the Great Sphinx was its *temenos*. The *temenos* becomes the site-memory, the sacred place, that which the European garden aestheticizes and distances. The temple forecourt was an intermediary space between the sacred place's mummified body and the people; it was a space where priests could carry out ritual functions. Here the priests, rather than garden strollers, enact the rituals that will bring clarity through a mortal and divine communion, but the aestheticizing exercise of judgment is the same: the space of mediation before the impure can approach the pure remains in place. Kant's aesthetic enlightenment thus embalms its Egyptian origins, its archaic and sublime ground.

V. APOCALYPTIC MEMORY

Egypt was, for Romantic-period culture, doubly referenced as a textually knowable biblical site, and as a cultural vision anterior to the Hellenic world. As the eighteenth-century excavations at Pompeii and Herculaneum were increasingly publicized, this new information about the Classical world fueled a growing interest in the Near East as a locus of seductive cultural alternatives to western manners and mores. Arab and Turkish cultures achieved an atemporal cohesion in the western cultural imaginary: past and present were conflated, as were national and cultural differences among Near Eastern peoples, to produce one entity of "Oriental" otherness. This entity could be distinguished from the other cohesive and atemporal "others" of the Indian subcontinent and of the Far East (similarly consolidations of all regional, national, and historical differences). The same cohesive classificatory system organized African peoples into a largely unified imaginative concept. These forms of otherness, created by epistemological categories of genre rather than species, informed the general public's understanding of the foreign. More scientifically oriented knowledge informed political negotiations, trade relations, and scholarly pursuits, particularly in linguistics. But specialized knowledge, which dialectically interacted with more specialized classificatory strategies, only entered public understanding in very diluted and filtered ways so that the large categories of atemporal and mysterious cultures remained fairly intact. Romantic writers and thinkers were drawn to both forms of eastern otherness, the generalized and the specified. The generalized eastern other was seductive merely for its coherence, compounded nature, unknowability, and imperviousness to time. The specified eastern other was alluring in the very details of the constitutive difference between eastern and western beingness. Both ways of knowing the Near East were further filtered through the biblical lens of Old and New Testament descriptions, from the Exodus story to Paul's Epistles, and from knowledge brought back by travelers to Jerusalem to 'Oriental' travel writing.

Egypt's visibility both as locale and as memory therefore fluctuated between knowledge and mystery depending on the choice of parameter, biblical history or Classical history. Biblical history presumes eschatology, an apocalyptic imagination that figures Egypt as that which precipitates final causes. Classical-age history presupposes a backward glance, most likely because Greek authors were already depicting an Egypt shrouded in anterior time, knowable only through the remnants of its fragmented greatness. These remnants were still available to Romantic-period readers in Herodotus's fifth century BC *History*, represented as the slipping away of a colossal presence that haunted both the Alexandrian and Hellenic imagination and then the Roman Empire. In these pre-Christian perspectives, Egypt is the sphinx itself, the haunting of first causes, the precursor spirit. Once biblical narrative intercedes, Egypt is read through the Judaic misprision of pharaonic evil and mysterious knowledge. The western medieval imagination was stimulated by this mystery, the result of stories about the Alexandrian Library, the medical knowledge of Alexandria that was famous throughout the Hellenic world, and the mystery of the hieroglyphic code. The symbology of the pyramid, the mummy, the obelisk drew the medieval magus well into the Early Modern period as the search for eschatological and alchemical knowledge was fed by the increasing circulation of Egyptian artifacts such as papyri and mummy parts.

These images of past greatness and great mystery were countered by new information arising from geological discoveries about the age of the earth, the new archaeological experiments arising from excavation sites such as Pompeii which gave birth to a more scientific understanding of the past, and new astronomical information arising from refinements in telescopy and other observational instruments. These changes in epistemological assumptions provided a new key to biblical intimations. The past could now be viewed as a future tense, an apocalyptic provision. Egypt could be the grounds for a general coming to judgment, a weighing of souls, a passage to something new.

For the Romantics, the bifurcated directionality of the unknowable past and the unperceivable future is somewhat blurred by the attachment of apocalyptic thinking to either end of the historical spectrum. The antique is catastrophic both in the sense of diluvian, as in the paintings of John Martin, or ruined, a lost history needing to be reinvented or reimagined, as in the odes of John Keats. It is also manifest as final judgment, as a return of the historical repressed such as Mary Shelley imagines it in *The Last Man* (1826). In that novel, the narrative itself is presented as a futuristic remembrance, a posthistorical text that somehow survives in a weird time warp through the visionary dream of an ancient Delphic oracle. This future-past story is at once a dream vision, like Volney's *Ruins*, in which the past is reviewed from a cosmic stance, and a remembering of eye-witnessed events from a time yet to come. Both the Delphic seer's past presence and the narrative hero's future presence are unimaginable, while their existence is verifiable through the extant fragments of their textual lives. This is the essence of Ancient Egypt, verifiable only through inscriptions that have managed to survive, however fragmented, through the centuries. John Martin imagines the last man in Mary's Shelley's sense, albeit the concept was a popular one during the Romantic period, in his painting of that title (1849) depicting an old man looking down on the nearby ruins of a vacated town, with a ghostly female form lying at his feet. (He produced a study for the painting as early as 1826 and a watercolor rendering in 1832.) Others were also fascinated by the idea, but by the time Nietzsche was writing toward the end of the nineteenth century the idea had turned sour. In *Thus Spoke Zarathustra* the last man is a ruined, eviscerated being who illustrates death-in-life, the very opposite of the *Übermensch*. Like him, Thomas De Quincey's English opium-eater is also a ruination of a man, a verisimilitude who can only imagine a stronger yet somehow both past and not-past existence, while his present life is somehow already posthumous.

With Napoleon's Egyptian Campaign, the fragmented nature of Egypt's past offered yet a third version of the antique. The accelerated removal of ancient forms, an export industry under scientific guise in statuary of all kinds, was not just a grasping at "the shadow of a magnitude," as Keats puts it in "On Seeing the Elgin Marbles";[52] it was the radical decontextualizing of the already decontextualized, it was the assertion of a fully lost ground. The removal of obelisks to Paris (predetermined by a variety of similar imperial removals to Rome and Constantinople through the ages of the mysteriously shaped and inscribed columns) was the preempting of any possibility of an obelisk having relevance to Egypt, a task already begun under Augustus when he had obelisks moved from the religious centers of Heliopolis and Thebes within Egypt to Alexandria, and then to Rome. The obelisk lost its religious significance altogether when it was made to symbolize Rome's conquest not just of nature (moving the monumental) but of culture (reinventing Egypt). Under later removals, including Napoleon's, the new ground the obelisk encountered forced a new meaning on that imperial ground borrowed from an incomprehensible past. Yet if Egypt is thus reinscribed, no new meaning could be affixed to the artifact itself precisely because of its presumptive unknowingness and illegibility. In this artificially consumable version, decontextualized and stripped of transformational meaning, the apocalyptic association is no longer applicable. It is rejected except as a sentimentalized echo of loss, the sad ghost of dead gods.

All three of these perspectives are selective visions, looking at Egypt by looking away. But the appropriative view sanctifies and mediates ancient otherness, denying the apocalyptic associations that prejudice the biblical and classicist views. The presumptive objectivity of this view, its cleanness, lies behind the nonchalance with which Egyptian artifacts entered British life. London's Egyptian Hall, the sphinx head atop Sotheby's front door, Wedgwood's sphinx and lotus motifs for his Egyptian ware, the periodical reportage of the colossal head of "Memnon" in the British Museum: all represent a sanitized encoding of the Egyptian into the semiotics of British culture. It is a vision of denial, and as such troubled writers who intellectually could not but entertain all three perspectives at once. Texts that confront the antique as apocalyptic, such as Wordsworth's Simplon Pass episode in *The Prelude* VI, and that explore the further othering of the antique represented by Egyptianness, particularly the antique as hallucinogenic, such as De Quincey's crocodile in *Confessions of an English Opium-Eater*, reveal how the cultural and artistic appropriations of Egyptiana problematize the uses of the antique for the Romantic imagination.

These uses require interpretative structures that surround and lie down with the appropriations of antiquity for cultural and imperial purposes: these are the structures of aesthetics, which I briefly explored above through Kant's third critique, and art itself. It is worth revisiting Hegel's *Philosophy of Fine Art* for its intertextual articulation of this view. Hegel's thinking about art history reveals a teleological and therefore appropriative worldview that was already in place, fueling the developing antiquarian interest in Egyptian, Assyrian, and Indian art. Hegel's theory reflects how Romantic-period thinking about antiquity, and particularly the alien antiquity of eastern cultures, reverberated in commodity fashions, popular culture, archaeology, the scientific and aesthetic debates that constructed museum studies, and literature.

For Hegel, art, religion, and philosophy are the three domains through which the history of the split between subject and object and its spiritual healing can be traced. Although art provides an inadequate vehicle for the expression of spirit, the dialectic of subject and object is readily legible in it: In "Symbolic" art, by which he means Egyptian, Hindu, and Hebrew art, the material form dominates the spiritual content, unbalancing the desired reconciliation; in "Classical" art, such as that of the ancient Greeks, form and content balance historically, but not transhistorically or transcendentally; and in "Romantic" art, the art of the medieval and contemporaneous time period, spirit predominates over form but in a way that ultimately cannot match the expression available by other means. This kind of thinking, compounded by Winckelmann's historicizing theories of Grecian art aesthetics,[53] and productive of Enlightenment and Romantic evolutionary and teleological discourses, was very much in evidence in the displays and approaches designed by the British Museum's curators of ancient art. Greek antiquities received an emphatic and prioritizing placement and positioning *as art*, while the Egyptian, Etruscan, and Assyrian antiquities provided historicizing context and background to the progressivist achievement visible in the Hellenic statuary. We also see this kind of thinking proceeding from such displays into cultural expression. Alan Bewell, for instance, shows how the primitivizing of Egyptian culture in relation to the progressive Greeks is a touchstone of the periodical press, and readily apparent in Keats's *Hyperion*.[54] Such a *telos* allows Keats to imagine the symbolic order of Egyptian art as representing the spiritual hobbling of older gods such as the Titans in relation to the more powerful Greek pantheon. It is a view, however, that he would have absorbed from merely walking through the British Museum galleries toward the display of the Elgin Marbles with the painter Benjamin Robert Haydon. In fact, in prefacing the Greek with Egyptian art, the British Museum replicated both the order in which Museum acquired its collections, and the direct precedence the acquisition of Napoleon's Egyptian collection provided Lord Elgin for his removal of the Athenian sculptures. It was only because of Nelson's decisive defeat of Napoleon, which so impressed the Ottoman Sultan with Britain's "saving" of Egypt, that just three weeks after the surrender of Cairo Lord Elgin was granted the firman for the Greek marbles.[55]

But Keats's imagining of the British imagining of Egypt's place in a cultural heritage is representatively more confused and conflated than a stroll through the halls of the British Museum should have suggested. Rather, it imitates the meandering of the garden toward the enlightenment of the folly. Theresa Kelley examines the passage in Keats's *Hyperion* where Thea's "face was large as that of Memphian sphinx,/ Pedestal'd haply in a palace court,/ When sages look'd to Egypt for their lore"[56] and then considers Keats's understanding of the bust of "Memnon" in the British Museum as a "Sphynx." However, she does not consider where in his visits to the Museum the head of Ramesses would have been, noting only that "Keats's 'Memphian sphinx'" probably responds to the arrival of several Egyptian pieces of statuary and sculpture at the British Museum during 1818. Certainly in 1819, Keats and his friend Joseph Severn saw the sculptures, including one Keats called a "Sphinx," which Kelley notes was reported by the *Annals of the Fine Arts* to be "initially identified as a 'Colossal Head, said to be of Memnon,' an 'enormous fragment' transported with difficulty down the Nile from Thebes to Alexandria."[57] The conflation in Keats's work and letters between the colossal head of Ramesses and the smaller sphinxes viewable in the Museum makes it difficult to know how he is considering these "fragments," but his reference to a sphinx "Pedestal'd haply in a palace court" in the magazine's description raises either an image of a smaller sphinx figure as emblematic of the Great Sphinx (and of the British Museum as another kind of "court," with important ramifications for thinking about the allegorical nature of overlapping Egyptian/British past/present cultural imagery and identifications), or of the ancient court of Ramesses being so absolutely enormous that it could contain the Ramesses head. The colossal head still inhabits the museum's entrance hall, just as it was first placed for fear that its weight would not having adequate floor support elsewhere in the museum, making the forecourt analogy even more striking to the poetic imagination. Kelley also points to the lines in *Hyperion*, of Hyperion as "a vast shade/ In midst of his own brightness, like the bulk/ Of Memnon's image at the set of sun,"[58] lines that, however unconsciously, realize the Memnon as participating in the sun rituals associated with the obelisks in Ancient Egypt as well as other monumental objects and tombs, and the necessity of the sun's rays touching them, and hence their relation to atemporal time frames that Keats sees as sadly defaced and imperiled.

But Romantic culture's absorption of the Egyptian as prior ground to the accumulating evidence of the integrity, coherence, and spirit-content of the proto-Christian world enfolded another appropriative view, that of Napoleon's Enlightenment need to measure, record, and remove—to look in order *to see elsewhere*. The folding of one view into the other charted a new Romantic epistemology; looking retrospectively and looking in order to see elsewhere become the hallmark of the Romantic aesthetic. This was an artistic imagination finally resistant to the contemplative one established by the Dilettanti Society's aestheticization of ruins, in which a stoppage of time and a meditation on ruins is the required aesthetic response (one already practiced with the antiquarian's cabinet of curiosities). Romantic culture and art, by contrast, reflect the doubled viewing of the past as a looking aslant in order to authenticate a precarious present and an even more precarious future. Romantic views of temporality, particularly as an intercourse between past and present, present and future, provide a relativist, destabilizing and ameliorative approach that greatly contrasts with Enlightenment endeavors to record, pin down, identify, and objectively "know" the remains of the past.

The volatile debate over the Elgin marbles—whether or not to purchase them, whether or not they are authentic (as Robert Benjamin Haydon held)—illustrates how the Romantic relativism allows for a resistance to appropriation as acquisitive colonization. The past cannot be simply acquired; its adoption puts in place a necessary adaptation which destabilizes subject and object (a rift which had not been as healed as Hegel hoped in his theorizing of Romantic achievement). The absurdity of appropriation, appreciable only under a relativist perspective, is its predatory impulse that cannot contain the magnitude's shadow, and that cannot assimilate the radicalizing differences in conceptual dimension, much less the mystery of cultural and historical identity. Lord Byron knew this when he modeled his Albanian dress: appropriation changes the taker's identity. Furthermore, the transport of cultural commodities as a commercial concern increases the crises of identity boundaries. The seductive appeal of the commodification of otherness can gloss over the entanglement of self-other distortions, a horrifying thought to a writer concerned with the limits of sanity like De Quincey. Byron's joke about putting a pyramid in Piccadilly Circus, which hinges on England's appropriative and commercializing attitude toward antiquity, was only one of many such jokes that partook of an ongoing cultural resistance to the importation of Egyptiana, both on the issues of scale and age. Moreover, it problematizes subjectivity: It is one thing to travel to the Orient and "go native," as several as the most noted early travelers did and as Byron imagines doing in his Turkish Tales; it is another to import nativeness to London. Such responses reveal how Hegel's categorical primitivism, as an attempt to contain and estrange the past—by importing antiquities to decorate urban centers for instance—is subverted and resisted by Romantic views of the temporal, not only in the intercourse between antiquity and modernity, but in the confluences and disturbances between the now and the elsewhere, the western and the eastern. To 'decorate with' is to partake of the symbolic order of that art, and not to leave it safely in its category of failed or impotent signification. To put it more succinctly, when Romantic-period notions of temporality are complicated by eastern otherness, the fragility or fragmenting quality of time becomes apparent, and frighteningly associable with the ruinous quality of remains that might be antique, but that speak to the present's inherent capacity to be ruined—especially in a time of war.

The problem of subjective and cultural intersections and disjunctions inhabiting the antique's seductive appeal is made a specifically Romantic concern by the effects of Napoleon's encyclopedic and cartographic interventions in Ottoman Egypt. That Enlightenment project of accounting brought home objects which were instead absorbed into the British fabric; the most common response to Egyptian artifacts was the dissemination of Egyptian motifs in fashionable fabric, furniture, and architectural decoration as an acculturation of the strange into the familiar. But grounding this confrontation was a century of slowly developing interest in Egypt: Rev. Richard Pococke described his 1737–1738 trip to Egypt in his two folio volume *Description of the East, and some other countries* (1743–1745);[59] Colonel William Lethieullier donated his collection of antiquities to the British Museum in 1756, among which was the first Egyptian mummy. By 1785, the Museum had acquired antiques from Egypt, Pompeii, and Herculaneum, heralding the increasingly rapid acquisitive projects of individual explorers and political appointees such as Sir Joseph Banks, Sir William Hamilton, and Sir Henry Salt.

These serious forays into what had been a land of mystery, a mystery attenuated by long-held superstitious beliefs about mummies, culminated in Napoleon's capture of Alexandria in May 1798. As Peter Clayton notes in *The Rediscovery of Egypt*, a direct consequence of the scientific focus Napoleon brought to bear on Egypt was that "Mummies began to be robbed for their papyri rather than broken up for their pharmaceutical properties."[60] Along with General Bryueys, Admiral of the Fleet, Napoleon was sent to take Egypt from the Ottoman Sultan, ostensibly to open up new possibilities for colonies and trade. Their real mission, however, was to redirect Napoleon's alarming energies away from Europe. Egypt became at this moment Britain's mirror text, since Napoleon's original target had been England, but when necessary resources were lacking, the Directory decided on Egypt instead since this would gain control of Britain's overland trade route with India. It was in this sense, perhaps, that Felicia Hemans remembers the Battle of the Nile, fought several months later, as the story not so much of Nelson's victory, but of Casabianca's captaining of Napoleon's starship *L'Orient*, and of the ship as the death vehicle of the French captain's young son. For Hemans in "Casabianca" (1829), it was the sacrifice of the dear one for the sake of empire that provides the telling allegory for the loss of the margins as a stab to the heart, a warning of rechanneled peril. Here the French subject accommodates both identity and otherness for British readers through the screen of vulnerable childhood, allowing a temporary erasure of Napoleon's imperial project in the face of eastern encroachments on western sensibilities, and the dangerous contamination of Ottoman and Egyptian acquirement.

Important to a less sentimental reception of Egypt was the fact that also on board the *L'Orient* was the Commission on the Sciences and Arts—"167 scientists and technicians, including many eminent scholars representing virtually all the sciences of the day, under the leadership of Baron Dominique Vivant Denon."[61] These men were to establish the scientific principles of what would soon become Egyptology, and they were aided as much as was possible by Napoleon himself, who amassed Egyptian antiquities for his own collection, and founded an "Institut d'Egypte" in Cairo for the study of Egypt past and present.[62] After the British acquired the expedition's amassed antiquities under the Treaty of Alexandria, George III presented them as war trophies to the British Museum in 1802, including the Rosetta Stone.[63] Alexandria was, of course, the location of the greatest loss of ancient knowledge, the burning of the library that housed many records and histories of Egypt, including the thirty-volume *History of Egypt* in Greek commissioned by Ptolemy I.

As replacement text, the Rosetta Stone reductively emblematizes the character of Egyptian mystery, both encoding a civilization and decoding itself. Although its value would not be fully known until Champollion deciphered hieratic script in 1822, it can functionally redirect our reading of a Wordsworthian text not usually associated with Egypt. I want to consider the possibility that the allusively biblical and apocalyptic nature of Wordsworth's Simplon Pass vision is resonantly Egyptian. The transportation that does occur there, versus the transportation that did not occur in crossing the alps, probes the association of biblical apocalypse as something yet to come, with ancient miracle revised as a kind of modern day Dead Sea crossing—not an escape from Egypt, but an invocation of its haunting force. The effect, which is a recurrent gesture in *The Prelude*, is to cast the future as a vision of the past; but the passage also effectively casts the present in terms of an Egyptian historicity, a quality of unknowable time. The vision is of a curiously downward movement, an archaeological descent into the earth's transtemporal truths. Looking up from these depths, he sees the "immeasurable height/ Of woods decaying, never to be decayed,/ The stationary blasts of waterfalls," images that capture the ruined yet unerasable quality of the antique as colossal, and which also imply the ancient geometry of first civilizations, the manipulations of "time and space" with which Book VI begins: "With Indian awe . . . did I meditate/ Upon [geometric science] . . . /And made endeavours frequent to detect/ The process by dark guesses of my own."[64] The darkness of these speculations expresses not just a knowledge lack, but the inefficacy of knowledge in the face of such old mysteries. It is a riposte to Hegel's absolute knowing.

The waterfall passage is typically read as an expression of the necessity of an apocalyptic imagination to understanding the French Revolution as both aestheticized and politicized. But the apocalyptic and the aesthetic are terms that, particularly in conjunction with politics, can be made equivalent to the religious (not surprisingly, the "Imagination" passage ends with the invocation redirected to God); this is a shift in emphasis that moves away from radical social conflict to radical cultural and temporal confrontation. In the first interpretation Wordsworth rejects a Napoleonic reading of social change; in the second he is rejecting a Napoleonic reading of antiquity by emphasizing the conflation of the first two perspectives—that of the oriental antique as both forward and backward, as both old time and the collapse of past and future tenses—in order to reject the third as represented by Napoleon's attempt to categorize, classify, and collect such time and space. Importantly, Wordsworth's invocation to imagination in Book VI ends with the comparison of the visionary mind to a soldier whose "prowess" is compared to the most fertilizing Egyptian reference available: "The mind beneath such banners militant/ Thinks not of spoils or trophies, nor of aught/ That may attest its prowess, blest in thoughts/ That are their own perfection and reward—/ Strong in itself, and in the access of joy/ which hides it like the overflowing Nile."[65] Here, Napoleonic acquisitiveness is rewritten as the mental absorption of such mysteries, while the self-renewing power of Ancient Egypt's imaginative life force becomes synonymous with poetic creativity or "joy."

Mary Shelley viewed with concern the analogy of Egypt's renewability with poetic virility, a subject of that Keats, Hunt and Shelley toyed with as part of the sonnet competitions that were themselves tests of such "prowess," to use Wordsworth's term. In *The Last Man* she finds the origin of the decimating plague to be Nilotic Egypt itself.[66] The ruins of old civilizations contain the germ of their ruin, the precipitant of final causes. It is a problem, finally, of sanitation, of the contaminating of the domestic familiar by ancient mystery, and makes strange the accommodation of oriental to occidental through Egyptian motifs on buildings, furniture, and even Wedgwood ware.[67] Mary Shelley's aesthetic response encodes a fear of subsuming biblical and Classical views toward Egypt into poetic valor as Wordsworth has done.[68]

When De Quincey encounters the Egyptian motif as similarly contaminating, for instance when a crocodile chair leg that, like a revitalized mummy, comes ferociously to life, his reaction is not the fear of what happens when Egypt's past predicts a British future, but a fear of the consequences of a Hegelian reading—the return of the contained. This is not a return of the repressed, but of the transformed or accommodated, the object of appropriation—the ingested. The problem De Quincey's hallucination raises is how acculturation as commodification changes the appropriator in indelible ways, as Byron saw so clearly. The question of Egypt as fertility and ruin, nightmare and empowerment, is: does raising Egypt's ghost divert Britain's progressivism and estrange its *telos*? If the ruins of Egypt brought home as something beforehand—before even Hellenic ruins, and because ritualistically unknowable, aesthetically unknowable as well—could preside over nineteenth-century Britain's relation to historical and cultural otherness, then the end of the world, or the end of a sane world, is a plausible imagining.

It is true that the British became crazy for Egypt. The work of Giovanni Battista Belzoni, John Gardner Wilkinson, and others, who popularized Egypt well into the nineteenth century, brought about the new field of Egyptology, its birth closely allied with the cultural adoption of Egyptian decorative motifs, funerary procedures, and mythic borrowings in Romantic culture. This new scientific romance with Egypt had to come to terms with the colonization of the past that Napoleonic invasion, archaeological retrieval, and Hegelian system represented. The consonance between all three suggests the political implications underlying Hegel's *telos*. It is available not just in the French army's reputed uses of the Sphinx as practice target—believable if not true—but so much more so in Sir John Soane's candle-lighting for dinner guests of the alabaster sarcophagus he acquired from Sir Henry Salt's collection when this item was refused by the British Museum. (Henry Salt, the Consul General in Egypt at the time, and his agent Giovanni Belzoni—formerly a circus strongman and hydraulic specialist—amassed a collection of Ancient Egyptian colossal sculpture, including a head of Ramesses II, known as "the younger Memnon," and a head and arm from a colossi of Thutmose III, both on display today in the British Museum, whose trustees purchased several choice pieces from Salt in 1819 for a disappointingly small sum of £ 2,000, refusing the sarcophagus that Soane was then able to acquire.)

The associations between the funerary and dining that Soane's entertainment suggests are fully resonant of the death/food economy of the Egyptian tombs, playing with its contaminating potential. The antique is ready for desecration, consumption, internalization, but the uses to which it is put may exact their vengeance. For Keats, the Egyptian eats time, for De Quincey it eats mind, for Mary Shelley it devours flesh, for Wordsworth it engulfs revolution gone wrong, for Hemans it signals a sacrifice of family to empire. There is a fear here of *telos* itself, of what gets lost when the symbolic is dismissed as unreadable, unpronounceable, irrelevant. If Hegel finds the spiritual unavailable in "Symbolic" art, these writers find the alien antique more than expressive in its spirit. The younger German Romantics, however, found the archaic appeal of Ancient Egypt and its priority stimulating. Even more so was the more recent but still ancient phenomenon of Alexandria and the mystery cult of Isis, based in Säis (in which the Egyptian deity is translated into universal Nature). Whereas Ancient Egypt functioned as a prior ground as well as a nowhere place for German Idealism, Alexandria represented an encyclopedic imagination at work in which poetry and science commingled to generate universal principles, verities about the cosmos and the world. Here was a model for the German Idealists' own encyclopedic endeavors, an alchemical basis for re-membering the material world as well as the cosmos. Isis represented the entirety of Hermetic wisdom concerning universal Nature, wisdom derived from Thoth, god of writing, and translated into gnostic associations with Judeo-Christian theology. In the Turin manuscript, which contains a variant of the Isis-Osiris myth, Isis steals power from Ra, the "self-created" divine being, by stealing his name. Isis had gained her power and her words from Thoth, the personification of the mind of the Creator; thus, her words are divine, for she is "Isis, the lady of words of magical power."[69]

These ideas will play out further in the next chapter, "Geographica," in which the mapping between celestial and terrestrial worlds, between the spiritual world of intellect and the material world of phenomena, is mapped onto each other, and in which infinite nature and finite nature are understood to mirror each other. These are all objects of study for encyclopedic knowledge, as figured by the Alexandrian Library.

NOTES

1. Novalis, "Logical Fragments I," 65.

2. Hegel, *Phenomenology of Spirit*, 14; emphasis his.
3. Aristotle. *The Basic Works of Aristotle*, Categories1b, 10–11.
4. Ibid, 981b. 22–24.
5. Ibid, VII.14.
6. Hegel's understanding of Spirit or consciousness as part of the movement of World-Spirit: "Since the Substance of the individual, the World-Spirit itself, has had the patience to pass through these shapes [the moments in the dialectical process] over the long passage of time, and to take upon itself the enormous labour of world-history, in which it embodied in each shape as much of its entire content as that shape was capable of holding" (*Phenomenology*, 17), then consciousness at the universal level as well as the individual level requires cognitive forms that dialectically ground Hegel's Romantic philosophy.
7. Canfora, *The Vanished Library*, 3–12, 100. For more on the unique culture of Alexandria during this period, see Hala Halim's *Alexandrian Cosmopolitanism*.
8. Budge, *Egyptian Magic*, 143.
9. Reginald Eldred Witt is helpful on the relation between Manetho and Timotheus, 21.
10. Although the rediscovered works of Plato were readied for translated before the *Corpus Hermetica* was recovered from Macedonia. See Yates, *Giordano Bruno and the Hermetic Tradition*, 9–14.
11. Ficino lived his classicism: he was, like Pythagoras, a vegetarian.
12. Keats explores this myth in his "Ode to Psyche."
13. Ficino had only 14 mss. to work with (Yates, *Giordano Bruno and the Hermetic Tradition*, 12).
14. Buried and worshipped at Saqqara; the earliest discovered was buried in reign of Amenhotep III by his son Thutmose. Ramesses II built the Serapium for the bulls' interment and worship, which was used through the reign of Cleopatra VII.
15. Yates, *Giordano Bruno and the Hermetic Tradition*, 7.
16. For a history of Alexandrian science, see Lucio Russo, *The Forgotten Revolution*.
17. Egyptians believed that certain priestly rituals called the god to its statue, bring the deity into presence.
18. Clark, "Lost and Found in Translation," 161.
19. I'm indebted to Tilottama Rajan's work on philosophical encyclopedic systems here.
20. He is best known for his cosmological theories, which went even further than the then-novel Copernican model: while supporting heliocentrism, Bruno also correctly proposed that the sun was just another star moving in space, and claimed as well that the universe contained an infinite number of inhabited worlds populated by other intelligent beings.
21. Although Bruno himself knew little Hebrew (Yates, *Giordano Bruno and the Hermetic Tradition*, 239, 258, 262).
22. In Sloterdijk's *Derrida, An Egyptian*, Egypt is a site of Judeo monotheistic origination. My usage of "Neo-Egyptian" departs from Derrida and Sloterdijk's definition, in which it refers to the Jewish identity Moses compelled his people to adopt after the exodus.

23. Nils Roemer, *Jewish Scholarship and Culture in Nineteenth-Century Germany*, 64.

24. Writing, or inscription, Derrida explains, is a conflict between vacancy and excess that demands an inaugural event or originary violence (*Writing and Difference* 8–10), which we might call the chemical spark.

25. Walter Budge, in his museological capacity at the British Museum, translated this in 1895 as *The Egyptian Book of the Dead: The Papyrus of Ani in the British Museum*.

26. Yates, *Giordano Bruno and the Hermetic Tradition*, 11.

27. See Pierre Hadot, *The Veil of Isis*, and Reginald Eldred Witt, *Isis in the Ancient World*.

28. Schelling, *Bruno*, 137.

29. *Bruno*, 119. Schelling is using the dialogue form to argue with Fichte; this is exactly how Bruno uses the dialogue form in several of his works to argue with his detractors; Bruno uses Hermes as the primary instructor in these dialogues.

30. Qtd. in Yates, *Giordano Bruno and the Hermetic Tradition*, 212.

31. Volney, *Ruins*, 21.

32. Ibid, 22.

33. Ibid, 23.

34. Ibid.

35. Celadon, *The Golden Age, or The Future Glory of North America*, 7.

36. Volney, *Ruins*, 33.

37. This internal and external structural enforcement reveals the existence of two different conceptions of British Empire, which David Armitage has analyzed as overlapping phases of imperial nationalism rather than a historically separate Elizabethan maritime empire and a second colonial expansionist empire. It is this second expansionist phase that is most associated with the British Empire, particularly in its colonization of India. Although it is the colonial that will be the primary identity of British Empire in this study, it is worth noting that, taking Armitage's argument, Britain was ideologically premised on empire through England's prior conquests of Wales, Cornwall, Scotland, and continued in its aggression against Ireland.

38. See in particular Laura Doyle, *Freedom's Empire: Race and the Rise of the Novel in Atlantic Modernity, 1640–1940*, 43–87.

39. Morgan, *Kant Trouble*, 71.

40. Ibid, 97.

41. "In the earlier times to which the history of human reason extends, mathematics, among that wonderful people, the Greeks, had already entered upon the sure path of science . . . on the contrary, I believe that it long remained, especially among the Egyptians, in the groping stage (*beim herumtappen geblieben ist*), and the transformation must have been due to a revolution brought about by the happy thought of a single man." Kant, *The Critique of Pure Reason*, cited in Morgan, *Kant Trouble*, 66. Morgan does not comment on Kant's dependence on the genius of one man to create the revolution in thought, but clearly Kant is comparing here the Greek ideal of individualism against Egypt's supposed valuing of communal identity and group thinking, a value also associated in Hegel with ancient Chinese and Indian cultures.

42. Kant's argument about regicide.
43. Morgan, *Kant Trouble*, 25.
44. Derrida, *Glas*, 105.
45. Rancière, *Mute Speech*, 64.
46. Kant, *The Critique of Judgment*, cited in Morgan, *Kant Trouble*, 24.
47. Morgan, *Kant Trouble*, 109.
48. Qtd. in Ibid, 108.
49. Paul Guyer's *Kant and the Claims of Taste* is the best treatment I have encountered of Kant's theory of aesthetic judgment.
50. Ibid, 6.
51. Qtd. in Ibid, 229.
52. See Paul Magnuson's explanation of Keats's response to the Elgin Marbles in *Reading Public Romanticism*, 189–192.
53. Winckelmann begins his chapter "On the Imitation of the Painting and Sculpture of the Greeks," by explaining,

> To the Greek climate we owe the production of Taste, and from thence it spread at length over all the politer world. Every invention, communicated by foreigners to that nation, was but the seed of what it became afterwards, changing both its nature and size in a country, chosen, as *Plato* says [in *Timæo*], by Minerva, to be inhabited by the Greeks, as productive of every kind of genius. But this taste was not only original among the Greeks, but seemed also quite peculiar to their country: it seldom went abroad without loss. . . . There is but one way for the moderns to become great, and perhaps unequalled; I mean, by imitating the antients. (*Reflections on the Painting and Sculpture of The Greeks*, 1–2)

Winckelmann's treatise, widely read, became the basis for both art history and, as Jenkins points out, modern empirical archaeology (21).

54. See Bewell, "The Political Implication of Keats's Classicist Aesthetics," and Theresa M. Kelley's use of Bewell's argument in "Keats, Ekphrasis, and History": "As a colossal goddess who might easily crush Homer's Greek heroes, Thea's alliance with Egyptian sculpture [in *Hyperion*] destabilises the evolutionary model of history and culture that dominates Enlightenment and Romantic aesthetics," in the sense that the poem "momentarily collapses Egyptian and Greek antiquity into a single frame, both cultures exist only as massive, broken fragments, and both offer equally moving evidence of the ravages of time and decay . . . mak[ing] it possible for Keats to put aside Haydon's anything-but-silent claim that the Elgin Marbles are the highest expression of antiquity" (220–221).
55. Jenkins, *Archaeologists and Aesthetes in the Sculpture Galleries of the British Museum 1800-1939*, 14–15; St. Clair, *Lord Elgin and the Marbles*, 88.
56. Keats, *Hyperion* I. 31–33, in *Keats's Poetry and Prose*, 476.
57. Kelley, "Keats, Ekphrasis, and History," 220.
58. Keats, *Hyperion*, II. 372–375.
59. He records monuments already missing in the French and German records made a century later. And James Bruce cleared the tomb of Ramesses III in the Valley of the Kings some twenty years later. Preceding their work, a medieval revival of

interest in Egypt based on biblical accounts had stimulated exploration, although the hostility of the Turks to Christian travelers since their takeover in the seventh century limited opportunities for engagement. Interest increased during the Renaissance, and by the eighteenth century there was beginning to be more extensive travel (Clayton, *The Rediscovery of Ancient Egypt: Artists and Travellers in the 19th Century*, 13–14).

60. Clayton, *The Rediscovery of Egypt*, 14.

61. Ibid, 15.

62. The French were able to accomplish a great deal in the collection, charting, copying, and study of Ancient Egyptian monuments and art before the Battle of Alexandria in 1801. In the Treaty of Alexandria, the French scientists were finally allowed to keep their notes, originally to be commandeered by the British, but all the assembled art objects became British property. No one considered returning any of it to Egypt, and indeed, the native Egyptians only worried about the export of their heritage when it meant a loss of revenue to them.

63. The Rosetta Stone proved to be the key to the hieroglyphic script of dynastic Egypt. However, the museum needed to create new space for them, and Banks, Hamilton, Charles Townley, and George Saunders collaborated on designing a new building, which was begun in 1804. By 1810 the middle class began asserting pressure for better access to the Museum (now 120 people a day) and for a more scientific approach to running the Museum. After 1810 the Trustees permitted 'persons of decent appearance' to wander unescorted on certain days.

64. Wordsworth, *The Prelude*, VI, II. 142–143, 149–150.

65. Ibid, II. 543–548.

66. "That word, as yet it was not more to her, was PLAGUE. This enemy to the human race had begun early in June to raise its serpent-head on the shores of the Nile; parts of Asia, not usually subject to this evil, were infected" (Shelley, *The Last Man*, 127).

67. Interestingly, Wedgwood himself didn't make dinnerware with the Egyptian motifs he developed. He revised Egyptian figures as Classical ones, and even so reserved his adoptions to decorative ware such as candlesticks, lamps, urns, and inkwells.

68. See Landor's 1798 heroic poem *Gebir* in response to Clara Reeve's "The History of Charoba, Queen of Aegypt," included in her 1785 *The Progress of Romance*; both poems allegorize Egypt as western myth, using the weak female ruler as a revision of the Cleopatra story to serve as Egypt's metaphoric history.

69. Budge, *Egyptian Magic*, 141–142.

Chapter 2

Geographica

Egypt, that ancient cradle of the sciences, where the wonders of art and those of nature contended for the prize of admiration, has been the object of philosophic excursion in ancient as in modern times. From Herodotus down to Volney, writers of equal celebrity . . . demonstrate the curiosity which it generally excited.[1]

"Geographica" is a term I am using to regard Egypt somewhat as Volney did in his *Ruins; Or, Meditations on the Ruins of Empires*—a book Thomas Jefferson translated into English after Volney's two-week visit to Monticello in 1796. The *Ruins* impressed Jefferson with its Enlightenment principles but post-Enlightenment perspective.[2] That dual perspective maps onto Volney's holding the east and the west in combination in his philosophical travel book: and as for the ancient Alexandrians, who similarly held the western Greek and Middle East worlds together in their Egyptianism, Volney also, like the Alexandrians, holds the cosmic and terrestrial perspectives together. The terrestrial is fully within Enlightenment principles, the cosmic fully within Romantic ones. It is in this sense of the dual perspectival quality that Egypt signifies for the west, that I will use "geographica" to refer a speculative cartography that maps the cosmic onto the terrestrial in such a way as to read deep history—indeed, prehistory and archaic ground—into and onto the ground and its foundation, the *Ungrund* or pure potentiality.[3]

Volney's *Ruins* provides an early vision of a Romantic geographica; it begins with a cosmic, post-Enlightenment philosophical perspective that entertains a value for dream and prophecy, rather than the empirical science of geography per se, and yet it fully presents the geography on the ground. Although it is geography that determines Volney as philosopher and Orientalist in recounting his travels to the Ottoman east in *Voyage en Egypte et en Syrie* (1787), a geographical science that categorizes, charts, and distributes the world, the *Ruins* provides a different perspective and cartography: not the terrestrial focus on land formations as such (though the historical geography is firmly in place) but an exo-terrestrial vision of a land's essence and imaginative status. It is a philosophical history or cartography that appears to arise from the land of Egypt itself, extending toward the other ruined empires of this middle region between Asia and Europe. During his lengthy stay in Egypt, Volney could witness the coexistence of archaic past and Ottoman present as commentaries on each other, commentaries that are given voice in the *Ruins* through the spirits that speak to the dreaming philosopher.

Dream vision and prophecy, deeply allied with poetic vision and speculative histories, also corresponds to the forms of knowledge revered in the mystery cults of the ancient world that were revived in Freemasonry (to which Jefferson also ascribed, having joined during his stay in France). The *Ruins*' theme, that there is a common truth underlying all religions as well as a cyclicity to the revolutions of deep time, is another way of parsing a cosmic truth of the kind Masonic self-enlightenment is supposed to attain. The cosmic vision of how empires revolve—how, like religions, all empires are in the end the same truism—is a different form of geography, a different way of charting how land and knowledge are mutually encrusted, place and wisdom coconstitutive. The formations that occupy the spatial dimensions of "Egypt" (primarily the ancient sites associated with centers of power, and so the capital cities and the necropolises with all their monumental ruins) embody the wisdom, the ways of knowing, and the achievements that though lost to time, nevertheless determine the imaginative power of Egypt's role in western prehistory.

How the Romantics, through the project of envisioning Egypt much as Volney did, pieced together the "wisdom" of Egypt is the concern of this chapter. The connections between empirical achievements of Greek thought and the cosmic wisdom reflected in Volney's vision of an underlying cosmic unity or common truth can be seen in something like Democritus's theory of the atom as the basic particle of all matter, which makes all sentient and nonsentient bodies mere variants of the same substance (a theory known to the Renaissance through antiquarian's rediscovery of Lucretius's Epicurean poem *De Rerum Natura*, and so also known to the Romantics). It is not Democritus that concerns me here, but how the Romantics understood knowledge, both empirical and speculative, in terms of Egypt. The mystery cults of Hellenistic Greece and the Hellenistic synecdoche for Egypt, Alexandria, carried and transmitted this understanding not only throughout the Greco-Roman world, but also ensured its continuance into the Christian overthrow of Roman theology. Geography in this sense involves time as well as space: a borderless as well as temporally spacious domain. These connections require a bit of prehistory preparatory to focusing on Alexandria as the occasion for this geographica.

A brief prehistory of this chapter could well begin with Plato (although the Pre-Socratics offer an earlier starting point), since Romantic thought is heavily imbued with Plato's dialogues, and because both the most daring scientific thought and the secret wisdom of the cults are at play in Plato's dialogues. What Renaissance intellectuals discovered was that Plato's authoritative use of reason and logic did not obviate the combinations of science and magic inherent in medieval alchemy and underground Hermeticism, but rather reinforced their ancient lineage. The Romantic interest in *Naturphilosophie* (nature philosophy, but as entwined with natural philosophy or alchemy), both as the study of nature and as the philosophical understanding of the cosmological implicit in the terrestrial, begins not with medieval alchemy or Renaissance Neoplatonism, but with the west's earliest appropriations of Egyptian science, magic, and medicine. The importance to Platonism and Neoplatonism of the Hellenistic mystery cults and their veneration of unknowability lay in these cults' mapping of cosmic truths onto terrestrial realities. This kind of cartographica was central to all the mystery cults.[4] Such cosmography had its roots in the even more ancient worships of Chaldean and Egyptian deities that required an interlacing of astronomical science, astrological beliefs, and mathematics as practiced by temple priests (and later by Pythagoras and his cult). In both the Chaldean and Egyptian religions, such practice was also associated with magic: magic for healing, for the passage from death into the afterlife, and for measuring geophysical events such as annual floods that were connected to rites ensuring continuation. In the Egypt of the Alexandrian period, the mystery cults of Isis, Serapis, and Harpocrates, which replaced the ancient worship of Osiris, Isis, and Horus as the main trinity of the Egyptian pantheon, retained some measure of this heritage of scientific knowledge—especially of nature—and magic. It eventuated in the early Christian mystery cult of Hermes Trismegistus known as Hermeticism, so important to the scientific beliefs of medieval alchemy, which spread through the Roman Empire as far as Britain. The relevance to Romantic-period Europe of these early idea systems, evidenced in Epicurean atomism and the Hermetic teachings, is that the few extant texts that carry this wisdom, particularly the *De Rerum Natura* and the *Corpus Hermeticum*, were deeply influential all the way up to Descartes and his decisive break with unknowability. And indeed, their significance survived Descartes's dismissal of not-knowing.

Part of the argument of this chapter is that Egypt is central to a cosmo-geography as imagined by the Romantics because in such a geographica, the mapping of time and history onto space—as applied by Schelling, Hegel, William Blake, Mary Shelley, and others—reveals that history is also cosmic, something the Egyptians knew. The past is still here, still alive. How to understand time, space, and history as entangled with the cosmic domain, or rather, as not two but one becoming that endlessly repeats, returns to haunt the Romantics in ways that stem from Ancient Egyptian cosmology as it was renewed in the Alexandrian production of knowledge. I locate the Alexandrian Library centrally within this alternative cosmo-geography, partly because Alexandria was the Romantics' main source of information about Egypt before Ottoman rule other than the biblical account. But I do so also in order to identify the mystical character the Library had attained as *the* Egyptian site of lost knowledge within a Romantic-period geographica.

My project here is to revisit the nature of knowability in terms of the Romantic encyclopedic imaginary and Romantic nature philosophy, in which the speculative philosophical thought conjoins with scientific knowledge. However, the antecedent of nineteenth-century nature philosophy lies in the achievements of scientists and poets at the great Library of Alexander's foundational city. Michel Foucault points out that the nineteenth-century restructured knowability as natural history;[5] certainly, nineteenth-century travel guides treat Egypt as an object of natural history, with accounts of Egyptian geographical features, tables of hieroglyphs, measurements of ancient monuments along with ethnographic observations of modern Egyptians and their culture. In the alternative geographics I propose to study here, natural philosophy is more to the point, as is natural religion; therefore Romantic-period imaginative geography, such as Schelling's *Ages of the World* (1811), in which geohistory is recoverable through a Hermeticized poetics, and Mary Shelley's *The Last Man* (1826), in which the spread of Egypt's cultural ruin seems an inevitable outcome of its geography, carries forward the Alexandrian project in significant ways. The connective tissue between Schelling and Shelley is Blake's mythopoetic construction of an archaic prehistory. Blake's mythopoetics provides an analytic of the imperial contamination that, for instance, helps explain why Shelley locates the archaic in Egypt's Nile River and its pandemic-infested mud. From Blake comes the problem of empire, which I will treat through the lens of the Alexandrian Library as a problem of museology, that is, as one of many Romantic attempts to encyclopedically catalog otherly knowledge. The argument here is that the Romantic encyclopedic is the modern version of the Alexandrian project to map a celestial to a terrestrial geographica of knowledge and phenomena. This last section will conclude with Hegel's cataloging efforts to trace the mystical engagement of spirit through art in his *Aesthetics* as the Romantically acknowledged form of cosmic knowing (aesthetics as that which joins empirical and speculative knowledge[6]) that necessarily begins with Egypt's monumental spirit.

Behind Neoplatonism's Egyptian revival, illuminatingly revealed in Giordano Bruno's "Egyptianism" (briefly treated in chapter 1), lies the mystery of the great Library of Alexandria, synecdoche for the new Egyptian capital's intellectual empire. Ptolemy I, one of Alexander's three generals, received Egypt as his share of the conquered territories after Alexander's death. Scholars such as Lucian Canfora have shown the correlation between Greek research to assure successful conquests and Ptolemy I's dream of intellectual empire. Yet the historical evidence reveals that although Ptolemy and his heirs extended their Egyptian holdings to include coastal lands stretching to the east and islands such as Cyprus, Ptolemy I (also known as Ptolemy Soter) did not, in this enlarging of empire, seek to wrest territory away from Alexander's other general Seleucus, who took the eastern third of the Macedonian Empire including Persia. Ptolemy Soter appears to have been in search of a more globally and celestially oriented conception of knowledge and its uses. The belief in the possibility of universal (territorial and celestial) knowledge and intellectual empire persisted despite the later destruction of the Library's books under orders from the Caliph Umar ibn al-Khaṭṭab, for whom ʿAmr ibn al-ʿĀṣ had wrested Alexandria from the Byzantine emperor Heraclius in AD 640–641. The fate of the Library under Umar's rule is told by the Egyptian historian Ibn al-Qifti in his *Ta'rikh al-hukama'* (*History of Learned Men*, translated into German by Julius Lippert [1839–1909]). Despite this erasure of the Library's symbolic importance through the burning of its books, the intellectual inheritance was not entirely demolished; enough of the significant books had been copied and transported either to elsewhere in the Roman world or to the Islamic world. Of the rest, we can only speculate about the riches lost. According to al-Qifti, after receiving the Caliph's order to destroy any book not the Q'uran, the Byzantine Alexandrian philologist and Aristotelian commentator Yaḥyā al-Naḥwī (also known as John Philoponus, or John the Grammarian) asked ʿAmr if the scientific books written during the reign of Ptolemy Philadelphius could be saved for him. Informing "the Prince of the Believers 'Umar ibn al-Khaṭṭāb" of Yaḥyā's request, ʿAmr asked for instructions. The response was decisively negative: "As for the books you mention, if there is in it what complies with the Book of God [Q'uran], then it is already there and is not needed and if what is in these books contradict the Book of God there is no need for it. And you can then proceed in destroying them."[7] John Philoponus's thirst for knowledge had inadvertently consigned it to an oblivion beyond not-knowing. By al-Qifti's account, the books, parchment codices by this point, were still numerous enough that it took six months to burn them as fuel for the 4000 public baths of Alexandria. This is the heritage of Ottoman Egypt during the Romantic period: an unbearable weight of lost knowledge, doubled by the loss of Ancient Egyptian cultural achievements apart from the visible architectural and statuary ruins. The half-buried status of these ruins—including the Great Sphinx at Giza, buried up to its shoulders until the 1810s—was emblematic of the veiled and illegible nature of Egyptian knowledge and its correspondent cosmic wisdom; now the Library's holdings joined this vast reservoir of lost knowledge and wisdom. Not-knowing presumes having an inkling of what might eventually be known, given the necessary indoctrination, or philosophical perspective, or imaginative insight. As for the full extent of the Great Sphinx—its body but also its meaning—what enormity of books and the discoveries they charted the Library had held could only be the object of speculation.

Historians today differ as to whether the Library's collection at the start of the Ottoman conquest still contained the originals of previous centuries or only the patristic scholarship of the Christian era. Luciano Canfora believes it was more or less intact; Roy MacLeod, following the standard theory, states that the major works had burned in the fire set by Caesar's troops in 48 BC, a concept difficult to believe since the book warehouses were not adjacent to the Museum or Library, nor does Caesar mention burning the Library's collection in his memoir (nor do other contemporary Roman chroniclers). For centuries Marc Antony's gift to Cleopatra of the library at Pergamum (approximately 200,000 volumes, half that of the Alexandrian Library) was thought to be a replacement for the books Caesar burned, a hypothesis made questionable by the lack of scholarly mention of such loss and inadequate restitution of precious originals.[8] The Library was begun with acts of theft from Greece in any case, especially from Athens. As these instances of imperial thefts, gifts, and destruction suggest, the treasure of knowledge is as valuable in its symbolic presence as its symbolic absence. For none of these rulers was reading anything the Library contained significant; what was important was the theft-gift-destruction formulation underlying knowledge's capacity to lay claim to a particular kind of empire, one that is unknowable in its scope and therefore unobtainable except piecemeal (empirically) or in theory (speculatively). The fulcrum of knowability/unknowability is firmly entrenched in the emblematic role the Alexandrian Library has played in the western imaginary even before it was subsumed to Muslim knowledge by al-Qifti, and to Ottoman control of what can be known and what must be lost to history.

Geopolitical empire, then, mirrors intellectual empire in important ways. The Library as a database was under threat well before Ottoman conquest, as Julius Caesar's disastrous takeover illustrates; even more destructive was that of the Coptic Christians who feared scientific work as magic and witchcraft. The work of eighteenth-century encyclopedists, building on the efforts of Renaissance scholars to amass associated materials, and of Neoclassical scholars to classify and catalog them, recapitulates the Alexandrian idea that knowledge correctly systematized creates intellectual empire. And intellectual power instantiates power as convincingly as political empire. Yet Enlightenment thought was also haunted by the other strain of Alexandrian thought, involving different ways of knowing such as a belief in invisible substances like atoms and voids, and the truths taught by the mystery cults. Thus, despite the stranglehold of Cartesianism, an undermining current of belief in the truth-system of mystery cults continued. This different order of knowledge relies on insights gained through a different perceptual system, one in which bodily experienced sensations, rather than empirical data, are actually experienced and thus interpreted according to a cosmic rather than human schema. Such belief was preserved in the publications of Paracelsus, Jakob Böhme (known in England as Jacob Boehme, and his followers Behemists), Ramon Llull, and Giordano Bruno; but importantly, all of these intellectuals participated in a network of European thinkers that included Duns Scotus and Erasmus von Rotterdam; and extended to Leibniz (who, in addition to his theory of monads, served as secretary to an alchemical society in Nuremberg), Athanasius Kircher, Goethe (who attempted to practice alchemy[9]), G. W. Hegel (whose understanding of Ancient Egyptian architecture is highly mystical), Schelling, and British Romantics such as William Blake (through English antinomian cults[10]), S. T. Coleridge (through his knowledge of Goethe and Kant), Percy Bysshe Shelley (through his research on Ancient Greek knowledge), and John Keats (through his theory of negative capability).

The genealogy for these threads can be traced back in some degree to the particular form of Epicurean thought and mystery cult practiced at Alexandria under the rule of Ptolemy Soter. Ptolemy I invited Greek scholars to reside at the Library in order to write new books on every subject, but also to collect and transcribe all extant publications of the known world. He even resorting to stealing books from the library at Athens when possible; his project created an empire of knowledge that could map onto the terrestrial empire of Alexander at the time of his death. Although library schools were begun at temples in Egypt and later in Greece in order to create a class of learned men,[11] Ptolemy's vision was grander. To contemplate such a grand project as a way of enlarging his share of the Hellenistic empire beyond Egypt to the intellectual realm rehearses in a literal way the teachings of the mystery cults: that the human is a reflection of the divine, therefore for Ptolemy, extending human knowledge is a reflection of divine knowledge. This version of universal knowledge is not far from that of the French encyclopedists, who *did* combine material knowledge with speculative reasoning based on universal principles, just as the alchemists did, just as the mystery cults did, just as Hermeticism did, just as Freemasonry did and still does. A literalization of this reflection can be found in the Renaissance-era globes that were produced for the great libraries, and the Romantic period still showed evidence of being influenced by them. These globes were always made in pairs, with the terrestrial globe mapping easily onto the celestial globe so that similar patterns were more readily visible. Such paired concurrence reflects Hermetic teaching: the cosmos is reflected in human mentality such that its reflection can be discerned in the world. Indeed, in late Egyptian burial practices, a celestial map drawn on papyrus and mounted on linen—the hypocephalus—would be placed under the deceased's head to keep warmth in the body, its round configuration as the pupil of the Eye of Horus filled with the mapping that was to guide the deceased in the dangerous journey through the afterlife.[12] This, too, is a pairing of mapped globes of human and divine knowledge of space-time, a literalization of geographica.

I. ARCHIVAL FEVER

For the eighteenth century, Herodotus's history was a major source for much of what was known of Ancient Egyptian culture; he visited Egypt c. 450 BCE prior to Alexandria's founding and during the Persian rule of King Cambyses II (d. 522 BC). Herodotus traveled to major cities and ancient sites, and possibly down the Nile as far as Aswan before returning. He collected his data by interviewing priests, who were the historical chroniclers as well as the keepers and practitioners of ritual-oriented and sacred knowledge in magic, medicine, and astronomy. But though he had viewed his previous historical inquiry into the causes of the Greek-Persian wars as a methodological one, he had no hesitation in his Egyptian account of accepting the tall tales of priests, and even his geography and ethnographical material was not always gathered firsthand. In 1890, Wallis Budge (Keeper of Oriental Antiquities at the British Museum) noted, for instance, that Herodotus never traveled to Thebes (previously burnt severely by Cambyses) and therefore his account is "not satisfactory."[13] Like so many British and European writers, Herodotus's work on Egypt was much indebted to the descriptions of others. He relied in particular on the world history of Hecataeus of Miletus, one of the several previous chroniclers whose methods Herodotus improved, although he also corrected Hecataeus and his other source materials as much as possible through on-the-spot observations. But he also recorded the myths interlaced with oral tradition of the priests with the same credulity as more factual matter, perhaps in order to produce a more readable yet authoritatively written account. Thus, as with any account of Ancient Egypt up through to the twentieth century, misinformation was legitimated by an authoritative account.

Although Herodotus's history survived, even the latest period of Ancient Egyptian culture under the Ptolemaic pharaohs and then Roman rule was not preserved in any absolutely reliable source after the final destruction of the Library. Even prior to that devastating loss however, Hecataeus of Abdera and other Greek scholars who consulted Egyptian priests and their temple records documented their findings through a syncretic version of Ptolemaic realities and ancient history. Later scholars such as Diodorus Siculus relied on earlier works in the Library so heavily that Egyptian history was further perplexed and obscured. But the royal Library of Alexandria, which housed the erudition of the historians, scientists, and poets who worked there, was beset from the beginning with obscurities. These were due to a temple-like treatment of Library initiates, who had to learn shelf locations by memory. Once library holdings swelled under the bibliomania of the first three Ptolemaic pharaohs, no degree of memorization could locate those texts doomed to be lost to time within the growing labyrinth, despite heroic efforts of classification and cataloging which occupied the careers of some of the greatest scholars of the Library. Under later pharaohs, degradation of the Aristotelian method that had characterized Alexandrian erudition set in, becoming reduced to editing original works through textual criticism that often-distorted works, as well as to the onerous cataloging tasks of the librarians. Both kinds of labor involved expending tremendous time and effort on minutia instead of on the production of new knowledge and new works. Perhaps precisely because both the collection and the scholarship stagnated, no effort was made to uncover a more considered history of Egypt.

Such a history had begun on the wrong foot in any case; Ptolemy Soter arranged for a collaboration between Manetho, a historian and priest of Heliopolis, and Greek scholars who Ptolemy invited to come live at the Library. Together they were to produce *Aegyptiaca*, Egyptian histories that would provide a foundation for Alexandrian legitimacy within Egypt and within the Macedonian Empire. Manetho, however, had to rely on various sources to provide information and to prepare his own king's list, necessary for a proper chronology. His last was accurate enough to be considered authoritative until relatively recently; however, temple records and monument inscriptions had often been rewritten and recarved multiple times by earlier pharaohs, altering factual history with a revisionist version. While this created inaccuracies in Manetho's account, these weren't detected until the twentieth century. But it is worth noting that even the sources Manetho used for his own *Egyptian History*, which he also provided to Ptolemy's scholars, were themselves unreliable. We have here a problem of unknowability, where empirical data is inadequate to the task. In addition to inaccurate or altered king's lists, Manetho suffered from the same problem of illicit information as Herodotus earlier. But unlike the earlier pharaoh's revisionist inscriptions and records (often done to align themselves with powerful forebears, and as imperial decrees that overwrote priestly knowledge), the priests of the Alexandrian regime who relayed inaccurate information, or infused their historical knowledge with myth and folklore, did so because the old knowledge had been largely lost, and increasingly even a real familiarity with reading hieroglyphics was gone. Guesswork replaced factual information, and histories of Egypt such as that by Hecataeus, who himself traveled no further than Thebes and Saqqara (just outside modern Cairo), were inaccurate to a degree alarming today. Later Roman histories would distort the Egyptian perspective even further than the Grecian, whether through revisions of the original distortions, or through interpretations of historical events according to the customs, practices, and new cults of a Romanized Egyptian culture. These histories are the best preserved, but are hallucinatory in their mediated versions of Egyptian history. They circulated misinformation that lasted for centuries, exchanging celestial knowledge and unknowability for fictions. This is one detriment of the dynamic of unknowability/knowability: human limitation of knowledge gathering can taint celestial knowledge. The dyadic structure of attained understanding and wisdom can suffer from effacement, erasure, and fictionalization. This gives such Hermetic knowledge a bad reputation, something to be refuted and corrected. Succeeding generations attempted to do just that, primarily by ignoring Egyptian history in favor of what Egypt represented.

Although most of the Library collection had been lost, there were a few rare survivors such as Aristotle's books, which were preserved through a set of bizarre circumstances that kept them out of the Library's collection until they eventually came to Alexandria during the Byzantine period. Other exceptions included those authors whose works scholars like Diodorus Siculus excerpted. Diodorus copied extracts directly from these works during a stay at Alexandra for his section on Egypt for Books I–V of his *Bibliotheca Historica*, literally the "bookshelf of history" but known as the *Library of History*. Other exceptions were those works by non-Alexandrians that the Library held only copies of. Although the idea that Julius Caesar accidentally burned 40,000 of the Library's books in his conquest of Alexandria has endured through accounts by Livy and other historians, Canfora persuasively rereads Classical sources in a vein favored by recent scholars to argue that the main holdings of the Library were never touched. Instead, Caesar's torching of the Egyptian ships in the city's great harbor in 48 BC had accidently spread to dockside warehouses storing grain and books, so the only books destroyed were elegant editions prepared for the lucrative booktrade with Roman nobles. Similarly, Canfora shows that the destruction of books credited to the Alexandrian Christians who pillaged the city's pagan temples and murdered Hypatia, the woman philosopher and physician they took to be a sorceress, only included copies held by the 'daughter' library belonging to the Serapeum, Alexandria's main cult temple. Even Diocletian's sacking of the city did not destroy the books then held in the museum's royal Library. When the Alexandrian scholar Yaḥyā al-Naḥwī, better known to western history as John Philoponus, was working on his commentaries on Aristotle before the Ottoman invasion destroy the Library's holdings, he still had a plentitude to consult. Unfortunately, Philoponus's attempt to preserve the books through political intervention was the very act, as noted above, that brought them to the Caliph's attention, sealing their fate as worthless and even blasphemous combustibles for the public baths.[14]

Histories of Egypt at any period were doomed to misinformation, lost records, politicization, and different forms of bias. In her biography of Cleopatra VII, Stacy Schiff explains that no single account of the great Ptolemaic queen can be relied on since all were written after her lifetime, or incorporated Roman prejudices against eastern cultures; the same can be said of the mainstay of the third person accounts of Egypt that make up the western tradition. Even where accounts concur facts can be doubted if, like Herodotus, historians relied on other scholars' versions. For Alexandria in particular, because of the loss of the great libraries of some 400,000 volumes (the Romantic-period Rev. Richard Polwhele, citing Gellius, puts the total number of volumes at 700,000[15]), as well as the ancient city's repeated destruction by human and natural forces, Classical accounts including those of the early church fathers must be understood to lie in the same realm of indeterminacies as Homer's own historicizing epics.

It is perhaps odd, though, to posit Alexandria as the first stop on a mapping or geographica of Egypt when the two capitals of Ancient Egypt, Memphis and Thebes, held the temples of the major cults and therefore the temple holdings of written accounts. However, because of the importance of Roman history for Britain, it was the latest period of Ancient Egypt, the Ptolemaic Dynasty, with which the eighteenth century and Romantic era were most familiar. Scholars working today can rely on substantiated facts about Egypt's past resurrected through two centuries of Egyptological research, but Enlightenment and Romantic scholars and poets had no such factual ground on which to walk. Moreover, both the Bible and Classical works were taken as accurate accounts of historical realities and were used as reliable tools even for the task undertaken by numerous antiquarians of deciphering hieroglyphics. It is therefore with Alexandria that an account of the abyssal ground of Romantic Egypt must start, even though the city and its culture represent one of the least "Egyptian" periods in the country's long existence. Despite what has been lost, vital information is still available in important accounts by Allus Gelius, Hecataeus of Abdera (not to be confused with Hecataeus of Miletus), Heraclitus, Livy, Porphyrius (who worked with Plotinus), Diodorus Siculus, and other scholars concerning Alexandria and Ancient Egypt itself, in addition to what Herodotus documented about different parts of the country. Alexandria, which was translated by Alexander's senior general and childhood friend Ptolemy Soter into a different kind of conquest, was thus the center for a late versioning of Ancient Egyptian culture. The flowering of Alexandria was also the end of an Egyptian culture expressing a continuum from its first legendary king Menes.

To begin a geographica with the final phase of Ancient Egypt makes sense in that Alexandrian culture as preserved in extant Hellenistic and Roman texts and biblical representations of Egypt was the only way in which early modern and post-Renaissance Britons and Europeans "knew" Egypt in any real sense. After Shakespeare's *Antony and Cleopatra*, Alexandria was the synecdoche *non plus ultra* for Ancient Egypt. Moreover, Alexandrian culture as practiced by the Macedonian, Greek, and Alexandrian intellectuals who worked in the great Library and Museum—a culture based on Socratic, Platonic, and Aristotelian methods and ideals—created the foundation of modern philosophy, science, mathematics, and engineering as the Romantics knew these fields of knowledge, and as we know them today. Particularly interesting for thinking about geographica here is the fact that Alexandrian scholars originated the sciences of geography and astronomy (in its western sense as measurable fact and accurate charting of stars and planetary distances, disentangled from astrology as in Chaldean and Ancient Egyptian astronomical practice). These Alexandrian sciences, the measurement and description of the earth and of the sky, both producing astoundingly accurate calculations of diameter, mass, distance, and field population of stars, retain their paired meaning making through the paired terrestrial and celestial globes so popular in the Renaissance and Neoclassical period. It was this legacy, rather than the mysterious and illegible remnants of an even older Egypt—the pyramids, obelisks, colossi, and temples—that recalled "Egypt" for the Enlightenment and Romantic age. Yet without these more ancient remains, without the archaic grounds that gave birth to them, Alexandria would have been unimaginable even to Alexander. Egypt was the necessary site, the fulcrum itself, between west and east, between known and unknown, between ancient Persia and the new empire Alexander intended to spread through to the Indus River. Of all his conquests, however, Egypt alone was reformed for history in Alexander's image; the land's ancient culture lay masked behind the Alexandrian one, which even as it transformed from Macedonian to Greek, and then to Roman, remained the face of "Egypt." This is the force of geographica: the time-space horizon is unstably grounded in the land itself, coarising with the mentalities that reform the ground from what can be empirically seen to what is experienced both imaginatively and on the ground.

Alexandria was also the site of the first of three historical correspondences that illustrate the interrelation between material and imaginative ways of understanding the world in the history of the west's version of "Egypt." When Alexander decided to locate his namesake city at a site described by Homer, behind the island of Pharos on Egypt's Mediterranean coast, he had his Homeric epics with him; when Columbus embarked on his westward mission across the Atlantic he had his Claudius Ptolemy, who theorized that India could be reached by sailing west, with him; when Napoleon arrived where Alexander had also landed to initiate his Egyptian Campaign, he had his Volney's *Ruins* in his pocket.[16] In each case the thinker mapped out the terrain that the conqueror took to be his challenge; if for Columbus his textbook provided geographical and mathematical aid, for Alexander and Napoleon the imaginative impetus of their textbooks provided a lens through which to accomplish a territorial end. Both soldiers were thinking more of the gateway to the east that Egypt would provide them (as well as its grain production) than of the mental world it embodied; nevertheless, the mental world was part of the gain. For Alexander that mental world was the priestly tradition of Ancient Egypt, which was particularly rich in esoteric, astronomical, and medical knowledge. For Napoleon it was the intellectual legacy of Alexandria combined with Volney's rumination on the cultural ruin that both it and the ancient land itself represented. These correspondences denote the relation between the mental and physical, spiritual and material, cosmological and terrestrial that have organized and structured the west's inheritance from Egypt.

Napoleon's Egyptian Expedition provides an apt exemplar of political ambition informed by the literary imagination: his campaign incorporates both of Volney's books, not just the visionary *Ruins* but also the on-the-ground tour guide and memoir of his *Travels Through Egypt and Syria, in the Years 1783–1785*. Together these volumes, made even more valuable with the inclusion of Syria and its ancient relation to Egypt, deliver a metaphysical conception: the idea that the land is a liminal or threshold space for something larger. Although Napoleon's scientific team, which included engineers as well as artists, was primarily charged to make the military scheme more efficient, its long-lasting effects by all members of the team depended on a metaphysical encounter with Egypt. In measuring and recording the ancient past, the team also brought it back to life in the celebration of its monumental achievements through beautifully illustrated large folio volumes.

However, for each of the conquerors—Alexander, Columbus, Napoleon—their ultimate vision was too material and land-defined to constitute the real mental geography that Ancient Egypt and its Alexandrian incarnations represented. What the ancients knew, and Alexandrian scholars demonstrated through astronomy and geography, was the essential correspondence between celestial and terrestrial knowledge. Without scientific proofs much of the ritualized beliefs concerning such correspondence were too highly mystified and androcentric, resulting not just in something like Chaldean magic (the magi's combination of astrology and astronomy, which was a combination of Zoroastrian and Babylonian priestly knowledge) as the combination of prophecy and worship without the mathematics. In other words, something like Hermeticism without the speculative wisdom embodied in that practice; something closer to witchcraft. Even alchemy, often associated with witchcraft, was probably of Egyptian origin as a cult practice, for it correlates heavily with the priestly rituals for burial and the instructions in The Book of the Dead. It also closely parallels the Pythagorean conception of reincarnation which, like The Book of the Dead, required remembering secret passwords and road marks for safe passage in the underworld.[17] In contrast, the majority of works housed in the great Library were of the Aristotelian school, with an insistence on empirical observation and experimentation whether scientific, mathematical, or philosophical and artistic. Lost in the sequence of fires that devastated it, the west spent the centuries after Alexandria's demise attempting to recover its discoveries. The loss was irreparable but assimilable in the sense that lost knowledge can be as valuable for being known to be lost. Alexandrian knowledge, like that of Ancient Egypt, became the metonym for knowledge itself, for all that can be known. The imaginative reconstruction of Alexandrian or Egyptian knowledge—as opposed to the empirical method employed by the equally philosophical scholars of the great museum and Library (Euclid, Aristarchus, Eratosthenes, Claudius Ptolemy, as well as Ammonius whose works were foundational for Theosophy)—could only remain just that—imaginary—about such knowledge. Athanasius Kircher is a prime example of a scholar who, at least in his research on some of the mysteries he attempted to elucidate, depended too heavily on imaginative and cosmological resources without the empirical element so necessary to sustain the dynamic of knowability/unknowability. He produced these treatises in addition to those on his remarkable inventions and his scientific treatises, but they are works that are fantasy rather than science, especially his attempt to decipher Egyptian hieroglyphics. Although Kircher was convinced he had correctly translated the inscriptions on the Egyptian obelisks brought back to Rome and still one of the best sources of hieroglyphic use in his day, his translations are decidedly colored by his Jesuitical beliefs and overshadowed by Christian theology.

Unhappily for scholars such as Kircher, achievements such as the mathematical calculations of Alexandrian scholars Eratosthenes and Claudius Ptolemy, who were known to have produced a more scientific mapping of the cosmos onto the known and unknown parts of the terrestrial world, were lost to the world. The loss of Eratosthenes's work is especially terrible: he came to Alexandria as tutor to Ptolemy IV and as librarian of the great Library, and his scientific efforts included demonstrating the curvature of the earth, and accurately calculating the circumference of the globe as well as the distance from the earth to the sun. His immense productivity resulted from an adherence to two principles: love of empirical study and the Platonic ideal of the philosophical path to spirituality. The two together reveal how closely the material and spiritual, worldly and celestial, were intertwined for these men. But the connection could not have been pursued outside of

Egypt. Even Pythagoras did not make his mathematical discoveries without spending time studying in the east with Chaldean magi, and most probably although not verifiably spending time in Egypt—resulting in the concurrences between his secret cult of mathematical mysticism and Egyptian priestly rituals.[18] In part the intellectual strides of Greek scholars who came to Egypt were the result of having in one place—the great Museum with its Library—a community of like-minded individuals devoted to a philosophical way of life that embraced all fields of knowledge. But equally important was the interchange of Greek with Egyptian scholarship, as much of the Alexandrian knowledge that was produced depended on the esoteric and scientific knowledge that Egyptian priests had accumulated over the millennia. That Homer was their starting point illustrates the confluence of history and geography with literature as an imaginative and aesthetic realm that could enworld them.[19]

It was that enworlding effect in both a mythic and transcendental sense (i.e., the creation of a comprehensible universe to the worshipper of the eternal as well as the beholder of manifested appearances) through discursive form that also impelled Ptolemy Soter to be able to imagine realizing Plato's vision of an ideal republic in which philosophy and politics could productively cohabit. This vision was embodied in the Alexandrian Museum (the house of the muses), to which the Library belonged. Plato, Aristotle's teacher, Aristotle as tutor to Alexander the Great, were the godfathers of the Museum. In chapter 3 I will discuss how Plato associates the model for an ideal city with the Egyptian city of Saïs in the *Timaeus*: it was Alexander who was educated to build and rule that ideal city. Ptolemy I was well equipped to flesh out the skeletal city Alexander laid down and to rule it in his stead. He had been brought to the Macedonian court of Philip II as a youth to be part of the young Alexander's entourage, and as such he had also studied with the royal tutor, Aristotle. Trained in the Athenian school, Aristotle made sure his charges were educated in the forms of enlightenment that combined philosophical inquiry with empirical study. But he added a love of reading that, unlike Plato, included the literary. If Alexander was a voracious reader, never satisfied with the quantity of books that accompanied him on campaigns, Ptolemy—and more particularly, his son and grandson—were voracious book collectors. The first three Ptolemaic pharaohs had texts borrowed from elsewhere copied, translated, and edited; Ptolemy III also had them seized or stolen in order to make the Alexandrian libraries (both the great Library and the secondary library of edition copies at the Serapeum) the greatest in the world. But the work of collection for Ptolemy Soter had to be combined with the production of texts, and to this end he created the conditions for what rapidly became a true university, a community of scholars who studied every discipline possible and invented new ones.

The impetus for Ptolemy's vision for his new capital as the center of an intellectual empire had two prongs: the first was the need to attract the attention of the Greco-Macedonian world, and the second was the essential need to yoke of Greek and native Egyptian populations. The first would turn Egypt's enormous grain surplus and trade items such a papyrus, linen, and unguents—along with Alexandria's uniquely protected yet large harbor—into the elements to make his domain a commercial giant, insuring economic stability, while the second would prevent civil unrest and possible native rebellion against his rule. Ptolemy could only quell unrest once the prior and much hated Persian rule that Alexander defeated could be forgotten and the new Ptolemaic regime assimilated into the larger cultural frame of the Egypto-Hellenistic world. Once established, Ptolemy would have the necessary precondition for the production of a universal history, terrestrial and celestial, of both old accumulated knowledge and wisdom, and newly generated empirical and speculative knowledge.

Although Hellenistic Egypt never extended much further along the Nile than the Delta, Ptolemy was able to configure a synthetic Neo-Egyptian religion to achieve both strategies for a civic peace. Helpfully, through a convincing collusion with the Egyptian oracle at the oasis of Siwa, Alexander had had himself announced the son of Ammon and thus a god in the tradition of the pharaohs. Ptolemy had to rapidly develop a similar but more believable strategy, for despite the site of the Siwa oracle, Ammon was a cult deity of Upper, not Lower Egypt (which is borders the Mediterranean), and it was the more powerful Lower Egypt that mattered politically. It was to this end that he enlisted the aid of the Egyptian historian Manetho to write—in effect, to create—a synthetic history of Egypt that would accommodate the new regime. But Manetho was also asked to help orchestrate something far more powerful: a new religious cult that could synthesize Egyptian *and* Greek religious beliefs and rites. He was a powerful ally, and with the aid of Greek scholars whom Ptolemy invited to Alexandria, as well as the aid of the priesthoods of the major cult centers Memphis and Thebes, Ptolemy developed the new cult of Serapis that both Egyptians and Greeks could worship.

The god Serapis was named from combining the name of the Apis bull after his death ("the Osiris Apis") for "Osorapis" or "Serapis," and would be composed of many elements recognizable to both Egyptian and Hellenistic cultures. The cult of the Apis bull was one of the oldest of Egypt, and the most important of three bull cults (the others were of Buchis and Mnevis); each living bull, carefully chosen and venerated during his lifetime, was considered a manifestation of the pharaoh and a herald of the god Ptah. On his death he was mummified and buried as a king-god in Saqqara, and his successor chosen. Although Greeks could not accept animal worship, the synthesis of Greek and Egyptian deities overcame this difficulty, while the Apis would ensure Egyptian acceptance despite the amalgam of Serapis as both Osiris and Zeus. The Egyptian priests were powerless to resist Ptolemy in locating the new deity's cult center in Alexandria rather than Memphis (which was Ptah's cult center and therefore where the Apis was worshipped), but this did not hinder Ptolemy's achievement in establishing the Serapis cult as powerful enough to be elevated above traditional cult centers and their gods. In order to enhance this relocation, Ptolemy had the Serapeum strategically built near the Soma, Alexander's mausoleum. Ptolemy's vision of Egypt as a wealth generator and thus a powerhouse, especially as it extended its reach to the east, was realized by his heirs: in the Romantic period the Ptolemaic pharaohs were known to control an estimated 330,000 cities, according to *The Monthly Review*.[20] The cult of Serapis, together with that of his Egyptian goddess spouse Isis, would spread throughout the Classical world, and Alexandria would remain the intellectual center of that world until the death of Hypatia in AD 415 in a victory of Christianity over "pagan" philosophy and science.

One of Ptolemy Soter's first strategic acts was to invite renown Greek philosophers to his new but as yet incomplete city, and he aimed no lower than the successor of Plato at the Athenian academy, Theophrastus, who had inherited Aristotle's extensive private library. Although Theophrastus declined, he sent his student Strato of Lampsacus, who would follow in the tradition of enormous erudition set by Aristotle. In inviting Theophrastus, Ptolemy was vying for a brilliant tutor for his son, which he got, but he also wanted to attract enough scholars of mark to the new capital that others would come of their own accord. These philosopher scientists, historians, artists—many of them polymaths—would form the community of scholars that Ptolemy envisioned living and working together. For this he planned a museum, or temple to the muse, within the royal quarter (which was indeed one-quarter, and eventually one-third, of the entire city's expanse). Unfortunately, little of this history was intact by the late eighteenth century, and even in the twenty-first century the achievements of the museum's scientists are still known only through references by much later Classical writers, the texts themselves mere fragments or ruins. What does remain of the vast learning accumulated in the Museum and its Library is the Alexandrian entwining of the cosmic and the worldly in an absolute rejection of the independence of either. This entwining is also the trace of Ancient Egypt writ onto the plan of Alexander's cosmopolitan city. The other trace of Egyptianism inherent in this plan is the reverence for ancient wisdom; the librarians who guarded the accumulated papyri were overtly enacting the role of Egyptian temple priests in protecting their temporal and spiritual histories—in the librarians' case, histories that were a direct result of Ptolemaic archival fever.[21]

The archival fever, theorized by Derrida but beginning earlier than he suspected, can be traced at least as far back to Mesopotamia, initially as a matter of royal bookkeeping and then of individual traders. The oldest texts known, c. 3400–3000 BC, discovered at the ancient site of Uruk (now Warka in southern Iraq), were clay tablets.[22] Importantly, the great library of Assurbanipal, although missing the all-important temple or museum, was in intent a forerunner of the later Alexandrian one, for "its contents were representative of the sum total of the learned tradition of ancient Mesopotamia" (Potts, 23). In *Archive Fever*, Derrida articulates the principal acts that constitute library-ness. These were so clearly the foundational acts of Ptolemy's Library that Derrida could have predicated his theory of the archive on it. There must be the "commandment"; this Ptolemy gave when he charged Demetrius Phalereus with creating the collection, as well as when the regal command came for subsequent scholars to catalog the unwieldy and growing holdings (prior to the first attempt by Callimachus in c. 250 BC they had to be navigated by sheer memory). The establishment of an archive also demands a place from where the things "commence"; the archive places and historicizes all else. By planning the Museum and its Library on the floor plan of the Ramesseum, Ptolemy Soter ensured the necessary religious and ritualistic aspects for such authorized scholarship and scientific research (as opposed to the politically entangled nature of Athenian philosophy, conducted and taught in the public space of the agora). With commandment and placement, according to the "law" of how and in what place things are ordered comes the "nomological principle" (from *"nomos,"* law).[23] In this way the Alexandrian Library, in the tenuous form of its extant fragments, provides the epigraph, citation, inscription (the "exergue") for the early modern and modern eras, though only in the sense that the exergue "capitaliz[es] on an ellipsis."[24] Insofar as we can only know a fragment of what was lost (the ellipsis), and in the Library's synecdochal status, it is the exergue for the founding law of what can be known both empirically and speculatively, both dialectically and metaphysically.

After the Alexandrian Library established itself as the world's largest library, it acquired rivals, the first being the newly established library at Pergamum under Seleucid rule (the dynasty established by Alexander's general Seleucus in the eastern portion of the Hellenistic empire). Seleucus replaced the ancient Chaldean temples and seats of learning with a library of his own. The results were somewhat disastrous for the Alexandrian Library, which was by this time weighted down with conservation and textual editing that made no room for innovative thought; indeed, the rivalry encouraged the acquisition of spurious texts and forgeries. For Pergamum, by contrast, the scholars invented a better parchment when Alexandria enacted an embargo on papyrus in order to starve its rival library. The rivalry, and a more long-lasting parchment, served to disrupt, fragment, and bring to ruin the Alexandrian legacy of universal knowledge, although the spirit of archival fever would be forever associated with it as the lost place of learning.[25] The distinction between the two libraries is also part of the transformation of a highly scientific intellectual legacy into a highly mystified one. Alexandria represented the Platonic way of life, in which one seeks spiritual purification and enlightenment through reasoned philosophy and a continuous search for ideal forms and Truth, whereas at Pergamum the Stoic approach as practiced in Asiatic Greece was in place. Here Chaldean mystical-astrological thought offered valuable insights and a source of recognizable and transferable patterns. This displacement, along with the loss of the Alexandrian texts, became syncretic, contributing heavily to the later reception of Alexandrian "Egyptian" knowledge as mystical wisdom rather than Aristotelian science. If the Platonic enlightenment sought by Alexandria's Aristotelian scholars provided a legacy and footprint for Renaissance and Enlightenment intellectuals, Pergamum's Stoic practitioners, with their intermingled Greek and Near Eastern thought, provided a shadow legacy that in some ways rivaled the Aristotelian one. This was a legacy and footprint that often had to go underground in its more excessive manifestations, such as Hermeticism, but that also had well-received, as well as suspect, embodiments in early modern alchemy and Enlightenment Freemasonry.

The connections between this more mystical use of insight at Pergamum and the admixture of reason and mythopoetics of Neoplatonism, the Alexandrian legacy, lie in the rites of initiation held by both the Persian and Babylonian magi and the mystery cults of the Greek world. These rites ensured the transmission of a collected ancient wisdom, literalized in the Alexandrian Library but also collectively accessible in the Jungian sense when correctly approached through initiation. For eighteenth-century scientists intrigued by these legacies, Nature was the veiled Isis, the Egyptian mother goddess reincarnated through the Serapis cult as the deity who only allowed initiates to view her secrets, particularly the secret of life itself. As such, she provided an intriguingly mysterious symbol of what could be known if properly approached. As the Alexandrian goddess Isis, whose cult spread throughout the Greco-Roman world had never entirely died out, she is the maternal ground for the rise of interest in Hermeticism and Freemasonry among European intellectuals from Goethe to Thomas Jefferson, men for whom rites of initiation seemed in line with other forms of tutelary knowledge. But for some Romantics, such as Blake, Hölderlin, Percy Shelley, and Schelling, an approach even more deeply related to mystery cult practice was necessary to interpenetrate cosmic truths, the most important of which was origin, or the law of founding, and its precondition, the archaic ground. It was Schelling who strove hardest to explore this conditioning ground.

II. SCHELLING'S GEOGRAPHICA

The 1815 *Ages of the World* (*Die Weltalter*) is Schelling's third attempt to retell the biblical story of cosmic origin through natural philosophy in the German Behemist tradition, which gained wide popularity in England as Boehme's influence spread. It is a philosophical poem, an attempt to re-create through form the sense of what Schelling is conceptualizing for his planned history. In this sense it is a revision of Lucretius's *De Rerum Natura* and Plato's *Timaeus* together. Both earlier works illustrate that while there is a "boundary between theosophy and philosophy" that must be "chastely . . . protect[ed]," as Schelling explains of his own project, it is also necessary (and this is the problem with Enlightenment universal histories) that such a history pass through the dialectic between art and nature.[26] Certainly this requires a return to mystical wisdom, Behemism as much as Bruno's "Egyptianism," in order to begin at the beginning with the question of origin.

Schelling's project in the *Ages of the World* (*Die Weltalter*) was to write correlative philosophies. He would show how the empirical can be traced as it ascends into the cosmic or ideal, and the history of how the ideal enters into the forms of nature. This mapping of celestial onto terrestrial ground, like the Renaissance celestial-terrestrial globe pairs, reflects Hermetic thinking about the alchemical relations between the divine and mundane. What is particularly compelling about the *Weltalter*, and what connects it more closely with the projects of universal history as poetry/science, or speculative science symbolized by the Alexandrian Library, is that it is a philosophical poem. The *Weltalter* makes its form the embodiment of its idea—creating, in a manner, an alchemical mixture of truths. In this it resembles a religious artifact more than a scientific analysis, although in the sense of the poetico-mythic character of many of Plato's dialogues or the poetic form of Lucretius's atomistic philosophy and universal history (*De Rerum Natura*), or even in the tradition of theological reflection that would have been familiar to Schelling through his study of the German mystical tradition, particularly Meister Eckhart. It is also allied to the negative theology that Derrida explores in his treatment of apophasis,[27] a negating approach that interested Schelling particularly because Plotinus was the first to transform Plato's account of a divine genesis in the *Timaeus* into negative theology in his Neoplatonist system.

Apophatic (or negative) theology, which focuses on what God is not and on what God does not know about himself, is highly allied with mystical thought; it concerns unknowability at both a cosmic and divine scale. More importantly for imagining Egypt, negative theology corresponds closely with the tipping point between knowing and not knowing, between the ideal and its enmeshment in the real. That tipping point is something Freud located in the unconscious, and it is intriguing to see Schelling theorizing

God's unconscious through this lens. Combining God's unconscious and mysticism allowed Schelling to develop a cosmogenesis, a history of a time so archaic it is time out of mind. In this sense the *Weltalter* is what we might call a Neo-Egyptian work, or a reworking of Alexandrian knowledge systems: the pairing of speculative and empirical thought so that together the cosmic principle could be theorized. As Joan Steigerwald points out, Schelling thought that the positive life force (the productive aspect of the cosmic principle) not only can't be known, but "he even contended that language has no term for it, and hence made use of the poetic expression of the ancient philosophers, the 'world soul,' to indicate metaphorically what eluded conception."[28] Schelling takes the term "world soul" from Plato's account; although Plato and Lucretius draw on received traditions from mystery cult beliefs about the origin and nature of the universe, what Schelling is not reflecting in his cosmic account is the cultist's assured tone of insider knowledge. Instead, he reflects the struggle with negativity that is the process of becoming.

Although this negativity differs from that of "the negative" in Hegel's dialectic of becoming that eventuates in absolute spirit and absolute knowledge, Schelling and Hegel share the German Idealist conception of love as a creative force. For Hegel: "the Spirit is the whole, and not just one or other of the elements for itself. Or to put it in terms . . . of feeling (*Empfindung*), God is eternal love, whose nature is co have the other as its own."[29] The relation between a God whose creative principle is "love" within the context of the debates about German mysticism, pantheism, and other alternative knowledges, and Egypt can be traced back to two sources. First, the Hermetic strain of conceiving the cosmos that dates back to Alexandrian speculative thought; and second and even more historically, in the Ancient Egyptian conception of Amun-Re, the principal god represented by the sun, who was a god of light and love. To worship Amun-Re, depicted on tomb and temple walls that Romantic era excavations were beginning to uncover, was to worship the gift of life itself.[30] However, Schelling complicates both Hegel's and Ancient Egyptian notions of a god whose first principle of love. For him, God both loves and rejects, both yields up love and retreats into himself (his account is very similar to that of Blake's depiction of a cosmology determined by the movement between positive and negative passions). In imagining that God must become himself through his own dialectical movement of love and retraction, of desire and ego, Schelling employs the principles of poetics— not as mythopoesis but as the struggle between form and self-expression that poetry concentrates into a formative act. Unlike the discourse of logic, the poetic enables Schelling to trace the evolution of spirit, since soul is the excess within the form, an indwelling force that can de-form. The dialectic between soul and form is the formative pain of becoming.

Schelling finds the groundwork for this dialectic in Boehme's *On Generation and the Logos* (1622). Boehme, highly influential for the German Romantics and for English Romantics such as Blake and Coleridge, was a Neoplatonist and himself deeply influenced by the alchemical writings of Paracelsus; he speculated on the chemical reactions that caused cosmic generation, and conceived of God as fire, Christ as light, and the Holy Spirit as the life principle. Part of Boehme's larger theoretical system is to posit an *Ungrund* that becomes separated from God in the formation of the world; this saves him from the charge of pantheism, but it is equally important for Schelling in thinking about the ways that God can be divided from himself. Further, wisdom (Sophia) is also separate; God is not all-knowing but is divided in what He knows and can't know. Boehm's dialectical system, however, describes God's becoming; as the Trinity, Sophia—who is inseparable from *Logos*—is related to the divinity in each of his three aspects. For God the Father, Sophia is revelation; she enables Him to come to self-consciousness. But it is the Spirit that, through the *Logos* and Sophia, creates the world.[31] Boehme's system provided Schelling with the germ seed for his speculative universal history. Instead of Volney's cultural revolutions, the cosmos and the earth would develop through revolutions of spirit that were a divine coming to knowledge and then to self-knowledge. By mapping out the world's prehistory in this way, Schelling uses Boehme's conception of the *Ungrund* to understand the archaic as such, and for the Romantics the archaic ground is no other than Egypt.

The fragment of the *Ages of the World* that Schelling published is actually only the beginning of his unwritten universal history, presenting the terms for understanding the divine creative principle. This principle, containing Being and the necessity of Being, as well as Freedom or choice, is always at once a dialectical opposition of an "eternal no" and an "eternal yes," a positive and a negative drive (a life force and a destructive force). This dialectic does not work in the same way as Hegel's, in which negativity propels the accession to the absolute by challenging thought to move forward toward absolute knowledge. Schelling's divine principle is more fundamentally challenged by negation, which is incorporated into its earliest expressions of divine consciousness. Neither Hegel nor Kant can provide the basis for thinking with God in this account, for such a struggle cannot be preresolved as it is in orthodox Christian theology. To forestall a resolution was essential, since Schelling's *Ages* in some ways responds to the destructive force of the Napoleonic wars; he therefore turned to the apophatic discourse of German mysticism, and to Boehme in particular, for an alternative model of encountering struggle as *logos*. The notion of the Word as the meeting of sensible and supersensible, developed in Boehme's negative theology, was compelling for the German Romantics generally, but Boehme provided special inspiration for Schelling's philosophy of "the indeterminate."[32] This in-between state allows for the transition between opposites (positive/negative, sensible/supersensible, matter/form, finite/infinite, activity/constraint). In analyzing Schelling's view of indeterminacy in 1801 prior to the *Ages* project, Hegel explained that the indeterminate both precedes and follows the determinations of thought; for every positing there is something that resists it, that can't be done away with.[33] Discarding the standard self-other model of Cartesian thought, the *logos* rests on an ineffable otherliness, an indeterminacy that resists reason's (or the word's) power to resolve. Steigerwald's points to the problem with *logos* in Schelling's positive principle as itself indeterminate, with no word to accurately describe or contain it.

To apply Schelling's formulation of the divine principle to the sensible world as a contrasting theory to Coleridge's famous distinction of the primary and secondary imaginations reveals that one of the most important differences between the two theories would be that for Schelling, knowledge has agency. Like spirit, it discovers and reveals itself, it unfolds from its organizing concepts. Spirit is the hero of the story, and knowledge (rather than Coleridge's primary Imagination) expresses its agency: "it is the development of a living actual being" that has no predate, no foundation before its existence.[34] Instead, it develops in and with primordial life. Therefore knowledge, particularly esoteric (speculative, mystical) "knowledge," *is* history; the conscious and spirited examination and discovery of history is a recreation of the past's becoming that reveals knowledge. Here is the Alexandrian legacy in full force, yet with a touch of Pergamum's shadow legacy as well.

This is the vital point that cosmic wisdom is history. Volney's philosophical history in the *Ruins* is extended in Schelling's *Ages* to a grander scale, but it is the same thought. For Schelling, it's not the revolution of empires, but the revolutions of dialectical processes that take the form of gestational phases. Similarly, the process of revelation occurs by a dialectic between opposed principles that force the first principle to respond to a different part of itself (as in Boehme) and thus to more than itself; such an account of primordial self-difference presents a model of self-consciousness answerable to other ways of knowing, to others as otherness. In pursuit of this fundamental struggle for self-knowledge that is at the heart of becoming, the philosopher must be absorbed into the vitality of the age he writes about: "the recollection of the primordial beginning of things . . . [must] become so vital that knowledge, which according to its matter and the meaning of the word, is history, could also be history according to its external form."[35] This is the very essence of mystery cult understanding: to see that universal history *is* knowledge; that prehistory (*die Vorzeit*) as recorded in geology is only an actualized history; and that there is no before-time that is prior to this vitality, to this struggle that is the frisson between creative thought and the threat of death. The intervention of the human in this account is that of a spirited absorption, somewhat akin to Percy Shelley's poetic attitude: a purposeful affinity rather than an analogy to the divine.

Had Schelling completed his speculative history of the cosmos, Egypt would have provided the jumping off point for a primordial collusion of negative with positive, of prehistory as history, and in its expansive, synthetic polytheism, of nature with ideal form. I will return to Schelling's project, but will turn for a moment to an important predecessor universal history, one that does take man as its hero, to illustrate the difference that late Romantic thought makes to the conception of what can be known about the suprasensible, about universals, about history itself. In his 1766 *Philosophy of History*, Voltaire had previously continued the direction taken in Classical universal histories, especially Eusebius's *Chronica*, and Renaissance world histories. Using Classical sources for his guide, Voltaire does begin with the geological, asking,

> Can the moving sands of Northern Africa, and the coasts of Syria, bordering on Egypt, be any thing else than the sands left by the sea, on its gradual retirement from those countries? Herodotus (who does not always romance) tells us, without doubt, a great truth, when he relates, that, according to the account given by the priests of Egypt, the Delta was not always land.[36]

But as this passage suggests, by relying on classical rather than geographical information, Voltaire necessarily shifts his attention from prehistory (a term not yet in use, leaving Voltaire little to schematize) to the producers of history, the races of man. Remarking the predilection of people to settle in fertile lands, he postulates the origin of cities and moves quickly into his survey of ancient cultures. Notably his 1829 English translator's purported interest in publishing Voltaire's work, supported by the names appearing in the subscription list, was to promote an understanding of God's purpose. The *Philosophy* is to be understood by its English readers to contextualize the Old Testament's accounts of the creation and development of humans and their activities.

Yet despite this orthodox interpretation of the *Philosophy*, it is clear that Voltaire's self-conscious approach does not let him discover the history of spirit; he has no form through which to discover the excess of form. In discussing Egypt he cannot understand Egypt, and views its worship of nature as neither dialectical nor synthetic, but as commonsensical. Their hieroglyphics and monuments are obvious solutions to pressing problems, but were developed without art, that is, without spirit. In his chapters on Ancient Egypt, Voltaire is most interested in the promise of the body's resurrection: Egyptian priests "persuaded the nation that the soul would return to, and reanimate the body, at the expiration of a thousand years. They wished, therefore, to preserve the body, . . . and, to protect it from all accidents, they enclosed it in a mass of stone, without an aperture, or outlet of any kind. . . . We have, at this day, Egyptian mummies more than four thousand years old. The bodies have endured as long as the pyramids themselves."[37] Voltaire's emphasis here is on the priests' supposed ability to delude their kings and people not only through the use of hieroglyphs to mystify meaning, but with their dogma on bodily resurrection. This is not natural science but human politics; however, once the question of a singular deity intrudes, Voltaire does appear to begin tracing the rise of Christianity.

> Did the Egyptians, at first, acknowledge a God supreme? If this question had been put to any of the common people, they would not have known what answer to give;—if to young students of Egyptian theology, they would have discoursed a long time without coming to a conclusion;—but, if the question had been put to any of those sages consulted by Pythagoras, or Plato, or Plutarch, they would have answered, plainly, that they worshipped only one God. As the groundwork of their opinions, they would have referred to the ancient inscription on the statue of Isis,—"I am that I am;" and to this other,—"I am all that has been, and all that shall be; no mortal can lift up my veil." They would also have pointed to the globe, placed over the door of the temple of Memphis, which represented the unity of the Divine Nature, under the name of *Knef*.[38]

In this passage on the Temple of Serapis, Voltaire reflects Masonic and Hermetic interest in the Egyptian mysteries and a cult that flourished in Egypt's Late Period, rather than on the Mosaic version of Egyptian monotheism. Spirit, for Voltaire, takes on a Hermetic, mystical sense that he further explores in his chapter on the Egyptian mysteries. The fact of Egyptian polytheism is explained commonsensically: no peoples are "constant and uniform in their opinions."[39] This is not a conflict between state and secret religions or between poly and monotheism but a reflection of man's variability. Similarly, he believes that mystery cults cannot be traced to a single origin, citing all the ancient cultures with such cults. But of the Egyptian rites recorded in Apuleius he asks, "Can we possibly have stronger proof than this that the Egyptians in the midst of all their detestable superstitions yet acknowledged the unity of one only God?" As his final word before turning to the superior Greeks, Voltaire's skepticism appears to diminish, but not as a loss of self-consciousness (the "detestable superstitions" reveal his bias) nor as a discerning of the dialectical progress of knowledge. The detestable has been subsumed by the admirable, which he associates with the Greco-Roman adoption of the Isis cult and not with the vacillating, even unprincipled Egyptians.

Schelling, by contrast, sees vacillation, cyclicity, and lack of dialectical rigor as the positive cosmic drives that created the universe and our world.

Will and first principles are not Enlightenment axioms as explored by Voltaire and Kant, but cosmic forces that propel history toward revelation. Although Schelling only completed the "past" section of *Ages of the World*, leaving the present and future unfinished, it may be that Schelling's attempts to complete the work were foiled by his very conception of time in eternity: "that life was posited God as past or in concealment is always what it was before," he writes.[40] The life he describes, which has a beginning that is an eternal beginning and an end that is an eternal end, is the cosmic life as much as the particular life; it is always what it was and what it will be because the process through which it comes to be and sustains itself is one whose rhythms and cycles are determined by the fact that a thing's whole, its completeness, is contained (as in Hermetic and alchemical doctrine) in its smallest part. The whole tree is discernible in the seed, as the return to the seed is discernible in the mature tree (an idea that Goethe sought to prove). The rhythms and cycles of life, which are not cycles only but do progress, are constrained and liberated by the rhythmic alternations of the life forces, which Schelling (after Boehme) calls "potencies."[41] The potencies interact and energize one another first through what Schelling terms "rotary movement," which is both cyclical and generative, and through this movement the potencies are liberated into a higher state of existence, becoming 'principles.' Although the *Ages* is organized progressively, it cycles through the key ideas in a rotary fashion, bringing the reader again and again through the revolutions as these ideas build up a conception of cosmic and earthly creation.

Die Weltalter thus presents the terms of understanding the divine creative principle. This principle, the godhead, which both does and does not have being (a main tenet of apophatic or negative theology), holds out the necessity of Being and is in itself "eternal freedom." God is always at once a dialectic of opposites, of an "eternal no" and an "eternal yes." The "no" belongs to the contracting, dark principle of ego; this is the wrathful God of Moses.[42] The "yes" belongs to the light, outstretching principle of love, the God of the New Testament, but also of ancient cults like that of Isis. Schelling was also familiar with both August Schlegel's and Humboldt's translations into Latin of the *Bhagavad Gita*, and drew on the rich tradition of apophatic theology in eastern thought for his ontology. However, Schelling's dialectic is progressive because the no precedes the yes: if love were instead succeeded by a wrathful denial, then the process would be driven by necessity, which is not possible since God is eternal freedom. In this way the rotary motion does proceed forward. Love succeeds denial because it is then a voluntarism, a giving and thus a free choice or movement toward freedom. Because the crisis or "cision," in which one of the potencies "sacrifice[es]" itself to the whole by giving way to the other's essence, necessity is from the beginning subject to freedom. The sacrifice belongs to the yearning of the potencies for the eternal freedom that is God in his completeness;[43] the process as the completion is the One that is All, the Whole that is Many.[44] "[A]fter it [God] has become the All out of One," "[t]he One becomes the All with reference to a higher One [the Godhead] and the inexpressible becomes the expressible in relationship to what is for it the word."[45] "One in All" is the recently resuscitated pantheistic motto that Hölderlin, Hegel, and Schelling enthusiastically embraced as students, *hen kai pan*.[46] It is associated not just with Boehme but also with the eighteenth-century revival of the Cult of Isis—Isis as the threshold to the divine mysteries that Schelling is mapping.

In a manner very akin to Blake's prophetic poetry, Schelling devised a form for describing his conception of cosmic history, of a true 'universal history,' that poetically embodies his divine vision. In this, he recapitulates the Alexandrian combination of poetry and science, speculative and empirical thought; but unlike the Alexandrian example, Schelling determined the aesthetic to be the highest form of consciousness, as art is the locus of true understanding. Indeed, the "universal soul," which is "the essence that wavers beyond [or between] nature and the spiritual world," "we may now consider . . . as the artistic wisdom of that which dwells in the Whole."[47] What communicates between nature and spirit is artistic insight, expressible only in the aesthetic. Therefore, it is in the aesthetic that philosophy can find its own insight, its own access to cosmic truth. (Hegel, by contrast, determines philosophy to be the highest mode of the aesthetic and therefore aesthetic form is in a sense beside the point.) Schelling understands the aesthetic to consist of both form and poetic language, and his account is rife with metaphors drawn from alchemy (which he calls "chemistry"), magnetism, botany, and astronomy. Fire, lightening, chemical reaction, magnetic attraction, phylogenesis, and comets are all important metaphors for his ontology. Poetic language provides the form through which understanding can be achieved. Soul is an excess of form within the form, an indwelling force that can de-form or disorganize productively. Like the human soul, the creative essence of a work vitalizes it; this soul will emerge from the work's own principles. Such a work is produced by the genius out of freedom but invoked by the divine's requirement for expression (necessity as divine articulation of Being). It takes the attentive eye, the re-creative eye, to allow a work's living concept (its soul) to emerge from and transcend the form; the theoretical and critical eye are too ego-centered, too self-bounded, to do so. As Schelling remarks, his conception of the godhead (a variant of Boehme's divine trinity) "does not let itself be grasped in a short explanation nor circumscribed with limits like a geometrical figure."[48] Rather, it must be experienced as a work of art is experienced, not least because it is the divine creative principle.

For Schelling's representative prehistory of the archaic, at both the universal cosmic level and at the natural and human levels, there is a progression, an urge forward ("yearning," "desire") toward the transcendental or creative imagination. This is what Coleridge, reading Schelling, called the "primary Imagination" in the history of his own creative life, the *Biographia Literaria*. The transcendental imagination is, in Coleridge's reading of *The Ages of the World*, "esemplasy," the plastic imagination, or in Schelling, "*Ineinsbildung*."[49] All things yearn for the transcendental, procreative imagination, that which will bring them into being through its own free choice and only after a thing's voluntary sacrifice of its selfish principle to a larger unity. The primary Imagination acts out of freedom, and it is for freedom that the thing sacrifices itself in order to escape the rotary movement of necessity. Coleridge, however, grasped the plastic imagination and the primary Imagination as central concepts with his artist's affinity for the creative principle; for Schelling, these are secondary concepts to that of eternal freedom, the pure essence of the godhead. God creates voluntarily in an act of freedom as the will that does not will; it is a creation that need not take place, and does so as an expression of joy, as "the lightening flash of freedom."[50]

That flash condenses movement and energy into electricity. Indeed, "the oldest state of all matter and of all celestial bodies in particular, is a state of electrical dissolution," a "two-fold fire" of radiation (+E) and negation (−E) (96). These forces, the same that activate the "voltaic pile," also activate all matter, "a decisive proof that matter is capable of an electrical spiritualization and dissolution . . . in which it also discards all other corporeal qualities." The very fact that comets refuse system, functioning by the same "systole and diastole" that powers earthly cycles, makes them "so to speak, living witnesses of that primordial time, since nothing prevents the earlier time from migrating through later time via particular phenomena."[51] Electricity, then, is a scientific phenomenon, a cosmic force, and also a spiritual activant: the alchemical "Flash" of Boehme translated into Romantic terms.[52] Its analogue is magic, a conceptual energy that appears frequently in the *Ages*. Magic, for Schelling, is both mystical and alchemical, spirit magic. In his volume on Hindu mythology, he relates it to the Sanskrit word "Maya," meaning "the veil of illusion" (Blake calls it "Vala").[53] This is the same veil Isis draws over the wisdom of divine Nature. Both the European term "magie" or magic, and the Zoroastrian term "magus" or priest and dream-interpreter denote human mediation between the natural and the spiritual, the *hen kai pan*. As Assmann points out, *kai* in this Greek motto has the same meaning as Spinoza's term "*sive*":[54] Spinoza's importance for *Ages of the World* cannot be understated as the philosopher who more convincingly than even Bruno assimilated pantheistic thought to Christianity. "Perhaps, of all the modern philosophers, there was in Spinoza a dark feeling of that primordial time of which we have attempted to conceptualize so precisely," Schelling remarks of Spinoza's so-called pantheism.[55] Magic connects the primordial to the temporal; for Boehme, "Real magic is not an essence but rather the desiring spirit of essence," or yearning.[56] Because for Schelling yearning connected to freedom represents wisdom, it is through its etymological and mythological (pantheistic) connections with "maya," "magus," and *Möglichkeit* (possibility) that yearning is energy, the electrical Flash. This is the insight that is the "holy madness" of the artist but also the crisis or "cision" of magnetic sleep, Schelling's version of spirit magic. In the Hermetic tradition, magic was what the hieroglyphs hid from noninitiates. Egypt's "mute seriousness" concealed the wisdom of its magician priests, encoding that wisdom on and in monuments built for eternal time, but magnetic sleep or spirit magic unveils the hieroglyphs' mysteries, their archaic wisdom which is also what Isis keeps veiled.

III. MARY SHELLEY'S RUINOUS GEOGRAPHY

For Mary Shelley, unlike Schelling or Boehme, electricity is coded with an inappropriate lifting of Isis's veil; the "flash" of brilliance experienced by Victor Frankenstein is a holy madness gone wrong. Although the unholy vision arising from Victor's improper initiation into nature's secrets is not the subject of Shelley's *The Last Man* (1826), the novel is nonetheless filled with deviant uses of magical thinking (made explicit in the figure of Merrival the astronomer, who madly ignores the plague while calculating a millennial future). More important to Mary Shelley is the association between the kind of ancient Chaldean and Egyptian knowledge embodied by Merrival and the ruinous energies figured by Egyptian ground. Like Hegel, Shelley views Egypt as coterminus with living death, a necropolis of death-in-life. This is not the apocalyptic view of a Mosaic Egypt depicted in the Bible but rather a return to the Classical Greek view of Egypt: for the Greeks the Nile represented the site of primordial contagion rather than the source of all life. Plutarch notes this prejudice in writing of the Apis bull: "They are said also to give the Apis drink out of a well of his own, but to keep him away from the Nile; not that they hold the Nile water to be polluted by reason of the crocodiles, as some think, for nothing is so venerated by Egyptians as the Nile" ("Isis and Osiris," 4). The crocodile problem looms for Shelley as well as Thomas De Quincey as if contamination is synonymous with an improper antiquity, an archaic knowledge that should not be disturbed. Schelling reflects a sense of this eerie taint when he writes "Darkness and closure are characteristic of primordial time," noting "This is the way it is with the mountains of the primordial world and this is the way it also is with the oldest formations of the human spirit. This same character of closure approaches us in the mute seriousness of the Egyptians and in the gigantic monuments of the Indians that seem to have been built for no particular time but rather for eternity."[57] Unlike Schelling, Mary Shelley's universal history spans a past that eschews eternity, incorporating, even digesting, both a present and a future anterior that is overwhelmed with spirit and yet unredeemed by it, unless the erasure of mankind and of history is a cosmic redemption.

The sibylline cave that inaugurates *The Last Man* is a post-prehistory, a variant of Schelling's speculative cosmography. The author, in her *propia persona*, enters the cave with her companion, an undisguised Percy Shelley, as her guide. Like the novice at the Temple of Saïs, Mary as initiate must be inducted into the sacred precepts through guided exploration in order to discover the truth, which in the novel's case is the dynamic intersection of past, present, and future in a conflation that reveals the folding back of one upon the other. This is a past inhabited by the future anterior, a future that plays the evolutionary schema backward to a desecrated, or perhaps deconsecrated beginning. The paradox of the novel's temporal Möbius strip is explicable only in its realization of the empirical meltdown that would occur if Ideal and Real were to coalesce. The apocalyptic vision of the novel results from the materialization of Adrian's Idealism in his political activities (Adrian is the character associable to Victor Frankenstein, both of which are based on Percy Shelley's personality). The dangers of a spiritualized politics that Adrian attempts to put in place of the pragmatic, empirical approach of the other politicians are dramatized in the tension between realizable and idealistic goals that the Byronic Lord Raymond confronts in his leadership role. In Percy Shelley's Idealist political projects the actual battle between liberal Whiggism and the Tory party is understood as human vulnerability to self-interest and party politics. Mary Shelley saw in her husband's Idealist politics an apocalyptic dynamic that, at least as *The Last Man* envisions it, was more dangerous in the long term than the revolutionary devastation that had overwhelmed French Jacobinical idealism. At several key points she foreshadows apocalypse by figuring the impassioned plight of Perdita, the narrator Lionel's sister, who feels her love for Lord Raymond to place her on 'a precipice,' ever in danger of the abyss. Perdita, representing the creative and generative soul of Schelling's "yes," illustrates the losses to humanity that an unmediated idealism can bring to bear. The abyss itself is that fall into the apocalypse which is not the future of the Ideal realized, but that of the archaic. And it is the archaic to which Lionel, the titular last man, is returned at his narrative's end. Here there will be no written records or writing after his death, and thus no history. The return to prehistory (for Schelling, as for Shelley, this can only be geologically inscribed) is the moment of Saitic truth, rather than the Ideal realized; it is this revelation across which the veil has been drawn, and which the initiate needs guidance in understanding.

Mary Shelley sought to temper her vision by insisting on the need for an enlightened monarch, an Alexandrian leader whose spiritual purity could ensure cultural continuity. By doing so, she was initiating readers into this sacred knowledge. If Isis represents the divinity whose statue at Saïs, according to Plutarch in "On Isis and Osiris," bore an inscription that famously read "I am all that has been and is and shall be; and no mortal has ever lifted my mantle," then the conflation of historical temporalities in the novel is an empirical representation of that sacred truth.[58] Moreover, in one of the supposed Sibylline Oracles discovered in the preface's cave, and written on papyri, this formula has been integrated with that of Yahweh to provide a self-description that prophetically orients Shelley's vision vis-à-vis Schelling's convergence of Ideal and Real: "I am the being one, recognize this in your spirit: I donned heaven as my garment, I clothed myself with the ocean, the earth is the ground for my feet, air covers me as my body, and the stars revolve around me."[59] Plutarch's account supports this convergence, since he refers to the sacred knowledge of Isis as the *"Word"* which is symbolized by priestly vestments, since the truth should *"wrap"* one up, that is, immerse one in realization.[60] This oracle from the Sybil does away with temporality, its full realization providing a way in which future and prehistory could not only touch, but in the final analysis be the same thing. Mary Shelley finds form in prophetic gestures, whether that of her persona in the Sibylline Cave or of Perdita's sense of precipitory doom. By entering the Sibyl's cave she has immersed herself in the rituals of sacred knowledge, and thus discovers the vital energy of the 'age' she is recreating, as Schelling requires. But *The Last Man* is a negative vision of Schelling's system, a devastating rather than transcendent realization of Hermetic Egyptianized knowledge. The end is inscribed in the beginning as a reflection of the unity of the system, but in mystical thought such as Boehme's beginnings and endings are ongoing, everything revolves in circular motion continued through the "flash" of love and desire. Neither Schelling nor Mary Shelley accept this nonlinearity, although Shelley holds out the possibility in *The Last Man* that Lionel's singular survival in a world emptied of humanity might spell a new beginning, one that recapitulates the sibylline temporal cyclicity of the preface.

Indeed, the time-bending of the sibylline cave's space can be interpreted in terms of the Saïte period, with its backward/forward-looking perspective. The Saïte Period, Dynasty 26 in Ancient Egypt's chronology, was one that encapsulated the Romantic-era bifurcated vision of Egypt as both archaic, originary ground and as colonial terrain. The Saïte pharaohs ruled from Saïs in the Delta area, springing from a local Assyrian governor who as Necho I of Saïs (c. 672–664 BC) continued to rule after the Assyrians ended Nubian control of Egypt and then withdrew. The Saïte Period is marked by its in-between status, its pharaohs (belonging to a single native family) looking backward to Old Kingdom stability and strength while remembering too well Egypt's recent colonization by Nubia and Assyria, and older conquest by the Hyksos in the Second Intermediate Period and the Libyans in Dynasty 22. Despite the 130-year duration of the Saïte Period, Egypt was not the strong international power it had been during the consolidation achieved in Ramesses II's long reign, focusing its resources on maintaining a unified nation. At the other end of the period would come the Persian invasion, and the Saïte kings must have sensed that their strength was oriented toward the archaic past, their weakness toward a colonial future. In this the period embodied corruption-in-progress, the very character Mary Shelley ascribes to Egypt and its Nilotic mud. Their nation-building strategies included a strong building and reconstruction program that embraced Old Kingdom monuments, forms, artistic style, and culture. It was during this period that the Great Sphinx at Giza was repaired, its cult revitalized, and its godhead perhaps best representing the Saïtic image of Egypt as archaically strong and wise, and as already lost to the future.

The Old Kingdom pyramids at Giza, which the Great Sphinx guards, represented the condensation of Egyptian genius and wisdom as embodied in the later-deified royal vizier and architect Imhotep. He was responsible for building Djoser's Step Pyramid at Saqqara and was thus the "father" of the Giza pyramids. Those next pyramids, the three monumental structures with their perfect coordinal alignment and precision-fitted stone blocks, provided a site for the wisdom of the ancients. That Khufu's Great Pyramid remained the tallest architectural achievement for thirty-eight centuries, proudly signified by Khafra's pharaonic Great Sphinx, reinforced the centeredness of Old Kingdom knowledge, and created a site for the retrospective view. The Saïtic Period held such a Romanticized view of its own ancient world in its sense of backward/forward-looking perspective, which the Giza sphinx concretized. For the Saïtes, as for later generations, the sphinx was the iconic figure whose Old Kingdom identity as archaic, riven from the limestone quarry for the great pyramid of Khufu, was lost and then reinvented by a late-period pharaoh, and intermittently forgotten and reinvented following that renaissance. Its fate was to be yoked—like "Khufu" to the Greek name of "Cheops"—to the Greek sphinx with her sibylline riddle of human identity that also dealt with cycles of interrelated time. Several Romantic texts reflect a similar backward/forward gaze in different ways that are interesting for this identification of Egypt's spirit: Schelling's *The Ages of the World*, Mary Shelley's *The Last Man*, Hegel's *Aesthetics*, Novalis's *The Novices of Sais*, and William Blake's prophetic books. Like Schelling, Blake did not single Egypt out in particular for such a backward/forward gaze, but also like Schelling, the ground of Blake's poetic vision lies in the long history of mystical appropriations of Egypt to create a return path to archaic wisdom.

IV. BLAKE AND EMPIRE

Blake's idiosyncratic mythopoesis developed as a synthesis of antinomian elements, including Swedenborg's new biblical history, his parents' practice of private biblical interpretation, texts associated with antiquarian thought such as Paracelsus and Boehme,[61] and Blake's own contact with pagan mythologies through his book illustration work. Boehme's works (all of which had been translated into English by Morgan Llwyd between 1645 and 1662) deeply influenced antinomian thought and were a particular inspiration for Blake.[62] Blake's cosmic universal history, developed in tandem with his mythopoeic vision, creates an alternative prehistory of the world told in interfolded layers in *The Book of Urizen* (1794), *The Book of Ahania* (1794), *The Book of Los* (1795), and *Milton: A Poem* (1804; c. 1810–1818). This prehistory recounts the decisive turn from the eternals to sensible forms, and the division of essence and spiritual fragmentation; the resemblance to Schelling's *Ages of the World* in several of its elements is notable, especially the self-difference initiated in divine essence. The division of the eternal and the sensible is also part of the lineage for cosmic historiography, particularly clear in Plato's *Timaeus*, and is a structural aspect Blake would not have taken from the Pentateuch but rather from pagan sources. In *Jerusalem* (1804; c. 1821) Blake depicts the history of the sensible and ideal city of Jerusalem; in the ideal city the highest state of being, Eden, predominates over lower, increasingly sensible and materialized states. In Edenic being, the originary division that begets the beginning is healed but without recurrence to originary ground; the return is to the prior, before-ground of origin. As for Mary Shelley, the origin seems to be the problem that Blake's vision strives to resolve, whereas Schelling views the narration of origin as in itself a reconstructive, even magical practice.

Blake's work that worries most about origin is *Milton: A Poem in Two Books* (c. 1804–1811), with its anxiety about the "eternal death" of worldly materialization embodied in Milton's return from his afterlife to the sensible world on a sacrificial quest. Milton's contamination[63] (both the fungus-like cloud that emits from Blake's left foot where Milton enters him, and the Polypus, or horrific "vegetated" systems of the lowest level of being) are revulsions at the dark matter of origin.[64] Blake may have appropriated the term "vegetative" from Paracelsus's discussion of the "vegetative soul" *Neun Bucher Archidoxis*, since his works, widely read in the seventeenth and eighteenth centuries, were still circulating among Hermeticists and would have appealed to esoteric thinkers like Blake and philosophers like William Godwin, Mary Shelley's father.[65] I will focus on Book I of *Milton*, where the comparisons with *Ages of the World* and *The Last Man* are most apt, and not only for the role of poetic vision in all three works, and where the critique of empire begins at the level of improper seeing. Whereas the contaminated Nile in *The Last Man* lets loose the cholera-like plague that decimates the entire world's human population, the contamination of the vegetated world allows Milton and his self-divisions (his physical embodiment in the narrator "Blake"; his shadow; and his specter) to redeem the fallen world. Blake's is a dark poetic vision with a prophetically promising future anterior. This redemption of the origin begins anew with Milton's self-sacrifice (reentering the mundane world, he sacrifices his eternal life) that reenacts the initiation rite of the mystery cults. Like Milton, the novice must enter a dark labyrinth that leads to self-discovery as well as a higher truth and therefore a higher state of being. But as Mary Shelley clearly shows, this is an ancient path to knowledge, already revealed in sibylline prophecy recollected in the sybil's cave. Blake puts it thus: "And Los thus spoke . . . / I recollect an old Prophecy in Eden recorded in gold; and oft/ Sung to the harp: That Milton . . . / Should ascend forward from Felpham's Vale," that is, embodied as the poet Blake, "& break the Chain/ Of jealousy from all its roots."[66] Unlike Shelley's narrator Lionel, Blake's hero Milton can effect radical change, in his ability to reverse the negating rotary motions of descent and devolution that empire's contagion brings on.

Yet this too is a prehistory, one of 6,000 years, about the length of time Shelley's astronomer Merrival speculatively calculated of the earth's posthistory and the fate of the universe. "Such is the World of Los the labour of six thousand years" Blake writes.[67] Indeed, Merrival's astronomy is not irrelevant here, for Blake understands the lower three levels of being (Beulah, Generation, Ulro) as mediated by science; science is the only lens by which the material world is made intelligible, whereas "Poetry, Painting, Music" exist in eternity. But the fourth art, "Architecture which is Science" exists materially: "only/ Science remains thro Mercy: & by means of Science, the Three/ Become apparent in time & space."[68] Here Blake departs from Pythagorean tradition as recorded in Plato's *Republic* in which the four "sister" sciences are astronomy, arithmetic, geometry, and—importantly—music, although both Pythagoras and Blake would agree that music's importance to either schema is its reflection of the harmony of the spheres.[69] Due to this visual defect in the perfectibility of the material sensible world—the inability to see beyond the five senses or 'gates'—the unifying arts cannot actually be known but only imitated cursorily by humans, while nature itself cannot be comprehended, its mysteries shrouded. "Thus Nature is a Vision of the Science of the Elohim,"[70] a fact about the eternals (the Elohim) that emphasizes the problem of cosmology in general: humans who are not endowed with prophetic powers have recourse only to the telescopic, distorting, and fragmenting lens through which nature must be viewed. The veil of Isis must not be lifted, and nature will always look horrifically "vegetative" to human eyes that cannot see or fully comprehend *hen kai pan*, One in All.

The problem may indeed have originated in Egypt with its monumental, crystallizing architecture—the one art, because reducible to science, that exists in the world within Blake's Mundane Egg. (The mundane egg is itself a concept traceable to Hermetic beliefs, showing Blake's familiarity with at least some of the principles of Freemasonry, along with elements such as the initiation rites of the labyrinth quest.) Blake's repeated image for Egypt is of the emblem of enslaved humanity, the pyramid, derived from the biblical narrative of an Israel in bondage, but Egypt's ancient association with architecture, particularly mortuary architecture that entombs the spirit, underlies this emblem. Egypt is the origin of science as practiced from the temple roofs of cult centers and mortuary temples; in its Alexandrian period Egypt was the Mediterranean's scientific base, especially associated with Euclidean geometry and the parsing of nature via mathematical and classificatory divisions. In Blake's imagination however, Ancient Egypt stood as every originary roadblock to a reunified soul that would unweave the "veil of human miseries" that is "the World of Los," a world in which Isis has lost her footing.[71]

V. MAPPING EMPIRES

Egypt represents the conjoining of science, magic, poetry, myth, and esoteric wisdom. It also stands in for the birth of art, man's creative act that imitates the divine creative principle. As Blake's critique unfolds of the scientific vision that empire compels (with Egyptian enslavement as a key emblem of that perspective), not only in *Milton* but throughout his works, so does an alternative, cosmic point of view as well as a different form of mapping realities and what can be known. The issues raised in literal cartography, and more importantly, the classificatory work of empire, can help justify Blake's view that Egyptian science created a ruinous legacy. In art collection, these problems come to fruition as collectors attempted to create not just cabinets of curiosities, but representatively universal collections that conserve the history of the world. Since such collection, also attempted by Lionel in *The Last Man*, is doomed to lapse into rubble when collectors die (or the present vision becomes decayed), and since such a history is already by its artifactual nature nonrepresentative of any spiritual reality, as *Milton*'s critique of erroneous seeing shows, the very idea of an ideal collection seems a contradiction. But the Romantic encyclopedic imagination, such as Hegel's, valued such conceptual maps of universal knowledge and its products quite differently. It was an immersion in form that yields the vision of form that the French art historian Quatremère de Quincy felt was fully historicized and fully 'true' (1755–1849), thus taking Johann Joachim Winckelmann's art history a step further. For de Quincy, cosmic mystery is recoverable in the art of antiquity, which is itself oracular, and this positive historiography (contra Mary Shelley and Blake) begins with the Egyptians. De Quincy's universal history, however, was (as for Winckelmann) tightly defined in terms of art production. An adamant opponent of the national, imperial museum, de Quincy felt that museums were problematic on two counts: first, they presented art in fragments instead of an entire field of similar pieces; second, museums denuded the land from which the art was taken.

In an early work, the *Lettres à Miranda sur les déplacements des Monuments de l'art de l'Italie* (1796), de Quincy points to a positive version of the museum that differently maps the world: Rome, the prerevolutionary cultural capital of Europe and center of the western world as a museum city. This form of museum is, unlike the national museum, valuable and worth visiting because not only is a school of art presented whole and in context, but the continuum of art and of schools is presented. Imperial Rome expropriated the artwork of Egypt and Greece to decorate its landscape; subsequent eras saw both more artwork brought to Roma for the Papacy, and the revitalization of Classical art in modern art production. Collectively, Rome before Napoleon represented the only positive model for a museum: a three-dimensional and interactive timeline of art and available knowledge about history and intellectual production. Like the Library of Alexandria, Rome was a complete repository of human knowledge. Scholars can produce treatises on this knowledge and disseminate it, making the museum an invaluable cultural and intellectual repository:

> For a truly enquiring mind, the city of Rome is an entire world to be explored, a sort of *three-dimensional mapamundi,* which offers a condensed view of Egypt, Asia, Greece and the Roman Empire, the ancient and modern world. To have visited Rome is to have made many voyages in one. Consequently, the disperse the works of art collected together in Rome would be to deprive scholars of both their instruments of learning and the object of their research.[72]

De Quincy thus points out the mapping potential of the ultimate repository, which would enable scholars to write a universal "history of the human intellect and its discoveries." Significantly such a study could trace the developing realization of spirit in the sense Hegel would pursue and that the Freemasons found in the Egyptian mysteries: "the artistic monuments of Antiquity are an even greater source of inspiration as to the methods of recording history . . . resolving its inconsistencies, completing its omissions."[73] With this statement de Quincy has essentially laid the groundwork for Hegel's *Philosophy of the Fine Arts*, the plan for which was a history that would resolve inconsistencies and complete omissions, and to do so with principles grounded in "the artistic monuments of Antiquity."

De Quincy's antimuseum becomes the philosophical history of Hegel's *Aesthetics*. But to fully understand the grounds of Hegel's museology, I want to return to mystical terrain particularly as it relates to Ancient Egypt. Hegel could address the aesthetic not just because Kant had theorized the mental faculty necessary for understanding it in the *Critique of Judgment*, but because Winckelmann, whose work provided the most important locus for the Romantics of the concept of a western art history, had already begun the project of mapping that Hegel would theorize. Winckelmann found a purity in Classical Greek art to which moderns had to return in order to revitalize western civilization. Like Hermeticism's Egyptian revival, Winckelmann's Classical revival was a determination to reinvigorate culture itself, a much stronger claim for antiquity and its art than de Quincy's localized argument for Rome and its regenerative art production. But, just as de Quincy's Rome was a jumble of past and present, so was Winckelmann's, and indeed, so was Hermeticism's. Hegel puts an end to such historical jumbling and Kant's Egyptian "groping" after knowledge with his architectonics. The neat grouping in triads of related knowledges that Hegel structures at both the macro and micro levels of his system belies his reliance on Hermetic thought, with his fundamentally alchemical dialectical history. In Hegel's *Philosophy of History*, Herodotus is the "*Father*, i.e., the *Founder* of History."[74] This makes him the foundation, the origin of the architectonic that is grounded on Egypt, which Herodotus visits and records. "Original history," such as Herodotus and Thucydides wrote, has "no suppositious system of ideas" (as opposed to "critical history," the form of "reflective history" that is idea-driven and thus blinded to true history). Hegel's triad of historical approaches distinguishes "original history," a subjective approach exemplified by Herodotus as that written by an historical participant; "reflective history," which in its critical form he excoriates as pretending to objectivity and to knowing more than the historical record; and "philosophical history," which is what he presents. Whereas Schelling and Blake wrote mythopoetic prehistories that aspire to cosmic history or cosmography that is also a geographica, Hegel's project is "Universal History," by which he means a history of the unfolding of the World Spirit (Nature plus Spirit as the Hermetic path to self-knowledge).

History is the progressive realization of the "Idea," which is the Spirit's Idea; Reason is the Idea's manifestation and therefore the Spirit's agency in the world. As the Idea struggles toward realization, that is, toward Freedom, its highest embodiment is in the perfection of human community, which is the State. None of this would puzzle an Alexandrian scholar for whom the enclosed campus of the museum and great Library literalized the Platonic republic. The State is "that form of reality in which the individual has and enjoys his freedom; but on the condition of his recognizing, believing in, and willing that which is common to the

Whole,"[75] reflected in both the communal life of the Alexandrian scholar and his pursuit of knowledge as the path to spiritual freedom. For Hegel too, freedom is a pursuit of the Idea, which is itself spiritual. Those who participate to the highest degree—"World-Historical Individuals" such as Alexander, Julius Caesar, Napoleon—sacrifice themselves to the Idea. The same can be said of Blake's most heroic protagonists, Milton and Los.

In contrast to Winckelmann and de Quincy who valorized Greco-Roman art, Hegel took Hellenistic art to be only one step in a lengthy spiritual journey. Egypt is where art proper begins, with architecture as the crystal within which spirit must begin to recognize itself. Greek antiquity is a place marker in the evolution of a realized spirit. If Schelling had stopped short of the merging of Real and Ideal in an unimaginable future, Hegel was ready to pronounce the appearance of Spirit in the highest achievements of his contemporaries. In his *Aesthetics* he redefines the anesthetic of Enlightenment science, a science determined to rid itself of what Nietzsche called "conceptual mummies."[76] Hegel's philosophy of art will recuperate Egyptianism by treating Egypt's ruins as spirit-inhabited remains and positioning them in the first step of a dialectical theory of material translation. He repositions archaeology as comparative anthropology, and science as dialectical aesthetics. His *Aesthetics* situates things as in-process, as occupying states of betweenness rather than as dead matter that is completely othered. In Hegel's three-stage history of art, the grounding civilizations symbolize spirit through form. Egyptian architecture crystallized spirit, Classical art balanced spirit and form, and Romantic art subordinates form to spirit. Greek sculpture belongs to the middle ground, since despite the beauty of Greek matter-spirit harmonies in its sculpture, there is an equivalence here that suggests the spiritual has not yet achieved its full translation in the material. In Romantic art, objects, and especially poetry, achieve the fullness of their spiritual expression, and are the opposite of the deadening and mummifying weight of object over spirit. This schema, which in this summary appears to be historically progressive, is actually dialectical. The Egyptian stage posits the Idea of spirit as and in art; the Classical stage mediates the Idea by a process of reflection so that the spirit moves further inward, and is not so completely mobilized by the form itself; the final stage in which the problem posed by the Idea is resolved into the fullest expression of spirit's self-awareness and enlightenment is Romantic art.

In this respect, Hegel's treatment of objects or thingness is not unlike John Keats's dialectical resolutions in his odes, which his poetics render dynamically synthetic, a presentiment of spirit. For Hegel, Egyptian art is exemplary symbolic art, a riddle that cannot know its own solution:

Egypt is the land of symbol, which proposes to itself the spiritual problem of the self-interpretation of Spirit, without being able successfully to solve it. The problems remain without an answer; and such solution as we are able to supply consists therefore merely in this, that we grasp these riddles of Egyptian art and its symbolical productions as this very problem which Egypt propounds for herself but is unable to solve.[77]

Symbolic art begins in the originating point of wonder that should conjoin human thought and nature, but instead reveals how wonder begins over time to ossify in worship. Wonder as riddling, like the ciphering Sphinx, "the symbol of the symbolic itself," gives way to the self-consciousness of artistry that is Classical art.[78] Hegel's interpretation of the dialectical unfolding of spirit through art is an Egyptianizing of western art, because he presents an Egypt that veils its own being from itself, mystifying its own relation to spirit by encoding it as hieroglyphs or making it monumental and so beyond life-size, beyond the human. The problem presented by Hegel's schema is to understand how the negative in the Egyptian stage does not perform its remedial function as well as it should: "The shapes remain colossal, serious, petrified."[79] Instead, they eventually become contagious and fatal through the drive inward, for pyramids are not legible but riddling; they are "prodigious crystals which conceal in themselves an inner meaning," so that in "this realm of death ... an inner meaning rests concealed."[80]

In "The Pit and the Pyramid" Derrida clarifies the relation between symbol and the realm of death that is concealed meaning when he unpacks Hegel's theory of the sign, set out in part three of the *Encyclopedia of Philosophical Sciences*, "Philosophy of Spirit," and in the third part of that section on "absolute spirit." The sign arises in thought's dialectical-ized movement as it returns divorced from nature: having "lost the consciousness and meaning of itself in nature, in its Being-other," the sign designates a "form or a movement of the Idea's relation to itself in the element of spirit, a mode of the absolute's Being-near-to-itself."[81] Hegel's relation of the sign to the Idea in its movement toward truth is, Derrida notes, belongs to a "phantasiology," having derived from Aristotle's definition in *Peri Hermeneias* of "signs, symbols, speech and writing ... [as] the states, affections or passions of the soul."[82] Signs represent images, kept in reserve by the intelligence in a kind of "night pit, silent as death" from which a path leads "to a pyramid brought back from the Egyptian desert," a sepulchre that stands between the night pit and the divine as feminine law.[83] Derrida's reference to Hegel's interpretation of *Antigone* here as a contest between the feminine divine of the hearth and the masculine divine guiding reason and the state situates both the night pit and the sepulchre or pyramid in the unconscious: "what is unconscious ... is the other essential power, and is therefore not destroyed, but merely wronged (*beleidigt*) by the conscious Spirit."[84]

Thus, the sign, as represented by hieroglyphics, can be said to belong to a "fantastics," a fantasy in which unconscious or feminine knowing is pitted against the light of reason or the Idea: the hieroglyph hides its knowledge in the dark pyramidal enigma of its soul-affecting quality.[85] Feminine law of the family may be an essential power, but it is a "rebellious principle" that fights the universal and self-conscious spirit to the death; in this sense it represents contamination, a stain on the universal (which "easily knocks off the very top of the pyramid").[86] What has been "brought back from the Egyptian desert" is not just the pyramid, not just the hieroglyphic sign, but the unconscious itself. For Hegel, as for Mary Shelley and Blake, Egypt represents contamination and dark enigma ("the pyramid becomes once again the pit that it always will have been—such is the enigma") not the purification that the mortuary rites enact.[87] Thus, the sign itself, as the hieroglyph, is suspect in that it hides knowledge from the Idea and the self-aware spirit. The archaic ground is not all it should be and needs to be retranslated in order to serve its purpose—much in the way that Hermeticism translated Egyptian mystery, and then was itself translated again by alchemical philosophies.

Hegel's depiction of an Egypt obscured from itself merely replicates the western tradition of viewing Egypt as archaic, and therefore unself-conscious. Symbolic art ends when the balance between form and signifying presentiment proclaims a self-conscious freedom in Greek sculpture and the human form—a freedom from mystification, from dark uncertainties, in short from all the things Keats, ironically, claims for poetry in the Chamber of Maiden-Thought.[88] Keats's poetics resembles Hegel's dialectic as an Egyptianizing of western thought, but with a far different conclusion. Keats values the relation of wonder to the cosmic questions of life and death, potencies, and the spiritual power of embalming. The "embalming" of the poet's imaginings in "Ode to a Nightingale" ("I cannot see what flowers are at my feet" "... / But, in embalmed darkness, guess ..." [ll. 41, 43]) provides a far different picture from Hegel's own conceptual mummies, in which dead matter symbolizes the spirit at an impasse, unable to be released or to express itself in consciousness. For Keats, the unseen and the embalmed give flight to the imagination: dead or ungraspable things assume the agency of threshold, of entrance into the third chamber of poetic thought, which is for Hegel the third stage of matter-Spirit integration.[89] Keats's thought is synthetic whereas Hegel's is encyclopedic, pushing him toward a determinate reading of history. But the synthetic imagination finds a dynamism in embalmment in the Egyptian sense, a life that, so worth living, must be enabled to survive after death. Keats's manuscript poem "This Living Hand" (c. 1819) is, in this sense, an Egyptian poem.

This living hand, now warm and capable
Of earnest grasping, would, if it were cold
And in the icy silence of the tomb,
So haunt thy days and chill thy dreaming nights
That thou would wish thine own heart dry of blood
So in my veins red life might stream again,
And thou be conscience-calm'd—see here it is—
I hold it towards you.

The Egyptians viewed life as what is to be so valued that death must not inhibit its fullest duration; mummification and entombment were meant to allow the spirit to perdure after the body's death. Keats's spontaneous poem, written in the margin of another poem he was composing, is the opposite of Egyptian architecture, especially pyramids, which required decades to complete. There is a similarity of sentiment, however, with the Egyptian view that troubles Hegel's schema of a dialectically progressive historical development. Keats's poem represents an identity with the Egyptian view of life, in that what is so full of life now—this warm, capable hand—will still be capable of "earnest grasping" after death, will still be spirit-imbued and in correspondence with the beloved. The poem suggests an imagining of how the dead experience the offerings of loved ones, a visit that temporarily stages a renewed life through candles, flowers, and gifts of fruit. Keats would not have known of this Egyptian mortuary practice, but it is hardly different in its humanity and desire for contact beyond death from how the dead were remembered during the Romantic period.

In fighting the effects of temporal change through mummification, most Romantics would think, Egyptian priests denied the becoming that is history, thus denying the body its progress through time. The mummy is hermetically sealed, stuffed, and preserved against erosion and decay, a thing without bodily significance or transcendent possibility. Hegel must reread this embalmment (what he calls the "Egyptian view and representation of the dead")[90] as a signifying turn inward. That in itself, as well as the Egyptians' own view of their history, must be understood as monumental in accordance with the gigantic scale of their memorials to the dead. Egyptian monumental time, which like their representation of the dead, is not on the same scale as Hegel's tripartite art history, but Hegel can revise Egyptian history because for so long it had been lost, had been represented solely by monuments or the comments of travelers lured by its allusive mystique. The loss of Egyptian chronicles is significantly the product of a loss of translatability, which is the key to change, to history, and to the liminal. Without a way to read the hieroglyphs, an erroneous dynastic history interpolated by Greek and Roman historians was taken by the Romantics as Egypt's incongruous and incomprehensible, mummified history. Not until Champollion broke the hieroglyphic code in 1822 was a correct dynastic chronology available, allowing Egyptian time to be rescued from the monumental, the living death of Egyptian afterlife (however, even now scholars debate the chronology and correct identification of pharaohs).[91] Hegel believes he, too, can rescue Egypt from its ciphering monumentalism, producing a reading of its remains that translates it from its archaic ground. Hegel's geographica, in its dialectical revolutions, does not differ so drastically from Schelling's account of rotary movement in *Ages of the World*. But both Mary Shelley's and Keats' versions provide a more flexible model in which the past and the present, as in Quatremère's Rome, are inextricably bound to each other in ways that escape the frameworks of time and balance more loosely on the archaic ground rather than being bound to it and its Isis-like promise.

NOTES

1. de Manoncourt, *Travels in Upper and Lower Egypt*, Vol. I, 8.
2. Jefferson translated all but the final four chapters, which were translated by Joel Barlow; it was Barlow's name, however, that became attached to the English translation. For Jefferson's connections with Volney, see Furstenberg's *When the United States Spoke French*, 355–367. For an approach with deep affiliations to my own, but with an eye toward the effects of Romantic literary and philosophical thought on modern geography studies, and a focus on German Romanticism only, see Chenxi Tang's *The Geographica Imagination of Modernity*.
3. Jacob Boehme coined this term to refer to God, the ineffable, the abyss, or the absolute; it lies behind or founds the determinate, differentiated, potentiated, finite.
4. Bowden's *Mystery Cults of the Ancient World* provides a comprehensive history of the development, central beliefs, and importance of these cults and cult centers. Bowden investigates the role of the major cults in transmitting cosmic wisdom through initiation rites and strict protection of secret knowledge concerning the origin of the universe and the matter-spirit synergy that maintains its order; these traditions can be clearly detected in eighteenth-century Masonic practices. "Cartographica" is the title of the journal of cartography that, fittingly, publishes articles that sometimes juggle contemporary philosophical theory with problems in geographical mapping.
5. Michel Foucault, *The Order of Things*, 131.
6. This is the bridging mental faculty that Kant in his third critique claims joins the other two faculties of pure and practical reason. Kant calls this faculty "judgment," but his argument is by way of what we might call the aesthetic faculty.
7. The English translation of the section from al-Qifti's history concerning the burning of the Library, first posted on the webblog hosted by Roger Pearse (roger-pearse.com), is available on the Blog of Coptic Literature, Culture & Politics.

8. For a detailed account of this legend, see Schiff, *Cleopatra: A Life*; a brief account is in Pollard and Reid, *The Rise and Fall of Alexandria*, 170. See also Chauveau, *Egypt in the Age of Cleopatra*.

9. See Ronald Gray's excellent account and analysis in *Goethe the Alchemist*.

10. For a succinct discussion of Blake and Antinomianism, see Mee, "Is there an Antinomian in the House?"

11. Brouzas, "Libraries in Ancient Athens," 13.

12. Budge, *Egyptian Magic*, 116–119.

13. Budge, *The Nile: Notes for Travellers in Egypt*, 12.

14. For the standard account of this event, see al-Qifti, Ali Ibn Yusuf. *Ta'rikh al-hukama' (History of Learned Men)*.

15. Polwhele, "Notes on Theocritus," 292. *The Idyllia, Epigrams and Fragments of Theocritus, Bion, and Moscus*.

16. Napoleon had intended to make Volney one of his scientific team on the Egyptian Campaign, but the *Ruins* had to substitute for the man (Furstenberg, *When the United States Spoke French*, 376).

17. "For the Pythagoreans recollections meant, first of all, remembering one's previous incarnations (as Pythagoras himself was reported to have done) and secondly, remembering the secret passwords and road markers coommu7nicated to the initiate for a safe passage in the realm of the dead." Kahn, *Pythagoras and The Pythagoreans*, 51.

18. Kahn, *Pythagoras and The Pythagoreans*, 5–13.

19. I use this term in the sense given it by Merleau-Ponty in *Phenomenology of Perception*: intentional life requires self-apperceptions that locate it in the world, but with an added element of imaginative distortions of that world that affect apperception.

20. *The Monthly Review*, vol. 74, 527.

21. As with Mesopotamian and later Persian archives, the Alexandrian Library grew large enough to need cataloguing. There seems to have been no shared tradition regarding this practice or one of categorizing, and until the reign of Ptolemy III Alexandrian scholars had to memorize where books were idiosyncratically shelved. The scholars holding the post of Librarian from Demetrius on considered their main task to be one of acquisition, not order; the first scholar assigned (by royal command) to the task was Zenodotus of Ephesus (283–245 BC). One of his several gifted assistants was Callimachus of Cyrene (c. 305–240 BC), who created an organizational system for the Library's holdings by subject. Earlier, Ptolemy II had ordered Lycophron, a member of the group known as the Pleiades, to organize and catalog the Library's comedies (Pollard and Reid, 88). Perhaps because he was a poet, Callimachus's catalog only treated literary texts; it is not clear whether or not he built on Lycophron's contribution. Using categories still used today (drama, epic and lyric poets, legislators, philosophers, historians, orators, and rhetoricians), Callimachus listed and summarized 120 scrolls, and gave biographical and scholarly details for each author (MacLeod, *The Library of Alexandria*, 5; Pollard and Reid, *The Rise and Fall of Alexandria*, 146). This did not account for even half the Library's holdings, which were never fully catalogued so that the full extent of the Library's holdings has never been known.

22. See Potts, "Before Alexandria: Ancient Libraries of the Ancient Near East," 22–23.

These contain both arithmetic accounts and lexical lists of what the king and his kingdom possessed. Archives were established for record-keeping, with the scribal room adjoined; libraries arose later, with the first known royal library assembled by Assurbanipal. The Alexandrian Library is the first Greek library assembled under royal patronage and not belonging to a school or individual; it combined several elements of Mesopotamian libraries, such as wooden shelving and pigeonholing to categorize different kinds of texts in the small chambers leading off the central, communal room.

23. Derrida, *Archive Fever*, 1–7.
24. Ibid, 7.
25. In *Archive Fever* Derrida uses the concept of the exergue to argue for the "violence of the archive," that is, the way in which the cataloguer classifies, denominates the most valuable works and obscures the others, and conserves these orderings through an authoritative catalog. The exergue "accumulat[es] capital in advance and . . . prepar[es] the surplus value of an archive." The capital enables a lexicon through which to "lay down the law and *give the order*," a nominative and classificatory principle that Alexandrian librarians attended to with varying degrees of success for so vast a collection. But it is the violence of the archive, at once "institutive" and "conservative," "the violence of a power (*Gewalt*) which at once posits and conserves the law" (Derrida cites Walter Benjamin here on his *Philosophy of History, Zur Kritik der Gewalt*) in a manner that is "unnatural" (*Archive Fever*, 7). Derrida's meaning of "unnatural" here is in reference to the violence of the acts of keeping and "put[ting] in reserve" (Ibid): the archive keeps its objects and texts apart from the 'over there' of the social order as it plays out. This, too, follows the pattern of the Alexandrian Museum and Library, reserved for the museum's patronized scholars and not available to other scholars or the public; moreover, texts could not be taken from the premises, they were unconditionally "on reserve."
26. Schelling, *Ages of the World*, xxxix.
27. See Derrida's "Sauf le nom (Post-Scriptum)" for a treatment of apophasis that directly treats mystical thought; and see "Post-Scriptum: Aporias, Ways and Voices" for Derrida's engagement with the tradition of apophatic theology.
28. Steigerwald, "Epistemologies of Rupture," 555.
29. Qtd. in Derrida, *Glas*, 31.
30. Amun-Re is the later manifestation of the patron deity of Thebes, the capital of Upper Egypt. His huge New Kingdom period temple of Karnak was one of the temples documented by Napoleon's team. In his earlier incarnation as "Amun" he was the creator god, and Mut, the mother goddess, his consort, with their child the moon (Khonsu) completing this divine family known as the Theban Triad. When Egypt was unified, Amun was promoted to Amun-Re, a syncretic deity that combined the father with the sun god, Re. It was this combined deity that Akhenaten reformed as the "Aten," the monotheistic god that Assmann and other Egyptologists argue influenced the shaping of Jewish monotheism.
31. Stoudt, *Jacob Boehme*, 216.

32. Rancière, *Mute Speech*, 35. See also Brown, *The Later Philosophy of Schelling*, and Bowie, *Schelling and Modern European Philosophy*, for the importance of Schelling's revival of negative theology.
33. Hegel, *Between Fichte and Schelling*, 95.
34. Schelling, *Ages of the World*, xxxv.
35. Ibid, xxxix.
36. Voltaire, *Philosophy of History*, 2.
37. Ibid, 124.
38. Ibid, 130.
39. Ibid, 132.
40. Schelling, *Ages of the World*, 49.
41. See Boehme's *De Signatura Rerum* (The Signature of All Things) (1621).
42. Schelling, *Ages of the World*, 86.
43. Ibid, 38.
44. See Magee, *Hegel and the Hermetic Tradition*, 76–78.
45. Schelling, *Ages of the World*, 31, 37.
46. Magee and others treat *hen kai pan*. For its significance to Hellenism, see William Davis's account in *Romanticism, Hellenism, and the Philosophy of Nature*.
47. Schelling, *Ages of the World*, 56.
48. Ibid, 49.
49. See Wirth's editorial note, *Ages of the World*, 146 n.98.
50. Schelling, *Ages of the World*, 56, 102.
51. Ibid, 97, 96.
52. See Benz, *The Theology of Electricity: On the Encounter and Explanation of Theology and Science in the 17th and 18th Centuries*.
53. Schelling, *Ages of the World*, 143–144 n. 71. Vala appears insidiously in *Jerusalem* as a corruptive force.
54. Assmann, *Moses the Egyptian*, 142.
55. Schelling, *Ages of the World*, 104. For Hegel, the difference between superstition and "proper Pantheism," as he calls it in the *Aesthetics*, is that proper pantheism such as that held "primarily in the East," is an intuition of "the unity of the Divine and the thought of all things as comprised in this unity . . . as unity and All" (*Aesthetics*, I. 365). Specifically, this is an agency of power: Wirth notes that the root of magie, to which Schelling connects *Möglichkeit* (possibility) along with "maya" in his *Philosophie der Mythologie* (1842), means "being able" or "having power" (*Ages of the World*, 143n). That essential power, that energy or spiritual intellectuality and creativity, is for Boehme a "will" or "desire" that is "the mother of eternity," "the essence of all essence."
56. Ibid, 143n.
57. Ibid, 83.
58. Plutarch, "On Isis and Osiris," 8.
59. Qtd in Assmann, *Moses the Egyptian*, 120.
60. Plutarch, "On Isis and Osiris," 3.
61. See Raine, *Blake and Antiquity* for Blake's understanding of Paracelsus and Boehme, both of whom he rejects along with Swedenborg in *Marriage of Heaven and Hell*; see also Mee's *Dangerous Enthusiasm* for Blake's antinomian influences.

62. See Hessayon and Apetrei's *An Introduction to Jacob Boehme*, particularly ch. 10 for the English Romantics' reception of Boehme.
63. Blake, *Milton*, pl. 14: 30–33.
64. Ibid, pl. 21: 4–7, pl. 17: 8–10. I use the plate numbering in Erdman's *The Complete Poetry and Prose of William Blake*, 95–144.
65. Paracelsus, *Paracelsus, Essential Readings*, 68.
66. Blake, *Milton*, pl. 23: 32–38.
67. Ibid, pl. 29: 54.
68. Ibid, pl. 27: 55–59.
69. Kahn notes that Plato's explanation of the four "sister sciences" is "apparently a quotation from [the Pythagorean] Archytas, fragment 1" (*Pythagoras*, 55).
70. Blake, *Milton*, pl. 29: 65.
71. Ibid, pl. 29: 62, 64.
72. de Quincy, Letter VI, qtd in Déotte, "Rome, the Archetypal Museum, and the Louvre, the Negation of Division," 222; emphasis mine.
73. Ibid, Letter III, Déotte 218.
74. Hegel, *Philosophy of History*, 3; italics his.
75. Ibid, 38.
76. Nietzsche. *Twilight of the Idols*, 35. My thanks to David Clark for pointing me to this passage.
77. Hegel, *The Philosophy of Fine Art*, I. 74. I intend "the anesthetic" literally, as the incapacity for or insensitivity to feeling, thus as a rejection of the object's potential to hold spirit.
78. Hegel, *Aesthetics*, I. 360.
79. Ibid.
80. Ibid, I. 356.
81. Derrida, "The Pit and the Pyramid," in *Margins of Philosophy*, 74.
82. Ibid, 76, 75.
83. Ibid, 77, 77n.
84. Hegel, *Phenomenology*, 286; qtd. in Derrida 77n.
85. Derrida, "The Pit and the Pyramid," 76.
86. Hegel, *Phenomenology*, 286.
87. Derrida, "The Pit and the Pyramid," 77.
88. Letter to J. H. Reynolds, 3 May 1818, in Gittings, *Letters of John Keats*, 95.
89. For Keats's understanding of Egypt as archaic and embalming, preliminary to Hellenistic imagination, see Bewell's discussion of the Egyptianized shadows behind the Hellenistic forms in Keats's *Hyperion* in "The Political Implication of Keats's Classicist Aesthetics," as well as Kelley's use of Bewell's argument ("Keats, Ekphrasis, and History," 220–221).
90. Hegel, *Aesthetics*, I. 354.
91. See the four-volume series by Emmet Sweeney, *Ages in Alignment*.

Chapter 3

Ruins

Monumentality, Rubble, and Cities of the Dead

In *Ages of the World* Schelling dramatizes a Christian version of the Egyptian conception of a divine immersion in form, the god manifesting in the cult image in the inner sanctum of a temple dedicated to that deity. James Boswell manifests this incorporation of Egypto-Christian blending when he imagines his biography of Samuel Johnson through that lens: "I tell every body it [the Life] will be an Egyptian Pyramid in which there will be a compleat mummy of Johnson that Literary Monarch."[1] This need for the deity to inhabit or to create a terrestrial place to express itself, whether Egyptian colossi and cult statues or the earth itself, is already a part of the western imaginary as Boswell's sentiment indicates, but in a superficial or metaphorical way compared to the more strongly yoked expression of Romantic and Egyptian notions of mystical habitation in the knowable world. What distinguishes these notions is that for the Egyptians the pharaoh was the mediator between the gods and his people, whereas for the Romantics it was the philosopher and poet (not Johnson metaphorically conceived as the embalmed mummy, but the Romantic poet-seer as a living and vocal mediator). Coleridge as philosophical poet also takes on this Egyptian conception of divine immersion when he writes in *Confessions of an Inquiring Spirit* (in "Letters on the Inspiration of the Scriptures"):

> Thoughtfully have I put the question—why should I not believe the Scriptures thoroughly dictated, in word and thought by an infallible Intelligence? . . . Because the doctrine in question petrifies at once the whole Body of Holy Writ . . . that I had seen "stand on its feet as a Man with a Man's [heart?] given unto it"—the Doctrine in question turns at once into a colossal Memnon's Head, a hollow passage for a Voice, a Voice that mocks the voices of many men and

speaks in their names and yet is but one voice and the same!—and no man uttered it, and never in a human heart was it conceived![2]

Coleridge's conceptualization of the Ideal in the Real is imagined in an ancient rather than future terms, when the text was indeed the Word and spirit embodied, and likewise this body has a voice. At least the Memnon colossus does, renowned since Classical times for the sound it makes at dawn, thought to be a prophetic or divine utterance by the embodied pharaoh. This is not Mosaic law or even the body of Christ but the sacred manifesting itself in formed matter, the divine creative principle that is also the locus of cosmic wisdom.

For Schelling this embodiment expresses a divinely fallible and evolving coming to self-consciousness and self-knowledge, a process that takes place through the creation of reality, time, space, and history. For Coleridge the formalization, whether in law or statuary, of the Word is a desecration because then the Word is no longer living; already interpreted and mediated by man, it has been desacralized. It seems natural that Coleridge should envision an Egyptian colossus, particularly the Memnon with its oracular voice that history had separated from the actual pharaoh it represents; here is indeed corruption, a broken form attributed with a mystical voice, a false word that is both petrified and petrifying. Implicit in this passage is a question of how much better the poet-philosopher would be at transmitting the message of spirit. Coleridge may have conflated the Memnon head with the head of Ramesses II that Belzoni brought back for the British Museum; like that head, Coleridge imagines his head separated from the Memnon colossus. The Memnon (head and body intact but cracked) was anciently believed to speak at dawn, its song-like sound emitted when cooled stone and the sun's heat first meet already long interpreted as the voicing of spirit as Herodotus records. Coleridge imagines the isolated head still speaking its archaic prophecies, but rather than viewing this act as realizing Spirit he interprets it as petrifying, mummifying the voice. Like the Egyptian mummy, Memnon's voice has no heart because it comes from the dead and not the living spirit.

In the chapter epigraph Boswell takes the opposite approach, using the Egyptian metaphor to construe Samuel Johnson's knowledge as a cosmological and terrestrial complex, a complex mapping of knowledges that can only be understood as vocalized spirit. This spirit must dwell with itself in a preserved state, in the pyramidal casing of Boswell's biography where reification and petrification are held off by the power of that monumental voice. In these two approaches to Ancient Egypt as form that embodies spirit, one positive (Boswell and Schelling) and the other negative (Coleridge), we have a Romantic bifocal vision of Egypt as a land of ruins in which it is both the grounding of the living spirit and the denatured ground of spirit's possibility. A third approach entered Romantic thought with Hegel's concept of the negative as the instigator of movement and conceptual life: Ancient Egypt as ruins, as remains, provides the ground for the negative in which one must tarry in order to recognize the dialectical movement of spirit, its evolutionary progress toward absolute knowing.

I am arguing for understanding Hegel's interpretation of the role of the negative in *Phenomenology of Spirit* as a way to understand Egypt's place in the dialectical becoming of spirit in his *Aesthetics*, but more largely, as a way to understand Egypt's place in Romantic-period self-realization. Hegel offers an interpretation of Egypt as a cultural stage in the evolution of self-realization in which spirit is not petrified, as for Coleridge, but caught in a negative moment. The negative is the moment in which the "idea" is questioned, doubted; perhaps Hegel is imagining Egypt from the Hellenic perspective when the Egypt of pre-Alexandrian dynasties could be known only from remains and the biblical and Greek accounts of foreigners. For Hegel, spirit is negation of negation in the dialectical process, so that "there is an identity of formal structure between spirit and time, i.e., the negation of the negation." In this account, time is "an entity standing there in front, facing spirit," as Derrida explains.[3] The negative produces history in that the archaic confronts spirit's movement in a manner not unlike Schelling's rotary movements of God's thought and drives that bring creation into history. In this reading Egypt is the repository of the negative in being the nonwestern or archaic of the other, but the negative as that which the west has to engage in order to self-realize as subject. This might be literally illustrated by Sir John Soane's acquisition in 1824 of the alabaster sarcophagus of Seti I, brought back to England by Giovanni Belzoni but rejected by the British Museum. Soane hosted a three-day dinner party in his museum-like London house to celebrate his triumph, lighting the entire basement level housing the sarcophagus by candlelight so that it could be seen from every floor in the house through a central open area. A literal enlightenment for Soane's initiates, the translucent sarcophagus functions as a self-actualizing space, since it is both the translative medium of light and a space of generative, creative energy. As such, it is a monumental embodiment of spirit that Hegel's *Aesthetics* interprets as negativity. This third Romantic adoption of Egypt as conceptual matter takes the negative as a positive, creative and motivating; it both creates the conditions for knowable history and maintains the grounding of history through its unknowable past.

From a Hegelian conception of the subject's necessary encounter with the negative, Egypt is no longer the *Ungrund* but the ground as condition; no longer a reliquary of esoteric knowledge but a land that begins to become measurable despite its deep relation with spirit and its reserves of ancient wisdom. Nor is Egypt any longer the beginning in the sense of an archaic begetter of the west, since there is more than one beginning: for most historians of the period Ancient India and Ancient China are the other civilizations claiming equal status for the human spirit's generative beginning. But for Hegel only Egypt is the archaic ground of the negative: if it is the ground of the life-in-death state symbolized by the pyramid as habitation for its mummy, it is so as the condition of self-becoming. Ancient Egypt as it was encountered through the ruin-strewn ground in the Romantic period was legible as both past and ongoing; seemingly knowable in its visible remains, but unknowable when the dimensions of these remains as well as their purpose and hieroglyphic legends defied speculation. On leaving Alexandria and Cairo it was possible to ignore, even not see, the contemporary Muslim world by focusing on the ruins as did explorers, adventurers, and Napoleon's engineers and draftsmen. It was even more possible to do so for those not experiencing Egypt firsthand who, like Hegel, gained impressions from the descriptions and drawings provided by adventurers, travel writers, and Napoleon's Commission of Science and Art. I will begin with this aspect of Egypt's ruins, their knowability such as it was during the Romantic period, before moving to ruins as the unknowable, providing the condition of possibility for Romanticism's self-becoming.

I. RUINS

Napoleon's team approached Egyptian monuments and ruins with the same opposition of open-ended unknowing and systematicity that generally characterized the west's approach to Egypt's mysteries. Ruins set within wasteland vistas evoked the expansive and contractive "potencies" that dominated Behemist ideas (Behemism was the legacy of Boehme's thought that characterized so much of Romantic speculation), and that structure Schelling's *Ages of the World*. The *Description de l'Egypte* is replete with oppositions or antitheses beyond this basic organizing principle of not-knowing and knowing—of what might be called "gnosesis" or suspended knowledge—and epistemology, or the urge toward systematicity and closure. This is a different conflict than that between the Renaissance system of ordering by resemblance and the Classical age's system of analytic order; the suspension between open-ended and closed approaches in gnosesis is deliberately sought and is characteristic of the west's approach to Ancient Egypt in the Romantic period and shared by Napoleon's team. In the illustrations for the *Description*, in which Vivant Denon incorporated the work of the team's four architects and eight draftsmen, both approaches are apparent. Many of Denon's drawings are of ruins as ruins, sometimes with contemporary Arab and French figures peopling the drawing. These figures are for purposes of scale, but they also provoke a contrast between ancient and modern, living bodies and dead ruin, the known and the unknown, the simple human figures and the grand architectural statement. These are the same oppositions apparent throughout the *Description*. Moreover, the drawings also compare the habitable to the unhabitable or ruined space, extreme ruin or rubble versus relative preservation, fragments and body parts that contrast and resist reimagined wholes. In each antithesis, the two urges of a will toward closure and an openness toward the ruin can be sensed. The first urge is a closing down on the ruin, a reification of it *as* ruin; the second suspends this judgment in order to consider the ruin's unknown-ness as something complex, a gnostic awareness that may well remain beyond reach. Several of the views are of reimagined interiors fully intact, peopled by ancient priests, and vibrantly polychromed. These scenes express both urges at once: they visualize Ancient Egyptian ways of knowing, imagining the ritualistic space as light-filled splendor; at the same time, the desire to complete the ruin back to totality, to create a perfect image of it, brings the ruin back into a western epistemological system as in Soane's Englishing of the Seti I sarcophagus.

These antitheses structure what might seem to the western reader a somewhat random series of sites and monuments, not organized by either the Classical, Aristotelian system of taxonomy or that of eighteenth-century natural history. Instead, the *Description* at first appears to be an accumulation of overwhelming detail, each minute particular drawn with the same care given to clearly politicized drawings such as the interior views of the Egyptian Institute. Drawings of papyri and inscribed stones are so detailed that the hieroglyphs could later be translated. What is striking about the accretion of detail is that previous images of Ancient Egyptian ruins had stressed their simplicity, their rudeness that was both antique and primitive. The *Description* presents a fantastically complex civilization; both the intricate temple floor plans and renderings of surface ornamentation reveal a highly refined and sophisticated culture. The drawings intimate that this culture might be again known—that indeed, the Commission's scientists were already proceeding to accomplish this task—or that it might be beyond the epistemological veil.

What is most interesting about the drawings aside from their organizing antitheses and their extraordinary depth of detail is their representation of ruin. This is a particularly Romantic obsession, but it equally fascinated the Enlightenment arts scholars in the Commission. For the Romantics, the ruin is ontologically linked to the fragment. The fragment form, as has been well explored starting with the Romantics themselves, is intimately linked to the Romantic imaginary. The dream vision, for instance, in Coleridge's "Kubla Khan," links interior vision with a larger wellspring and a primordial moment in the genesis of creative being. Coleridge's lyric-maiden gives form to that which preexists, to the archaic and eruptive rhythm that Julia Kristeva means by poetic language. The fragment allows us a brief glimpse of the invisible; it registers a synaptic moment with the infinite other. These are all aspects of the Romantic intimation that there is a larger palimpsestic reality beyond normal frames of reference that recent geological and archaeological discoveries were beginning to uncover. If this larger reality is so layered that its depths will forever remain unplumbed, this in itself attests to the effects of the remainder. When the remainder itself is immeasurable—Mont Blanc, for example, as a remainder of ancient geological upheaval—its sublimity arises from that monumental embodiment of the fragment of a lost whole. Similarly, Ancient Egyptian ruins pose the problem of the irredeemably lost, the fragment of the whole, the sublime referent. In "Shadow of a Magnitude" Paul Hamilton demonstrates the conceptual importance of monumentality and its formal realization of the sublime. Both of these formal concerns—the lost whole and the inexpressible whole—are linked with ruin in the aesthetic theory of Edmund Burke, Kant, and the German Idealists. Political historians such as Volney also found a compelling case to be made in the consciousness of ruin, ruin as a speaking effect of the remainder.

Before turning to monumentality, fragmentation, and their relation to a Romantic Egypt, I need to distinguish some key aspects of the ruin. Ruin can connote either dead ground or generative ground. Again, these are expressions of the opposed mentalities of closure and of openness. Geologically speaking, ground can be linear and progressive, as in geological strata. But it can also be catastrophic; ground can be violently disrupted, destroyed, or simply ruined. This is the metaphor Volney and other Enlightenment philosophers used for Ancient Egypt, to oppose it to continuous cultures such as those of Ancient India and China. Rome was similarly catastrophically disrupted, but because it was reclaimed by Christians and its archives transmitted relatively intact compared to the "lost" cultures of the ancient Near East, Rome offers a model of interruption more than termination, and thus knowing rather than not-knowing.

The opposition between interruption/disruption or termination is one between disorder and suspension, or *aporia*. In the subjective experience of disruptive catastrophe, one is ungrounded, severed from normal contextual cues that provide everyday normalcy. The subject, as in post-traumatic stress syndrome, is disoriented and feels disembodied and beyond any form of systematic knowledge, any grounding. There is a sense of haunting a terrain rather than inhabiting it, and of being severed from the community. Alternately, there is a sense of the haunted terrain that speaks its palimpsestic runes of past lives and activities. Both understandings of the land are alienating and yet the alienation that comes in the moment of safety is that of being at home within oneself, "*chez soi*," to use Emmanuel Levinas's term. Being at home in disorientation provides the moment when otherness can enter into or become intimate with us, providing a "glean of exteriority or of transcendence."[4] Transcendence, interpreted as the sublime, provides a landscape of ruin with a grandeur that is compelling to the Romantic desire to reshape prior understandings of the world and its cosmic role. But when this sublimity is understood as devastating loss instead—as an alienation effect or profound self-alienation—then the land becomes a haunted and apocalyptic memoryscape of the end of things, the end times as already achieved. For William Wordsworth, in his Egyptianized vision of the apocalypse in Book VI of *The Prelude* ("Characters of the great Apocalypse,/ The types and symbols of Eternity,/ Of first, and last, and midst, and without end," ll. 637–40), and for Mary Shelley in her vision of an apocalyptic end of humanity in *The Last Man*, Egypt provided the originary source of the end of things, a ruin-strewn and ruinous landscape. For both of them, Egypt both as ancient culture and colonized Ottoman land tropes the abyss. This alienated experience of the abyss, an alienation effect always in place, can be troped as the ruin in its signifying capacity of the loss of knowledge and spiritual wisdom, and literalized in the architectonic material ruin. In either case, whether inspiring terror or suggesting existential calm or surrender, the ruin haunts us because a greater magnitude lies behind it.

The ruins of Ancient Egypt, however, are symbolic markers not just of abyssal erasure but of the creative void, the negative in Hegel's sense of negativity; this is the *Ungrund* of Boehme's and Schelling's philosophies, the nonground of potentiality, of coming forth. Both the negating and negative potentiality of Ancient Egypt's ruined past provided the Romantics with a compellingly fertile ground for artistic inspiration. Its fragmentation allows for endlessly suggestive ways to re-present what has been so completely lost or buried.

In contrast to the disrupted/terminated life, the interrupted life still belongs to the material and spiritual community, and thus represents a way of knowing (which the abyss cannot, in its gesture toward excess and the infinite). Ancient Rome as a cultural phenomenon, unlike the ruins of its physical manifestation, was not erased from history as was Egypt; it remained legible through its extant literature, and therefore also remained omnipresent as a back-presence in the historical life of Rome through the ages. That continuity is represented at the level of the individual in the devastated person who survives tumult or revolution; they continue, but on a different, diminished scale and in a different relation to the community. Architecturally, when the inhabited dwelling is reduced to a ruin, it may still be habitable for the recluse, who is still (as a ruined human) an acknowledged member of the community. Even when no one dwells in the ruin, its former habitation determines it to belong to that category; the ruin participates in the material articulation of space at the level of dwelling. As poets and authors of the Romantic era generally, regardless of nation, wrote about ruined lives—the human remainders of social injustice, revolution, and misfortune—it was an easy stretch to similarly imagine the last survivors of a lost culture, figures walking among ruins as they contemplate what has been taken away. That which is taken or has disappeared remains as an absent presence, a runic figuration that might be called into presence through one's contemplative invitation, one's openness to interpellation by otherness or by what might appear its glimmer of exteriority that Levinas calls "signifyingness itself," into which something must be read.[5]

Only when the ruin is reduced to rubble may it lose its habitable quality, be returned to sheer materiality that is neither haunted nor a palimpsestic layer. Yet the Romantics did see in material ground what Schelling calls the "indwelling spirit": rubble could be the same as Lucy for William Wordsworth, for both are figurations of a remainder. In Wordsworth's poems "The Leech-gatherer" and "The Thorn" the encounters between speaker and other begin as a meeting of subject and object; the leech-gatherer, indeed, serves as an apt object lesson to the poet-subject just as ancient ruins typified for Enlightenment writers a reflection on history and progress. In Wordsworth's speaker's case, the stony debris unfolds itself, revealing itself to be a man habituated to stillness, trained by life's vicissitudes to endure. Habitude equals the right to inhabit the land here; endurance allows the man a place in the landscape. In "The Thorn," Martha Ray offers a different test case; she inhabits a landscape that also contains speaking objects, particularly the mysterious pond and the ambiguity-laden tree. Her victimization has made her an outcast from the human community, but in inhabiting marginalized land her possible guilt has also imbued the landscape with gothic hauntings that teach no lesson. If the leech-gatherer is a remainder that gestures toward a greater immanence, a sublime insistence, Martha Ray is a ruination, human rubble. Yet for both figures, as each poem's telling of the object's story unfolds, revealing it to be a human object with a history and a community that have somehow become disrupted, the unfolding can be seen as occurring in the speaker-subject, creating something new that both is and is not part of the object itself. It is the speaker who is affected, in whom the unfolding occurs. This is the phenomenon that called forth the eighteenth-century travel writer, especially the traveler to the Near East where one could more readily encounter the origin of things. Things are inhabited by spirit, the Romantics intuited, in a return to older patterns of thought; if human things are their own historicized subjects, natural things are similarly temporally present but also alive at a different level. Disrupted things have been ruined, have become fragments of their former selves, but are not severed from their context. Even the thing-like Martha Ray continues in the vicinity of her village unwilling to cut herself off entirely from it. So too do ruined homes, ruined monuments, ruined temples and tombs inscribe a continuity with the past, however lost or buried. This continuity is also a potentiality, a contribution to the archaic *Ungrund*'s fertile spaciousness.

In habitable or habitual ruin and disrupted experience, the Romantic imagination found a clearer articulation of the life force underlying all communal integrity. Wordsworth's "A Slumber does my spirit seal," for instance, expresses the relation of the habitual ruin to a spiritual community. It is a participatory relation, one more clearly articulated in "We are Seven." In this last lyric, the gravestones are markers for the included community of the dead, which outnumbers that of the living at the moment of intervention by the outsider-speaker. "A Slumber did my spirit seal" interestingly raises the question of magnetic sleep, which so intrigued Schelling, as well as an "ensouled world" and the idea of "soul sleep." The speaker's vision of the dead Lucy as an eternally present entity arises from his own mesmeric insight; Lucy belongs to the ensouled world, and both he and she are translated into participants in the encircling, universal strata via soul sleep. The spiritual community of the poem includes these strata; the silence, aporia, or abyss between the two stanzas which signals tremendous loss and yet not-loss; the rubble of rocks and stones and trees with which Lucy has become identified in the second stanza. In the dialectic between materiality and spirit (in Schelling's terms, the dialectic between the three potencies), Lucy as ruin becomes part of the habitat and its spiritual life.

Despite her inconsequential death, Lucy has not been lost to communal memory within the world of the Lucy lyrics. Even those who terribly, disastrously disappear are remembered by those they leave behind. When there is no tie, when all removed from the calculation, then we cannot talk of ruin but only of a cutting off of the human; but even then, the ground holds the possibility of rediscovery however illegible the remains. What holds real terror for the Romantic imagination is the possibility of total loss without ground, without the potential for rediscover, remembrance, or rebirth. Severance belongs to the alienated experience of catastrophe, the apocalyptic loss of connection and community. For those interested in antiquity, Ancient Egypt represented both the possibility of disrupted habitude—either of ruin or rubble—and of apocalyptic severance. Extreme loss can barely gesture toward the infinite; its condition of silence and nonfigurability removes it from the palimpsest, and any trace left of it must exist in categorical translation, placing it in the purely imaginative realm of possible pasts. The lost world of Atlantis retains just such a cultural trace. Ancient Egypt was not similarly catastrophically lost to memory, yet Egypt's ruins did not speak to the observer in the same way as Roman ruins or medieval European ruins could. A colossal hand or arm lying on the ground was an uncontextualized body part, its counterparts unimaginable.

II. SHELLEY, HEGEL, AND THE MONUMENTAL

Percy Shelley was particularly intrigued by the ruins of ancient civilizations. Egypt, for him, represented both a lost world and a clear example of the erroneous use of power; for him, the biblical account of Egypt's practice of enslaved labor explains the downfall of its civilization and provides a parallel to English labor practices. In thinking about institutional agency, Percy Shelley shared with Hegel the idea that Ancient Egypt could provide a cryptogram that, properly viewed, would reveal institutionalized power as an embodiment of the culture's character. For Shelley, institutional power was abused and provided its own undoing. For Hegel, it revealed the coming forth of human spirit in its progress toward self-consciousness and self-knowledge. Both accounts, representing oppositional perspectives, are premised on empire as a way of being in the world, as well as on the assumption that despite our ongoing inability to heed their messages, change and redemption (for Shelley) or realization (for Hegel) is possible.

Yet for both Shelley and Hegel, Ancient Egypt represented more than a hieroglyph.[6] Ancient Egypt was a Hellenized or at least classicized riddle, its sphinx-like wisdom a tantalizing world of secret knowledge that could recover humanity's spiritual birth. Decoding meant assessing empire and its loss of innocence as Britain spread itself eastward, swallowing up ancient civilizations like they were heritage livestock. The cultural critique of empire in its eastward spread is most legible in the productions of the younger Romantics, but empire was fantasized everywhere, saturating mentality as well as everyday objects.[7] Yet with news of Napoleon's Egyptian Campaign, the subject of much political caricature, and with the British capture of his looted antiquities including the Rosetta Stone, the British became even more intrigued by Ancient Egypt, as were German intellectuals such as Hegel. The dominance of India in our own reconstruction of Romantic-period and nineteenth-century Britain makes us sometimes forget the impact that the ancient ruins, not just of Egypt but of other ancient lands in the Near East such as Palmyra, had on the forward-thinking as well as on larger cultural imaginaries.

Ancient Egypt and the Nile River were poetic topoi among the second-generation Romantics, to say nothing of a topic for poetry contests such as the one between Hunt and Keats: Keats wrote "To the Nile," Leigh Hunt "The Nile" and "A Thought of the Nile," Percy Shelley "To the Nile," Edward Lear "There was an Old Man of the Nile," and William Lisle Bowles "The Battle of the Nile." Although most of these efforts were topical, almost reference points for British Romantic thought, Shelley's focus in "Ozymandias" on the ruins of civilization rather than the age of the world as represented by the Nile and its civilizations went deeper. Shelley is interested not in the terrestrial so much as the effects of cosmic not-knowing on those who presume to know, and who acknowledge too late the consequences of such presumption.

Percy Shelley locates his unease with empire and its cultural dreams most succinctly in his sonnet "Ozymandias," but it is a poem that has been so over-read as to become shrouded by interpretative accretions. The poem demands renewed attention because within the framework of cryptology and ruin, the sonnet's own funerary ritual offers a way to reconnect what is temporally dismembered, even as the sonnet structure demands that it withdraw deep within itself. "Ozymandias" is not just a traveler's tale, nor a version of Byron's Middle Eastern romance-critiques, but an emanation whose voicing when imaginatively decrypted still has something to tell us about the east-west confrontation and about institutionalized identity. Shelley's and Hegel's fantastic and phantasmatic renderings of that 'antique land' provide a way to re-member and reface Romantic Egypt.

"Ozymandias" was published in 1818, the same year Thomas Young published his *Encyclopædia Britannica* article on Egypt, although the Shelleys used the 1814–1817 new edition and likely would not have known it. Four years later Jean-François Champollion would decipher the hieroglyphs, surpassing Young's attempts by recognizing elements within a pharaonic cartouche, which allowed the French linguist to develop an accurate theory of the Ancient Egyptian language and writing system. Several years before Champollion, and still largely unacknowledged, a young British traveler, William John Bankes, would likewise decipher Cleopatra's cartouche on an inscribed stone with both Greek and Egyptian versions of the same text. Egypt, it seems, was an amateur's dream, the amateur an unacknowledged— or if he published his memoirs, an acknowledged—arbiter of the state of things as they might have been. The translative amateur fills in for poet, philosopher, linguist through the act of imaginative interpretation, pre-scribing hermeneutic acts to come.

The arch amateur Shelley himself fills all these roles, his poetry a rich complex of insight, theory, and linguistic interplay. His visionary poem goes beyond a culturally reflective, trance-like and translative evocation of ancient days and men, although it, too, translates old meanings and words into the here and now. "Ozymandias" provides a vision that is also prescient in that it, as if to presage the translative agent of the royal cartouche, gives the pharaoh's name through an inscription that is embedded in the sonnet itself. The pharaoh repeats his image throughout the land through the reiteration of self-presencing statuary: Ramesses II's omni-present colossi. Aestheticized, he becomes an art form that speaks merely by representation. The statues' invocatory strength demonstrates his dominion while the pharaonic power of self-proclamation transcends the temporal order. But like the historical king who must finally die and be entombed, in Shelley's sonnet the pharoah's self-presencing name is also encrypted within the third quatrain that also proclaims his defiance of death and time: "'My name is Ozymandias, King of Kings:/ Look on my works, ye mighty, and despair!'" The poem's formal structure asserts the literalizing and reifying agency of the ancient cartouche, a hieroglyphic entombment of the pharaoh. Shelley's poem is an invocation as powerful as the encircled throne-name that enacts the pharaoh's authority. The sonnet's embedding is a nod to the suggestibility of knowledge claims and the elusiveness of actual knowledge in what can be said to be true about another culture and another place; at the same time, it pays tribute to the pharaoh as a funerary rite and offering. If the pharaoh has been so aestheticized that only the artist's rendering communicates to us, if he himself as monumental identity has not transcended time, nevertheless we may read from his ruins something contained within the aesthetic realm that has meaning for us. Drawn to his ruins, we approach a comprehension of empire and desire.

What can be known is indeed the problem: who was Ozymandias, and what did Shelley know of him? A network of naming, an illusory nomination, and a mash of languages underlie the poem that names the pharaoh, or "king of kings." Shelley's source and probable traveler, Diodorus Siculus, covers Ancient Egypt in Book I of his universal history the *Bibliotheca Historica* (translated by George Booth in 1814). There Diodorus transliterates the inscribed name as "Osymandias," a classicization of a form of Ramesses II's throne-name (later Anglicized as "Ozymandias"). It is thus a code name, desacralized and detached from its source of power. The other main historical source for any knowledge of this ruler would have been Herodotus, who uses the name "Sesostris" for this pharaoh. (This is the appellation Leigh Hunt gives him in his sonnet "The Nile.") Herodotus does note that this ruler, who built many statues of himself, may also be called "Memnon," a name that shared with Ramesses II the two best-known identities of this New Kingdom warrior pharaoh (biblically known only as "Pharaoh"). Champollion would identify his temple complex, which we now know as the Ramesseum, through hieroglyphic decipherment, but not until 1829. Instead, Shelley would have— with his Egyptological friend Horace Smith in their sonnet competition— based his vision on old accounts and on recent drawings, especially Richard Pococke's well-known *A Description of the East and some other Countries*, and the *Description de l'Egypt*, 1809–1829.[8]

Therefore, Shelley had a nesting of names and identities to work with: Ozymandias, Ramesses, Sesostris, and Memnon. Part of the historical riddle arises from Diodorus's inaccuracies. Although he provides invaluable details such as figured columns and the many bas reliefs depicting Ramesses's military victories in the temple complex, he also attributes the colossi's creation to Memnon of Sienitas without giving his source; the reference to an artist when such information was as a rule lost to history, clearly appealed to Shelley. But more importantly, Diodorus provides a questionable description of the colossus, explaining that there are four colossi, not one, with only the largest a representation of the pharaoh, the other three being that of his daughter and two of his mother.[9] As Diodorus notes himself, his description is based on reports by other travelers, so that although he gives precise measurements for the Ramesses colossi and a description of their careful craftsmanship, details that Shelley utilizes, his account is inaccurate in its assertion of a single Ramesses colossus instead of the three whose ruins still stand in the Ramesseum and the fourth, removed by Belzoni.

In describing only this first of the pharaoh's colossi as seated, Diodorus creates a possible confusion for readers with the two colossi of Amenhotep III on the Theban plains nearby, which also include female family members at the base; these were known to the Greeks as "Memnon." Memnon was Homer's Ethiopian King in *The Odyssey*, and a real-life hero, Memnon of Rhodes (380–333 BC), who commanded the Greek mercenaries under Darius III. If Diodorus is correct about the name of Ramesses's sculptor, then the Memnon identity becomes a richer field for Shelley's vision than the biblically pejorated Ramesses.[10] The Englishing of Ramesses, deflected through the classicizing of Amenhotep, creates a hermeneutic puzzle of identities that, for Shelley, spells out the costs of self-aggrandizement and its institutionalization: nothing but the undecipherable ruins of human monument can remain, not even the correct name. The aesthetic provides the visual space for moral calculation, while nonaesthetic seeing dismisses the ruins as incommunicable. The disarticulation at the heart of Shelley's sonnet can best be represented by the unrecognizable name "Ozymandias."

Horace Smith had engravings of the Memnon colossi for Shelley to view, and these visuals would have provided the imagery for Ozymandias' "Two vast and trunkless legs of stone" that "Stand in the desert" rather than lying fallen the inner court of a temple complex, while "Near them on the sand,/ Half sunk, a shattered visage lies," on which are stamped the passions of pharaonic heart and hand. The Ramesses visage is not, in fact shattered: it is his crown that has been lost and his body that has been dismembered. Indeed, it is the north colossus of Amenhotep that was shattered in ancient times and repaired. These two colossi originally guarded the entrance to the largest mortuary temple complex ever built.[11] They provide, both in their shattered state and proof of time's devastation to the desire for immortal repute, a stronger imagery for Shelley's critique of tyranny and hubris.[12] Shelley had even more food for thought than this, however. Although Herodotus identifies the conquering pharaoh with his self-proclaiming colossi as Sesostris, Herodotus, Diodorus, and Strabo, all treat Sesostris so as to conflate historical memory. Sesostris, it turns out, is a confabulation of Ramesses II with his father Seti I, although possibly a figuration of Senusret III instead, and what the Greek historians so matter-of-factly record of this mythic personage is astonishing: as a kind of ur-king, Sesostris is supposed to have conquered the known world, and to have institutionalized the caste system, administrative districts, and codified law in Egypt. He is indeed a creator of great works, providing Shelley with perhaps a better model for his pharaoh than Diodorus' Osymandias. And Diodorus providentially provides this pharaoh with a strikingly similar epitaph: "Sesostris, king of kings, and lord of lords, subdued this country by his arms."[13]

A reconstruction of historical and contemporary witnessings, none of them Shelley's own, makes his sonnet's movement back in time while presaging the future a provocation, a pretended enigma that denounces the tendencies of the present. It is Ramesses who has been encrypted, renamed by Greek historians and diminished by the British to a false heritage as "Memnon the Younger." He is further fragmented through the British Museum's display of the decapitated synecdochic head, cut off from its body of signification and metonymic sets of codified knowledge, and exhibited as disembodied artifact. Shelley's denunciation of power's entrapment—that institutionalization dehumanizes, decontextualizes, and destroys spirit—is as ironically boldfaced as Ramesses's colossi as well as his inscription proclaim him to be. "'Look on my works, ye mighty, and despair!'/ Nothing beside remains." As the poem's ending reminds us, "Round the decay/ Of that colossal wreck, boundless and bare,/ The lone and level sands stretch far away." Tellingly, this description only fits the Amenhotep colossi, yet conflating Memnon to both Amenhotep and Ramesses, and Ozymandias to Memnon, allows Shelley to pronounce on the futility of institutionalized power which reduces the individual to an empty symbol of ruin: reduced to the biblical "pharaoh," so stripped of all metonymous contextuality, the god-king is now a signifier irreducible to anything other than foreign intentions and time, unreadable on its own terms.

Yet Ozymandias speaks, associated as it is with the Memnon colossi, via its inscription. The words that command the viewer to "Look on my works" and to despair, are words of power still, despite the statue's and the monarch's ruin. Derrida traces Hegel's version of the Memnon colossi's ability to "speak" in this way:

> This element is called voice: the spontaneous outside production of an inner sense filling with presence[,] from then on the form of its emission. The spontaneity, the production of self by self gives voice. The sound, resounding ever since the blow struck from the outside, does not utter itself. The sound announces and represents the voice but also holds it back, too much on the outside or too much on the inside.

This moment of the half-voice sculpts its paradigm in the statue of Memnon, son of the dawn, adored by the Ethiopians and the Egyptians. The "colossal sounding statue (*kolossale Klangstatue*)" was ringing under the first rays of the sun. The stroke of light on the block provokes a species of voice, extracts, evokes a voice that is not yet a voice, even when Memnon (*tönend und stimmgebend*) thanks "with its voice" the faithful who come to offer it sacrifices . . . the human face presented there is *tonlose*, noisy but mute: "Therefore the work [of the artisan], even when it . . . wears only the shape of self-consciousness, is still the soundless shape which needs the rays of the rising sun in order to have sound which, generated by light, is even then merely resonance (*Klang*) and not speech (*Sprache*), and shows only an outer, not the inner, self."

The Klang of the stony block is not yet the voice that it already is: neither inside nor outside language, a mediation or an excluded middle.[14]

As Shelley's ode has it, the ruin's command to worshippers of its sublimed majesty is more than merely the shape of self-consciousness, it is self-consciousness itself, and a morbid reflection of it at that. Ozymandias's voice *is* "voice that it already is," and yet also is "neither inside nor outside language, neither a mediation or an excluded middle." The prescience of Shelley's vision, its graphic manipulation of new science into old mysteries, makes even more sense if compared to yet another text, published after his poem, which takes an entirely different position on Egyptian monuments and their interpretive possibilities for a critique of empire, conquest, and cultural domination: Hegel's *Aesthetics*, not published until 1835. These lectures were, however, written and given during the 1820s and their thinking is very much of a piece with both Shelley's critique, and those who, like Giovanni Belzoni and Napoleon, considered Egypt grounds for innovative science and colonization. Belzoni, circus strongman and engineer cum archaeologist, colonized Egypt for England through the acquisition of grandiose artifacts, including the British Museum's head of "The Younger Memnon"; Shelley colonized Egypt imaginatively through his visionary adaptation for political critique; Hegel employed intellectual colonization, turning Egypt into a rich field of conceptual symbols for his aesthetic theory.

Taking archetypal monuments such as the pyramid, obelisk, and colossi to typify Egyptian architecture, Hegel reads into them constructions that potentiate spirit rather than reify and destroy it, as Shelley's sonnet does.[15] His pyramid takes on the potentiality of the crystal as a spirit-focusing instrument: "they are prodigious crystals which conceal in themselves an inner meaning and, as external shapes produced by art, they so envelop that meaning that it is obvious that they are there for this inner meaning . . . and only in relation to this meaning."[16] Nevertheless, the pyramid as spiritual achievement remains "mysterious and dumb, mute and motionless" because instead of distilling and subliming inner life, Egyptian pyramids represent "the inward indeed as the negative of life, as death . . . in . . . a concrete shape."[17] The pyramid, the aboriginal icon of Ancient Egypt, the symbol that best identifies Egypt with itself and its spirit, is more than an architectural feat, more than a sublime object as eighteenth-century aesthetic discourse describes it. For Hegel it is also, as Derrida explains, "Spirit produces itself as object, does not retake itself, does not recognize itself entirely," and is compared to the pyramid.

> The pyramid erects itself immediately. A lack, however, is remarked there—and thus a representation of what will appear only a little later, the curve, roundness, the curvilinear that can be produced only by the living spirit. Cold, formal, and death-dealing, the understanding proceeds geometrically, cuts and secures angular forms. The artisan religion is the history of a rounded angle, the passage from the pyramid co the column, from mathematics or calculus to the incommensurable grace of the spirit. And this passage is a *(re)(ful)filling*. The round and curvilinear form is more full-of-spirit. . . . The crystals of pyramids and obelisks, simple combinations of straight lines with plane surfaces and equal proportions of parts, in which the incommensurability of the round is destroyed . . . these are the works of this artisan of rigid form *(der strengen Form)*. On account of the merely abstract intelligibleness . . . of the form, this form does not have its signification *(Bedeutung)* within itself, is not the spiritual self.[18]

Another such symbol of spirit as entombed or encrypted is evident in the Memnon colossi of Amenhotep III, which Hegel treats as similarly inspirited matter. For him Egypt is a land in which "almost every shape is a symbol and hieroglyph not signifying itself but hinting at another thing with which it has an affinity." Hieroglyphic symbols are worth scrutiny because networked within an affinity of a "more fundamental and deeper kind."[19] He demonstrates here Foucault's reading of nineteenth-century writers as looking back to the Renaissance treatment of signs in order to listen for the murmur of "another, deeper, discourse" beneath the disjunctures of contemporary language.[20] Taking his information from Tacitus, although Hegel himself confuses his source and believes it to be Herodotus, Hegel recounts the mystical quality of both Memnons to emit a musical sound at dawn. According to Strabo, whom Hegel does not consult, it is only the northern colossus that does so, having been shattered by a first-century earthquake, after which it produced the oracular sound until the statue was repaired by the Roman emperor Septimius Severus, the repair ironically silencing it. Giving both the superstitious and scientific plausibilities, Hegel then casts both out in order to assert the priority of the symbol as inspirited. In ignorance of the fact that only one colossus ever sounded, and was then silenced, Hegel reinscribes the Memnon with significance: if the spirit-sound only emanates at the touch of the sun's rays, "the meaning to be ascribed to these colossi is that they do not have the spiritual soul freely in themselves and therefore, instead of being able to draw animation from within, from what bears proportion and beauty in itself, they require for it light from without which alone liberates the note of the soul from them."[21] Whereas a pyramid contains human form, colossi only represent it. Uninhabited by spirit, colossi are only spiritually awakened by the touch of celestial light. Rendering this hermeneutic reorients the colossi from institutionalized power, the cult figures of Amenhotep's godhead, to a failed cultural achievement in which the spiritual is eclipsed by the symbolical which cannot "portray its own inner being."[22] It is a necessary failure; however, a precious first step in the human progression toward enlightened self-knowledge.

Hegel's meditations on the importance of the monuments, the spirit crystal of the pyramids and the spirit-veiled colossi, conceptually mirror in reverse Shelley's formal and metaphoric project in his sonnet on empire and its consequences. Whereas Shelley provides a negative depiction of colossal testimonials to human power and achievement, and to the riddles and visions these monuments provide, he also concedes their grandeur. Hegel gives a positive depiction, but in comparing Egyptian achievements with those that came after he belittles them, using their examples to prove that what might have been, but in the end was not achieved. Hegel does read Egyptian cosmology as positive in that Egyptian belief in the immortality of the soul is a form of self-knowledge that is itself "the principle of freedom."[23] But it is an incomplete achievement, a fragmentation, a reaching of "the threshold of the realm of freedom" only.[24] Nevertheless, it is the necessary first step. Where Shelley sees the end times of spirit, Hegel sees its birth. Hegel and Shelley both accord to history their mythologizing confusion and conflation of Egyptian identities, achievements, mysteries, and monuments received through Classical sources, displacing onto another discipline their reorientation and reintention of Egyptian relics. History's seeming factuality allows the philosophical poet and the poetic philosopher to covertly deny Ancient Egypt the true sublime in which "the strictly symbolical character vanishes."[25] Reduced to its ruins, Egypt becomes the cryptographic text for political and aesthetic pronouncements, a broken cipher mired in, rather than transcending, death. And yet, such fertile soil.

III. RUINOUS SPIRIT

Shelley's *Alastor* (1815) concerns a haunted poet who chases poetic vision by chasing Egypt.[26] As his prefatory note explains, the poem "represents a youth of uncorrupted feelings and adventurous genius led forth by an imagination inflamed and purified through familiarity with all that is excellent and majestic, to the contemplation of the universe." In the abstract this sounds like a condensation of western thought about Ancient Egypt as a mythos to which one can imaginatively if not physically return; certainly he is not a reference to another mythic figure, alastors, avengers of evil deeds.[27] That this poetic youth attempts a physical return as well accounts for his demise: "drink[ing] deep of the fountains of knowledge," he "is still insatiate" we are told. It is not enough to know, he must experience what Egypt represents; his failure to do so is formalized in his tomb, which is composed of "mouldering leaves" that the winds have piled "o'er his mouldering bones [in] a pyramid . . . in the waste wilderness."[28] The poet's bones as leaves, conjoined through their mutual moldering, will reappear in Mary Shelley's *The Last Man*, as the sibylline leaves appear to be read as bones of the future anterior. On the poet's wanderings he encounters "The awful ruins of the days of old" in Athens, Tyre, Balbec, and Jerusalem, then went to what is present-day Cairo where he visited the nearby "eternal pyramids" of Giza, as well as "Memphis and Thebes." In Thebes, modern-day Luxor, he must have visited the great temple complexes of Luxor and Karnak, for he was compelled by "whatsoe'er of strange/ Sculptured on alabaster obelisk,/ Or jasper tomb, or mutilated sphinx" although these Shelley places in "Dark Aethiopia" or Nubia.[29] "The Zodiac's brazen mystery," a reference most likely to the zodiac taken from the Temple of Dendera during Napoleon's Egyptian Campaign and famously depicted in the *Description de l'Égypte*, represents a more solid version of the cosmic knowledge the poet seeks in his "contemplation of the universe." Not surprisingly, it is soon thereafter that the Arab maiden reappears to him in his dreams as the veiled maid, the representative of Isis and Nature in her infinite knowledge and wisdom. As such, she robs him of sanity and surety of knowledge of any kind. Although she also represents the anima of his Jungian unconscious, tormenting him with her unavailability, she also represents the Hermetic wisdom of the ancients, the spirit of Ancient Egypt encrypted in its hieroglyphs and zodiac, its mystical ruins and closed tombs, that is, in its remainder.

The ordinal precept of the necropolis is the remainder, that which exceeds the end of life. A necropolis ensures that extinction will not take place, that bodily remains and living memory will be inscribed on the land in such a way that continuity is demonstrable. The necropolis in ruins, however, demonstrates the opposite, becoming for the Romantics a set-piece of the unremembered, of lost time, of human fragility. When Alastor conducts his flight into the unknown, he begins that journey as an extension of his expedition to "The awful ruins of the days of old," from Athens and Tyre to "the eternal pyramids,/ Memphis and Thebes, and whatsoe'er of strange/ Sculptured on alabaster obelisk,/ Or Jasper tomb, or mutilated sphinx."[30] It is a journey begun in alchemy, extended through the hieroglyphs of ancient knowledge, and ending in the alchemical transformations of nature, an entirely Romantic quest. But it is also a journey conducted "Among the ruined temples . . . / Stupendous columns, and wild images/ . . . [where] dead men/ Hang their mute thoughts on the mute walls around."[31]

In the British imaginary the necropolis was a contained whole, a body of knowledge populated by entombed bodies, and a ruin at the same time—troping the paradoxical figure of forgotten memory, of what can only be reimagined but never recovered. The most ruinous necropolis is the Valley of the Kings, the tombs of which were historically violated and lost to memory. The Valley of the Kings, hardly understood in its enormity during Shelley's lifetime, finds its expression in *Alastor* (1815) as the cavernous and labyrinthine end of the boat flight taken by the hero, the Poet. Here his Orpheus-like journey remaps the underground and labyrinth of passages and chambers underlying the Valley of the Kings as much as it traces the boat and stream episodes of *Alastor*. The water-based episodes consume nearly half the poem, emphasizing the frenzied flight of a poet lost in mazes, but they are also and interestingly analogous to the lengthy and arduous trials of the Egyptian Book of the Dead, trials that represent a dangerous quest which is symbolically replicated in Masonic initiation rites, and therefore not unavailable for poetic resonance.

As an exemplary necropolis made for both continuity and forgetting, the Valley of the Kings treads on necropolitics. A term that summons up the eighteenth-century attitude toward Ancient Egypt as a culture consumed by its supposed death cult, necropolitics is related to the "border thinking" that Walter Mignolo theorizes in order to reconceive the colonizer/colonized relationship. Mignolo's intervention is necessary, he argues, in order to show how subaltern ways of knowing adjudicate both native and colonial epistemologies. The border zone between local ways of knowing and colonial "knowledge" is fluid rather than rigidly dichotomized;[32] the known and the unknown bleed into and inform each other. Necropolitics concerns a state in whose borders one is on different conceptual terrain and inhabits a different form of subjectivity. In this state the idea of individuality loses its mortal inference and becomes lost within the restrictions of the communal enterprise. When this enterprise becomes ruinous, its circuit of life-death-renewal is lost; it no longer figures continuity and spirit, instead prefiguring world-death and nullity. But the conceptual space between continuity and nullity may be contiguous rather than an absolute rupture; this is the space exhumed in Shelley's long meditation on death and ruin in *Alastor*, a poem that begs for a necro-political reading of individual excess, subsumption of the individual to the habitus, and wasted life.

Shelley structures *Alastor* as an epic account of poetic genius as embodied spirit: the poem's speaker calls on the "great Mother," "Mother of this unfathomable world!" for inspiration to tell the story of Alastor, whose "untimely tomb" is built of a leafy "pyramid" constructed by "Medea's wondrous alchemy."[33] The equilibrium between beginning and ending references to a pyramidal tomb, punctuated by Alastor's quest among ancient ruins, with a protracted account of the Egyptian pyramids, tombs, and temples he studies, provides the kind of balance between nature and art that Georg Simmel discovers to be the key attribute of ruins: on a fulcrum that exists between natural materials and human design during the life of the architectonic which has toppled in the ruin.[34] For Simmel, the fulcrum only becomes truly visible in a ruin that retains, and thus extends, the monumentalism of the built space; Shelley notably records only monumental ruins for Alastor to ponder—pyramids, obelisks, temples, the Great Sphinx. But Shelley also includes the signs of strange knowledge, the origins of alchemical science: specifically hieroglyphs and "The Zodiac's brazen mystery,"[35] the Egyptian brass zodiac at the Dendera Temple in Luxor having been made famous when sketched by Napoleon's scientific team during the 1798 Egyptian Campaign (which was torn from the temple's ceiling in 1820 and added to the Louvre's collection). These references to human infiltrations of the Great Mother's 'unfathomable' mysteries do not reflect a disappointed attitude toward such knowledge; clearly Shelley felt such mystery was both compelling and yet still beyond human reach, embodied in the poem by the seductions of the veiled maid, who is a clear reference to the alchemist's Mother Nature but at the same time an emblem of poetic desire and vision.

The veiled maid herself, coming in the middle of Alastor's quest, projects the qualities of the architectural fulcrum, balancing the poetic subject between forgotten and desired knowledge; between lost and reimagined life; between the positive space of the home and city, and the negative space of the ruins of those, represented in the poem by the cavernous underground structures of nature's labyrinths and burial chambers. In associating Simmel's fulcrum in his meditation on ruins to *Alastor*, the cemetery as *locus classicus* for such ruminations comes into the foreground, a ruinous terrain Shelley in fact carefully avoids in his poem, and yet which haunts the entire work. The cemetery is a place carefully located with a demarcated but extendable perimeter that encloses the sacred, consecrated, or ritual ground. It is clearly these demarcated limits that are the problem for a poem about transgression and overreach. The necropolis, therefore, provides a more apt figure for the poem's haunting, since it creates the space of continued life and retained knowledge through its symbolic houses and underground structures for the dead. When these become ruins, when the whole no longer holds, what is the significance of the remainder for life after death, and the continuity formally ensured through ritualized symbolic practice? How does the abstraction of life as life-in-death relate to that remainder which is the cultural and spiritual excess correlating to negative space within architectural design, and which is available to the visitor hailing from a different time and culture?

It is this remainder, this excess, that Shelley explores through Alastor's ruin-hopping as he seeks a sustaining vision for his poetic energies. The dissipation of those energies and Alastor's failed quest is due largely to the failure of these ruins to provide imaginative sustenance; yet Alastor's relation to the ruins is largely what is at fault here. Rather than opening himself up to the "excendence" of the ruins, to use Levinas's term for keeping one foot on the ground, Alastor demands a transcendent experience. That is, Alastor hopes to leverage the ruins, using them as the fulcrum for his own departure from earthly matters into spiritual poetic vision. In misunderstanding the poet's relation to vital energies and vital matter, believing that only a spiritual project is necessary and that any remainder from that excessive devotion is unnecessary, Shelley's creative artist resists coming to terms with the ground for which he believes himself to be the figure. Believing that ground or field are merely locations for his vision to represent itself, he ignores the importance of ground for figuration, and thus ignores the figure's own vital design and agency. In other words, he ignores the importance of negative space for the figure as and in the veiled maid and for the architectonic design that he is constructing through the mapping of his quest for knowledge. It is for this reason that the logic of the necropolis haunts both him and the poem. It is not until the Poet is relieved from his imaging project, maddened by passions that transform his mental state, that he experiences a different relation to ground and field, and begins to absorb the importance of wasteland, ruin, and negative space.

In thinking about vital energy and vital matter, the question arises: does life indeed end with death? Such speculation rehearses some of alchemy's most interested points, particularly with regard to vitalism, the belief that living organisms are regulated by some vital force beyond the synchronization of atoms and organs (a belief in existence at least as early as Ancient Egypt, and developed by the Greek physician Galen into his theory of humors). But what is vitalism in the abstract? We might consider how Shelley redefines that scientific theory in light of the ordinals of *Alastor*. These are not just east/west, but material/spirit, life/death, lack/imaged, dull/vibrant, excess/waste. These dynamic contraries relate back to the necropolis in the sense that the necropolis is bounded and yet open, secreted and yet seductively beckoning, and a structured habitat for life-in-death.

Dynamic contraries are precisely not what an allegory should be about. Nevertheless, Shelley's Preface characterizes the poem as an "allegory" of the human mind "inflamed" by imagination in "contemplation of the universe," indicating his orientation to such ordinals:

> He drinks deep of the fountains of knowledge, and is still insatiate. The magnificence and beauty of the external world sinks profoundly into the frame of his conceptions, and affords to their modifications a variety not to be exhausted. So long as it is possible for his desires to point towards objects thus infinite and unmeasured, he is joyous, and . . . self-possessed. But the period arrives when these objects cease to suffice.[36]

Alastor's mind begins to desire "intercourse with an intelligence similar to itself." Therefore, "He images to himself the Being whom he loves." The Poet is no longer a self-enclosed, inwardly focused monad, to use Leibniz's conception of vital force which he so resembles; he is now an actant, one who is capable of his own engendering thoughts that set bodies in motion. The Poet can only *image* that which he already loves, but which is not preformed and is not therefore his soul mate—or at least not within a Leibnizian universe. More apt would be a Platonic conception of the division of souls into gendered pairs, set into motion through the quest for their missing half. The Poet's imaging capacity allows him to project both the ideal other and the ideal world, in a unification of "all of wonderful, or wise, or beautiful, which the poet, the philosopher, or the lover could depicture." However, in attempting to locate this ideal other within the material—searching nature, known and unknown landscapes, ruins and waste—he is "Blasted by his disappointment." Thus, while deploying a Faustian ability to conjure his vision into form, he has also accessed the negative space of that construction, an experience he finds annihilating. A Leibnizian subject, or indeed an alchemist, is not activated by imagination, only the algebra and calculus of reason, for the creative imagination alone belongs to God; Shelley's Poet takes his imaging to the highest achievable level, an act that explodes his very atoms when he discovers that unlike God, his creative act is not mirrored in material reality.

Earl Wasserman has argued in *Shelley: A Critical Reading* that the poem explores the dynamics between the human need for love and community and the Idealist's quest for universal truths and ideal love. In this reading the Narrator relates his own search for ultimate knowledge through nature in a Wordsworthian manner, before narrating the visionary Poet's contrasting Idealistic quest. But in the critique of alchemical research that inhabits the poem, played out in a blasting of the subject, we are given a visionary Poet who cannot realize his own images, since though he clearly sees the ideal other he has imaged, he cannot materially locate her, and finds recognition only in the material ruins of others' visions and other lives. He not only fails to achieve epiphanic transcendence by communing with the Good, but he fails to transcend his own and others' materiality in the consecration of his ideal world. The point is not that the overreaching Poet causes disharmony in the monadic universe through his transcendent desires and must, like a diseased or disruptive body, be eradicated, but that, contra Leibniz and indeed Wordsworth, great truths and universals cannot be ascertained by their mirrored revelation in material nature. Nature, as Simmel reminds us, is quick to destroy design and reclaim its elements and materials for its own processes. To this end, it is the wastelands and ruins of the poem's many terrestrial and mental landscapes, as the Poet ranges over the known and unknown worlds in his quest, that best reveal the deficiencies of Leibniz's and Wordsworth's vision of a harmony between hierarchically orchestrated monads and an activating vital force rather than the deficiencies of a transcendent project.

Shelley notes that the Poet's demise is due not to his failed quest alone, but also to his "self-centred seclusion" which was then "avenged by the furies of an irresistible passion pursuing him to speedy ruin." Here the human imagination constitutes the basis for ruin, for waste. Aligning the ruins of vision with that of architectural visions in ruin, Shelley provides terrain for the Poet's wanderings that signifies material disruptions, points of blasted relations between atomistic levels. Moreover, the manifest (rather than bodily) sites of ruin harbor points of continuity between seen and unseen subjectivities or spheres of action, serving as referents to the tomb and other liminal spaces where life and death are connected not through monadic hierarchies or atomistic dynamics, but through a more creative act of memory, vision, and other faculties that "have their respective requisitions on the sympathy of corresponding powers in other human beings" as Shelley writes in his Preface of the Poet's mental faculties. This sympathy has an alchemical element to it, one derived from the intimate connection between magic and philosophy as "corresponding powers" that informed the intellectual achievements of the Renaissance and post-Renaissance periods.[37] Shelley's point as the Preface gives it is that generative imaging can achieve its transcendent project only in a world of corresponding and sympathetic faculties that transcend bodily limitations—a kind of electrically or neuron-networked sphere in which communicative imaging can structure its reality. A necropolis then, which connects the spirits of both living and dead.

Although such a world of ideal communion might only be possible in life-after-death, as in the continuities made possible by the freeing of spirit from body, in the material world of intransigent barriers to mental imaging, it is better to have attempted to realize the artistic vision than to refuse the creative act altogether. Those who refuse "live unfruitful lives, and prepare for their old age a miserable grave," that is, a grave with no afterlife, constituting in death what they have constituted in life, "the lasting misery and loneliness of the world." But as ruins teach us, the creative act is not eternal: instead, it is subject to the forces of nature in an ongoing struggle over intention and necessity.

In Simmel's mediation on ruins, when the fulcrum no longer enacts its mandate the structure de-forms as nature reclaims its materials from a no-longer performative design. Simmel accords a presence to the balancing of nature and art as if the natural elements of the design are vital matter, not quite in the sense of an animating vitalism, nor in the sense of a Benjaminian aura, but in a suggestive way, giving life to the negative space of the ruin that corresponds to and enables the afterlife of the subject. It is this dynamic of continuity between the realized and the envisioned, between the corporeal and the ideal, even between the Leibnizian subject and its predicate, that Shelley's Poet enters by a radical act of self-blasting. In disrupting his own harmonies, such that his passion is externalized as "furies" intent on "avenging" his externalized desire, the Poet radically destabilizes the balance between nature and design, decentering the fulcrum, and thus creating or at least creating the conditions for the possibility of entering into the continuities of afterlife, negative space, and wasted life otherwise defined. Violent rupture rather than transcendence provides the pathway that both the poet and the poem seek. Thus, the unbalanced structure of the poem itself is an articulation of the ruin's unbalanced relation between positive and negative space, thus speaking to the rupturing required to enter an altered state. This life-before-death that the Poet experiences both prior to and in the act of his self-blasting creates for him a kind of agency that resists nihilism, that is, we cannot read the Poet's quest as a death-wish or a commentary on the death of ancient cultures. Rather, it is a vision of an alternative life, a figure-ground reversal, or life lived in the negative space of the design.

In *Alastor*, the Poet's seeming affinity for nature is contradicted by his increasing sense of estrangement from it and his recourse to a different calculus from that of the phenomenal world. Although *Alastor* begs to be read in terms of excess and wasted life, it is truer to say that it has to be read in terms of ruins and the necropolis as conditions for the remainder, which is the key element in catastrophe. Catastrophe essentially concerns the remainder, which is not just the remaining, or remainders in the sense of rubble. The remainder is what is left over after division, that which is indivisible/resistant/required; and yet before catastrophe it appears to be the nonnecessary, the other-than in the ratio of necessity and being vis-à-vis nullity. Indeed, necessity and being in the face of nullity might begin to get at a way to understand wasted life as that which resists extinction but refuses transcendence. It is the life that in recognizing its own failure to transcend, commits a failure in generative imaging. Or rather, it refuses to leave the remainder. To read *Alastor* in terms of the necropolis, negative space, and the remainder is to see in the Poet's self-blasting not a blasting of his dream state—as if all the electrical and neural networks had exploded, destroying his being—but the translation of what was essential in his existence and quest into a different sphere, that of negative space or life-after-death. The remainder—his nongenerative imaging—not only kept him from death-in-life, which is what the majority of Shelley's world chose to experience according to the Preface, it is the agent of his translation into that experiential realm associated with the tomb and ensured by the built space of necropolitan community.

That the Poet recognizes the sympathetic correspondence between the remainder in his own creative agency and the remainder visible in necropolis ruins is evident from his honing in on such sites early in his quest. What he does not stop to consider after the veiled maid appears to him is that he is searching for the wrong thing in those sites; the soul mate cannot be found in positive space, only in the negative or alternative space of continuity and return. Only in the act of dying into that alternative space, only in his self-blasting, can the Poet be returned to himself. That return, a transcendence that incorporates a dust-to-dust ratio, keeps one foot in materiality. Rather than a secular version of Christian transport, what Shelley describes in *Alastor* is a positive reading of the remainder, of wasted life, of extinction. This is a Neo-Egyptianism: *aporia* and exile as the necessary condition of western life.

When Alastor is chased by his own externalized passion, that objectification of his nonmental drives divides him from the object of his poetic desire, the soul mate. He is infuriated, driven mad. However, that maddening also helps accelerate the Poet's translation into a flight toward death. After his death the Narrator comments "—but thou art fled—," emphasizing that fleeing problematizes the nature of this catastrophe: does the Poet erase the passion or himself?[38] In the last two lines concluding the poem, which overshadow the lament that the Poet's death left "Those who remain behind" not with "sobs or groans" but in "pale despair and cold tranquility,"[39] there is no indication that the Poet has been assigned to nullity or separated from those who remain. Rather, the passionless grief of remainders for the Poet translates them into the negative space of the necropolis, just as his externalized passion translated him into that reversal of fields. Translation brings remainders from a Leibnizian algebra into alignment with Alastor's new calculus. In their paleness, coldness, quite despair and tranquility, the remainders have entered the grave's world of life-after-death and become associated with its alternative aesthetic and sociability. This new formulation of life as the wasted life, or as negative living, provides an antidote to the death-in-life of the Preface's disparaged "meaner spirits" who are "morally dead," their "destiny . . . more abject and inglorious as their delinquency is more contemptible and pernicious" as members of the "unforeseeing multitudes who constitute . . . the lasting misery and loneliness of the world."[40] Against these the Poet's mourners register a decided community of spirit that begins with the sympathetic circulation of vision and culminates in the necropolitan community of the negative life.

IV. NECROPOLITICS:
THE CITY OF THE DEAD AND REMAINDERS

Within the boundaries of the concept of a necropolis, catastrophe is the ordinal precept. The necropolis, literally a "city of the dead," whether located in the Far East, Near East, India, or Africa, was for the British imaginary a contained whole and a ruin at the same time—an eternal city and yet a forgotten culture. Ancient Egypt presented a special case since, unlike Ancient China, India, or Persia, the Egypt that predated the Hellenistic empire created necropolises at several sites whose purpose was to outlast eternity, to create a sovereign nation of the dead whose postmortal purpose was to mediate the lives of their descendants. Yet their very existence was predicated on forgetting; only those priests in charge of the necropolis could know the forensic secrets and locations of the tombs or tomb entrances, ensuring that what was lost with them would remain lost—at least as an entirety—and what fragments could be recovered, would be so in a different context, their signs providing different interpretations and misreadings.

The Giza plateau was itself a city of the dead; the three great kings originally entombed there were accompanied by their various wives, whose tombs were the secondary pyramids, and officials buried in the small mastabas. It is the city hall, as it were, of Saqqara, the vast burial grounds for Memphis, the capital of Lower Egypt. Saqqara was filled with tombs and catacombs that developed around the early Step pyramid of Djoser, the architectural forerunner to the Giza pyramids. As participants in life-in-death, Lower Egyptian pharaohs, nobles, and court officials were both contained by the boundaries of the necropolis and freed to converse with the gods; they were both restrained by the limits of mortal remembrance and, despite that memory trace, liberated into cosmic life.

The most famous necropolises are that of Giza and the later Valley of the Kings, but what distinguished royal necropolises from other forms of burial was that their mummies were pledged to intercede for the Egyptian people. Yet it was these very kings whose tombs had been violated by their people, which meant their memory was then lost. These were the true remainders in that their trace remained even when the connection to life through the mummified body was gone. The violations of sacred trust were carried out by those for whom the royal dead interceded, or at least those specializing in tomb robbery, and those willing to purchaser the stolen goods. In this sense Giza and the Valley of the Kings, as exemplary of all Egyptian necropolises and even of the late cemeteries of Hellenistic Alexandria, tread on necropolitics. "Necropolitics" is a term associated in political theory with states of exception and internment camps;[41] the latter is irrelevant to the Egyptian necropolis, but the former is not. The cultural politics of Romantic-period interest in

Egyptian necrology and its most famed burial sites bear intriguing relations to another necropolis Romantic-period travelers to Egypt would have encountered: Cairo's enormous Moslem cemetery, known as the "City of the Dead."[42] Both ancient and contemporary Egyptian cemeteries functioned as states of exception, where subjectivity was delimited by a different set of rules; where subjectivity was given to both the dead as well as the living, but under different terms. Cairine law does not apply to the cemetery, and so Cairo is the only Muslim capital that has historically tolerated women going en masse to the cemetery to pray while the men attend the mosque on Fridays.[43] Along with early Christian use of catacombs for worship and survival, and the erection of Roman mausolea to line the Appian Way, Egyptian necropolises from ancient through medieval and Romantic periods combined the funerary and the domestic in houses of the dead. Consolidation of the home as life-and-death allows a housing of the catastrophic: the home contains an element of the remainder, a remainder which is always the exception to the private/public divide that the home demarcates. The home/tomb intimates catastrophe rather than sublimity; it is always uncanny rather than transcendent. The conceptual space of the living tomb as home had particular resonance for the Romantics in the ruinous landscapes of a war-strewn Europe. Egypt provided singular symbols for this space, and pyramids and hieroglyphs were repeatedly repurposed as literary reference points in Romantic-age literature; Mary Shelley's Victor Frankenstein sees icy pyramids in the Alpine glaciers, Byron imagines a pyramid in London's Piccadilly Circus.

Necropolitics concerns a space in whose borders one is on different conceptual terrain and entertains a different form of subjectivity: that of the catastrophic and ruinous. The remainder, that which is left apart from the numerical whole, is the rubble, the ruin, the outsider. It can be applied to the dead, the ruined, the enslaved, the underprivileged, the exiled. In this space the idea of individuality—whether subjective or objective, whether a person or an entity—loses its mortal inference and becomes lost within the restrictions of the communal space. Not only the inhabitant, but the very habitation, undergoes transformation in this exceptional space. When Egyptian mortuary temples that had been viable cultural spaces lost their objective identity, it was cotemporary with the loss of the dead's identity; the home and its inhabitant are colegible. In consequence of their illegibility, their loss of identificatory signs, they became buried in sand themselves, or their stones repurposed for habitations of new inhabitants bringing different cultures, or they themselves become homes—as when the mortuary temple still standing at Giza in the 1830s was the abode of a saintly Muslim hermit; or when the harem of Mohammed Ali, Viceroy of Egypt, was encamped in his mausoleum during the festival of Bayram; or when C. Rochfort Scott visited the principal tomb at Beni Hhasan in 1834 and discovered it was "occupied as a dwelling place by a French artist and a young Greek, who, after presenting us with some coffee, kindly volunteered to act as Ciceroni."[44] Rochfort Scott fully accepted these transformations of dead space in recounting his trip, his sensibility only outraged on discovering that at the famed Temple of Luxor, "the French *savans*, (lately employed to superintend the abduction of one of the obelisks that stood in front of the edifice,) have converted [a part of the temple] into a modern white-washed villa, with glazed windows, green jalousies, and brick chimneys!"[45]

The concept of domestic tranquility available in dead space was fully in place in 1860 when Basil Cooper remarked in an article on Egyptian chronology for the *British Quarterly Review* that "the Great Pyramid . . . [was] built by King Cheops nobody knows how many centuries ago, as a snug and rather roomy resting-place for his mummy."[46] This domestic description presumes the Cheops or Khufu pyramid to be a home of sorts, both snug and roomy, and although others thought the burial chamber to be cramped instead. The Ancient Egyptian conception of the pyramid as a living space for the deceased continued to influence how the pyramids were viewed by the west in the eighteenth and nineteenth centuries. When Lake Williams, for instance, commented in 1815 in his "Letter" to the Royal Antiquarian Society that "the stupendous pyramids and palaces of Aegypt . . . surpass almost human conception," he is equating pyramids and palaces, the common denominator in this equation being a habitation, one for the reigning king and one for the afterlife.[47] And when Rochfort Scott describes the Ptolemaic temple at Edfu, noting that "Access to" the grand pylon's "summit is gained by stone staircases in the towers, on either side the gateway, from which passages lead off to no less that *nine* tiers of apartments," his astonishment is not at there being any apartments there, but at the palatial number of them.[48]

It would seem to be much of a continuum, then, that the twenty-first century Cairo cemetery is literally a city within a city. Present-day Cairo offers a window on the Romantic-period city and its necropolis. The City of the Dead is distinguished by two main features. The first is the presence of family mausolea, 1,000 hectares of them taking up a thirtieth of modern-day Cairo. The more elaborate of these mausolea might be typified by this description: "My father's family tomb was like a villa, with high stone outer walls surrounding an open courtyard on either side of which there stood two single-story rectangular buildings" one of which was the oratory. "Up four steps and across a veranda was a front door flanked by symmetrical windows and leading to a room with three ceremonial sarcophagi marking the places where the vaults were located below ground. . . . Across the courtyard stood the building for the living: a tomb keeper's lodge, which was occupied year-round, and reception areas equipped with washrooms and a kitchen: everything but a bathroom."[49] Lesser mausolea might simply have tombstones set around a courtyard and a covered gallery for visitors. The second main feature is that a vast number of people don't solely visit for a funeral or Friday prayers but actually live there, either squatting in the mausolea, carrying on their trades, and sending their children to the nearby schools, or living in homes near their family tombs if they are better off. However, the City of the Dead was not known as such in the late eighteenth or early nineteenth century. Rochfort Scott refers to it, as well as the mausolea of the sultans, pashas, and Mamluk Beys, only as the Muslim burial grounds, commenting of the tombs of the elite, however, that the rulers of Egypt "from the time of Cheops down to the present day, appear to have been in the habit of saving their successors the trouble of raising monuments to their memories."[50] Those memories, it is acknowledged, are invariably ephemeral.

When a westerner or other cultural intervener uncovered ancient temples in the eighteenth century, in a few years the structures would be recovered with sand, disappeared again as effectively as temples whose stones were moved to new cities and new buildings. This disappearance—marked by a cultural memory—is similar to the phenomenon of individuals being disappeared, guillotined, forced to flee to an exiled life, his or her home and goods taken as so much loot, so that nothing remains but familial memory, a noumenal trace. In this way, the temple, the mummy, and the pharaoh retain a cultural memory, a trace of existence as it awaits rediscovery through the ages, however mistaken the orthography of its retracing. Even cities can be mummies: Rosetta or Al Raschid was a debilitated city for the Romantic tourist: "In fact, nothing bearing the semblance of a town can well be more miserable. It may be called the mummy of a once flourishing city—one half the houses are in ruins, the other inhabited by paupers. . . . Even the tombs and burying grounds, usually preserved with great care by Mohammedans, are dilapidated and neglected."[51] The habitation, the body, and the city are all subject to the transformations of life into the vestiges of life, their traces to be found in something other.

If Rosetta is disappointing, incapable of providing translation, such waiting and such rewriting more typically excited the British Romantic imaginary which sought in natural landscapes those hidden traces of waiting memories, subjective and objective entities hovering over the possibility of recovery. Catastrophic ruin was seductively infused with Gothic romance and tourism for the British, whereas for the Egyptian it was normative, part of the rubble and dust of everyday life. Romantic period archaeology, ignited by the potential for discovered treasure, was also impelled by the sense that what was lost could be regained; that what is in the present now could forestall its own future loss through the recovery of past ruin. Thus, digging up the ruins of catastrophic loss in Egypt could tell the bones of England's own future empire, could tell the fortune of cultural death and prospective necropolitan terrains.

It has been a long-held assumption that the pyramids were built with slave or peasant labor. Herodotus maintained that the Jews in captivity built the Giza pyramids and since then it was long believed the pharaohs treated their people just as any monarch or emperor would, enslaving them in all but name to ennoble themselves. Only relatively recently has the theory of fallow-season agricultural labor, well paid with beer and bread, been posited, but the yoking of slavery and empire, monumental statements and ruin, mistreatment and catastrophe, was a persistent Romantic-era theme. So much so that Rochfort Scott's travelogue naturally blends a description of the Aswan-area quarries, where the prized rose-colored granite was cut and floated downstream, with that of the nearby "vast plain, strewed with the mouldering walls of countless tombs and mausolea; all nearly in the same ruinous state," and that of "a wretched Arab village" nearby opposite the Island of Philae which was "a grand depot . . . for slaves. We found a large assortment just arrived from Kordofan. They were offered to us [at] great bargains. . . . A poll-tax, which is levied here, and a second at some other place, ere reaching Cairo, occasioned the poor creatures to be disposed of at so cheap a rate. The Island of Philoe is about four hundred and fifty yards in length, and two hundred wide; and is completely covered with ruins."[52]

Necropolitics in the Romantic Age, then, was a way of thinking empire; the past was embodied in the ever-ready image of disaster by which the foundation of power and control as the subjection of peoples was understood to be ruinous, and empires such as the Ottoman, dependent as it was on deeply institutionalized slave economy, were destined to sink into the quick sands of their destabilizing practices. Ancient Egypt was considered to be founded on a similar politics of systematic abuse. But if the Ottomans provided a telling version of Volney's *Ruins* about to come true, it was far too uncomfortable for an Englishman to see any clear analogy between Britain's and the Ottoman's empires. Although Rochfort Scott is quick to denigrate the Egyptian slave trade in the early 1730s, George Baldwin, who had served as Consul-General in Egypt, had in the 1790s sought to persuade British slavers to adopt the Egyptian system, whereby slaves taken from other African countries were treated kindly as domestic servants, whereas slaves taken from the Balkans were trained as Mamluks and taught to rule the Egyptian populace in the name of the Porte.

Baldwin also warns, however, in an 1801 letter to the Commander-in-Chief of the British Forces, that "The ambition and hope of the Mamaluk is to reign; to recover his sovereignty: The [new], and now become necessary, policy of the Turk, is to annihilate the Mamaluk, and to despoil the country of its wealth."[53] Empires then, built by slaves and powered by abusive systems, produce an uneasy tension between freedman and bondsman, citizen and servant. James Thompson also makes this clear in his lines "Rule, Britannia, rule the waves:/ Britons never will be slaves" (II. 5–6).⁵⁴ The thin line between imperial subject and subjected counterpart also seems clearly delineated for Rochfort Scott in his retelling of the history of Memphis, the ancient capital for which the vast necropolis of Saqqara developed. Repeating the legend that the city was founded by Menes (or Narmer), "the first king of mortal race who governed Egypt," Rochfort Scott explains that,

> Captured and plundered by Nebuchadnezzar, (B.C. 567),⁵⁵ it had not time to recover from that misfortune, under the peaceful reign of Amadis, when it fell a prey, under that of his successor, to the ferocious Cambyses, who, though he permitted the city yet to exist, destroyed the temples, and scattered their priests. It [Memphis] again experienced the fate of a conquered city, in the attempts made by the Egyptians to throw off the Persian yoke, during the reigns of Darius and Xerxes—and, finally, of Artaxerxes Ochus (B.C. 355), by whom, probably, its walls were destroyed, as it appears to have been incapable of offering resistance to the victorious Alexander.
>
> Ptolemy Soter having made Alexandria his capital, Memphis sank into insignificance, and probably owes its final destruction to some unusual rise of the Nile.⁵⁶

Basing his history mostly on Herodotus and the Old Testament, Rochfort Scott's account shows how much was erased and forgotten in the spiral downward of conquest and subjection. Indeed, he ends this passage with the afterthought that, "I have no doubt but that any person, who would incur the expense of excavating to some depth in the neighbourhood of Metraheeneh, would find very extensive remains of the ancient Memphis, of which the plain about Sakara was, perhaps, merely the Necropolis."⁵⁷ Not only has the capital of the first nome of Lower Egypt disappeared; its necropolis is no longer known as that, the city of the dead having disappeared along with that of the living, leaving only the Step pyramid with its unknown history and forgotten original occupant. Rochfort Scott speculates that "The principal pyramid at Sakara, which by the way is rather a series of frusta of pyramids, (six in number) placed one upon another . . . appears to me . . . [to have] been originally built as a perfect pyramid, and that the steps, or frusta, were formed afterwards by the addition of successive coatings, commencing near the top, and increasing fourteen feet in each gradation."⁵⁸

So much history is conflated or lost, as in the example of Saqqara, that Rochfort Scott remarks on a small structure near the great temple of Philoe that it is "usually called Pharaoh's Bed," correctly surmising from its design that it was from a later period than the temple. But the popular name for this edifice, which so oddly contrasts with the fact that except for a single tablet inside, the building "is not sculptured either with figures or hieroglyphics,"⁵⁹ coalesces the connections both ancient and Romantic between pyramid and temple as habitations, the domestic spaces of gods, mummies, and squatters; slaves as the constructors and servants of those domestic spaces; and both the dead imperial subject and the subjected slave as the inhabitants of dead places. These ideas appear to be transhistorical in the accounts of British Romantic travelers. Rochfort Scott reveals as much when he notes that,

> Amongst the ruins [on Philae], fragments of statues, sphinxes, &c. are here and there perceptible; but the surface of this stratum of the handworks of the ancients is covered by so thick a layer of the filth of the moderns, that it is only by great labour anything can be excavated. From the same cause, the utmost difficulty is experienced in tracing the foundations of the various temples, or other buildings, every spot on the island where a mudhut would stand having been formerly built on; but the island is now altogether uninhabited.[60]

Ironically, unlike Scott's island of Philae the twentieth-century City of the Dead *is* inhabited; its habitation in some sense replicates that of the caliphate tomb custodians and Sufi mystics of the original cemetery, or the mortuary temple priests of ancient Saqqara, or even the French *savans* living in the Temple of Luxor—these are not a remainder nor outcast yet are also within the exception, still living within the walls and therefore not part of the whole. The whole might indeed be the ability to live in ruin, as Wordsworth suggests in "The Leech-Gatherer" and as Shelley suggests in *Alastor*. That is, the whole requires incorporating the negative in the Hegelian sense, death-in-life and stymied existence as well as the promise of life-in-death and the infinite.

V. TARRYING WITH THE NEGATIVE

In the Preface to *The Phenomenology of Spirit* Hegel claims that the negative step in the dialectic is not only essential, but requires tarrying within its negative force:

> Lacking strength beauty hates the understanding for asking of her what it cannot do, but the life of spirit is not the life that shrinks from death and keeps itself untouched by devastation, but rather the life that endures it and maintains itself in it. It wins its truth only when, in utter dismemberment, it finds itself. It is this power, not as something positive, which closes its eyes to the negative as when we say of something that it is nothing or is false, and then having done with it, turn away and pass on to something else; on the contrary, spirit is this power only by looking the negative in the face, and tarrying with it. This tarrying with

the negative is the magical power that converts it into being. This power is identical with what we earlier called the Subject.[61]

Spirit is the power that doesn't shrink from death or keep itself untouched from catastrophe: it endures death, as the pyramid attests, but it also endures something like the void, which from Hegel's perspective might be imagined as both vacuum *and* dark matter, the void as generative. The negative is not only generative, it is also a force or movement that tends toward conversion and translation, and therefore has alchemical properties. Hegel's mature conception of the negative concerns each aspect of Spirit's self-investment, from thought to historical process. In this it differs from the mystical worldview developed by Schelling, Hölderlin, and Hegel in their student days of an inexpressible life force. Schelling treats this force in his 1799 *On the World Soul*; it is based on Platonic concepts (particularly those given in the *Timaeus*) in which the world is "a single visible living being."[62] But Hegel's negative, which he intends to be entirely rational, nevertheless contains remnants of his student exploration of the mystical; the negative has an inexplicable, generative capacity. One must give it the time to do its work; therefore, it demands tarrying in its seeming negation in order to yield the products of spirit's potencies. Although the processes of spirit can be demonstrated through reason, that is not how they are experienced. This is not another way to describe the imagination's workings; rather negativity names the spiritual/mystical aspect of mentality that belongs to unknowability.

As Frederick Beiser notes, Hegel came to this formulation of philosophy's role in analyzing the progress of human self-consciousness only after revising his organic worldview in light of the necessity of a discursive treatment of mystical experience (88–89). But Hegel gives priority to the mystical experience obtained through the negative movement that precedes discourse and organizes it. This black hole of spiritual experience models the ways in which conceptual thought and historical movements proceed, according to Hegel, but it is the nearly originary role he gives to the negative that concerns me here. In *Tarrying with the Negative*, Slavoj Zizek explains that the Hegelian negative is a "noir" predicate that allows the "proper" to "arrive at its truth."[63] Zizek suggests that this black predicate includes a state of amnesia in which the symbolic community is dissociated from the proper subject. Loss, ruin, and rubble are other terms for understanding the amnesic aspect of human consciousness: what happens when we forget and are forgotten? Aren't tombs and memorials, pyramids and obelisks erected precisely in order to prevent the forgetting of names and achievements? And yet forgetting inevitably happens; in Hegel's dialectical movement it is even necessary. Amnesia applied to Hegel's scheme helps image the role of the negative in supplying what for Hegel is a tension between "Notion and reality," which is "its irreducible Other encountered in the sensible."[64]

The negative is the place of tension in which the self-as-intellect takes a step back from its initial idea, dissolving its certainty and giving room for doubt and contradiction. It is the space of not-knowing. "But it is precisely here that Hegel cautions us to stay with negativity, to linger in this experience of contradiction, and not to rush precipitately towards what he calls 'the magical power that converts it into being,'" that is, "merely transferring a naïve positivity to the level of consciousness' own relation to itself," Raphael Foshay explains.[65] Rather, we should linger in negativity to learn its lessons, not to take it up in Cartesian, positivist propositional logic, but to give space to this moment in which "the power of self-moving subjectivity" appears as self-determination. That is, the negative allows for the insight "that the alterity of the object is not external to us, between the world and us, but rather within our own relation to ourselves."[66] This coming to self-consciousness is the achievement of dialectical thought. The most important element of the dialectic then, from a history of Spirit's movement in the world, is that of absolute, self-relating negativity, for it is the moment of self-reflection in which finite spirit appears. In terms of the finite spirit's comprehending its relation to what Hegel calls absolute spirit, and absolute spirit's relation to absolute reason, we get the transcendent form of Spirit in its self-movement through historical time. And that moment of comprehension, of absolute knowing, is the moment of the recognition of death. Absolute negativity, which is death, is therefore both finite for the subjective consciousness, and spiritual in its role in Spirit's self-movement. Egypt's necropolises, long understood to represent an Egyptian religion as both a death cult and necromancy, transformed Ancient Egypt for the west into a synecdoche for both the archaic beginnings and for absolute death, absolute negation. Ancient Egyptians called their kingdom "Kmt" (meaning Black), as the land of black earth; it was therefore, and particularly for post-Kantian thought, a particularly charged form of negation in which to tarry.

Hegel considered art as well as religion and philosophy as belonging to the absolute mind.[67] In Hegel's *Aesthetics* the role of the absolute in self-relating negativity is apparent in the section on Egyptian or Symbolic art where he discusses the function of the pyramid as a spirit crystal. Although Hegel is analyzing the development of spirit through the characteristic artistic expression of a civilization, the concept of a spirit crystal is a Hermetic and alchemical one, his own philosopher's stone. As I suggested above, it is tempting to consider Ancient Egypt itself as the negative with which the west must tarry in order to realize itself; Egypt's buried identity is a grounding agent that works like amnesia in order to recall the west to its spiritual realization. This is the force, at least, of Egypt's fascination for the Romantic period. Hegel treats the aspect of Egyptian remains that is less susceptible to his dialectical process, hieroglyphs, with less certitude in the *Aesthetics*. Nevertheless, it is there that he might have profitably tarried longer, since his brief remarks on them concern spirit and its mystical progenitors. The small section Hegel does devote to hieroglyphs focuses principally on the role of animal symbols in Egyptian thought and cultural realization, presumably for their representation of life force. However, his interest in the hieroglyphic characters relates almost exclusively to their use in decorating and inscribing representative Egyptian art. He finds the symbols and other animal depictions to be flat, falsely coded, unaesthetic; he is aware though, through Herodotus, Tacitus, and other historical records of equally symbolic animals that were kept and ritually killed as temple animals sacred to particular gods: ibises, baboons, crocodiles, bulls, and cats. These animals, like the pharaohs and court officials, were also mummified. Their double identity as hieroglyphic signs and sacred beings marks them as special cases: highly aestheticized, they are the remainders he can't account for. These mummified forms, translated into beautiful hieroglyphic signs, are themselves representations of negativity, of the conflict between remembrance and amnesia, of knowing and not-knowing.

Although Hegel does not devote much attention to mummified animals, the liminal status of sacred animals in Ancient Egypt appears to haunt his discussion of hieroglyphs and other religious symbols; they and the subterranean labyrinths in which their mummies were buried enrich his discussion of Egyptian burial sites by providing a glimpse into the ground beneath the pyramid or temple complex, the labyrinthine territory of the negative that is perhaps more a space of otherness than that of the pyramid structure. Sacred or ritual animals remediate Spirit on an order of magnitude disturbing to a Hegelian schema that depends on teleology and a human capacity for divine communion.

In the *Aesthetics*, Hegel introduces the concept of the "degradation of the animal" in his discussion of the development from ancient symbolism to the Classical aesthetic, signaling the proper demotion of animals from the sacred as either symbols or embodiments of the divine.[68] The ancient Hebrews, as he notes, correctly did not invest nature with symbolic presence, although they did revere animal life through ritual sacrifice, but "as it were accidentally," so that animals are merely "the remains of reverence." But the Ancient Egyptians, Indians, "and Asiatics in general" were steeped in the "unconscious symbolism" of the sublime and as such used animals to identify divine presence either alone or in connection with the human, Hegel argues, "at a time before the human and only the human came into consciousness as what is alone true. The self-consciousness of spirit is what alone makes respect for the dark and dull inwardness of animal life disappear."[69] If the Egyptian use of the symbolic is an "unsatisfied urge" of spirit,[70] this is because Egyptian symbolism "confusedly intertwines meaning and shape" so that "the associations are ambiguous";[71] but the development of the Subject requires that animal inwardness diminish so that the individual consciousness can "come close to that inner subjectivity." Because of the ambiguity of the animal, the Egyptian is doomed to failure, in part because the symbol reduces to mystifying "riddle," and in part because he denigrates himself in venerating the animal.[72]

Although the artistic rendering of animal symbolism is only peripheral to Hegel's focus on Egypt's principal symbolic art form, architecture, animals reappear throughout the *Aesthetics* as a delimiting of spirit by the animal. For the Egyptians, architecture gestures toward the "inner kernel," but animal worship externalizes the intuition of spirit. Hieroglyphs further distance this process by generalizing from the specific animal to a universal sign, or worse, an alphabetic associated with its initial letter. Hence "In Egypt, on the whole, almost every shape is a symbol and hieroglyph not signifying itself but hinting at another thing with which it has affinity" and that a superficial one. "Yet symbols proper are only really complete when this relation is of a more fundamental and deeper kind."[73] The fullest expression of Egyptian misdirection and riddle is the sphinx, the mishmash of animal and spirit that is "as it were, the symbol of the symbolic itself."[74] The sphinx, "constructed out of the hardest stone, polished, covered with hieroglyphics," is riddle itself. The sphinx's human head signifies the human attempt "to push itself forward," but also its inability since it cannot come "to a perfect portrayal of its own freedom," remaining "confused and associated with what is other than itself."[75] We might consider the animal other here as a Not-I, a negativity that must be inhabited all the more because it is both hieroglyph as glittering sign and a symbol infused with mystical presence.

For Hegel, as for Derrida, the animal is both the possibility and the limitation of threshold for the human who realizes himself as "the animal that therefore I am."[76] But Hegel has made some reductive assumptions in his discussion. It is more correct to say that as symbols of the sacred, animals in Ancient Egypt disturbed the human-divine ratio by mediating it, bisecting the god figure so that animal head on top of human body represents the unknowable god's character. Even so, the relation of animal part to divine trait is itself mysterious: ibis head plus human body equals the god of writing, Thoth, the seat of intelligence and wisdom. The animal is a metaphor that figures the god, and yet that metaphor is literalized through the cult practices of sacred animals; both ibis and baboons were kept within Thoth's temple precincts as living points of spiritual access to the god. The literal animal, kept, paid homage to, and mummified is imaginatively transfigured into a spiritual aide to the god, and then refigured as a transparent metaphor of that god, a ghostly representation of itself as immortal. Other animals were sacrificed and mummified as offerings, but it is the sacred and not sacrificial animals that concern Hegel.

The animal is not only a spiritual aide to the god, but it also assists the human to reformulate the great void into a communicable interspace. In his main shrine in Khmun, later Hermopolis Magna, Thoth's priests fed the temple ibis as part of the daily rituals of caring for their god; the indirection of feeding to inanimate sculpted form to symbolic inscription traces a dissociation as much as an associative process, a peeling away of the animate body to reveal the living thought, the spiritual component that links animality and deity. It is this link from which the human has been barred, first through impurity, but also through fear of death as absolute negation, absolute ruin. Fear of mortality pressures the human imagination to view animality as naturally integrated into the death cycle and thus emotionally above it; at the same time divinity is immune to death as death's overseer or redeemer. Only the human is subject to death's great void, to the negation of everything. Therefore, the tomb is the sacred space of meeting this negativity in all its enormity.

In Egyptian tomb decoration, hieroglyphs are essential whereas the demotic (ordinary writing) is irrelevant. It is not information but inscription that matters, and gods must be multiply made present through pictorial representation, hieroglyphic naming, and prayers. These invocations accompany the dead person's autobiography as represented by inscription and pictures of his deeds. They are reinforced by the Book of the Dead which is made manifest through both texts painted onto and into the nested sarcophagi, and excerpts included in mummy wrappings. The animals deemed nonsacred—animals who labor or are a food source—are represented by paintings and clay figurines; they will feed the dead magically in the afterlife, a different order of transfiguration than that of divinely implicated animals. These representational animals will provide the sustenance for the continuance of the spirit, of both the *ba* and *ka*, the two Egyptian forms of the soul that are integrally yoked to the body. This is the difference then that gives Hegel pause: animals are a material source, animate matter, but at what point are they subsumed by the mystical, at what point can they be said to have shifted from matter to spirit, from literal to symbolic, or even from the perceived to the negative? It is in detecting something like a negative space that Hegel turns from this moment, in the end unimpressed and finding hieroglyphic inscription unequal to the task of spiritual embodiment.

Because conceptualization performs the categorical, it reduces an inscrutable being to an object of scrutiny, Hegel's finally uninteresting animal symbols. But I would argue, here Hegel has closed his "eyes to the negative as when we say of something that it is nothing or is false, and then having done with it, turn away and pass on to something else."⁷⁷ If the living animal and its symbolic counterpart are not conceptualized but held in mystery in esoteric, then it partakes of an indirection, a mystical path where there are no solid correlations of animal to god. It partakes of the "Spirit [which] is this power only by looking the negative in the face, and tarrying with it." This is the function of Thoth's ibises and baboons, both of whose animal parts are assimilated to his divine form, but it is also the function of the animal remains found in the ancient ruins, contemplative remains that continue to offer entry to the Subject's self-actualizing power. In Egyptian religion, the animal is not an other but, rather, mediates and incorporates sacral space, the subject-disturbing interstice between self and deity. It therefore resists, refuses, rebels against conceptualization, returning us to Hegel's youthful organic worldview and away from his discursive critiques. The animal does not animate the symbol but rather references it, pointing it in a certain direction on an uncertain path.

I take as the prime example of this the early Egyptian worship of the Apis bull in Memphis, recorded back certainly as far as the Second Dynasty according to Manetho, but most likely even earlier and worshipped as a fertility god. Giovanni Battista Belzoni's remarkable discovery in October 1817 of the great Seti I's tomb in the Valley of the Kings included a mummified bull. The bull mummy had been placed in its own room in the large tomb, indicating that the pharaoh participated in the cult belief that the Apis bull's spirit-force is aligned with the pharaoh's power. The Apis bull must be the calf of a cow that, or rather who, cannot have another, and the calf must also display distinctive markings especially on its head. Herodotus, albeit not a reliable source, reports in his fifth century BC *History*, that

> According to the Egyptians, a beam of light descends from the sky to the cow and from it she gives birth to Apis. This calf, which is known as Apis, has certain features: it is black, except for a white diamond on its forehead and the image of an eagle on its back, its tail hairs are double, and it has a beetle-shaped mark under its tongue.⁷⁸

This remarkable constellation of attributes signals the ritual animal whose special relation to humans is through Osiris, the son of the earth, Geb, and the sky, Nut. All three are represented anthropomorphically, Geg and Osiris as bearded men; although Osiris is mummified as judge of the underworld and granter of life, Geg could be represented as a bull, crocodile, or ram, and Nut as a cow or a woman with a cow's head. Through a process of imitative magic, Egyptian kings would hold communion with Osiris and with him be reborn into eternal life. In the New Kingdom this communion was available to all who could afford the rites. At Saqqara the Serapeum was built, a tomb complex for mummified Apis bulls, in which each was given his own stone sarcophagus and tomb chamber. The Apis bull is distinguished from other ritual animals in his embodied representation of divinity and as an oracle; he is the only deity represented fully as an animal and not anthropomorphized. Furthermore, he is connected with both Osiris and Ptah, the cosmic creator who is also represented as a mummified man. In the Memphite religion, the Apis bull's title was "the renewal of the life" of Ptah; later he is associated with the Hellene worship of Serapis, centered in Egypt at Alexandria. After death, the bull became Osorapis, the Osiris Apis, analogically coordinating with human communion with Osiris after death.

As the most important of all Egyptian sacred animals, the Apis bull poses a special problem for Hegel's meditation on animal symbolism. Because he confuses the Apis bull with all Egyptian temple animals, Hegel believes it to be like the ibis or cat, having "in it nothing symbolic, because . . . the actual living animal, Apis for example, was itself worshipped as an existence of god";[79] thus the problem can be skirted in *The Aesthetics*, but it nevertheless remains. Conceived by heavenly lightening, the Apis bull is treated as a deity on earth much like the pharaoh, and the ba of Ptah while alive, his "Spokesman" and "Herald." Unlike other temple animals, there is only one Apis bull at a time, and he is given his own house at Memphis with a court for exercise and a harem of cows. His behavior is studied for omens, his death mourned, his burial splendid and highly ritualistic, his successor when discovered widely celebrated. Like the king's list of pharaohs, records were kept of the bulls, including their ages at death, their birth and throne dates, their mother's name, and place of birth. Providing direct rather than indirect access to divinity through his presence on earth and the omens he provides, the Apis bull is both a sacred animal and an embodiment of the god. As such, he does present Spirit in the Hegelian sense, being closer to Hegel's highest terms, poetry and philosophy, since he demands the poetic imagination in order to see his gaze as that of a true Other. The animal, whose bond with the divine is entirely otherly, leaps into the void in order to lead the human spirit to realization. The Apis bull with his divine body and ancient worship disturbs Hegel's teleology of the "wholly discovered individual" by posing an alternative schema to his rationalized one; in the Egyptian schema, the supernatural determines the role of the animal in the divine ratio as the knowing subject while the human must wait for the afterlife to realize himself. The animal as negative force that facilitates human self-realization was already at work in Ancient Egypt long before Hegel erased it from his dialectical machine, but its presence as the animal remains in the ruins haunts his attempt to reconcile phenomenal remains with the Egyptian remainder of spirit.

Spirit and its magic will be the subject of the next chapter: spirit, which is Hegel's term for reason, can be rationalized or occulted, related to knowability and unknowability. How spirit as a philosophical rather than theological concept becomes entangled in the trope of Ancient Egypt will be my next focus for investigation.

NOTES

1. Quoted in Wendorf, *The Elements of Life*, 105.
2. Coleridge, *The Collected Works of Samuel Taylor Coleridge*, 11.2: 1133–1134. The internal quotation is a reference to Daniel 7.4, *The English Standard Version Bible*. In Coleridge's text a word is missing; the editors of the collected Coleridge suggest that the missing word is "heart." My thanks to Erin Goss for this reference.
3. This is from an argument concerning Heidegger's reworking of Hegelian spirit in Derrida, *On Spirit: Heidegger and the Question*, 26–27.
4. Levinas, *Totality and Infinity*, 40.
5. Ibid, 262.
6. That is, the signal embodiment of cultural time referenced by Roland Barthes. "In order to tell a story, the painter has only . . . the instant he is gong to immobilize on the canvas. . . . Necessarily total, this instant will be artificial . . . a hieroglyph in which can be read at a single glance . . . the present, the past and the future" in Barthes, *Image/Music/Text*, 73.
7. Through literary treatment and the East India Company's increasing economic and political importance for Britain despite its mercenary character and political imbroglios, empire became culturally pregnant with the imagined Near East and India. Even now we sometimes relegate to second-hand those other regions of cultural conquest or attempted penetration such as China, Japan, Africa.
8. Diodorus resembles Herodotus at this point in recounting priests' tales (such as that both Hercules and Perseus were Egyptians or Egyptian-born) and Egyptian mythology while translating gods into the Greek pantheon, and noting something of Egypt's history and its agriculture. Curiously he discusses the feats of gods like Osiris and Hermes as if they are pharaohs—as if taking the god-king conception literally. His account of Egypt provides rich material for Shelley's imagination. "From Osiris and Isis, to the reign of Alexander the Great, who built a city after his own name, the Egyptian priests reckon above ten thousand years" (Diodorus Siculus, *The Library of History*, Vol. II, 29).
9. Diodorus explains that there are two separate statues of his mother to show her rank as the daughter, wife, and mother of pharaohs.
10. A further cause for confusion, or perhaps imaginative conflation, was the news that Giovanni Belzoni was bringing the head of one of the colossal statues of Ramesses back to London, where it would be installed in the British Museum as "The Young Memnon," the Greek name for the Amenhotep colossi. Shelley would not, as is commonly assumed, have seen Belzoni's trophy head, since it was not installed until late 1818, after he had left London permanently. However, he certainly would have heard word of the head's journey and may have seen newspaper engravings of circus strongman Belzoni's heroic feats in dragging the Memnon head to the Nile;

there the tremendous head appears to defeat its modern conqueror through sheer magnitude, itself an aesthetic achievement, rather than through Ramesses's vaunted power and achievements. And again, the act of misnaming makes it unclear whose head is being dragged; for British newspaper readers, perhaps Belzoni has removed the Amenhotep head rather than taking an already fallen head.

11. A cult center vastly larger than the Ramesseum that was used to worship Amenhotep as a god during his lifetime, but which had utterly disappeared.

12. Moreover, the Memnon colossi is visually the statuary more likely to have the significant epitaph carved into its base, which in Diodorus's words as translated by George Booth in 1814, reads: "I am Osymandyas, king of kings; if any would know how great I am, and where I lie, let him excel me in any of my works" (Diodorus Siculus, *The Library of History*, Vol. I, iii, 53).

13. Ibid, Vol. I, iv, 60).

14. Derrida, *Glas*, 253.

15. Hegel conceives of the pyramid as a kind of spirit-chrysalis in a prescient vision of what Egyptologists later discovered as the belief that the pharaoh's ba will ascend to the heavens nightly from the two openings near the pyramid's apex, in order to intercede on his people's behalf.

16. Hegel, *Aesthetics*, I. 356.

17. Ibid, I. 354–355.

18. Derrida, *Glas*, 249.

19. Hegel, *Aesthetics*, I. 357–358.

20. Foucault, *The Order of Things*, 49.

21. Hegel, *Aesthetics*, I. 358.

22. Ibid, I. 359.

23. Ibid, I. 355.

24. Ibid.

25. Ibid, I. 363.

26. *Alastor* was composed in late 1815, two years after *Queen Mab* and one year before "Hymn to Intellectual Beauty." (Published in the volume of 1816 with eleven short poems including "Hymn," and "To Wordsworth," which critiques both Wordsworth's and Southey's conservative politics). In *Shelley: A Critical Reading* Earl Wasserman argues that the poem explores the dynamics between the human need for love and community and the Idealist's quest for universal truths and ideal love. In this reading the Narrator relates his own search for ultimate knowledge through nature in a Wordsworthian manner, before narrating the visionary Poet's contrasting idealistic quest.

27. According to Hesychius of Alexandria, Alastor was also one of Zeus's epithets.

28. Shelley, *Alastor*, ll. 52–54.

29. Ibid, ll. 106–115.

30. Ibid, ll. 110–114.

31. Ibid, ll. 116–120.

32. Mignolo, *Local Histories/Global Designs: Coloniality, Subaltern Knowledges, and Border Thinking*. See esp. chapter 1, and particularly 60–64 where Mignolo

discusses the European understanding of fourteenth-century Arab intellectual achievement, as opposed to the later sixteenth-century colonial adaptation and cooption of it.

33. Shelley, *Alastor*, II. 2, 18, 50, 54, 672.
34. See Simmel's essay, "The Ruin" in *Essays on Sociology, Philosophy and Aesthetics*.
35. Shelley, *Alastor*, II. 119.
36. Shelley, *Shelley's Poetry and Prose*, 72–73.
37. See Seth Loris, *The Virtue of Sympathy*.
38. Shelley, *Alastor*, I. 695. Flight problematizes catastrophe because, since the Poet's death is self-generated, artfully representing his flight through different scapes as a flight of translation, an allegory for his reversal of ground and figure. Since Shelley has alerted the reader to the allegorical nature of the poem in his Preface, it is important to attend to the levels of allegory available in the text. Indeed, the reader can locate literal catastrophe in the poem only by missing the positive message of both the Preface and the poem itself: the remainder that is signaled by the "surpassing Spirit,/ Whose light adorned the world around it," and whose death reveals that "Nature's vast frame, the web of human things,/ Birth and the grave, that are not as they were" (Ibid, II. 714–715, 719–720).
39. Ibid, II. 716, 718.
40. Shelley, *Shelley's Poetry and Prose*, 73.
41. See Achille Mbembe, "Necropolitics."
42. Cairenes generally refer to it as 'the cemetery,' and it is divided into the more habitable part and the slum, where the poorest live and where Cairo's recycling is taken. See El Kadi and Bonnamy, *Architecture for the Dead*.
43. Ibid, 15.
44. Rochfort Scott, *Rambles in Egypt and Candia*, I. 198, 275.
45. Ibid, I. 348.
46. Cooper, "Egyptology and the Two Exodes," 3.
47. Williams, "A Letter to Major-General John Briggs," 24.
48. Scott, *Rambles in Egypt and Candia*, I. 330.
49. El Kadi and Bonnamy, *Architecture for the Dead*, 9.
50. Rochfort Scott, *Rambles in Egypt and Candia*, I. 198.
51. Ibid, I. 60.
52. Ibid, I. 312–313, I. 313–314.
53. Baldwin, *Political Recollections Relative to Egypt*, 121.
54. *The Works of James Thomson*, II. 191. In 1740, Thompson collaborated with Mallet on Alfred, a masque first performed at Cliveden for Frederick, Prince of Wales.
55. Scott relies here on Herodotus and the Old Testament (Manetho, by contrast, puts Menes's founding of Memphis at 3000 BC). The date of Nebuchadnezzar's battle with the Egyptian army would have been nearer to 606, when Nineveh fell. Although sources differ in their accounts, Nebuchadnezzar's Egyptian Campaign was a border issue as Egypt attempted to reassert its prior control of Syria after the fall of Ninevah and the division of its empire between Babylon and Media, rather than an

aggression into the interior, and the battle was not against Menes (or Narmer), the first king to style himself king of Egypt, but against Necho I of the 26th Dynasty, whose dates are more in line with those of Nebuchadnezzar's. Scott's account of Memphis's decline belongs to the Middle Kingdom and the invasion of the Hyksos, around 1650 BC when they laid siege to Memphis. The Hyksos looted and destroyed Memphis monuments, taking some of them to their new capital at Avaris (in the Delta, finally destroyed by Ahmose I). It was not until the kings of the 17th dynasty that Egypt was regained by the pharaohs centered at Thebes.

56. Rochfort Scott, *Rambles in Egypt and Candia*, I. 253–254.
57. Ibid, I. 254.
58. Ibid, I. 255–256.
59. Ibid, I. 317.
60. Ibid, I. 318.
61. Hegel, *Phenomenology of Spirit*, 19.
62. Quoted in Beiser, *Hegel*, 87.
63. Žižek. *Tarrying with the Negative*, 10.
64. Qtd. in Ibid, 20.
65. Foshay, "'Tarrying with the Negative,'" 298.
66. Ibid, 299.
67. These occupy the last part of the *Phenomenology of Spirit*.
68. Hegel, *Aesthetics*, I. 445.
69. Ibid, I. 445.
70. Ibid, I. 354.
71. Ibid, I. 360.
72. Ibid, I. 445.
73. Ibid, I. 357–358.
74. Ibid, I. 360.
75. Ibid, I. 360–361.
76. Derrida's first lecture in *The Animal That Therefore I Am* concerns the ways that animals provide humans with the embodied contradiction of knowing and not-knowing.
77. Hegel, *Phenomenology of Spirit*, 19.
78. Herodotus, *The Histories*, 3. 28.
79. Hegel, *Aesthetics*, I. 357.

Chapter 4

Spirit Magic

In his *Moralia* Plutarch considers the cult of Isis not as the "mysterious treatment of nature science" referred to by Novalis when he jotted "The State of Nature is at once *res privata* (mystical) and *res publica*./ Mysticism of Nature. Isis—virgin—veil—Mysterious treatment of nature science./," but as concurrent with the goddess who is sister and wife to Osiris.[1] He identifies her as both the reanimator (her role in restoring Osiris to life after Set tears him apart) and the goddess of knowledge. This conflation, as with all speculative accounts of Egypt, draws a veil over what can be known about that culture. The veil of misconstrual is easily confused for the veil of truth, the first the target of the historian and the second the goal of the philosopher. The tension between history and philosophy, and their mediation by the poetic, structures the focusing of realized spirit and its magical instantiation on Ancient Egypt, particularly for the younger German Idealists and second-generation British romantics.

Plutarch's analytic description of the Egyptian cults and rituals focuses most heavily on the Saïtic beliefs. (The Saïte Period, 672 to 525 BCE, was the twenty-sixth dynasty of Egypt, when the capital was moved to Saïs; its pharaohs reconstituted Egypt as a single kingdom after the Assyrian invasion and destruction of Thebes.) Plutarch explains that because religious devotion aims for Truth, Isis (whose name, he assures us, is Greek, providing a confusing provenance for this principal Egyptian deity) is "especially well-pleasing" because "she is both wise, and a lover of wisdom; as her name appears to denote that, more than any other, knowing and knowledge belong to her."[2] The interweaving of myths occurs organically, with Isis's role in restoring her husband after his brother Set kills and dismembers him making her an allegory for truth: Set (in Plutarch's account, Typhon) is "her enemy, for he is 'puffed up' by want of knowledge and falsehood, and tears to pieces, *and puts out of sight, the sacred word* which the goddess again gathers up and puts together, and gives into the charge of those initiated into the religion."[3]

Plutarch also gives a quite different account of Isis's relation to the cosmic god Amun from traditional Egyptian mythology, which portrays her as a lesser goddess; it is Hathor (whose attributes the goddess Isis, along with another goddess Mut, took on beginning in the New Kingdom) who is the consort of the sun god Rā (later displaced by Amun), and mother of Horus. As a sky and solar deity she is also one of several goddesses who acted as Ra's female counterpart, the Eye of Rā. Plutarch, who ignores the older pantheon in his discussion of the Hellenic and then Roman worship of Isis, describes her as handmaiden to the cosmic god who is "the First, the Supreme, and the Intelligible": *"That which is*, the *All."* The *All*, which the Egyptians "call Amun," is "both by her side, and united with her" while her temple is called the Ision, "the entering-place."[4] She guides the (male) worshipper, bringing him knowledge of the cosmic god. The sacred story that is her wisdom is also the *"Word,"* and "the real Isiacist is he that is competent to investigate by the aid of the Word." For Plutarch, Isis is the key to decoding the symbolism behind the pantheistic myths; correctly understood, these deities and their rituals become an open book to he "who meditates upon the Truth which is involved in them." Plato, too, reads philosophical meaning into ancient myths, as will Schelling in his *Historical-Critical Introduction to the Philosophy of Mythology*. The question becomes, what is the ground of this symbolism and how must the disclosure of the spirit it represents inform its interpreter?

In Plutarch's account, as for all Hermeticism, Isis's role as Nature is one of mediation between the human and the divine. The Word is sacred knowledge in general, or the ground of that knowledge, rather than the divine creative power writ large or the revelation of the Son. But Isis is not handmaiden to the Christian God; she is rather the locus of the history of spirit magic, associated with Hermeticism and alchemy until Hermetic doctrine was redirected in the transitional years between the Classical and Christian empires. This is not the spirit magic Hegel uses derisively to refer to Cartesian positivist naïve thought, but the spirit magic of the alchemist Paracelsus, who (working with his theory of sympathy between cosmic and terrestrial entities) continued Isis's traditional identity as healer, magician, and holder of sacred knowledge. If for Hegel spirit has to do with reason and the subject, for the late Heidegger spirit is "fire, flame, burning, conflagration."[5] Hermetically, it is in this sense of spirit, light, and alchemical flame as their correlative that Isis must be understood. As the *genius loci* of spirit magic, Isis links the grounding of symbolism, its meaning for the history of spirit, and for the place of Ancient Egypt in that problematic.

I. THE GROUND OF ORIGIN

The Romantics trace the problem of origin, associated since the later Egyptian dynasties with Egypt's prehistory, back to Plato's *Timaeus*, his account of the origin of the universe. This discourse was written during the last gasp of Egypt's priority in Mediterranean affairs and was a signal text for the Renaissance's Neoplatonic revisionism of Plato's works after they were discovered, collated, and then given to Marsilio Ficino to translate. The *Timaeus* is a text that has served to anchor both early modern and modern thought, as well as twentieth-century philosophy, and its origin story serves as a reminder that to speak of the grounds of origin is to speak of Egypt.

The *Timaeus* can be read as the originary text for the *mythos/logos* dialectic of western discourse; the "whole history of interpretations," "the immense literature devoted to the *Timaeus* since antiquity" is one that "[w]e will never exhaust."[6] Schelling invokes the *Timaeus* (as well as Boehme, Hermeticism, and Pythagoras) in his study of the philosophy of mythology,[7] and even earlier it was a signal text for the student trio of Schelling, Hölderlin, and Hegel. Still the problem of the *Timaeus*'s encyclopedic prehistory, in which the cosmogony presented "runs through the cycle of knowledge on all things," so that its "encyclopedic end must mark the term, the *telos*, of a *logos* on the subject of everything that is," connects it from the beginning with Alexandrian encyclopedic projects.[8] This also connects it to Renaissance encyclopedism (as in the *oeuvre* of Athanasius Kircher), and Enlightenment and Romantic encyclopedism, particularly important to German Idealism. Even before this cosmological mapping, the *Timaeus*'s cosmogony asserts a prior place from which to speak: it is, as Charles Kahn notes, one of the two "supreme expressions" of Pythagorean ideas in Plato's dialogues (the other being the *Phaedo*) regarding the immortality of the human soul and mathematics as the key to cosmic knowledge.[9] I will focus on several significant features of the *Timaeus* for the history of spirit magic, leaving aside for now the problem of encyclopedism. The important elements here are its Egyptian beginning; its exhaustive discussion of the interval as the space between integers (as the gap between subject and object), whose function to introduce temporality and death while foreclosing the possibility of remainder; and its central discussion of the *chora* as mythic metaphor for the nowhere place of the generative interval or subject-object gap.

In Plato's account in the *Timaeus*, the highest cosmic caste, replicated on earth by social castes (the highest of whom operate in secret, as does Plato's God), is that of the gods, who as perfect beings are spheres in orbit, turning by themselves and moving in relation to the whole. These divine planet-beings, which follow Pythagoras's determinate cosmos of sun, moon, and the five planets (although Plato drops Pythagoras's central hearth and shadow earth from his schema), are ruled by earth, "the first and eldest of gods that are in the interior of heaven."[10] The earth is the eldest planet and guardian of the inner heavens in analogy to the caste of the magistrates in a perfect human republic; she is therefore "our nurse," and by this term has associations with the female womb. The *chora*, presented as a maternal metaphor, functions as a "nurse," which Derrida suggests is a "third gender/genus," the third genus also being the nowhere place from which artists and the itinerant Sophists speak, and from which Socrates affects to speak in the dialogue's beginning as he "receives" the speech of Critias and Timaeus.[11] The earth "cling[s] around the pole which is extended through the universe"; the pole allows her not only to guard and regulate the inner heavens, but to be "artificer of night and day."[12] For Giordano Bruno, it is this very universal pole that is the problem. For him, the pole—represented by the slanted rod that holds together the armillary model of the universe, its spheres and plants captured and held in strict relation to each other and to the whole by that spinal pole—is what keeps man in his place, unable to interact with the spheres, held down by his very caste of the lesser mortals. Bruno's "Egyptian religion" dismantles the armillary sphere of the inner heavens, allowing the inner and outer circles of the diverse, planeted regime and the outer, self-same, eternal regime to intermingle. (Plato takes the conception of a spherical earth centered within a spherical universe from Pythagorean beliefs associated with cult centers in Italy and Sicily, explicitly departing from the Ionian cosmos depicting a flat earth.)[13] Bruno's remapping of the universe unseats several entities in Plato's conception, including the soul, time, and the problem of being. At the same time, Hermeticism assimilates Plato's planetary rod to the Caducean rod carried by the Greek god Hermes as a symbol of healing and synchrony, as well as the magical rod used by Moses in Egypt, which became a symbol of division and righteous destruction.

What Plato's rod of stability manifests in the *Timaeus*, apart from its function in planetary orbit, is an organizing principle that makes sense out of the mathematical divisions, foldings, compressions, and compoundings. Its conceptual equivalent is the soul, a female element which prioritizes and sorts the universe while distributing and attending to the chaotic influence of "the affections."[14] Spirit-essence as the Platonic God is connected to but different from the universal soul: God made the soul "in origin and excellence prior to and older than the body, to be the ruler and mistress, of whom the body was to be the subject. And he made her out of the following elements and on this wise"—as a combination of the eternal/unchangeable, the material, and a "compounded . . . third and intermediate kind of being," that is, a triad of the "indivisible kind of" both "the same and the ["reluctant and unsociable"] different," plus "being" (which is the compound of those opposites as is found in proportion in material bodies).[15] Here, too, is a third entity; the soul aligned in its intermediary and therefore necessary status with the earth, the *chora*, art, and the place from which truth (philosophy) speaks. Like the *chora*, which Derrida explains is aligned with the necessary, the soul takes part in the distinction between two modalities, the true and the necessary.[16] The soul's *chora*-like mediation between the intelligible and the sensible—Paracelsus, tellingly, calls it the "matrix" or womb[17]—arises from necessity in order to ground philosophical truth. God then provided the means by which the rod of stability would be conceived: "he formed within her [the soul] the corporeal universe, and brought the two together and united them center to center."[18] This union, a kind of rigid umbilical cord, connects the eternal (ideal) universe with the material one of appearance. Thus, connected and organized, her involutions can be rationally apprehended: "The soul, interfused everywhere from the center to the circumference of heaven, of which also she is the external envelopment, herself turning in herself, began a divine beginning of never-ceasing and rational life enduring through all time."[19] Her beginning of never-ceasing, that which returns to itself, is another origin story springing from a nowhere place; the soul begins but does not end, encircling itself in order to mediate (in order to *mean* or *intend*) the correlation of the eternal universe of the outer circle of "the same" with the corporeal universe of the inner circle (that of "difference").

What marks difference in the inner circle of our world is its resistance; what marks the bodies and habitations of the cosmos and world of difference is numbers—their integers, intervals, compoundings, and means. The purpose of numbers is, literally, twofold (doubled, enfolded, involved): to rationally harmonize the corporeal universe so that it operates symphonically (to draw in Pythagoras here, although Plato himself emphasizes sight rather than hearing and music as the quality by which humans know that numbers and cosmic alignment exist); and to create time. Numbers are necessary, for they both orchestrate the corporeal universe and reduce triads (the same, the different, and being) into unity. In Plutarch's much abbreviated account "Isis and Osiris" (Plutarch acknowledging his deletion of "everything unnecessary and superfluous" of the mathematical formulation of the universe) he transforms the Egyptian myth of origin from one of division (as in Plato) to one of multiplication. It is the myth of a primal elopement, a dice game, and Hermes/Thoth's winning from the moon "the seventieth part from each one of her lights," or of each day, which he adds several times until he made the days of the year.[20]

Plutarch notes the same Egyptian ground as does Plato's *Timaeus*, explaining that not only did many Greek philosophers journey to Egypt—"such as Solon, Thales, Plato, Eudoxus, Pythagoras."[21] If Plato did not travel to Egypt, this only throws into relief the afterwardness of Plutarch's synthetic account, but does not discredit the additive principle, even if Plutarch's mythic version provides an element of chance, of craps, into Plato's rational account. Plato's deductive logic requires a divisive rather than additive principle: "Then, taking the three new elements, he [God] mingled them all into one form, compressing by force" the different with the same "mingled . . . with the intermediate kind of being and out of three made one, he again divided this whole into as many portions as was fitting, each portion being a compound of the same, the different, and being. And he proceeded to divide after this manner" so that mathematically "the double intervals [that is, between 1, 2, 4, 8] and the triple [that is, between 1, 3, 9, 27]" were filled up proportionately. Thus, by "cutting off yet other portions from the mixture and placing them in the intervals, so that in each interval there were two kinds of means, the one exceeding and exceeded by equal parts of its extremes [as for example, 1, 4/3 2, in which the mean 4/3 is one third of 1 more than 1, and one third of 2 less than 2], the other being that kind of mean which exceeds and exceeded by an equal number," God created a harmonious universe controlled by its numerical perfection.[22] The eighteenth-century fascination with Platonic numerical accounting can be seen in treatises attempting to mathematically measure the great pyramids at Giza (purely speculative endeavors), as well as the innumerable attempts to determine the precise date of creation from biblical textual evidence. In these accounts, as in Plato's universe, there would be no remainders. For Plato, each difference ("reluctant and unsociable") is "forced" into relation with its opposite and its mean, placed along a continuum that stabilizes its radical resistance and controlled by an interventionist mean.

This stabilized difference ("the other or diverse") was then placed in the "inner circle," the "outer circle" being left to the same, which moves clockwise and is eternal ("for that he left single and undivided"). The inner circle, made up of the diverse, moves counterclockwise, and in order to control it better God divided it into "six places and . . . seven unequal circles having their intervals in ratios of two and three, three of each, and bade the orbits proceed in a direction opposite to one another. And three [sun, Mercury, Venus] he made to move with equal swiftness, and the remaining four [moon, Saturn, Mars, Jupiter] to move with unequal swiftness to the three and to one another, but in due proportion."[23] It is these motors of time ("instruments," Plato calls them) with their differing movements that enabled ancient astronomers from the Chaldeans to the Alexandrians, to conduct their precise measurements of the cosmos and of their world. Ancient Egypt, with its temple astronomical observatories, produced calculations that depended on additive/multiplicative as well as divisive principles, spelling out the relation between Plato's and Plutarch's Egyptian origin stories: they must be taken together in order to reflect Egypt properly.

The choral burden of Plato's Pythagorean numerology, after he had accounted for the exceeding and exceeded fractions that occupy the double (1, 2, 4, 8) intervals and the triple (1, 3, 9, 27) intervals, is that God ensures that there *are no remainders*. "Where there were intervals of 3/2 and of 4/3 and of 9/8, made by the connecting terms in the former intervals, he filled up all the intervals of 4/3 with the intervals of 9/8, leaving a fraction over, and the interval which this fraction expressed was in the ratio of 256 to 243. And thus the whole mixture out of which he cut these portions was all exhausted by him," exhausted because the fraction left over, remaindered, is accounted for.[24] The accounted for, or compound mixture, is as in Euclidean geometry, best understood by a diagram that relates parts to the whole rather than parsing them: "This entire compound he divided lengthwise into two parts which he joined to one another at the center like the letter X, and bent them into a circular form, connection them with themselves and each other at the point opposite to their original meeting point, and, comprehending them in a uniform revolution upon the same axis, he made the one the outer and the other the inner circle."[25] As the X—a phenomenal, algebraic yet also genetic figure—becomes concentric circles, bending round and uniting its opposite ends, it does the chromosomal work of generation: what it generates is time.

Time, Plato explains, is merely what can be apprehended of the eternal; it is "a moving image of eternity" scripted by numbers: "Wherefore he resolved to have a moving image of eternity, and when he set in order the heaven, he made this image eternal but moving according to number, while eternity itself rests in unity, and this image we call time."[26] In this way we have past and future, which are "created species of time," whereas eternity resides in the unending now. Plato is willing to grammaticize this: "for we say that it 'was,' or 'is,' or 'will be,' but the truth is that 'is' alone is properly attributed to it [time], and that 'was' and 'will be' are only to be spoken of becoming in time." The grammatical rule proves the universal one: "These are the forms of time, which imitates eternity and revolves according to a law of number."[27] Being and becoming are thereby sorted: being is both an intermediate thing between same (eternal) and difference (material). It resides in time itself as the now—a shadow existence of the eternal now. Becoming belongs to the world of generation, of past and future, for which the law is death. It is the becoming which is always already death that Schelling, Novalis, and Keats will understand as the end of the possibility of the absolute. Becoming also instantiates afterness as the looking toward death that must always follow the beginning and the point of origin: no cosmogony can obviate the fatality instantiated by origin, as Wordsworth intuits even as a boy in the 'spots of time' chronicled in *The Prelude*.

Thus far, Plato has only been speaking of the interval. It is already halfway through his cosmogony of the cycle of knowledge before Plato overtly introduces the concept of the *chora*, as if it is difficult to speak of it, and indeed, he says he must only describe it metaphorically, mythically, as he installs it in the place of the cosmic interval. Derrida worries that the Platonic *chora*, troped as a mother or nurse and associated through a "relation of abyssal and analogous reflexivity" with politically determined marriages, darkens Plato's mysterious but positively generative *chora*.[28] Its reflexive quality is also mirrored in the *chora*'s role in generating three natures as the stages of translation from the abyssal into the sensible. "For the present we have only to conceive of three natures: first, that which is in process of generation; secondly, that in which the generation takes place; and thirdly, that of which the thing generated is a resemblance naturally produced."[29] The *chora* provides the translative key, but she does so from her intervention in binary oppositions; this gap, which is reflexive rather than one-directional trafficking, is both nowhere and "place itself, the irreplaceable place," that then gives place to others.[30]

The three natures all relate to each other through the in-forming space of the *chora*, which is itself "universal nature" as Plato says—not the eternal-intelligible nature, but the interval between the intelligible and the sensible natures, between the eternal idea and its resemblance; in other words, Isis (called "universal nature" in Novalis's *Novices of Sais*, and worshipped as such in Hermetic lore). Isis is the great magician who takes Rā's symbolic name into her own hands in order to regenerate the dead and to give form to new life. Like her, the *chora* possesses a natural magic, one that translates ideas into things by bearing them, awakening them to life. The choral interval, "the receiving principle," makes sense of impressions: it makes them sensible; they matter. The problem of the integer, which the choral interval mediates, is a problem of doubles (1, 2, 4, 8) and triples (1, 3, 9, 27); triples are synthetic formulations, and Hegel would agree with Plato that they describe the most "beautiful" of absolute forms, the triangle which forms and informs the universe and its inhabitants, materially perfected as pyramids.[31] Doubles (male-female, light-dark, eternal-sensible, immortal-mortal, outer-inner, life-death) as well as triples (triads, pyramids, reproduction) are dramatically important in the ontologies of both Boehme and Schelling, whether derived from the Bible's good-evil and father-son-holy ghost versions (as for Boehme) or from the *Timaeus*. But prior to both philosophers, these integers had magical properties for Hermeticists, alchemists, and Neoplatonists, for they not only form the universe but by them everything begins at one, everything resolves into unity ("the one only-begotten heaven"[32]), the All.

The *chora* herself mediates doubles and triples between them: she "gives place to the measure of the cosmos."[33] She is Isis resurrecting Osiris from the dead as the mediative principle, producing a child—the mean, Horus—on his re-membered body. In Christian theology Horus becomes the Son, the Word materialized; in Hermetic lore, as in Plutarch's account, Isis is handmaiden to the Word, chorally enabling its materialization as the speaker of spells. As the principle of the interval rather than the mean, the *chora* is the space of an otherness (Isis as magician) that occasionally is not just receiving but reactive: "the universal nature which receives all bodies . . . always receives all things, she never departs at all from her own nature and never, in any way or at any time, assumes a form like that of any of the things which enter into her; she is the natural recipient of all impressions, and is stirred and informed ['in-formed' is Schelling's term] by them."[34] Is the *chora* stirred in the sense of being impassioned? Stirred by love, as is the maternal body in response to its filling womb, in which informing and in-forming take place? Does Isis as the mother goddess in-form being with her passion, instilling a female element into the stirring of life?

What is the nature of this stirring, this informing, which Plato also refers to as a shaking conducted by the *chora* ("the four kinds of elements were then shaken by the receiving vessel"[35])? For Derrida the *chora/khōra* comes "as the name" which is not the name of the other so much as "the other of the name and quite simply the other, whose irruption the name announces."[36] It does not speak, resists naming until it irrupts, stirring or shaking as impassioning (desire and love in both Boehme's and Schelling's ontotheologies). This stirring is also a violence or resistance to the visible, geometrically formulated, knowable symbolic order; something unknowable is included. For Plato, the irruptive is disorderly and different, requiring a rule or intercession by way of a mean: finding the mean allows all exceptions to have less value. So, Isis's theft of Rā's secret name, which she tricks him of to enhance Horus's power, is primal disruption of the rule; an irruption into the symbolic. For Kristeva, 'irruption' is key to the *chora*'s formative role in the activation of linguistic potentialities (on a cosmic scale this is the creative power of the Word). Because the *chora* is characterized by "pulsating . . . in a rhythmic but nonexpressive totality," it precedes any signifying trace.[37] As Kristeva notes, "the semiotic *chora* has been separated from the 'subject'-'object' continuum";[38] thus it designates "a break"—the thetic—which works as a scission in the process that "sets up the symbolic thesis and an object." The *chora* as such is the "precondition" of enunciation and denotation, and it can only intervene in the subjective state via a stirring, an impassioning, in which sound and rhythm begin a dance that irrupts into orality, babble, the semiotic.[39] It precedes not only speech but the trace; inscription, translating impressions which gives way to speech, occurs *after* its intervention. Plato posits the work of the *chora* as a kind of preinscription, whereas the free play of Kristeva's semiotic posits such labor as prior to even that. Derrida views the *chora* as necessarily limited by its abyssal or interval position, the abyss itself imposing an authoritative "logic" on Plato, a "programme" that entangles Plato so that the mythic is the only way he can properly describe the *chora*'s mysterious functioning.[40] But Kristeva sees free play and resistance where Derrida sees "constraint." Artists return to the semiotic's priority in order to achieve "a constantly maintained ambiguity between the possibility of a *meaning* . . . and a *denotation*."[41] And it is through irruption that "Language thus tends to be drawn out of its symbolic function (sign-syntax) and is opened out within a semiotic articulation," so that "this semiotic network gives 'music' to literature."[42] Its pulsating, rhythmic quality in-forms the literary with the musicality of the poetic.

As Kristeva describes the *chora*'s pulsating quality, it resembles the bodily rhythms of the maternal womb. If at the conclusion of the *Timaeus* Plato for the first time associates the female human "womb" to a "matrix" that powerfully invokes the *chora*, he has already indicated that the *chora* should be considered as both a mother and a nurse: "The receiving principle" may be likened, Plato says, "to a mother, and the source or spring to a father, and the intermediate nature to a child." But the mother receptacle is "an invisible and formless being which receives all things and in some mysterious way partakes of the intelligible, and is most incomprehensible."[43] Her incomprehensibility, her otherness, gives room for understanding the *chora* itself as the site of God's self-othering, as in Schelling's *Ages of the World*. But Kristeva reflects on such an incomprehensibility differently: it is incomprehensible because before symbolic language only. Otherwise, it is responsible, as in Plato, for in-forming the new being with a heterogeneity in what is available to the human. By contrast, Derrida views the *chora* with suspicion as "quite simply the other" that casts doubt on Plato's confidence in the container-like *chora*'s containability.

But what of the *chora*'s role in soul-making, in spirit essence? For Schelling, this will also be part of her translative key, for she decisively differentiates God by her presence. Plato's first mention of a *chora*-like site of transformation is just after God has created the universe, and after it the gods and children of gods of the inner circle. To these "who are my works and of whom I am the artificer and father" he explains that what he has wrought is "indissoluble, if so I will." Yet only an evil creator would undo what is "harmonious and happy," indicating that universal synchrony is already at play, and that God is already hampered by constraints. These gods and their children, who are themselves of a lesser divinity, are tasked to fill the earth with mortals, while God "sow[s] the seed" of "that divine part" in them, the soul.[44] And at that moment he activates (again, we learn for the first time) "the cup," the first receptacle or container: "and once more into the cup in which he had previously mingled the soul of the universe he poured the remains of the elements, and mingled them in much the same manner; they were not, however, pure as before, but diluted to the second and third degree." This mixture he divides into as many parts as there are stars, assigns a soul to each star, and *teaches* the stars ("he showed them") "the nature of the universe and declared to them the laws of destiny." The souls were also "to be sown in the instruments of time," the planets, and into the first of the mortal tribes, man. It is in the ensouled body, this interconnected entity of immortal-mortal elements that sensation as a faculty resides; sensations are to stem from "irresistible impressions," while the other faculty possible in the ensouled body is "love, in which pleasure and pain mingle." Love is the faculty "in the second place," suggesting its connection with the *chora*-site as a "place" of informing, of information: love or passion is a formative agency. (By contrast, for Boehme, love is the first creative power, and not just a faculty.) In man, love mingles not just pleasure and pain, but fear and anger, and every feeling "akin or opposite to them" in doublings and dyads of affective challenges, for the emotions must be conquered for the soul, after the body's demise, "to return and dwell in his native star."[45]

Plato's association of universal nature with the divine principle situates stars as the dwelling places of souls; love is therefore an intervention in the universal–particular dynamic that grounds the ensouled body. The perfect body whereby God begins his new universe as the circle or sphere which returns to itself; and universal nature is thereby produced by the interval of the feminine *chora*. All of these are determinate elements of Hermetic belief, Neoplatonism, seventeenth-century mysticism such as that of Boehme, Rosicrucianism, and German and British Romanticisms. One aspect of the *Timaeus*, however, particularly haunts Romanticism: there are no remainders in Plato's cosmology. Plato's universe excludes voids, compressing until they disappear: although voids appear along with the four elements, the universe "being circular and having a tendency to come together, compresses everything and will not allow any place to be left void." The compression process is not merely exclusionary, but is a displacement.[46] Therefore, although there is a productive displacement, there is no external nonground, which Boehme and Schelling term the abyssal *Ungrund*, which is what I am connecting— through Plato's placement of Egypt as prior—to the Egyptian ground for any Romantic speculative system. For Plato there is nothing outside of the encircling universe, no "outside" properly speaking, and yet God creates this perfect sphere *in someplace*. The displaced voids must also go *somewhere*, and may provide a link to the incomprehensible mystery, the otherness of the *chora*, which as the interval of transformation serves not just as a receptacle, but as a vehicle, a metaphor, for the abyssal *Urgrund*. Like the *chora*, the void has its activating function: when compression occurs, "the contraction caused by the compression thrusts the smaller particles into the interstices of the larger." Thus, constant movement, displacement, and an essential "inequality" exist, generating the perpetual dynamism of "the elements in all time."⁴⁷ The "interstices" which situate void-ness are the intervals, spaces or gaps, musical or verbal pauses, which must be filled up between integers by fractions that resolve any remainders; they are also the receptacle that is the *chora*, which fills itself with impressions in order to "fulfill" the world, as Plato says in his concluding paragraph.⁴⁸ Moreover, the self-same, which is order and the symbolic (or the eternal, the intelligible), God designates as the outer circle of the universe; it orbits in clockwise concentric fashion, and encircles (and therefore contains, provides the rule, rather than enwombs), the counterclockwise inner circle of the different-unruly, which is the sensible world and its heaven.

And this unruly world is brought to bear through the rule of time, which is merely the moving image of eternity, connecting to that eternity through the soul-parts that are "sown in the instruments of time," the earth, moon, and other planets.⁴⁹ The past, as Critias's anecdote which begins the *Timaeus* explains, is itself unruly, open to forgetting, loss, and the necessity to begin again. The past is only a reservoir for intelligible wisdom if it has been recorded. Thus, Critias's anecdotal history, or rather Plato's, begins with the Egyptians and the loss of Atlantis. Atlantis is significant in the story as an emblem of resistance, of unruly aggression, which is lost in the universal history of cosmic intelligibility, remembered only by Egyptian priests but forgotten by the Greeks themselves, near-victims of the Atlanteans. Critias gives us an account of Egypt and its chroniclers that stems from the end of dynastic Egypt; its priests resemble the mythmakers and fabricators of Herodotus's Egyptian travelogue rather than those of a truly prior Egypt, which unlike Atlantis was already lost to memory by Plato's time. Derrida makes much of this Egyptian origin story, which he associates with Marx's "Egyptian model" for his master-slave dialectic. But Derrida misreads Egyptian history here, mistaking the "temple archives" by which the Saitic priest teaches Solon, which were stored on the temple bookshelf (as it was termed), for "writing on the walls of temples."⁵⁰ The Greeks, an oral culture, have deprived themselves of their own history and thus rely on myths that make them forget their political heritage based on war with the Atlanteans.⁵¹ Egypt is thus, for Plato and for Derrida, the place of preinscription.

"In the Egyptian Delta," Critias explains, lies "the district of Sais" as well as its great city; its cult deity is "Neith" (Nephthys, sister of Isis and Osiris, guardian of Osiris; Saïs is his supposed mortuary site). In this account Neith is the patroness of Saïs rather than Isis, and "is asserted by them [Saïs citizens] to be the same whom the Hellenes call Athena" for they share the same attributes of wisdom and protection.⁵² Derrida reads this Egyptian preinscription as a Platonic entanglement in *mythos*: reading Saïs as Ancient Egypt in general, Derrida describes the reflexive relation between orality and written record as a problem of history. The Saïtic priest informs Solon that Saïs is built on the model of Athens, the perfect city, a difficulty in chronology that Derrida reads as mythic entanglement: "As the myth of its [Athens'] origin, the memory of a city is seen to be entrusted . . . to the writing of the other," as preinscription. "It must thus *be made other* twice over in order to be saved . . . the living memory must be exiled to the graphic vestiges of *another place*."[53] By his reflexive logic Derrida asserts the priority of Egypt as that of the *chora*, the other or nowhere place that is also the third genus, the place in which Platonic philosophy, and thus truth, receives its impressions. From this Egyptian beginning Timaeus can then begin his monologue on the universal history that is Plato's origin story;[54] from the wisdom of Saïs comes the beginning point for early modern and modern thinking about origins, generation, becoming through time, and the fragility of that becoming.

II. DARK CENTERS

For Plato the sensible universe is geometrically reducible to triangles, as the most beautiful form to arise from integers and their intervals, so that even humans reduce to their "primary triangles."[55] Because of this the pyramid as a form has priority: at the end of his lengthy discussion of triangles, Plato writes "both according to strict reason and according to probability . . . the pyramid is the solid which is the original element and seed of fire."[56] Plato's fire, one of the most mobile and dynamic of the four elements, is thus seeded in the pyramid; if the *chora* is seeded in spirit as "the cup" in which the universal soul and the sensible soul were molded, enfolded, and interconnected, the pyramid is the receptacle not of spirit-soul but of fire. Why Plato denies the function of the pyramid as the resting place of the dead body has more to do with Ancient Egypt's own lost history by his day, and with the obvious connection between sun and pyramidal point at high noon (the moment of the sun's most present aspect as fire). But it is the importance of the pyramid's priority, its role in the original, that it finds its place in Hegel's *Aesthetics*: there he aligns the pyramid with the history of spirit as the increasing visibility of the soul in human consciousness and creative expression, than with the primordial quality of fire. And yet fire and spirit are not entirely differentiated in Plato's account, in which both are vitalizing powers necessary for nature's dynamism. It is this dynamism that Hölderlin celebrates in *Hyperion*, whose title also celebrates the sun.[57]

Hegel conceptualizes the importance of the pyramid as both a mortuary space and an expression of spirit. He knew of the pyramid's original purpose although not of the pharaoh's soul or *ka*, the vital spark (relating it to fire), having the ability to leave and return each night to comingle with the deities. And he describes the appearance of Spirit in a form that resembles the Platonic geometry of a triangularized universe in that he views the pyramid as containing crystalized Spirit. His point is that Egyptian architecture captures and reflects an important point in the development of Spirit (much as the pyramid captures and reflects the sun's rays); in the next period of development, Greek art will go further to harmonize the outer appearance of Spirit, but in Egyptian architecture the pyramidal tomb signifies an inability to depict inner-outer correspondences. The tomb contains Spirit, frustrating its own struggle to free itself. As Derrida explicates this concept, using the Antigone section of the *Phenomenology* rather than the *Aesthetics*, he makes it clear that the mortuary space is a creative one:

> Crypt—one would have said, of the transcendental or the repressed, of the unthought or the excluded—that organizes the ground to which it does not belong. What speculative dialectics means (to say) is that the crypt can still be incorporated into the system. The transcendental or the repressed, the unthought or the excluded must be assimilated by the corpus, interiorized as moments, idealized in the very negativity of their labor. The stop, the arrest, forms only a stasis in the introjection of the spirit.[58]

Hegel would have partly derived the Greek coincidental harmony of inner and outer from Johann Joachim Winckelmann's influential theory of Classical art, in *The History of Art in Antiquity* (1764). But Plato's concentric circles of outer-self-same and inner-different-other, inextricably bound together through the enfolded soul as the reflexive X bends around to encircle itself, also provide a precedent for understanding Hellenistic expressive art as coincidental harmonies of inner and outer. Plato's circles are encircling; the *chora*'s receptive principle, which is its enwombing, ensures that outer and inner forms will bear resemblance. Plato's circles have everything to do with Bruno's "Egyptian" memory wheels, in which forgetting is eradicated so that human oblivion (the obliviousness to all priors in the ruins of time) is transcended. In breaking himself free, through his concentric circles of universal symbols resonant with eternal wisdom and spirit presence, Bruno transcends the death-driven temporality of human consciousness, thus making himself an equal with the Egypto-Grecian gods, who he believes to be the truly divine entities prior to the Judeo-Christian God.

Boehme, although fascinated by the circular, was more drawn to the doubles and triples of Plato's integer sequences; for him, the universe is constructed of dyadic oppositions (good and evil foremost) and threefold models (father, holy ghost, and their mean as Christ—Devil being principal among these). But in order to make his threefold worlds comprehensibly interrelated, Boehme deploys a triadic system in which the light of love and the darkness of evil or resistance provide the opposition and its resolution in dialectical scales that preview Hegel's dialectical schema of an ongoing self-identical | negation | self-realization dynamic (commonly referred to as the thesis-antithesis-synthesis sequence). Boehme's influence on the German Romantics was widespread, although most followed Goethe in registering discomfort with any association with the writings of a magus. But for Schelling it is Boehme's dyadic oppositions, traceable back to Plato's concentric circles, which provide the model for a dynamic universal history as recalled from the beginning point of origin. Schelling's center of light and center of darkness structures this history, emerging from the deterministic good-evil dyad for a fuller, or perhaps more Platonic expression, while the rotary motion of *Ages of the World* (1811–1815) generatively plays the triadic scales of becoming so imperative to Boehme's mysticism. The first triad of Boehme's system as given in the *Mysterium Magnum* (1623) is "the wheel of anguish," consisting of a sour/negative force, a sweet/positive force, and a bitter compromise that make sensible the anguish of God's trinity of conflict. This is the triad of the unmanifest God (God-in-Himself), the 'birth of God' as the living God, and the birth of life itself. This triad founds the second triad of vital heat giving way to the heat of love, tone (love's seeking, the quest for harmony), and body (love manifest to itself). Both triads put together result in the seven source spirits that God holds in potential as *Ungrund*.[59] Schelling avoids the yes-no, presence-void logic of a dyadic structure by replacing a good-evil construct with Bruno's model of light and dark. It is important for Schelling that in Bruno's model darkness itself is the light, as Isis says in Bruno's *Spaccio della bestia trionfante*, but as she explains, only if one has the knowledge and wisdom to see it. The formative concept that permits Schelling's substitution, Derrida argues, is the *chora*, which "might perhaps" (because for Plato it is unintelligible) "derive from that 'logic other than the logic of the *logos*,'" or the symbolic.[60] The question of the *chora*'s role in creation lies in whether she creates originally or by replication: is she the vessel of ideation (merely translating the idea into form) or is spontaneity also part of her capaciousness? Is there an origin story to be told here?

In David L. Clark's reading of both *Ages of the World* and the *Freedom* essay, Schelling has already brought into question the problem of origin. "The origin is always already derivative," he notes.[61] Or rather, the origin contains at its heart its own supplement; that is, the dyad can never, as in Boehme, resolve into Platonic unity, into the "one" that starts off all integer sequences or that reduces in its fullness to the one God and the one heaven, which is Plato ends the *Timaeus*. The one simply contains its opposite just as, and Plato knew this too, the concentric outer circle contains the othering difference of the resistant inner circle. But as Clark points out, for Derrida the one does not simply contain its other, its supplement; the other is "en-crypted" much in the way that Hegel envisages the crystallizes Spirit in the pyramid, as "an inside heterogeneous to the inside of the Self . . . can only maintain in a state of repetition the moral conflict it is impotent to resolve."[62] To be "encrypted" is not just entombed or encoded—that is, not just contained or made replete with symbolic power—but the repetition at the heart of encryption, which reduces difference to a self-same semblance of unity, stamping a code on self-difference, turns the unruly into the ruled. Jan Assmann's theory of "presentification," so essential to cultural memory, helps explain this repetition: presentification is the combination of repetition and representation common to all ritual that ensures presence of Being.[63] Egyptian ritual, in other words, is presentification itself—the bringing into presence of what is ritually knowable—within the western cultural memory.

Schelling rises above the encrypting, crystallizing impulse of repetition by referring to a cyclicity of ground and existence: there is "no first and last, since everything mutually implies everything else, nothing being the 'other' and yet no being being without the other." Thus, "God contains within himself the inner ground of his existence" yet "God is prior to [his] ground" which requires his existence in order to exist itself.[64] Still, encryption as the problematic underlying entombment and priority becomes in Schelling's schema "God's dark ground," the dark center within God himself, which for Schelling means that "God others himself."[65] Thus, Clark explains, "God's being is primordially a conflictual site—turned inside out, as it were—that is constituted rather than compromised by otherness."[66] Encryption then as constitution, as Plato's generative interval, as the *chora*'s flexing of the X into the encirclement of being and universal nature.

The "turned inside out" of Clark's phrase is suggestive of the *chora*'s capacity for reflexive encirclement, enwombment, of the other place that exists within the female, an elsewhere that both preexists and posits the fetus, postexists and deposits it. Within the folds of that other place, the new being joins as one with the prior being, its primordial ground (in Boehme's and Schelling's terminology its *Urgrund*), to which it can never recur once identity is voiced. That proclamation, which occurs within the new being after the time of enfolding and depositing, who enfolds and deposits identity within itself as an always recurrent allusion to the beforeness of the other place. And because beforeness requires that its status be substantiated by an afterness, the beforeness of enwombment requires the afterness of entombment. The tomb can never *be* the womb and yet repeats its ontological otherness, its presentification (representation + repetition) as a religious rite. Because religious rituals transmit knowledge and conserve wisdom, the womb/tomb figuration that configures human self-identity also configures human knowledge of both the Real and of existence. The womb/tomb figures the "en-crypted" thing that lies at the heart of the mystery of the Real. Thus, the Real/*physis* distinction rests on an involution, a deep folding of ground and existence; these are not separate. To attribute the origin—or rather, the original—of that configuration as God's self-difference, his enfolding of otherness in order to know himself, is to understand origin as belonging to human knowledge rather than to that which is prior. Clark carefully unwinds Schelling's account in the *Freedom* essay to show that God's self-identity could not come before the ground of his knowing; he was not always already self-formed but differentiated himself from what was prior.

That prior, a thoroughly entangled relationality between the *Urgrund* of primordial ground and the *Ungrund* of the abyss, as Schelling (following Boehme) denominates it, becomes the elsewhere of cosmic mystery. Out of it—the knotted and unraveling circuit of *Urgrund* and *Ungrund*—comes life itself. This circuit functions, in Schelling's account and somewhat (echoing Plato) to his dismay, like the womb's dark knowing. Dark because secreted, not because in darkness' inevitable patriarchal construction, it is evil, unavailable to light, or fatal; dark because elsewhere, unavailable to the limited comprehension of existent life. The womb is the place of love, of maternal generosity, of the eternal yes. Only once the new being has divorced himself from coidentity, from the self-same of the mother-infant, during Lacan's Mirror Stage can he, the new ego, learn of the limitless "no" of the Symbolic/logocentric regime. It is at that moment that the "no!" uttered by the young language-learner receives its reply of the "NO!" of the father's law that darkness becomes defined as evil, as frightening, as unknowable, as fatal. In this redefinition of the beforeness that was dark into a haunting specter of potential harm, Schelling sees the moment at which human freedom is born; one can choose the light or the dark, it is not preordained. In that moment, or in any recurrence to that moment thereafter, one can choose the regime of the father or that of the mother. The regime of the father, constituted by the proclamations of the Law and its institutions, contests the viability of the regime of the mother, rendered invisible by the father's panoptic sightedness. According to this contestation, reverting to the maternal regime is a "descent," a devolution; a descent into madness, a death-in-life, an entombment. Madness is best defined as illegibility, as that which is incomprehensible; it closely resembles babble. I follow Julia Kristeva's theory of poetic language here to connect the babble of the mad with the babble of the prelingual baby. Babble belongs to the Semiotic, Kristeva theorizes, which is the place of poetic language, the wellspring of imagination and artistry which lies outside the domain of the Symbolic/logocentric.

Madness, as Boehme and Bruno practiced it, opens a space then for going over, going beyond limits. To be "Egyptianized" in Bruno's sense, but this applies to Boehme's Hermetic logic as well, is to be slightly mad—even more than it is heretical. It is to locate freedom as an archaic ground, as that which is without/beyond the logic of centeredness. When Schelling explains human freedom as resulting not from the traditional understanding of difference as evil and chaos, but rather defines identity as "an opposition between the 'light center' and 'dark center,'" as "interdependent contraries," he opens a space for the void which Clark defines as "lack and nonbeing."[67] The conception of centers, which Schelling borrows from Boehme, provides a motor for a cyclicity between the two places. The cyclicity, which in *Ages of the World*, is less a circuit than a rotary movement between the push-pull, gift and retraction, of love and ego (of mother and father?) that builds worlds. Existent human life and self-identity, along with its involuted self-depositing of self-identity and therefore of self-difference, not only repeats in rotary form the individual's relation to the maternal semiotic and the patriarchal Symbolic regimes. Lacan theorizes the Symbolic/logocentric regime as all that we *can* know.

It might be better to say, in the face of Hermetic wisdom, Boehme's mysticism, Bruno's wheels, even Plato's cosmology, that the Symbolic regime as the fiction we concur in believing, that this is the mythos we birth ourselves into on learning language. Its fictionality is the only way the human mind can exist in the face of the threatening Real; appearance is so much more bearable than its alternative, as Kant recognizes in refusing to speculate beyond the empirically knowable. Haunted as we are, as in Freud's uncanny, by a sense of the Real, we do not forget that we cannot remember what came before. We cannot remember the preexistent abyss of the *Ungrund* just as we cannot remember, because we have no determinate words for it, the state of enwombment, of the fetal. But always, humankind has been haunted by an almost-memory of the safety and beauty of the womb's love. Schelling acknowledges this haunting when he attributes to the *Urgrund* a feminine quality, yet he is scandalized by that gendering, unwilling to allow that God could enfold in himself, or posit himself from, the feminine. Yet the feminine dark center is absolute in its necessity for identity: as Clark puts it, "But as the essential pole within the ontological structure of God, the dark center is more primordially the necessary medium in which the light of his determinate being eternally comes into appearance."[68]

Because the feminine dark center is always already present, and knowledge is always already belated because it comes after, all that can be ascertained about the presentness of the dark center and its absolute priority is that its relation to the light center, God's "doubled ontological structure," and thus the relation of ground to existence, is dialogical.[69] Schelling's grammatological understanding of God's duality stutters, however, as he moves from the *Freedom* essay to *The Ages of the World*, from a conjunction or joint in God's identity. That is, in the *Freedom* essay there is still the problematic of ground | existence, rather than the circuit or cyclicity of ground | existence that structures the creation myth of *Ages of the World*. This suggests a still tendered adherence to hierarchical thinking of unruly | rule wherein Schelling suggests that the light orders the darkness: "it seems as though what had initially been unruly had been brought to order. This is the incomprehensible ground of reality of all things, the *irreducible remainder* which cannot be resolved into reason by the greatest exertion but always remains in the depths."[70] I will return to the problem of the irreducible remainder, but for the moment want to pursue the continuity that does exist between the *Freedom* essay and *The Ages of the World*, which is the dialogical rather than Hegelian, dialectical nature of the relation between the two centers of dark and light. Such dialogism—between two different ways of knowing, between alterity and identity, unknowability and knowability—whether it depends on a rule (the rule of the " | " relation) or a less regulated intercourse (the realm of love and a respondent desire)—opens up the possibility that the relation between the semiotic and the Symbolic/logocentric is not unidirectional, and that any resistance to the linear move from babble to speech does not necessarily result in madness or the return to babble and the pre-*logos*. The suggestion of a dialogical relation explains the poetical nature of Schelling's philosophical accounts: it is in poetic language that the remainder, that which lies outside of the Symbolic's logocentric control, speaks itself and speaks for itself.

III. NEGATIVE THEOLOGY

I briefly described in chapter 1 Bruno's memory wheels as interlocking systems of cosmic and terrestrial knowledges that are "Egyptianized" through the use of Egyptian symbols for deities and hieroglyphs as known through Hellenic and Roman authors and obelisks. These incredibly intricate wheels diagram an imaginary, a "place" in which ritualistic formulae speak a going forward, a way to transcend the normal logic of place and order. The various wheels use more than mnemonics; they inscribed powerful symbols drawn from the scripts of the living word such as Hebrew and Greek, Greco-Egyptian astrological symbols of divine power, and representations of Isis or universal nature. These symbols of Bruno's "Egyptianism," relating to each other via circles and circulations that look both Platonic and Egyptian, allow the user to mentally implant nature's animate and inanimate categorical plentitude so that the memory is cognate with the real, the intelligible eternal. Bruno's wheels are meant to function as an entangled motor for self-illumination and self-divination, allowing the mystic to disinter himself from the static placement of a geocentric and Pythagorean system of cosmic spheres and of armature. The free movement thus enabled means the mystic is no longer tied to the ground, capable not of transcendence but of enlightenment: cosmic knowledge within the terrestrial framework as a commingling of Plato's outer-ideal and inner-real circles. There is no need for the abyss of unknowing, for the mystery's interval or *chora* is accessible through the re-membering of such in-forming. Isis is the guide of knowledge and wisdom here rather than the placental mother. Both Boehme and Meister Eckhart envision a similar freedom, although not with Bruno's degree of self-authorizing that posits a real, not merely ideal, immortality of self.

The magus and the mystic share a skepticism of the Christian God as orthodoxly conceived. They are invested in the priority of the *chora*, that which receives intelligibility and renders it in sensible form. The concept in its traditional formulation makes no sense to them and they question its grounds. Derrida refers to the mystic's alternative vision as resembling apophatic discourse, which goes toward the absolute Other by "taking on a negative or interrogative form" that begins by declaring that Other both "one thing and its contrary, God that is without being or God that (is) beyond being."[71] Negative theology, or the *via negativa*, the way of denial or the way of speech, was theologized by John Scottus from his translation of the Greek philosopher Pseudo Dionysus. It appears in Plato's teachings, Neoplatonism (which focuses on the One, especially in the writings of Proclus), gnostic and other early Christian writers, and the Egyptian writer Philo of Alexandria. Apophatic or negative theology has affinities with mysticism, whose main proponent here is Meister Eckhart; mysticism seeks the perception of God beyond perception, beyond being, and so again, beyond knowing. Both theologies approach the ultimate unknowable as that which can be known only through the pursuit of unknowability.[72] Derrida's explanation of negative theology can be traced back to his important work on *différance*, a term that designates "a constitutive, productive, and originary causality, the process of scission and division."[73] Différance is the terrestrial method by which the One becomes the many: parthenogenesis. Perhaps mystics have been at once revered and condemned through history because "Nothing seems at once more merited and more insignificant, more displaced, more blind than such a trial" of the nothingness of being. But mystics are also inclined toward the poetic because an essential trait of negative theology is "beauty or sublimity";[74] more particularly, because in Greek culture it was the poet's responsibility to discover knowledge of the divine forms, often through epiphany. Beauty or sublimity are not merely degrees of the aesthetic here, they are evidence of a "going further than is reasonably permitted," a "passing to the limit, then crossing a frontier," which is also an essential trait of the apophatic voice.[75] The apophatic asserts through negation, describing God through attributes he (presumably) does not have; tarrying with the negative, the apophatic mystic asserts the unknowable through the knowably erroneous. Its sublimity resides not just in its bold language but in the manner in which it "attest[s] the desire *of* God," a desire that is at once our desire for God, God's desire in us, and God's desire for us. Because a relation to the other precedes any self-relation or self-consciousness, "all reflection is caught in the genealogy of this genitive." Thus, the apophatic also attests to an "essential and thus irreducible originality [that] would have to be recaptured" in philosophy generally[76] (286).

Bruno's wheels, as Schelling realized, are precise attempts to recapture the ground of that irreducible originality, with which through their magic Egyptian priests were supposedly conversant but which Plato's cosmogony mistranslated to drastic effect, as did Christianity's translations of biblical origin. The apophatic mode is a "singular movement" made by the soul, a "conversion of existence that accords itself to, in order to reveal in its very night, the most secret secret," Derrida writes, thinking of Augustine.[77] But Bruno's night, where in the most secreted knowledge also resides, is not the dark center of despair but rather is the maternal, Isis-like, or *choric* darkness of the mystery cults in which knowledge is conveyed and astrological or cosmic movement is clarified. "The possibility of the impossible, of the 'most impossible,' of the more impossible than the most impossible" leads Derrida to decide that "All the apophatic mystics can also be read as powerful discourses . . . on the (impossible) possibility of the proper death of being-there that speaks, and speaks of what carries away . . . its own [being]."[78] The moment of being-there and the death of Being are precisely the point of origin, the state prior to God's gathering himself up and reflecting on himself as being other than the 'before.' It is the moment before self-difference, before God's othering of himself. It is Plato's and the Church's refusal to acknowledge God's self-othering that Bruno decries, believing that this smoothing over of difference locks people into a subjected place (for Plato, its containment by the outer circle of the eternal; for the Church, the casting of internal self-difference as the Evil which is elsewhere).

Just as Bruno's wheels turn in order to free the magus from such placement and rule of the same, Schelling views divinity as returning to God's self. Here there is a connection with Plato's universe that Bruno would also condone as the encircling body that is self-sufficient, self-returning, and possibly nevertheless holding a privileged site of self-othering in the voids which must be constantly eradicated but whose displacement aids the dynamism that stirs life. It is this, rather than the soul's self-returning ("herself turning in herself") which "began a divine beginning of . . . rational life."[79] For Plato the void's radical instability cannot be tolerated, and Bruno's Egyptianism also endorses system over the radicality of nothingness. But the nothing of the void offers Schelling a way to understand remainders, which Plato eradicates by compressing voids and fractioning intervals until everything is mathematically accounted for. Schelling's remainders indicate that the mean is irrelevant since the rotary motor of devolving and evolving desire/love and ego must not be stabilized within any controlling continuum, or else the rotary movement of creative energy would cease.

Derrida offers a way forward, however. In speaking of what one must know even to come to a negative theology, or to judge it as either mad or insightful, he determines the starting point to be a preunderstanding that functions as "a fact . . . in relation to which we would be placed-after," making the readerly encounter with a negative theology through a language easily exhausted because the negativity negates the question of being, and of its verbal inflections. This exhaustion of logocentrism authorizes one to speak of the "apparently elementary" fact of our preunderstanding that is "perhaps indeterminate, obscure or void and yet hardly contestable."[80] A preunderstanding gives us knowledge of the void as a kind of interval, an obscurity, a darkness that is not the dark center so much as a *choric* moment in which things are shaken up, stirred, in which the affections have work to do. For one thing, it is a moment of "crisis," a "forgetting of the full and originary intuition, empty functioning of symbolic language, objectivism" and recognizing that emptiness as "the originary and final necessity of this crisis," recognizing that within the critical interval created by the origin and the end the question of being (*Dasein*), of God's being, and of origin can occur.[81] It is in this interval that works such as *Ages of the World*, Novalis's *Novices of Sais*, and Bruno's *Heroic Frenzies* arise.

The apophatic's negating work requires translation, but one based on love rather than the controlled (mis)translation of the creation in the *Timaeus* and Mosaic tradition. Plato himself speaks of the stirring up that occurs in the *chora*; Derrida likewise speaks of the "stirring up" of Augustine's *Confessions*, which inaugurates a mode of "doing the truth" that is a going forward, an "avowal" as much as a testimony.[82] If for Derrida the crisis indicates a negated moment "or some *khōra* (interval, place, spacing)" that relates the name of God to "the experience of place," the interval is located within as the self's dark center ("this place comes under no geography, geometry, or geophysics. . . . It is found in us"). At the same time, it is also located without as "an emplacement [that] displaces and disorganizes" what we thought we knew.[83] This suture of God to both an internal and a displacing place is the same that Freud identified in *Moses and Monotheism* as the always elsewhere of Judaic identity after Moses, which demarcates Egypt as that which is prior, as the elsewhere of any place. If for Plato the stirring up is the *chora*'s maternal love, and for Augustine it redeems spiritual crisis by invoking brotherly love, then (contra Freud and to an extent Derrida) crisis has been translated into potentiality. For Schelling crisis is both the negating withdrawal and positing love as the giving forth, the declarative power of God's "yes."

In Egyptian mythology this is the contest between Rā ("the self-created" whose two eyes are the sun and the moon)[84] and Isis and between Isis and Set (or Typhon), the yes-no that characterizes all creation, and that installs and redeems death. The apophatic questions the idea that God might reside *only* in the holding back, the egoistic "no" of God's self-return *or* in the positivity of his "yes"; negative theology opens the possibility that God might be of a doubled nature that is both/and. To entertain the possibility is to translate with love; it is to understand poetic language as the figurative potentiality for perceiving the irreducible and the singular. As Plutarch tells Clea, priestess to Isis and Apollo Delphicus, "the desire of truth, especially in what relates to the Gods, is a sort of grasping after divinity."[85] Although Plutarch believes that "reason" will lead to true knowledge, his text recites myths that recount an ancient, foundational magic requiring words of power, that is, the poetic. The poetic language of the apophatic, as evidenced in Bruno's *Heroic Frenzies* and Schelling's *Ages of the World*, illustrates the ritual magic of incantation and generative (re)presentation. The only thing that opposes "complete formalization," Derrida notes, is poetics.[86] As Kristeva's interventions in theories of symbolic language posit, poetry's oppositional power is to disrupt and disturb the symbolic forces of placement, order, and rule with the irruptive semiotic music of the *chora* and the mother. To her unpacking of the *chora*'s powerful agency I would add Nature, Isis, and all that opposes the Christian God, patriarchal system, and the erasure of the remainder.

In the Egyptian myths of Isis, the importance of the name founds her protective power against the darkness that threatens the light, especially the light of the sun and therefore of life itself. This myth in Plutarch's account is synthetic, condensing ancient and Hellenic traditions, but his account also helps to understand Isis's identity as universal nature hidden by the veil of mystery—the same understanding in play during the eighteenth-century revival of Hermetic thought, and apparent in works like Erasmus Darwin's *Temple of Nature*. As we saw early in this chapter, Plutarch characterizes Egyptian creationism as additive; this contrast to Plato's divisive version supplies an alternative principle for Schelling's exploration of his differences with Fichte in the natural and divine principles of things. But Plutarch mistakes Egyptian magic, something Bruno does not do; Bruno understands that the Egyptian principle is both additive and divisive, both/and. In the legend of Rā and Isis as transcribed in the Turin manuscript (one of the papyrus manuscripts that early nineteenth-century linguists used as a base text for their deciphering attempts) what Thoth enables Isis to steal from Rā is the sacred name "Horus the Elder," Rā's name at high noon. This is the moment of presentness when no shadow is cast, when pyramid and obelisk peaks connect directly with the sun's rays: the god is there in his being. Her power, which comes from dividing Rā off from himself, allows her to multiply other things in the most fundamental way. After Osiris has been slain by Set/Typhon, Isis uses her magic to impregnate herself upon her dead husband-brother, her self-return producing by the additive principle their son, Horus. By her enwombment of the intelligible the outside becomes inside, enfolded. Through the magic of repetition and difference, resurrection becomes a return onto itself in the most generative sense as an enfolding: Isis's doubling produces Horus who is himself a doubled entity (Rā/Horus the Elder, and Horus as Isis's son). Later connected with the Alexandrian Harpocrates, Horus will be associated with the Ptolemaic cult of Serapis, Isis's new Hellenized spouse (a version of Rā-Zeus) and their son, Harpocrates (the god of silence and the new version of the child-god Horus). Rā himself will retain a portion of his ancient identity in the new cult of Rā-Harmachis, centered on the Great Sphinx, which arose concomitantly with the renewed interest in the cult of the Apis bull that spread during the Hellenic period along with the cult of Isis. Isis's proven ability to multiply herself is reflected in the spread of her regenerated identity during the Ptolemaic period throughout the Greco-Roman world.

IV. SPIRIT LOVE

Yet the battle between Rā, who withholds his name, and Isis, who engenders (who loves) through the magic of that sacred name, is never over. The no-yes of this archaic struggle for a divisive or an additive universal principle is also the struggle between the silence that lies behind Derrida's apophatic voicing of the voiceless name versus Kristeva's semiotic *chora* as a heterogeneity that breaks up all silencings and erasures. It is also the struggle between light and dark with each being differentially defined. Light can be the life-giving sun or the love that steals the sun's name; either way light and/as fire is associated with sacred wisdom and the good. Darkness is either/and the denial of the name, a withholding or withdrawal, or it is mystery which holds a taint of the forbidden and thus the possibility of evil. For Schelling, darkness holds not that possibility, which was so real for Boehme although not for Bruno, but rather the possibility of freedom. But how does freedom begin in the withholding of the name, this withdrawal that is not the true secret of the night but the paternal prohibition, the "no" of the Father's law?

In "Post-Scriptum" Derrida speculates on the freeing potential of the poetic to transgress the limits of such withdrawal. He declares that God's name "names nothing that might hold . . . even a divinity," it "'is' the name of this bottomless collapse."[87] But that is the collapse of theology and ontology both, a collapse of ground; what lies elsewhere—the Egypt of the presumed ground—is the going forward that is the "bold language" not just of the apophatic voice but also of the mystic. For Bruno and Meister Eckhart, bold language is the poetic, which is the mode of going forward or beyond; it is how to engage dark centering with the irruptive power of light. The poetic is the same as magical incantation, of necessary repetition that is invocation. One of the magical formulae of Egyptian magic is "Rā triumphs over Āpep. Taste thou death, Āpep," with a pause between the two phrases and the entire line repeated four times (once for each of the gods of the cardinal points).[88] Bruno's works on magic similarly orient the reader so that each symbolic word matches a material object or an ordinal as the incantation is repeated. The incantatory reenacts the originary moment before the division into light and dark centers, and before the division of the intelligible from the sensible. In the effort to reestablish communications between them, the poetic act as incantation moves forward, exceeds a limit set on language, recurs to the semiotic of babble and repeated nonsensical phrases and sounds. Possibly it looks like madness, like what Ariosto and Bruno both term heroic frenzy, love madness.[89]

And yet it was in Bruno's works of heroical frenzy that Schelling found an inspiration for thinking about moving beyond the critical philosophy of Kant, and that made him work through his own "identity philosophy" in 1801–1802 with the *Bruno, or On the Natural and the Divine Principle of Things*. In conceiving his *Bruno* as a true dialogical conversation, not the disguised monologues in Plato's 'dialogues,' Schelling draws directly on Bruno's multiply voiced works to illustrate how a philosophy of nature could coexist with Kantian Idealism; how realism and idealism could cohere. One way of understanding his project is to say that Schelling attempts to Egyptianize himself, not by going mad (as Hölderlin did in his turn to the antique for identity), but as a way to reconcile Hermeticism with Platonism: Isis as *Naturphilosophie* without destroying the Kantian system, unknowability in balance with knowability. Although Schelling's later *Philosophy of Mythology* (1842) appears to systematize, to be a *Wissenschaft*, it adheres to an understanding of mythos as a form of knowing. Schelling seems to understand just how much the *Timaeus* grounds Platonic reason in myth and mythopoetics.

Bruno's magical incantation, and the poetic mode of his *Heroic Frenzies*, encodes the mode of difference as well as resistance to limit. In activating the differential power of the semiotic, of the womb-matrix and its 'stirring up' as Plato puts it, and its choric generation, Bruno takes the madness of poetic transgression, of the going beyond, to its limits. Although the *Heroic Frenzies* is aimed at the sun, at a burning up in the light-fire (literalized in his own death at the pyre), Bruno's magic is based more on the circular or reflective logic of Hermetic cosmology than of Plato's circles. His memory wheels are not the concentric, compressive circles of Plato's creationist myth, but rather something very like the rotary motions and in-forming/infolding of Schelling's *Ages of the World*. The power of this generative matrix of in-forming and information as a way of understanding a magic that is entwined with mysticism was a powerful concept for the Romantics. Like Volney's

Ruins, it drew out Napoleon's Romanticism to such an extent that his reason was at times overwhelmed by a preference for archaic magic. From 1801 when one of his soldiers discovered a papyrus manuscript in an ancient royal tomb until his defeat at the Battle of Leipzig, a manuscript that came to be known as Napoleon's *Oraculum*, or *The Book of Fate* ruled Napoleon's most important decisions. It was also known as *Napoleon's Oraculum and Dreambook* and was widely published after he left it behind at Leipzig; the connection between it and Napoleon was overdetermined by Napoleon's aspiration to be another Alexander the Great.

Napoleon would have felt the need of the *Oraculum*'s archaic ground and such an archaic aid: the early part of his Egyptian Campaign was a foreshadowing of the costs future campaigns would bring (his army's march to Moscow was perhaps Napoleon's version of Alexander's march to India in being the step too far). The military aggression again Egypt was twofold. On the one hand, it was an Enlightenment endeavor in the interests of empire; as the historian Juan Cole notes, the prominent politician Talleyrand had argued for the French Republic's need to replace the colonies lost in the Americas and Caribbean in order to increase its economic base, and now that Napoleon had added the Italian peninsula to France, the previously Venetian- and Balkan-led domination of the Adriatic Sea and Levant coasts were France's to take. The port city of Alexandria offered just such a vantage point for this takeover.[90] The second impetus was to stymy British access to the east, especially to India as one of Britain's most vital sources of wealth. Balanced against these Enlightenment and practical goals was the draw of Egypt itself, both as a gateway to the east and a gateway to the past. However, early in the campaign, Napoleon's troops suffered terribly from hunger and thirst, as well as from exhaustion and the ruthless conditions of heat; in addition, they had to fight the trained military class of the Mamluks.[91] What Napoleon did not anticipate, as Cole points out, is that taking the Mamluk strongholds—especially Cairo—meant unleashing the suppressed native resistance to Ottoman rule; if the Muslim population didn't want French occupiers, the native Egyptians didn't want any occupiers at all. Furthermore, by breaking the governmental structures of the towns, the French unwittingly opened up opportunities for ruthless attacks from Bedouin tribes. If reconstructing Egypt as a colony required Enlightenment practices and policies, wishing for guidance from nonrational sources was an entirely Romantic practice. In this, Napoleon was more than half a Romantic, which accounts for his two pocketbooks: Volney's *Ruins* and the *Oraculum*.

The *Oraculum* records Egyptian magical practices from the later period of Egyptian history, and unlike the priestly magic of the chant to defeat Āpep mentioned above, this magic works by a series of questions and possible answers, that is, as a dialogue, albeit one that works by a game of chance in which the random pattern of dots created each time by the user determines the possibility of response. In combining the logic of numbers (dots) with the logic of response (of the yes, of the giving forth), the Egyptian book of magic reflects the similar conditions of possibility underlying the Egyptian Book of the Dead. An oraculum allows the subject to navigate chance happenings and hard decisions; the Book of the Dead allows the subject to navigate the arduous journey of the underworld, where the dead face the horror of absolute nonbeing, of absolute lack. The ancient problem of lack and nonbeing, concepts that Schelling's *Ages of the World* and *Freedom* essay seek to negotiate, is essential to Egyptian religion as an *Ungrund*, an elsewhere state on which all else is predicated. It is horror of the *Ungrund*, of abyssal nonbeing, that forces Isis to transgress the limits set on all beings by Rā through his withholding of the sacred name even from the other, lesser gods. In her self-transformation, from limited being to preeminent magician, Isis anticipates Bruno's Egyptianism; she provides the *Urgrund* for an Egyptianized, rather than Hermeticized—alchemical and thus scientific, myth of knowing within unknowability.

Like Napoleon, Alexander the Great and his teacher Aristotle were likewise implicated in the imperializing problem of being and nonbeing, of yes and no. Like Napoleon, Alexander had his magic instrument—one provided not by long-dead occupants of a tomb (Napoleon's *Oraculum*) but supposedly given to Alexander by Aristotle himself. The thirteenth-century scholar Abu-Shâker reports that Alexander always carried with him a box of wax figures representing potential military enemies; in light of the increasing superstitious and paranoic nature that infected Alexander on his return to Babylon after the march to India, this account may well be true.[92] He was to recite certain formulae over the box that would innervate his opponents; this magical use of wax figurines is also associated with ancient religious practices in Egypt, including the ritual of invoking divine presence in temple idols and providing the dead with servants in the afterlife. Alexander's box of figures, then, like Napoleon's book of fate, serves both the living and the dead by creating an interested ground that serves to stave off the void and the gap between being and nonbeing, plenitude and lack.

V. MYTHOPOETICS

For Derrida Plato's *chora* is beyond category, it is aporetic; it is so because although it "is alien to the order of the 'paradigm,'" and is invisible, it "'participates' in the intelligible in a troublesome and indeed aporetic way (*aporōtata*, 51b)."[93] The aporetic here is the term Plato used to refer to paradigm and the invisible. Derrida draws on the work of Jean-Pierre Vernant to explore choral mystery as Plato supposes it. Vernant posits the binary *mythos/ logos* as an essential opposition that allows the very unPlatonic question: what lies outside the regularity and the law of *logos* yet does not belong to *mythos*? What then, to gather the threads of preceding sections in this chapter on spirit/God and Isis/magic, of the remainder and the *Ungrund*?

Derrida responds to the Platonic mystery by examining a "third discourse" (adding to the triads generated in the "cosmo-ontologic encyclopedia of the *Timaeus*"[94]) that Plato uses to describe the *chora*'s difference from the intelligible *logos*, the dream. Indeed, it is the connection between mythology and the dream that concerns the Romantics and that organizes some of their most compelling works. Schelling's logic-driven *Philosophy of Mythology* will provide the main points for this section; I will then turn to Novalis's *Novices of Saïs* and Keats's *Lamia* as Egyptianized texts, the first explicitly so and the second implicitly. The imaginative implications of dream vision for the Romantic poetic mode trace back to not just to Old Testament history with its magic and dream visions, but to Plato's *Timaeus*. For it is the *Timaeus* itself that mythically establishes Egypt as the philosophical prior ground, the place where true knowledge, now lost, had been possible.

In the late *Historical-Critical Introduction to the Philosophy of Mythology*, Schelling sets out the real value of myth in relation to science. Although it is not a systematizable subject in the sense of *Wissenschaft*, it is cognizable in terms of its traces. His thinking on the subject begins during what Jeffrey Bernstein has called "the interval" between Schelling's negative and positive philosophy.[95] Schelling's interval, in which publication ceased but he worked on his *Ages of the World* and began lecturing on mythology with an 1815 address *The Deities of Samothrace*, "effectively [began] the work of project of positive philosophy via the project of a philosophy of mythology," according to Jason Wirth.[96] Analyzing the value of mythic systems allows Schelling to correct the problem with Hegel's *Phenomenology of Spirit* and his theory of the graspability of absolute knowledge, which is the problem of history. The past does not teleologically unwind itself according to the concept of the idea, as Hegel claims, but rather—for Schelling, Novalis, and Hölderlin, as well as for Shelley and Keats—it is more asymptomatic, and productive of tension rather than resolution. The past generates only an irreducible inability to know about the future and thus the absolute, but also to know absolutely about pastness, which disappears all too quickly under the erasure of an encroaching present and future. It is related to both the *Urgrund* and to priority, to *Ungrund* not as the origins of the beginning, but in the shared characteristic of all three: their unknowability, their abyssal quality. All three are constituted by an essential break with the *logos*, with God's plan, and with the perfection of the circle of ideal forms, of absolute knowledge through geometric shapes and mathematical principles.

Schelling realizes the value of myth as a different kind of discourse, one that tells an impossible history that treats the *logos* as a matter of speaking rather than a rule of law, a contrary logic that that of reason's high position in Kantian and Hegelian thought. Schelling therefore "begins from the fact of the mythological and attempts to retrieve what is unthought—and in some sense inherently unthinkable—at its ground,"[97] a process Schelling theorizes as a "negative philosophy." Like negative theology, Schelling's "negative philosophy" begins in contrary movement to traditionally conceived metaphysics such as Plato's: just as negative theology works backward through negation, the negative philosophy opposes the "positive" philosophy of dualist thought, which begins with the ground of thought, which is it opposite—being—and then reflects that as having a mind-like structure so that it can be understood through thought. Unlike Hegel's philosophy, which arrives at the absolute by systematically negating all finite things, Schelling's philosophy works to explain how a finite world can exist in the first place; this is a world that cannot be known purely through thought. Further, the absolute also must contain that which cannot even know itself, as in God's faltering coming to self-consciousness which begins with the literal ground of the earth. God is not the all-knowing but unknowable divinity here. The connection of the mythos Schelling thus creates in *Ages of the World* relates in palpable ways to the discourse of dreams of Wirth's analysis but this is less obvious in Schelling's late lectures on mythology. What does correlate in the lectures to both dreamwork and the origin story of *The Ages of the World* is a new interest in origin as heterogeneous according to the varying and often self-revising histories that myths offer up. Heterogeneity as difference that is disruptive to the symbolic order belongs to both the *chora*'s productive semiotic processes and the *thetic* break or gap coupled to the interval. Schelling's first step in the *Mythology* reveals this connection to the poetic and the gap: to understand myth as "poesy," in the sense that it is fictive, has no scientific truth, but also in the sense that it is an alternative, allegorical form of knowing and of history (*Lectures* I–II). In assessing the philosophical "*essence*" of mythology, Schelling aims to establish poetic "representations" as existent "matters of fact" that out-survive "mute monuments (temples)" and "visual works," for "legends and stories . . . in general go beyond historical time."[98] These legends—and here Critias's story of Solon's tutorial by the Egyptian priest is illustrative—contain a "core, the primordial material onto which all of this crystallized, [which] consists of occurrences and events that belong to an entirely different order of things (not only than the historical, but also the human one), the heroes of which are gods," that is, "religiously venerated personalities who form amongst themselves a particular world." This "*polytheistic* moment" is "the *system of the gods.*"[99] In Lecture VI, Schelling queries the moment when monotheism and the belief in a universal God conquers polytheism.[100] But what is more interesting for the present discussion about Lecture VI is that the question of a universal God begins with the principle of original unity, of what was before self-division and the resultant filling in and folding that populates the universe.

Before Schelling can arrive at original unity, he must go "back further, [where] we initially encounter the Egyptians," whose system of deities is "petrified in massive works of architecture and colossal images," where a petrific crystallization is more akin to Hegel's crystallized spirit in the pyramids. However, neither the Egyptians or what Schelling takes to be their predecessors, the Phoenicians and Babylonians, have a mythic *Poesie*, unlike the "psalmlike poetry" of the "old Hebraic one." Nevertheless, this poor comparative between poly- and mono- does not disprove the poetic quality of mythology out of hand.[101] The quote from Hesiod proving that "there is no trace of poetry with them [the Egyptians]" enables Schelling to find poetic *mythos* perfected in the Greeks (Winckelmann's influence still being felt with the younger German Idealists, especially Hölderlin). But significantly, the myth Schelling uses to contemplate origin and original unity is the Greek myth of Io, who maddened by the jealous Hera, rushes forth in a *"crooked course"* eastward, where she finds and marries the Nile. The *"crooked course* [is that] of the deluge gushing forth," which is the Nile's annual deluge: "Io begetting Epaphus (*Occupus*) through the Nile means: via the water the Nile, *occupying* and *flooding the land*, emerges into being."[102] Thus, thanks to the Greeks, the Nile's annual fertilization of the land which allowed civilization such progress is "clothed in such expensive dress" by "the oldest poetic art." What Schelling proves by this comparative myth is that mythopoesis depends on "a contingent origin";[103] it is thus historical in an empirical way, since origin, like history itself, is necessarily contingent and not implicitly emergent or exteriorized.

The contingency of history is encoded in myth; Schelling shows this by deciding in Lecture V, à la Volney's racial theory in *The Ruins*, that "the oldest Egyptian population," the Nubians, "announced through their dark skin simply the mysterious disposition of their own inner selves" and a concomitant "fear that did not leave them; they felt the destruction of the original unity; a destruction that made room for a confusing multiplicity; and that seemed unable to end other than with the loss of all consciousness of unity and thus of everything human."[104] This contingency will allow Lecture VI to examine the question of monotheism and primal unity by showing that polytheism *follows from* originary unity and an all-knowing deity is not the necessary conclusion. This is an argument only made possible via the backward methodology of his philosophy. But what Schelling opens up here is the role of the fear of forgetting in the construction of logocentric historiography; *mythos* preserves what has been forgotten and thus it is the forgotten that philosophy, as in the *Timaeus* and *The Ages of the World*, can resurrect through a poetico-mythico-philosophical approach.

What Schelling's mytho-philosophy provides, despite its Hellenistic history of Ancient Egypt, is a way to come at the problem of time: of the already-prior and the always-elsewhere of the past and pastness. Because inherent in beginning and pastness is the problem of afterness and futurity, thinking about the utopic, primal origin—especially in the Napoleonic aftermath of the failed utopia of the French Revolution—is never a way out of confronting the problem of the real. And it is the all too problematic future that the younger German and British Romantics cast into doubt as a salutary *telos*. Alice Kuzniar argues that the tense Lacan isolates for articulating a traumatic futurity, the future anterior, is requisite for understanding the angst of these writers. It is the tense that will align the real of what has been and is now with the future resolution, and for Novalis and Hölderlin, the awareness of any future *telos* causes an "ironic awareness of nonclosure in language."[105] The dream discourse—and the dreamscape, demarcating the terrain of nonclosure—proves a salutary mode for both writers.

In *The Novices of Saïs* by Friedrich von Hardenberg (Novalis), the poet provides a dream version of what can be termed "magic idealism."[106] In this poetic novel, unfinished at his death, Novalis imagines a present-day Saïs that seems to be situated in Germanic territory rather than the Egyptian Delta; here a teacher instructs his apprentices in Hermetic wisdom (being at one with the natural principle) rather than in Egyptian magic. Thus, the Nature being sought by the novices is Isis herself, who at first seems to be discoverable only by way of an immersion of the self in the otherness of natural objects. Language as *logos* is a hindrance in this quest: "I heard a voice say from afar that the incomprehensible is solely the result of incomprehension, which seeks [only] what it has. . . . We do not understand speech, because speech does not understand itself . . . the true Sanskrit would speak in order to speak."[107] Sanskrit according to Sir William Jones was the originary language, the original precedent and key to universal understanding. If the origin is already redundant, preinscribed, then Sanskrit holds no priority over the language in which the novices of Saïs are taught: both contain revelation. Later travelers who had sought out Saïs to learn from the temple archives relate their discoveries when "they had gone out to seek traces of that lost primaeval race," they "had been lured above all by that sacred language," so that their very names "seemed to be the key to the soul of each thing in nature."[108] But without the key the apprentices must follow the example of their Hermetic teacher, who "knows how to gather together the traits that are scattered everywhere. A unique light is kindled in his eyes when he lays down the sacred rune before us and peers into our eyes to see whether in us the light is risen that makes the figure visible and intelligible."[109] Himself able to read natural objects as symbols, portals to divine presence, the Saïtic teacher can only wait for his novices' enlightenment. One apprentice does understand the integral unity of all things so that "Sometimes the stars were men for him and sometimes men were stars, sometimes the stones were beasts, and the clouds plants," that is, he was "attentive to the connections that are everywhere."[110] This is indeed the Hermetic basis of alchemical art that Bruno understood with his memory wheels, but also of Egyptian magic in which—as Bruno knew—gods were invoked in their statues as living presences.

The integral unity of all things, cosmic and terrestrial, is also the *hen kai pan* that Spinoza found to be implicit in the modifications of the One Substance, the monism that contains and integrates simple differences as "affections," we might say as stirrings of the primal matter, or affections as variations in *choric* desire.[111] The *hen kai pan* references another inscription, the temple admonition not to life the veil of Isis: "I am all that is, all that was, and all that shall be, and no mortal has lifted my veil."[112] Jan Assmann, who asserts that Spinoza *did not* use the phrase *hen kai pan*, attributes tracing the phrase "back to its Egyptian origin" to Cudworth; after him, Berkeley translated the phrase, making *Hen* equal to Osiris and *Pan* to Isis, and viewing the whole *as* an equation, "*Hen to Pan*, 'All *Is* One,' the world *is* God."[113] As Assmann notes, the phrase was resurgent in German Romanticism; it will have provided new meaning in light of the rekindled interest in German Pietism, Boehme, Hermeticism, and Freemasonry. The apprentice narrator is, however, unable to follow in the *hen kai pan* that enlightens his fellow apprentice: he instead follows his teacher's desire (an affection that modifies, leading to the truth by another path) that he go forth: "I, too, then will inscribe my figure, and if according to the inscription, no mortal can lift the veil, we must seek to become immortal; he who does not seek to life it, is no true novice of Saïs."[114]

In his desire to unite inscription with the originary desire to speak keyed into Sanskrit ("the true Sanskrit would speak in order to speak, because speech is its delight and essence," Novalis, *Novices* 5), the narrator desires to reconnect the trace with the manifest, the real with the existent. That is, he desires to "lift the veil" of Isis, but not in the sense of scientists who only "wish to learn this and that about her [Nature]" and do not understand that "cut[ting] into the inner structure and s[eeking] after the relations between its members" kills Nature, "leaving behind only dead, quivering remnants."[115] Science produces a false key, and "It is bombast to speak of one nature," for "The ways of contemplating nature are innumerable";[116] surely they follow modulations in the One Substance, or more correctly, follow the affections. Therefore, it is the fable of another youth, Hyacinth, told in dream-vision mode that produces the enlightenment for which the narrator quests: it enfolds the quest and replaces it. Searching for "the hallowed abode of Isis,"

Hyacinth one day "Amid heavenly scents . . . fell asleep, for only a dream could take him to the holy of holies."[117] After he traverses halls filled with "curious things," like the halls of Sir Hans Sloane's natural history collection, "the last trace of earth vanished as though dissolved in air, and he stood before the heavenly maiden." And yet when Hyacinth "raised the light, simmering veil," it was not Isis who stood before him but his beloved, Rose Petal. This allegory of the flowers, which the novices found illuminating, puts its trust in the inhering of the existent in the ideal.

The centrality of Hyacinth's story to Novalis, the purpose of its dream vision, is that the real—allegorized as "Rose Petal"—is ideal (Isis) all along. Although the teacher's instruction was to find the ideal in the real, the point of this dream is to locate the real in the ideal. Or rather, to discover their integrity through love, the affections, modifications of the One Substance. As Slavoj Žižek notes in *The Abyss of Freedom/Ages of the World*, Schelling's recovery of primal origin clarifies the role of desire in the real-ideal relation. "Jouissance as 'real' is that which resists (symbolic integration): it is dense and impenetrable," or rather it is mysterious and unknowable, as is Isis.[118] Desire, jouissance, should not be equated with love or the modifying affections however. "[T]he intensity of the real of *jouissance*" is an "encounter of the real [that] is always traumatic . . . I cannot simply integrate it into my universe, there is always a gap separating me from it."[119] The dream, the third discourse that Derrida isolates in the *Timaeus*, the discourse that can ruminate on the *chora*'s mystery and tackle the aporetic, is precisely the mode Novalis choses in order to find Isis in the real beloved.

To be Egyptianized, as Bruno's and Boehme's works both illustrate, is to be slightly mad. The madness of the semiotic, of the womb-matrix is the creativity of *choric* generation where the stirring and shaking have not yet settled out into a distinct genetics. To be Egyptianized is to use category errors productively, as when Boehme collapses the eternity-time distinctions in *The Aurora*: it is to ignore category, as when the mad Hölderlin addresses his visitors as "Your Majesty." This is a slight revision of allegory, a twist of the laws, so that Hyperion resides in present-day Greece and devotes his old age to Greek Independence. Allegory is a kind of madness, a stirring up and an epigenetics of the *chora*'s intermediation. They are repeated and half-remembered in the frenzied dances and rituals of the mystery cults, as in the Dionysian frenzies, but also an important aspect of the epiphanic illumination that occurs at the end of the *Corpus Hermetica* as the novice achieves his own transfiguration. Bruno's *Heroic Frenzies* uses the sonnet form for the same achievement, in order to take the madness of impassioned poetry best exemplified in Tasso's epics of love and heroic struggle and transform love-madness into self-illumination. The frenzy allows worshipper and magus alike to transcend rational categories that bind subjects into object-oriented understandings of the world; it allows a sacred escalation beyond reason into subject-subject understandings where the gap between subject and object is an interval that reveals itself to be the site of plentitude, of spirit. Without such frenzied illumination, the subject-object gap of the sensible world, where the intelligible is not manifest, appears as the gap Freud views as the site of desire, Derrida inflects with violence, and Žižek with the "slight" obscenity of an almost tangible, dreadful real.

How, then, does Novalis assert the real (Isis as universal Nature), as not only ideal beauty but real beauty in his fable of Hyacinth? The apprentice-narrator does not go mad; indeed, his dream-quest is a quiet search for the veil that Bruno's magic lifts at will, and without science's destructive effect. Kuzniar claims that the younger German Romantics (and the same can be applied to second-generation British Romantics, as we will see with *Lamia*) rejected the key to all knowledge as well as the key to all language: rather, their awareness of the nonclosure—and I would add, nondisclosure—in language "gives rise to pluralized, intermittent teloi."[120] Indeed, Novalis "defers the synthetic, third stage" the goal of Hegel's dialectic and the end-goal of absolute knowledge in the Hegelian sense as well as the Brunonian-Hermetic sense. And "poetic utterance—like time—is caught in a state of constant, unpredictable flux and transition."[121] Thus, the awareness of nonclosure, and so of the unpredictability of the present and of futurity itself, turns the poetic vehicle back on itself, returning to its dark center for priority (Isis in the temple), a prior ground or *Urgrund* of dream states and fables, and of an enlightenment about the real (Isis is Rose Petal). For Novalis, 'real' enlightenment does not dissolve into an encounter with the ugly, as Žižek asserts in his study on *The Ages of the World*, for Rose Petal is as beautiful as before. The referential haunting of the subject-object dyad is strikingly absent here though it does emerge in the *Timaeus* as the disgusting creatures of the sea (a disgust shared, Plutarch believed, by Egyptian priests who do not eat fish) in order to remember Typhon's (Set's) eternal attempts to destroy Rā. Set is the serpent who eats the sun, and his murder of both Osiris and the child Horus illustrates his destructive, evil power. But Isis resurrected both her husband and later her son from the dead; her restorative magic inserts itself in the place of the real (Set-Typhon as chaos) as well as of evil (Set as the dark power of ignorance and destructive ego).

Keats, however, fully embraced the implications of the fish-serpent Typhon, as well as "pluralized, intermittent teloi," the error of equating the real with evil, and the heterogeneity of the mythic in his Egyptianized poem *Lamia*. The dream, however allegorized and prettified in *The Novices*, finds a different, supplemental valence in Keats's *Lamia*. Both works are romances, the literary mode fully open to the possibility of dreamscapes, and as Spenser's *Faerie Queene* demonstrates, the romance explores the heterogeneity of the intersubjective encounter by pitting the real as both horrible and a mirage (Duessa, the hideous serpent-witch, appears as Una) that can (like the veil of Isis) be lifted. The trauma of encountering the real is the encounter with the ugly, Žižek argues, and "there is something at least minimally obscene about it."[122] The problematic of the ugly is that it locates the real; it is precisely not the ideal. However, in situating the real it exposes the gap between real and ideal, and this "is what 'intersubjectivity' is actually about."[123] Kristeva theorizes the problematic of the ugly and its relation to horror differently, as the objectification of the womb-matrix; the female interior (the real that cannot be unveiled) is transfigured into abjection.[124] Through what is in fact a disfiguration, the womb-matrix is associated with the vulvular, in which enfolding and in-forming hide a mystery that contains the horrible. Keats assimilates the abjected vulva, the horror of an uncertain *telos* and the ironic awareness of nonclosure and nondisclosure, to the beautiful ideal. In his Lamia both real and ideal reside uncertainly in the same body:[125] Lamia's serpent coils are both inherently beautiful ("of dazzling hue." I. 47) and transgressively so (she is "palpitating," "Striped like a zebra, freckled like a pard," I. 49). Her dazzling body recalls the vale in which Hyacinth falls into his dream in *Novices* (its flowers and heavenly scents), "this abode of the eternal seasons" as well as the Medusa's serpentine horror.[126] Lamia has a Saïtic priority, an Isis status. Like Isis, who learns magic with the aid of Thoth-Hermes in order to rejoin her husband Osiris, Lamia (herself possessing a "Circean head," I. 115) is aided by Hermes to bodily change herself into a woman in order to reunite with Lycius.

Most importantly, when Hermes chances on Lamia her serpentine coils are "cirque-couchant" so that she is "a Gordian shape of dazzling hue" (I. 46–47). The Gordian knot, famously entangled and emblematic of the irresolvable mathematical or philosophical problem, was just as famously severed by Alexander the Great with a single sword stroke. Severed, the serpent's swaying hypnotic motion: Lamia is "palpitating," its horrific mystery rendered ineffective, captive to the Aristotelian categories of a deciphered nature. Lamia's transformation from serpent with female features (she has teeth like pearls) to a woman is associated with severing; she must be divided from herself. Such self-alienation as disfigurement (defiguring her) causes inestimable pain to the objectified subject. Pain (expressed as Lamia's uncontrollable "fearful sobs" during her transfiguration, I. 138), particularly in the female subject-object, is evidence of a self-differentiation rather than an intersubjectivity. It is one that contrasts sharply with both the enlightenment of absolute knowledge and the rejection of the ugly, abjected thing. It assimilates to Schelling's distressed God rather than the normalized pleasure-pain dynamic of Plato's *chora*. By contrast, the intersubjectivity enjoyed by Lycius and Lamia produces a conjoined space—a womb/home—in which her luxury-filled palace is built and their dazzling dream life coils in self-returning fashion, "couchant" and "enthroned" (I. 46, II. 17). However, this dream life continues to exude sighs and tremblings: it is filled with what David Krell calls "the more languid moments of love and desire . . . *languor* and *languishment*," that is, a melancholic attempt to block time, and an awareness of the temporal becoming in which polar oppositions necessarily reproduce.[127]

The intersubjectivity between Lamia and Lycius, which takes place in both Žižek's subject-object gap and in an enwombed dreamspace of veiled appearance, is enabled not by Lamia's own magic so much as by her own painful transfiguration. That refiguring, as much as the circuit of intersubjectivity (which for Schelling's God enforces self-return through self-difference), allows the poem itself to query the severing of Lamia's inner serpent and its Gordian knot. This categorical rejection of Lamia's priority, her "elfin" status (I. 147), is accomplished by the coldly rational philosopher Old Apollonius. He interprets her, making her veiled Saïtic appearance legible, as abject and horrific by placing her in the category of Set-Typhon, the destructive serpent who eats the sun, rather than as an embodied form of Hermes's "Caducean . . . serpent rod" with which the poem associates her (I. 133, 89). This rod of healing is not Plato's rod of stability in the *Timaeus*, but a transformative, magic tool. Apollonius makes Lamia "shudder" on first sight (I. 369), a painful version of her earlier serpentine palpitation, implying disaffection and the very opposite of *choric* "stirring up." Keats's *Lamia* asks: who is the true serpent, and who is evil in the poem, Lamia or Apollonius? The light of reason very possibility aligns with evil in this romance of uncertain *telos*, while Apollonius's severing of Lamia's magical dream not only results in her vanquish and disappearance, but also kills Lycius. We are invited in the poem's concluding lines to hear in the description of Lycius's corpse as "wound" in its "marriage robe" not just as the shroud of the dead but also the serpent's richly hued coils, his outer garments replicating the way that she had "entangle[d], trammel[ed] up and snare[d]" their souls as in a "labyrinth" (II. 52–53). I have changed the literal inflection of the lines, which are Lycius's expression of how *he* would ensnare *her* soul in his, but clearly she has already done this to him, and his reciprocal wish is merely the articulation of the self-difference self-returning. It is helpful here to rehearse Krell's point that *Scheidung* refers to "all forms of cutting or sundering," and is etymologically related to the English "to shed," while "*Die Scheide* may be a limit or boundary, a watershed or a sheathe," all of which apply to the dead body in its burial shroud. Furthermore, in the Middle Ages *Die Scheide* became "the principal translation of the Latin word *vagina*,"[128] linking sheathe and vagina so that in *Lamia*'s concluding lines Lycius's dead body is visibly wrapped in Lamia's vulvular sheathe, speaking another moral through her labial folds. The only other image in the poem of vulvular sheathing is that of Hermes's serpent-entwined Caducean rod, symbol of healing rather than Set-like destruction. The reader is left pondering whether the bond between Lamia and Lycius has been severed, or whether their intersubjectivity endures as the wrapped body indicates. More importantly, perhaps, the Lamia-Lycius intercourse, in which the interval is productively *choral* in its dream state that can only be described metaphorically, resubjectivizes both parties; Lamia as serpent is not Set but Isis, not destroyer but the one who can enter the afterlife and exit again. Apollonius feels this altered state to be a crisis in its reassertion of the always elsewhere of nonrationalist knowledge, with its reference to the already prior. He comprehends Lamia's vuvular sheathing as a crisis of ontotheological proportions, not wanting to see in her an Isis (Lycius calls Lamia "Goddess" at first sight), associationally brought into the poem by Hermes's magical healing rod, nor as the magician-goddess who (as Isis does for Osiris) heals gaps and wounds in the body's fabric.

Keats's Lamia, even in her vulnerability to "ruin" and ruination (II. 16), allegorizes the problem of the irreducible remainder. She is a reminder of the signs that, instead of revealing symbolic knowledge, reveal what is left out of the symbolic's regime; she is a pulsating referent to the *chora*'s productive stirring up that should not be interpreted as the abjected female object. As such she refers back to the priority of the already elsewhere, of the Egyptian origin of history and of writing, for her coils and her charms inscribe on Keats's romance an alternate *telos* to the blocked futurity of "cold philosophy," and the piercing eye ("perceant") of affect-less rationalism (II. 230, 301). But her pain, and her "melancholy eyes" (I. 84), point us to another truth as well. The Egyptian *Ungrund*, in its abyssal priority, houses or entombs the history of original pain which is the condition of the creation of the world according to Schelling. The world comes into being through God's self-othering, an original suffering that models the world's tragic nature:

> And every tragic event that unfolds in the world's course is but a variation on the one grand theme that renews itself continuously. The deed in accord with which all suffering is scripted did not happen once and for all; rather, that deed *is happening* always and eternally.[129]

Lamia's suffering, both before and after the advent of Lycius, resembles Isis's suffering before Osiris's restoration, and after as she battles Set over her son Horus's life; Isis's story associates tragedy with maternal care, and healing with repeated crisis and wounding. If Lamia and Lycius's fable ends tragically, it is because Keats, like Schelling and Novalis, realizes the end of the possibility of an absolute; such a free unconditional is no longer thinkable.[130] Moreover, not only is the absolute absolutely inhibited, as Krell characterizes Schelling's God in his *Freedom* essay, but his self-othering is traumatically gendered and fatal: "The absolute is a mother, and he does not live forever. Essence, while majestic and manly in appearance, is needy and even squalid without its feminine counterpart," while Novalis's God is even more worldly, materialized as something "exceedingly strange, absolutely dense," completely enmeshed in matter.[131] Schelling's *Ungrund*, the dark center that in-forms divine essence, functions like Egypt in western mythological prehistory—as Isis, the essential mediator for the dead god Osiris, who reforms Rā's self-possessed light into regenerated life (Osiris), even new life (the child Horus). Yet, gods die in this fable, and rebirth occurs from tragic conditions. Like Lamia's womb-palace ("For all this came a ruin," II. 16), like Ancient Egypt itself, this can only lead to ruins and fragmentation.

In the next chapter, I turn to the Romantic period study of hieroglyphics as the attempt to end unknowability; it was an attempt thwarted by the very nature of the unknowable, and the benighted effort to efface it. Moreover, if the race to decode the hieroglyphs was conducted on largely scientific terms, it began in occultation, a beginning that left its trace in the work of linguists and amateur Orientalists attempting the decryption. By the end of the Romantic period, this occultation had obtained a hint of Oriental romance that was not far removed for the archival fever still strongly in evidence.

NOTES

1. Novalis, *Notes for a Romantic Encyclopaedia*, 146.
2. Plutarch, "On Isis and Osiris," in *Plutarch's Morals*, 2.
3. Ibid, 2; emphasis added.
4. Ibid, 8, 2.
5. Derrida, *On Spirit*, 83.
6. Derrida, *Khōra*, 94.
7. David Farrell Krell makes this point in *The Tragic Absolute*, 74.
8. Derrida, *Khōra*, 103.
9. Kahn, *Pythagoras and The Pythagoreans*, 49–50.
10. Plato, the *Timaeus*, *The Collected Dialogues of Plato*, 1154d.
11. Derrida, *Khōra*, 124, 109.
12. Plato, the *Timaeus*, *The Collected Dialogues of Plato*, 1169, 40c.
13. Kahn, *Pythagoras and The Pythagoreans*, 53. The use of Pythagorean cosmology is most clearly delineated in the *Phaedo*, "the most explicitly Pythagorean of all the dialogues," Kahn notes (52).
14. Plato, in the *Timaeus*, *The Collected Dialogues of Plato*, 1172, 44b.
15. Ibid, 1165, 34c–35.
16. Derrida, *Khōra*, 126.
17. Paracelsus, *Paracelsus, Essential Readings*, 59. The original title of the text discussing the womb-matrix is *Das Buch von der Gebärung der Empfindlichen Dinge in der Vernunft* (c. 1520).

18. Plato, the *Timaeus*, *The Collected Dialogues of Plato*, 1166, 36e.
19. Ibid.
20. Plutarch, *Plutarch's Morals*, 10.
21. Ibid, 8. However, he also explains that these philosophers did not always take the light of understanding from that prior ground: "for the most part of the Pythagorean precepts do not fall short of the so-called hieroglyphic writings in obscurity" (8).
22. Plato, the *Timaeus*, in *The Collected Dialogues of Plato*, 1165 35c–36.
23. Ibid, 1166c–d.
24. Ibid, 1166, 36 a–b.
25. Ibid, 1166, 36 b–c.
26. Ibid, 1167, 37d.
27. Ibid, 1167, 38 a–b.
28. Derrida, *Khōra*, 105. See Gasché for a study of Derrida's abiding interest in reflexivity in *The Tain of the Mirror: Derrida and the Philosophy of Reflection*.
29. Plato, the *Timaeus*, in *The Collected Dialogues of Plato*, 1177, 50c.
30. Derrida, *Khōra*, 110.
31. Plato, the *Timaeus*, in *The Collected Dialogues of Plato*, 1180–1182, 53c–56c, 1202, 81b.
32. Ibid, 1211, 92c.
33. Derrida, *Khōra*, 110.
34. Plato, the *Timaeus*, in *The Collected Dialogues of Plato*, 1177, 50b.
35. Ibid, 1179, 53a.
36. Derrida, *Khōra*, 89.
37. Kristeva, *Revolution in Poetic Language*, 40. For Kristeva's revision of Derrida's *khōra*, see 40–41, 239n11.
38. Ibid, 52.
39. For my earlier work with the Kristevan *chora* and irruption in British Romantic poetry, see my *Becoming Wordsworthian, A Performative Aesthetics*.
40. Derrida, *Khōra*, 106.
41. Kristeva, *Revolution in Poetic Language*, 53.
42. Ibid, 63.
43. Plato, the *Timaeus*, in *The Collected Dialogues of Plato*, 1178, 51 a–b.
44. Ibid, 1170, 41a–b.
45. Ibid, 1170, 41b–42b. Plato's woman is inferior in every respect including her access to impressions and love.
46. Ibid, 1183, 58 a–c.
47. Ibid.
48. Ibid, 1211, 92 c.
49. Ibid, 1170, 41d; 1171, 42d.
50. Derrida, *Khōra*, 114.
51. As Critias tells it in the *Timaeus*, Solon, "the wisest of the seven sages" learned the history of Athens, continually forgotten ("passed into oblivion") and rebegun, "through lapse of time and the destruction of mankind," in Egypt. Plato, *The Collected Dialogues of Plato*, 1156, 20e.
52. Ibid.

53. Derrida, *Khōra*, 114.

54. Solon questioned the Säitic priests about antiquity, for they were "most skillful in such matters," Ibid, 1157, 21e–22a. Their skill allowed them to understand when "a declination of the bodies moving in the heavens around the earth" occurs, resulting in "a great conflagration of things upon the earth which recurs after long intervals"—events the Athenians had only a faint memory of in their "myth" of Helios's son stealing his sun-chariot, resulting in dire destruction. The Egyptian priest who edifies Solon instructs him not only in the history of Athens itself, recorded in the Saisian temple archives, but also in the cosmology and meteorology of the world. In providing this beginning to Athenian time, the priest teaches Solon how Egyptian priority in-forms Athenian presentness by dividing it from its lost past (the sunken Atlantis).

55. Plato, the *Timaeus*, in *The Collected Dialogues of Plato*, 1196, 73b.

56. Ibid, 1182, 56b.

57. In Greek mythology Hyperion is one of the twelve Titans, children of Gaia the earth and Uranus the sky; Hyperion himself, god of light and wisdom, fathered Helios the sun, Selene the moon, and Eos, Dawn.

58. Derrida, *Glas*, 166.

59. In volume I of the *Mysterium Magnum, An Exposition of The First Book of Moses Called Genesis*, Boehme explains in his preface that we must question the biblical use of magic by Moses in Egypt, for "treatises of magic are histories of strange actions," xiii. Magee's discussion of Boehme's triads is especially helpful: *Hegel and the Hermetic Tradition*, 40–41.

60. Derrida, *Khōra*, 89; Derrida is quoting Vernant on binarity.

61. Clark, "'The Necessary Heritage of Darkness': Tropics of Negativity in Schelling, Derrida, and de Man," 84.

62. Ibid, 87.

63. Assmann, *The Mind of Egypt*, 12–16.

64. From the *Stuttgart Lectures*, qtd. in Clark "'The Necessary Heritage of Darkness,'" 88.

65. Ibid, 86.

66. Ibid, 89.

67. Ibid.

68. Ibid.

69. Ibid. Clark's rumination on belatedness and punctuality in "The Necessary Heritage of Darkness" has been generative for my entire understanding of beforeness.

70. Schelling, *Philosophical Investigations into the Essence of Human Freedom*, 7:359–60/34.

71. Derrida, "Post-Scriptum: Aporias, Ways and Voices," 283.

72. See Fagenblat, *Negative Theology as Jewish Modernity*, esp. the chapters by Sira Wolosky and Sarah Pessin.

73. Derrida, "Différance," in *Margins of Philosophy*, 8–9. See Derrida's "The Original Discussion of Différance," in *Derrida and Différance*, for a sense of the trajectory of this concept in his work.

74. Derrida, "Post-Scriptum: Aporias, Ways and Voices," 284.

75. Ibid.
76. Ibid, 285, 286.
77. Ibid, 286.
78. Derrida is thinking of Heidegger's *Dasein* here, where I have inserted "being." He notes that what Heidegger says of death concerns "the possibility of the absolute impossibility of *Dasein*." Ibid, 291.
79. Plato, the *Timaeus*, in *The Collected Dialogues of Plato*, 1166, 36e.
80. Derrida, "Post-Scriptum: Aporias, Ways and Voices," 295.
81. Ibid, 296.
82. Ibid, 286.
83. Ibid, 301.
84. "The Legend of Rā and Isis" in Budge, *Egyptian Magic*, 137–156. This is the legend that is transcribed in the Turin manuscript. It is this version that Derrida references in *Glas*.
85. Plutarch, "Isis and Osiris," 4.
86. Derrida, "Post-Scriptum: Aporias, Ways and Voices," 295.
87. Ibid, 300.
88. Qtd. in Budge, *Egyptian Magic*, 80.
89. Ariosto's *Orlando Furioso* depicts Charlemagne's heroic knight Orlando (Roland) in his struggle to overcome the madness brought on by his love for the princess Angelica. "Furioso" translates literally as "frenzy."
90. Cole, *Napoleon's Egypt: Invading the Middle East*, 12–17.
91. The Mamluks, a high-status group in the Ottoman regime who were nevertheless marked by their partial slave status as abducted Albanians, or boys from other Balkan states including Greece. See Abyu-Lughod, *Before European Hegemony*, 104–230, and Herold, *The Age of Napoleon*, 64–76, 330–331. See also Sanders, *Creating Medieval Cairo* on the identification of Medieval Cairo with Mamluk policing, 26–45.
92. Budge reports this tradition, commenting that Abu-Shâkir's sources are "clearly, derived from Egyptian sources." *Egyptian Magic*, 95.
93. Derrida, *Khōra*, 90.
94. Ibid, 113.
95. Cited in Wirth's Preface to Schelling, *Historical-critical Introduction to the Philosophy of Mythology*, ix.
96. Wirth, Preface to Schelling, *Historical-critical Introduction to the Philosophy of Mythology*, viii.
97. Ibid, xi.
98. Schelling, *Historical-critical Introduction to the Philosophy of Mythology*, 8–9.
99. Ibid, 9.
100. This is a problem recently reinterrogated on Egyptian terrain by Jan Assmann in *Moses the Egyptian*.
101. Schelling, *Historical -critical Introduction to the Philosophy of Mythology*, 21.
102. Ibid, 44–45; emphasis added.
103. Ibid, 45.
104. Ibid, 80.

105. Kuzniar, *Delayed Endings*, 49.

106. I have chosen to use the edition of Novalis, *The Novices of Saïs* translated by Ralph Manheim, which contains Paul Klee's illuminative drawings. These are placed on the verso side of each page, with the text on recto page sides (quoted passages will refer only to odd-numbered pagination).

107. Ibid, 5.

108. Ibid, 115, 111, 113.

109. Ibid, 5, 7.

110. Ibid, 9.

111. That is, Schelling's primal ground is itself both container and generative, affected by desire, and Spinoza's affections are the stirrings that activate such generation, an affection of bodies that allows them to undergo change.

112. Hadot, *The Veil of Isis*, 207.

113. Assmann, *Moses the Egyptian*, 142.

114. Novalis, *The Novices of Saïs*, 17.

115. Ibid, 27.

116. Ibid, 29, 31.

117. Ibid, 65.

118. Žižek, *The Abyss of Freedom/Ages of the World*, 24.

119. Ibid, 25.

120. Kuzniar, *Delayed Endings*, 49.

121. Ibid, 81, 94.

122. Žižek, *The Abyss of Freedom/Ages of the World*, 25.

123. Ibid.

124. Kristeva, *Powers of Horror, An Essay on Abjection*.

125. In Keats, *Keats's Poetry and Prose*, 413–429; parenthetical line citations refer to Part I or II, and line number(s).

126. Novalis, *The Novices of Saïs*, 67.

127. Krell, *The Tragic Absolute*, 70.

128. Ibid, 73.

129. From lecture 20 of those Schelling delivered on the subject of the philosophy of mythology, quoted in Krell, *The Tragic Absolute*, 14.

130. See Terrada, "Looking at the Stars Forever," for an extended discussion of this concept.

131. Krell, *The Tragic Absolute*, 5, 60.

Chapter 5

Hieroglyphica

"The first art is the study of hieroglyphs."[1]

Hence the fame of sculptors, painters and musicians, although the intrinsic powers of the great masters of these arts may yield in no degree to that of those who have employed language as the hieroglyphic of their thoughts, has never equalled that of poets in the restricted sense of the term.... Poets are the hierophants of an unapprehended inspiration.

Ancient Egypt stood in for and in the place of a prehistorical placing of language as knowledge. It haunted the historico-philosophy that eighteenth-century intellectuals were striving for, a natural philosophy that would fold the divergences of nature—both as natural history and as what lay behind the veil of Isis or Nature—into a general scheme that could also account for language, both as a general grammar and as language's divine origins. What ancient philosophers, mages, and alchemists strove to understand was the same thing that Medieval and Renaissance writers of universal history, and the same as Enlightenment writers of natural history, were attempting to solve: a universal plan that was apprehensible to the rational mind because it extended from first principles that could be learned from taxonomic classification. "Egypt" provided a first taxonomic class, a beginning place for knowledge as linguistically driven.

In the period between the Renaissance and the Enlightenment, scholars like Athanasius Kircher understood mind as intellectual intuition. Kircher's approach to hieroglyphs in particular followed a rule of "nonrecognition through assimilation," as Derrida puts it.[2] Kircher followed Aristotelian principles that drew generalizations from particulars in the natural and human world in such a way that, as for later eighteenth-century scientists, discordances only proved the general rule.³ However, Kircher was susceptible to the Renaissance system of ordering by resemblance as well, which allowed him a more malleable system of ordering things than later scholars would employ. This made his works susceptible to the ire of later scholars, and in particular of eighteenth- and nineteenth-century linguists. Nevertheless, Kircher's belief in intellectual intuition as a power of reason illustrates that such a historico-philosophy conceptual history began with a foregrounding of mind itself, with language functioning as an illustration of mental processes. During the Romantic period, Humboldt takes up this belief in his monumental study on language, particularly in his introductory volume *On Language*,⁴ and Diderot weighs in on the topic in his 1951 *Letter on the Deaf and Dumb*. Most intellectuals who, like Diderot, used hieroglyphs as a reference to early writing systems didn't worry about the grammatical function of the glyphs; instead, hieroglyphics served as a metaphor for the symbolization of spoken language. Some writers tended to invoke the mystical attributes of hieroglyphics whereas others focused on the hieroglyphic code itself; the first emphasized the glyph *as* glyph, and the cosmic wisdom behind surface meaning; the second emphasized the series, and meaningful representation. The first was the invocation of cosmic not-knowing; the second a terrestrial representation of knowledge and meaning-making.

Strikingly, Ancient Egypt was often invoked for the mind-language association as much as for the locus of encoded cosmic wisdom, while hieroglyphics were even more frequently invoked to stand in for first writings, originary traces of spiritual or divine presence, either pagan, Christian, or both. The grounding of language was a tool for magical thinking (as post-Kantians derisively referred to thinking by resemblance) as well as for reason (which works by predicates). This chapter traces the unfolding of the linguistic endeavor as it depicts a particular mind in transition from the eighteenth-century historico-philosophical model to the nineteenth-century scientific model, which begins the modern detachment of natural object from language. And yet this detachment, as Derrida argues, retains an unresolved residue of immediacy and presence—what Derrida calls the trace—that I see as traceable to ancient uses of ritualistic language in Egyptian magic as well as in the Renaissance belief in Hebrew's divine origin. I will begin by sketching the mental attitudes relating to Egypt, a renewed Egyptianism (Neo-Egyptianism), and shifts in approaches to language that grounded a late Romantic-era attitude toward hieroglyphics that led to Champollion's triumph. I will then focus the main part of the chapter on a particular figure: the amateur Orientalist, William Hook Morley. This case study of Morley illustrates the metaphysical pull of Ancient Egypt at the end of British Romanticism. Morley is the very model of an Alexandrian scholar, his studies combining scientific and practical research with a highly romanticized and occulted Orientalism. His Alexandrianism comes to bear full force in his own attempt to decipher Egyptian writing (the everyday writing known as demotic) during the race to decode the hieroglyphs, which breaks off suddenly once Champollion breaks the Egyptian code.

I. MENTALITY AND LANGUAGE

In contrast to the Platonic account of ideal and real or the Aristotelian scientific system based on essence and substance, atomism (a speculative understanding of the ground of all being) gained renewed interest with the more open and open-minded circulation of Lucretius's *De Rerum Natura* between the Renaissance and eighteenth century among philosophers and scientists. Rethinking the possibility of atomism only intensified the search for a key to the divine mystery that was already a principal feature of Alexandrian and Renaissance Hermeticism. And as a part of that key, Renaissance scholars began the work on historicizing languages even while they were busy decoding nature's signs. Hebrew was understood as the archaic, divine language given to men; Hebrew engendered "Syriac and Arabic; then came Greek, from which both Coptic and Egyptian were derived."[5] If Hebrew was the key for the Renaissance, the eighteenth century desired a more universal grammar by which to decode languages. The quest for such a key nevertheless retained mystical import and could be represented yet again as the Masonic version of the Eleusinian mysteries, and as the new alchemy as practiced by Goethe in his biological experiments or as expressed by Erasmus Darwin in his *Temple of Nature*. However, the key itself was always just beyond grasp, despite the eighteenth-century absorption of anomaly into its taxonomic systems. Unclassifiable species, such as the hydra (an exception to Linnaeus's system, it is the freshwater polyps that appeared to be both vegetable and animal), were more than anomalies to a systematizing that was meant to be both a universal mathesis and taxonomic system encompassing material phenomena. Grammar developed similarly vexing anomalies.

Antiquarians and linguists developed classificatory systems parallel to those of natural phenomena, so that languages and civilizations could be absorbed into universal structures that could then decode characteristic elements and ignore aberrant particulars. But ancient civilizations left few if any chronicles and historical narratives, records whose discrepancies, gaps, and contradictions could introduce doubt into any taxonomic system. Even so, unlike architectural ruins languages can be decoded, translated, compared once enough documents are made available, however fragmentary and random these artifacts are. The shift at the end of the Enlightenment to the nineteenth century was a shift away from believing a general grammar applicable to all languages could contain the key to all understanding (therefore still containing an aspect of the mystical belief in *Logos* as the key to life), and toward a belief that language is a historically specific medium for thought and experience that could recover a civilization's particularity. The Romantic period was situated precisely in this shift, longing for a general grammar while attuned to historical specificity. The result was often confusion arising from comparative linguistics: the theory that one could decode Coptic by applying the rules for the Chinese script, for instance. But progress was made in developing a historical understanding of different writing systems predicated on differentiated grammars. As Foucault notes, eighteenth-century general grammar depended on the classification of word roots and propositional elements derived from the study of documents and records in various languages. This was a reductively bifurcated system, but although reductive, this study was essentially "the constitution of a whole environment of history in which the nineteenth century was to rediscover, after this pure tabulation of things, the renewed possibility of talking about words . . . in a mode that was considered as positive, as objective, as that of natural history."[6]

Nevertheless, Egyptian hieroglyphics were a special puzzle, not only because of the west's longstanding superstitious attitude toward their magical capability, but also because they were the Linnaean hydra, the trans-species of writing systems. Hieroglyphs do not obey the rules of pictographs, characters, nor alphabetic writing, but seemed to be either all of these or none. But unlike other ancient scripts like Chinese or Hebrew, whose characters seemed to embody ancient wisdom accumulated by the civilizations they bespeak, Egyptian hieroglyphics appeared to have potential to actually embody and retain originary knowledge and ancient wisdom. Magic was the use the Egyptians themselves put to hieroglyphs, as was long known to the west through Hellenist documenters such as Herodotus: for the Egyptians the characters were believed to enable spiritual and physical action, cause events, and could intervene in both life and the afterlife. These ideas continued to circulate and be reported long after hieroglyphs could no longer be read in Egypt itself; they were revived by both Hermeticism and alchemy, and Hegel accords them a place in the coming to knowledge of spirit.

For the west, hieroglyphs have always been the writing of enchantment. For the Renaissance, "the face of the world is covered with blazons, with characters, with ciphers and obscure words—with 'hieroglyphics,' as Turner called them."[7] Renaissance resemblance depended on signatures: "The world of similarity can only be a world of signs," a "cosmology of signs" which must be deciphered.[8] The Renaissance, following this logic, understood knowledge as holding an equal status for erudition and magic, which are "not selected contents but required forms."[9] "Let us call the totality of the learning and skills that enable one to make the signs speak and to discover their meaning, hermeneutics," Foucault announces; and hermeneutics is effectively what the hieroglyphs represent, their Hermes-associated origins making the relation between divine *Logos* and men's words full of spirit.[10] (Hermes was the Greek name associated with Thoth, god of writing whose cult center was Hermopolis Magna.)

Eighteenth-century linguists, assuming a sharp division between pictographic writing systems and alphabetic ones, sorted civilizations out according to the presumably primitive nature of the first and the more advanced nature of the second. For the Rev. William Warburton, who viciously attacked Athanasius Kircher's theories of hieroglyphic decryption, pictographs such as the Mexican cultures employed were not true writing but only the crudest attempt to document events. Warburton's demolition of Kircher's work had powerful effects. Book IV, section 4, of the second edition of Warburton's *The Divine Legation of Moses Demonstrated* (1742) was translated into French with the title *Essai sur les hieroglyphes des Egyptiens* (1744). This was not an anomaly: Warburton's work on hieroglyphs in this section on Egyptian hieroglyphs, translated only two years later into French, had a huge impact on French *philosophes*, including Condillac and Rousseau. "Selected, sectioned, translated, copiously annotated, and furnished with a new title by M.-A. Leonard des Malpeines, Warburton's notions on Egyptian writing penetrated and permeated French thinking on the subject in the eighteenth century and marked a turning point in the history of decipherment."[11] As Derrida notes, Warburton's analysis of writing systems is grounded in "a theory of powers," whether political versus religious power, writing versus speech, words versus actions, or other combinations and divisions of the power of enacting.[12] Warburton announces another kind of power, a perversion of power in which the relation between nature and language (especially written) is distorted by European scholars in their analysis of hieroglyphics, most particularly in the case of Kircher: "The undertaking is extremely difficult owing to the general error into which we have fallen regarding the first use of hieroglyphs, believing as we do that Egyptian priests invented them so as to hide their knowledge from the common man. This opinion has cast over this part of ancient literature a shadow so large that one can dispel it only by unveiling the error completely."[13]

In *The Divine Legation of Moses* (first issued in 1741) Warburton developed three methods of recording thought in order to trace the development from pictographic to alphabetic writing as a historical progression; however, these were not to be the key to decrypting hieroglyphics, but only (inaccurate) descriptions of the three writing systems used in Ancient Egypt. Warburton combines his theories on the derivation of writing systems with his survey of "Aegyptian priests . . . the *Chaldeans* and *Magi* [from Persia]," Pythagoras, "the initiations celebrated in Eleusis, *Imbros, Samothrace* and

Delos; or wherever else, as amongst the Celts, and *Iberians*," and biblical and Classical history.[14] Kircher takes a more universalizing approach to hieroglyphs, and his belief that hieroglyphs were specifically devised by Egyptian priests to secrete their wisdom from noninitiated worshippers especially drew Warburton's ire; veiling and unveiling are central themes in the entire *Divine Legation*, but they don't reference God's works so much as man's.[15] Warburton's major claim for hieroglyphics is that they not only prove Ancient Egypt's use of science, but that they are no mere container for knowledge; instead, hieroglyphic writing "structures the content of knowledge."[16] And, contra Kircher, Warburton argues that hieroglyphs were meant for public consumption, as their use on public architecture such as temples, obelisks, and other monuments makes clear. Here is Foucault's summary of Warburton's three writing methods:

> True writing began when the attempt was made to represent, no longer the thing itself [as in the pictograph], but one of its constituent elements, or one of the circumstances that habitually attend it, or again some other thing that it resembles. These three methods produced three techniques: the curiological writing of the Egyptians—the crudest of the three—which employs 'the principal circumstance of a subject in lieu of the whole' (a bow for a battle, a ladder for a siege); then the 'tropal' hieroglyphics—somewhat more perfected—which employ some notable circumstance (. . . [God is] represented by an eye); finally, symbolic writing, which makes use of more or less concealed resemblances (the rising sun is expressed by the head of a crocodile . . . [at] the surface of the water).[17]

Warburton's theories exemplify the early Romantic approach to hieroglyphs and the other writing systems that Egyptian artifacts brought to the west revealed. He is correct to isolate the use of pictographs and ideographs (the "crude" and the "tropal" forms), but he has missed the alphabetic element, which will be Champollion's discovery. My interest at this point in Warburton's theory of language development is his introduction of metaphor into the theory of writing systems, a development that was of key interest to the Romantics, the French *philosophes*, and to modern-era linguistic theory as well. Foucault, for instance, sees in Warburton's tripartite system the three techniques that are "the three great figures of rhetoric: synecdoche, metonymy, catachresis."[18] Voicing Warburton, Foucault explains that these figures "become endowed little by little with poetic powers," and by the same virtue it is "also how esoteric forms of knowledge arose among those [priests] who pass on the metaphors to their successors . . . , and it is how allegorical discourse (so frequent in the most ancient literatures) comes into being." In other words, metaphoricity is grounded in the three forms of hieroglyphic writing.

For Derrida, writing in the Renaissance was "metaphoricity itself," but nevertheless "[t]here remains to be written a history of this metaphor, a metaphor that systematically contrasts divine or natural writing and the human and laborious, finite and artificial inscription."[19] By the seventeenth century, however, language as presence and metaphoricity gave way to an understanding of writing as the contrast between "the dead letter" of ordinary language and metaphoric writing: the "natural, divine, and living writing" that is "hieratic," associated with priestly ritual, perhaps because its more cursive form appears dynamic in comparison.[20] If for Kircher, hieroglyphs are "an ingenious linking of symbols . . . [that] proposes *at* once (*uno intuitu*) to the intelligence of the scholar a complex reasoning, elevated notions or some mysterious insignia hidden in the breast of nature of the Divinity,"[21] from Rousseau on, metaphoric writing contains *life*, an idea long associated with hieroglyphic writing as spirit. However, eighteenth-century attempts to read hieroglyphic metaphoricity were repeatedly frustrated, tinged with what Derrida, in reference to Kircher's mystical beliefs, terms "the '*Chinese*' prejudice."[22] This is a prejudice in which the Chinese script models "the philosophical language thus removed from history," liberated from voice (76). This prejudice is "a sort of European hallucination"; but simultaneously a "*hieroglyphist prejudice*" arose, producing "the same effect of interested blindness," and was also apparent in Kircher's work on hieroglyphs.[23] The occulting of hieroglyphics, in Derrida's Freudian reading, has to do with its combination of pictographic, ideographic, and phonetic elements. These should be read not as combinatory (as Champollion discovered was in fact how they should be read) but as stratification Derrida argues. Stratification, a concept he takes from Freud's work on dreams, allows for hieroglyphs to inscribe presence and to secrete it there. The glyphs are not immediately comprehensible as speech but as layers of symbolic and alphabetic writing,[24] hidden or disguised matter and manifest content. It is this stratified aspect, layers of packed meaning, that defer that meaning while insinuating spirit into the strata, giving rise to both an occultation and "an hyperbolical admiration" such as Kircher held for hieroglyphic writing. (Derrida notes that he "devoted his entire genius to opening the West to Egyptology.") Both the prejudice and the hyperbolical admiration are at work even in as late a scholar as William Morley.

II. ORIENTALISM

Drawing together the strands of practices, interests, networks, and forms of knowledge to reconstruct Britain's attitude toward Ancient Egypt in Romantic period, both as a historical matter and a speculative one, provides large overviews and intimate glimpses of British Orientalism. This is intensified when we add it that it was also a matter of romance, as in examples such as Handel's operas *Berenice* (1709) and *Tolomeo, re d'Egitto* (1719), Clara Reeve's *The History of Charoba, Queen of Aegypt* (1785), and Thomas Moore's *The Epicurean* (1827). Morley was interested in all of these aspects of his field, and Ancient Egypt was only one focus in his broad-ranging self-education in Orientalism. Nevertheless, it stimulated and contextualized his interest in attempting to decode Egyptian writing and played a significant role in his Egyptological researches.

William Hook Morley, barrister, Middle Temple (1815–1860) established a reputation as a self-educated Orientalist, and the process of his reading and dreaming provides an exemplary case study of the Romantic subject for whom Egypt was an object of mental travel, a virtual destination and a romance. Morley invested his time and labor in Oriental studies in the past decades of the Romantic period, but he was both more and less than that: most Orientalists spent time in India or the Near East while he most probably never left London; most Orientalists were colonial administrators, teachers, or had some empire-related post such as museum curator, while Morley was a barrister who evidently practiced little given how much time he devoted to scholarly pursuits. Egypt, the Near East, and India were not yet the easy destination of late Victorian- and Modern-period England for the health-poor and cash-strapped. Egypt itself was a land annually beset by cholera epidemics, corrupt government officials, arrogant Mamluk soldiers, bandits, and poor accommodations. Morley was a late Romantic, living on into the Victorian age as did Wordsworth, but he clearly remained influenced by the Romantic imaginary. He exemplifies the Romantic reader of travel literature, Oriental studies, and histories who participated in the romanticizing of Egypt. Morley's views of India appear to have been those of the progressive nineteenth century, but his interests in Persia, Arab cultures, Egypt, and surrounding areas were nostalgic, imaginative, and related more to eighteenth-century antiquarianism and Romantic nostalgia than to Victorian progressivism. Egypt was also still part of the larger schema of a biblical and Classical past to be recovered, annexed, Englished as Thomas Cook was soon to do with his popular tours. Ancient Egypt was more of a challenge, its language the most difficult code so far uncovered; by contrast, the Near East was in general nearer in time or had already been the subject of study, so that knowing its cultures and their pasts seemed manageable; one could imagine them. But Egypt was part of this map, and piecing the cultures, languages, traditions together would eventuate in knowing Ancient Egypt too. Morley desired both a nearer historical and a more ancient familiarity, knowledge of both Egypt on the ground and the ancient civilization that was so largely still buried in the ground. Still, his approach had something of Kircher's intellectual intuition and Romantic-period imagination in it.

Morley's overarching framework was, like most Orientalists, linguistic; he became fluent in Arabic and Persian, studied several other languages, including Hindustani, Hebrew, and Chinese, cuneiform and Egyptian hieroglyphics, but he was also fascinated by the cultures, histories, religions, and literature of the Near East, including India and what is now Pakistan, Bangladesh, Afghanistan, and regions north of Afghanistan up into Mongolia. He was less interested in the Far East, although he did seriously consider applying for a legal appointment in Hong Kong when that became available. In short, Morley was an Orientophile.

Not much is known about Morley, but he died very young, at forty-five in 1860, outliving his wife by several years, evidenced by his use of mourning stationary by 1850. Although her early death was difficult for him, even before that catastrophe he looked eastward not just in his hobbyist studies, but for a career move. Beginning at age fifteen, Morley began keeping extensive notebooks of his reading in Oriental studies; by the time his studies developed into clear evidence of his learning it becomes apparent he had set his sights on a judgeship in India under the patronage of the East India Company, to which the Royal Asiatic Society of Great Britain and Ireland was aligned. (The Society was founded in 1823 by a group of colonial administrators and Oriental scholars as the London sister of the Royal Asiatic Society of Calcutta—founded nearly four decades earlier by Sir William Jones.) It also becomes clear that the collections to which Morley had access for his reading and note-taking were institutions of the East India Company: the library of the India House in London, and the library of the Royal Asiatic Society. Morley became a Resident Member of the Society on April 17, 1847[25] but had long been associated with the Society and its library before this. When forty-three he was elected to the office of Librarian, two years before his death. According to the Dictionary of National Biography he was also a trustee of the Society. He was deeply concerned in the Society's business, and most of his Orientalist publications were commissioned by or carried out under their auspices, but his notebooks give evidence that his overriding desire in all of these pursuits and affiliations was to secure a post in Bengal where he could advance his career beyond what was available in London.

Little remains from Morley's legal career, what kinds of cases he worked on or clients he took on if any. The *Catalogue of Notable Middle Templars*[26] remembers him for his Oriental publications rather than his legal work, and his well-received *Digest of Cases decided in the Supreme Courts of India* (1849–1850). This was a study Morley undertook to prove himself qualified for a judgeship in the British Empire. Although no such appointment was made, it is the only trace I have found of his legal interests although he presumably had access to the library of the Middle Temple for his legal research. Following the example of his father George Morley of London, barrister of the Inner Temple, Morley studied law and was admitted in August 1833; he was called to the bar in January 1838. His stamp is that of the Middle Temple although his office was first at 38 Serle Street, then by 1840 at 15 Serle Street, Lincoln's Inn, perhaps because Serle Street was so conveniently near the Royal Asiatic Society and its printer (Cox and Baylis, printers to the Royal Asiatic Society, Great Queen Street, Lincoln's Inn Fields). He was born in Brompton, near Hyde Park, and probably lived there as an adult since he died at 35 Brompton Square. It is not until the end pages of notebook D273 in the British Library that Morley's career dreams are revealed: these contain pasted-in advertisements for foreign language classes offered privately (Hebrew) and at London's King's College specifically for those studying to pass the exams for civil service in the East India Company. Other ads indicate he was thinking of applying for a juridical appointment in Bengal, a post that required fluency in Persian, Hindustani, and Bengali. But that he never traveled for health or pleasure, waiting for a government-funded position to go abroad, suggests that his practice was not lucrative—not even enough, apparently to purchase his own books. This does not mean a man can't dream.

III. THE MORLEY NOTEBOOKS

In the majority of his notebooks held in the British Library and in his main publications, Morley remains a scholarly, logical man; the notebooks are for the most part collections of excerpts, copying rather than writing, and rarely resorting to the speculative thought of Coleridge's notebooks or De Quincey's essays. But two notebooks depart from this scholarly, even legalistic training. Each is in its way a romancing of the historical Near East, a passage into an antique past. One notebook, or rather a set of four thin volumes,[27] is a fair copy of his edition of a Persian manuscript of the *Jámi ul Hikáyát*, a collection of tales much like the *Arabian Nights*. The other notebook, *E115*, is a partial fair copy of Morley's own attempt to account for and practice the Egyptian hieroglyphic code by following the leads of the English physicist Thomas Young. The polymath Young was also an amateur linguist, following Warburton's methods and discoveries. He began work on the hieroglyphs starting in 1802 with a short list of demotic letters translated, half of them incorrectly, by Johan David Åkerblad. (Demotic is the everyday script developed for rapid writing, letters and documents; Åkerblad believed, erroneously, that the demotic is alphabetic only.)

However, Morley's notebook breaks off, suggesting that the Anglo-French contest over who could decipher the code first was finally over with Jean-François Champollion's decisive discovery of the Cleopatra cartouche.[28] Young's method, relying on a phonetic symbol system as for western languages, simply could not work, and Morley had no reason to continue his own efforts. Unlike Percy Shelley in *Alastor* or Mary Shelley in *The Last Man*, Morley doesn't envision the antique as holding the key to future unfolding. In both notebooks Morley's Orientalism reveals that linguistic translation is the key to a more universal but secret knowledge. In *E115* the usual interest in Egyptian artifacts, Egyptian décor, and Masonic Hermeticism are of no matter; the only code worthy of study is the linguistic one. And yet even that can only produce knowledge through romance, and a historical one at that. Language *is* culture for Morley, it is history; it is life as it was lived, its living expression and its spirit. That is what the mere collector of sarcophagi or excavator could never attain.

Morley's linguistic research seems to have two main foci: a philological interest in Asiatic languages, and an interest in the linguistic origins of ancient languages as these reflect cultural difference in Asiatic countries. The result is that his main research is on the ancient languages of these non-western cultures, with a linguistic interest in comparative and chronological arguments. Although it seems that the original stimulus to his study was to position himself for a legal career in the colonial empire, his romanticized and Romantically inspired interest in Egypt overtakes his more pragmatic study of British colonial territories. Although Morley corresponds with Sanskrit scholars, he himself seems less interested in mastering this language; indeed, aside from his fluency in Latin, his pursuit of at least two of the present-day languages necessary for a colonial judicial appointment appears quite purposeful. The excursion into Egyptian hieroglyphs was evidently a detour taken when Morley becomes caught up in the fevered race to decode the ancient characters: a romancing of Egypt's ancient spirit. Indeed, the reason for Morley's philological interest is borne out by a two-page advertisement pasted into the end pages of one notebook as well as by a letter to Horace Hayman Wilson.

The pasted-in ad addresses the requirements for those preparing to take the civil service exam for colonial posts as taught by a Professor Seddon, and notes which languages are necessary for different job classes or in different regions of India, but also indicating that fluency all of the required languages before leaving England is not absolutely necessary (though desirable). "Professor Seddon will, in November next, open classes in Sanscrit [*sic*], Persian, Hindustani, Bengali and Arabic," the pamphlet begins, and concludes with the professor's credentials: "It will be the Professor's aim to blend with the literature of India the results of a long local experience in the service of the Company, by pointing out the practical application of the subjects introduced in his Lecture," to which is subtended in italics, "*N.B. . . . Parties desirous of attending the Course are not required to enter as College Students, or to pay any fee but that for the Course.*" The languages to be taught address "the Oriental languages ordinarily proposed for the Civil and

Military Service of the Honorable East India Company; and two at the least, but generally three, according to the Presidency for which they are required, compose the test prescribed for their Junior Civil Servants or Writers."[29] Which languages for which specific region are clearly spelled out (e.g., "To the candidate for the Bengal Civil Service, a knowledge of Bengali is considered indispensable, as it is the vernacular dialect of twenty-five millions of people, while the Hindustani and Persian and deemed also essential requisites"), while "The Hindustani language being the prevailing medium of intercourse between the Europeans and natives throughout the British dominions in India, is absolutely essential to all." Perhaps most pertinent paragraph addresses Morley's own career plans:

> Under existing circumstances, therefore, it is impossible that a Judge or Collector in Bengal, can adequately perform his duties without a knowledge both of Persian and Hindustani, as well as of Bengali; nor at the other Presidencies, without a knowledge of Persian and the vernacular dialect of the province in which he may be stationed. Attention to this fact may prove the means of preventing, by timely application in this country, much fruitless regret in the other.[30]

Subsequently, Morley tipped in smaller advertisements after this announcing private lessons outside the university in Chinese and Hebrew. Chinese would have been relevant only for philological interest: generally, as linguists sought to determine which alphabets came first, and more specifically for how the transformation of sound into character occurred. Morley records notes on several theories as to this historical phenomenon and is interested in a universal theory of language development throughout the notebooks. But the philological aspect would become secondary if Morley's one extant plea for aid in seeking a colonial position could be realized. On January 3, 1844, he wrote to Wilson requesting just such aid:

> I see by the newspapers that the judgeship of Hong-Kong has been refused by several of my learned brethren & that there is some difficulty in finding any one to take it—You are aware, I believe, that it has always been my most ardent desire to obtain a legal appointment in the East & that with this view I have devoted much of my time to the study of the law of India—It is true that this has but little relation to that of China but still I think that the knowledge I possess of some of the languages & customs of the East in connection with my legal studies may give me some claim—With the public especially as to the world at large Chinese & Persian are not supposed to present many points of dissimilarity—I have little or no interest [i.e. influential connections] & know not to whom to apply—Have the Directors anything to do with the

appointment? If so & I might venture to solicit your influence with them I should entertain great hopes of success—I await your advice as to the course I should pursue—[31]

If the idea that an ignorance of Chinese is of less hindrance with a knowledge of languages "of the East," Morley had support from no less than Thomas Young in thinking so. In an excerpt from Young's letters, Morley records a similar conception of the earliest languages that reveals British facility for such speculative knowledge of ancient languages:

> Strictly speak[in]g there seems to be indirect mode of expressing the verb is or was in pure hieroglyphical writing; & if any such sign was employed in the Egypt^n or old Chinese hieroglyphics its introduct^n must have been arbitrary or conventional, like the employm^t of a postulate in mathematics—Every other part of a language appears capable of being reduced, with more or less circumlocut^n to the form of a noun substantive; & *the English language appears to approach to the Chinese in the facility with which all the forms of grammar may be shaken off*—[32]

Unknowability is apparently quite different in the Romantic period's version of "the Chinese prejudice": for this writing system it is what is not yet known, a decodable knowability.

Although Morley's notebooks lack an overarching narrative, they do include his own historiographic speculations in addition to the extracts from others' scholarship. But the volume dedicated to a grammar of Ancient Egyptian is an anomaly in that it is a fair copy of the book he appeared to be attempting to write and publish, probably for the Royal Asiatic Society, using Young's theory for deciphering the hieroglyphs. The fair copy notebooks for the eastern romance, by contrast, are purely a translation albeit accompanied by an editorial essay. However, read through chronologically, the journal volumes excepting the translated romance in general trace the intertwined institutional networks that this man represents, both formal (the Middle Temple, the East India Company, India House) and personal (the Royal Asiatic Society, the British Museum, Kings College), allowing a retracing of the neural circuitry of the suggestively associative entries in the notebooks. This circuitry shadows the network he established himself in his personal interinstitutional connections, a network that layers his formal and personal relationship to the institutions in different ways. It seems to me that the notebooks provide a deeper model of how individuals related to institutions in inventive and, sometimes serendipitous rather than purposeful, ways. In attempting to trace his mental world as this intersected with and was determined by the expediencies of the life he was living, I will map the armchair travels of William Morley onto the larger circuitry of a Romantic Orient, and move to its relational object, a speculative Ancient Egypt.

IV. THE ROYAL ASIATIC SOCIETY OF GREAT BRITAIN AND IRELAND

Because the Royal Asiatic Society, modeled on the Royal Asiatic Society of Bengal and located in London not far from Morley's Temple housed the embodiment of Oriental romance as a version of Romantic Egyptianism *and* Alexandria's legacy of knowability/unknowability as the structure underlying universal knowledge, I want to provide a sketch of this all-important gateway to the Near East for Morley and other scholars. The first meeting of the Royal Asiatic Society took place on March 15, 1823, at "the Thatched house, St. James's Street"[33] (George IV signed the charter on August 11, 1824). The Society obtained the lease for a house at the intersection of Grafton Street and Bond Street by the next January and began meeting regularly. By 1861, the year Morley's obituary was included in the Annual Proceedings, the society was in financial difficulties due to its increased activities while membership fees had remained relatively low. Moreover, until 1860 the authorities of the India Office halved the standing annual grant of 200 guineas the Society by the Court of Directors of the Honourable East India Company. "The Society's House, taken thirteen years ago on the faith of the permanency of the grant by the Home Government of India, . . . [cost] the Society for rent, rates, &c., nearly four hundred pounds a year," the RAS Council reported to the assembled members.

> It was conceived that, connected as are the researches of the Society with India, it might be possible to obtain from the authorities of the India Office, a set of apartments in the building to which the Museum of the East India Company has been removed. The Council caused a letter to be addressed, in consequence, to the Secretary of State for India, offering (subject to the approval of the Society at large) to add our Museum and Library to those of the India House, if apartments could be given to the Society for the transaction of its business.[34]

What these plans reflect is that, as national and colonial difficulties coalesced, funding of scholarly endeavors at home and abroad was reduced; moreover, the impermanence of the Society's housing and income as physical structures mirrored the increasing instability of the Alexandrian Library toward the end of Egypt's importance in the pre-Modern world. Publications by the Society's Oriental Translation Committee included volumes of disconnected translations that included religious texts as well as "cookery books" of "curry and khichary." Certainly there were men who were both colonial administrators and members of the Royal Asiatic Society, such as Horace Hayman Wilson (1786–1860), orientalist, who was in the Bengal Medical Services (1808–1834), Deputy Assay Master (1808–1816) and Assay Master (1816–1832), as well as with the Calcutta Mint; returning to England he was then appointed Boden Professor of Sanskrit, Exeter College, Oxford (1832–1860), as well as Librarian of the East India Company and India Office Library (1836–1860).[35] However, the intellectual and completely endeavors of the Society's members was idiosyncratic rather than systematic, and therefore less valuable to governing bodies at home and abroad. The Society was founded for practical more than intellectual reasons—to advance the linguistic acumen and cultural knowledge of those preparing to enter the East India Company's ranks, but by 1861 these goals were no longer of high priority. Translating ancient and medieval manuscripts had become an end rather than a means. Morley might argue even with this assessment of the Society's endeavors: if most of his publications are just that—translations of serendipitously discovered texts, with no rational organizing scheme in sight—his two fair copy notebooks reveal that in fact he had a different vision of the Orientalist's labor. It was one that required struggle and difficulty to be sure, as he points out in an introductory essay to the first notebook; but it also required imagination, the ability to transcend the limitations of mind and custom, of knowability.

Morley's own work with the Royal Asiatic Society began with his access to its library; when this began is unclear, but the notebooks indicate he is already reading in Oriental studies at fifteen. His borrowing of books and Oriental texts in the India House Library would have come later through contacts he made with East India Company personnel. Until his Arabic and Persian gain fluency, Morley's reading and note-taking are for the most part in the cultures, histories, royal genealogies, religions, and linguistic theories of the Near, Middle, and Far East. He tracks the translations made by the Bible translation societies as well: one notebook transcribes a multicolumn list of "Versions of the Scriptures in the Modern Oriental Languages," many of them translated by Baptist, but also Danish, Moravian, and American missionaries, and by the Mission of the London Society, and the Edinburgh Society Mission. Such tracking is important in its west-to-east translative direction; so much translation work in the east-to-west direction was necessarily religious in nature since these were the texts most replicated and circulated, and therefore most likely to be available either as historical or as present-day texts. Although in restrained moments Morley espouses a mainstream Anglicanism with a narrow view of the prophet Mohammed himself, his attitude generally toward eastern religions is scientific, open-minded, and generous. He is eager to learn of these eastern cultures and to be transported there in mind as a preparation for bodily transport.

By the 1840s when he is still in his twenties, Morley begins to participate in Oriental studies himself: first through letters to well-known Orientalists or to the Royal Asiatic Society, then by contributing to the work of others and to his own publications. This work was all done at either the early or latter Serle Street law office (mostly at number 15, Serle Street) rather than at home, and his notebooks continue to be stamped with his Middle Temple seal. His publications range from letters to the Royal Asiatic Society to full-scale translations. Letters to the Society would have been read at a meeting and then included in an issue of the Society's journal. One such letter described a Turkish tombstone that had been found, oddly, in the Temple garden; Morley translated its religious text and attempted an antiquarian description of the artifact as well as a guess at its age (it was disappointingly modern, but he could discover no explanation for its presence on Temple grounds). He also published an elaborate description of a "planispheric astrolabe" made for Husain Safawi, King of Persia in 1856; the astrolabe was in the British Museum's collection, and Morley included descriptions of twelve other astrolabes of both European and eastern construction.

The work on the astrolabe, like the tombstone, was of an immediately recognizable artifact, revealing how Morley's institutional connections were developing. Together these connections comprised the Middle Temple, where he would also become known for his legal contribution to the empire through his 1849–1850 two-volume digest of cases decided by the Supreme Courts of India (reissued in 1852); his work with the Royal Asiatic Society (one of his publications was a much-needed catalog combining both the Society's and the Oriental Translation Committee's libraries); India House and colonial administrators involved in Oriental studies; finally, he also developed ties with the British Museum. In addition to the research and report on the Persian astrolabe, Morley also successfully interceded on behalf of an Armenian priest in Alexandria for the acquisition of another set of culturally recognizable artifacts. The priest had first approached the librarian of the Royal Asiatic Society for purchase of his two rare Georgian religious volumes but had been declined; the librarian, a Mr. Norris, appealed to Morley, who wrote to the British Museum's Keeper of Manuscripts in 1837, urging acquisition of the precious volumes. Morley's arguments were powerful, and rehearsed the same twin motivations to be found in his notebook on the Egyptian hieroglyphic code: translating these texts would be an invaluable service to western knowledge, and the British need to acquire them before the foremost expert in the Georgian language, a Parisian scholar, were able to purchase them. "I am not aware that there are any ms. Georgian works at present existing in England," he writes, "& certainly not in the Ms. Department of the museum." Morley included a precise physical description of the volumes, and invited the Keeper to see them personally at the

Society's library: "Both these volumes," he notes, "are in the Khoutsouri or sacred character of Georgia & from this circumstance I imagine them to be either Lectionaries or works of a religious nature, there w[ou]ld however be a considerable difficulty in ascertaining the subjects as I do not think there is any one at present in England who is acquainted with the Georgian language—[.]" The Parisian expert, however, M. Brosset le Jeune had also been notified by Mr. Norris, and the race was on—and it would be a tragedy, he implies, to let the French win this one: "in all probability from their advantageous nature he [Brosset le Jeune] will accept [the volumes] either on his own account or for the Royal Library—."[36] In a note added to his notebook copy of this letter, Morley added that "our National Library" did indeed win this contest: "Immediately on receiving the above letter Sir Frederick Madden proceeded to inspect the mss. in question and purchased them on his own responsibility (without applying to the Trustees,) in order to avoid delay— They are at present deposited in the Library of the British Museum—W. M."

Morley's intercession with the British Museum appears both antiquarian and patriotic, but it was also a personal victory. Yet the circuits traversed— through the Royal Asiatic Society to Egypt, where Georgian liturgical texts brought by Mamluks came into the possession of an Armenian priest, back to the Society's Library and thence to the British Museum's manuscript librarian, as well as to a celebrated Parisian linguist—is replayed in a slightly different way by no less than Samuel Birch (1836–1886), Egyptologist and the museum's curator who did so much to further and popularize its Egyptian holdings. Before gaining renown Birch himself, like Morley, was driven to seek the interest of well-known and well-connected Orientalists. He too wrote to Horace Hayman Wilson in Bengal, requesting aid in applying for advancement. His letter is dated January 8, 1845, a year after Morley almost to the day that Morley had written.

> My dear Sir, An opportunity occurring for my promotion in the Museum I am desirous of obtaining testimonials as to the general services I have rendered to Numismatics and archæology in this Country. My labors have so often fallen under your notice in the Numismatic [Study?] that I venture to ask you for the expression of your good opinion in a letter directed to me.

The letter is signed, "Your[s] very respectfully[,] Samuel Birch[,] British Museum." Like Morley, Birch could consider making such a request because previous correspondence had involved matters of scholarly interest: Morley wrote to both Wilson and Elliot concerning questions of interpretation, provenance, and other matters requiring expert opinion. The world of British Orientalism existed via such connections, requests, and the sphere of letters; it was a world that mapped itself onto the world of colonial empire but with less legislated routes, fewer barriers of officialdom. What it reflects is the ascendency of knowability over unknowability that signals the last years of the Romantic period before a Victorian ideological attitude toward knowledge gained ascendency. Nevertheless, the intimacies of knowledge and of the drive for facts created subcircuits along which particular networks could be traced. It is from such circuitry and networks that mental travel can most actively be enacted.

V. MORLEY AND THE ROMANCE OF THE ORIENT

An example of one of Morley's best feats of mental travel is evidenced by another letter written to the Royal Asiatic Society, one which proved to be of serious consequence and elevated his reputation as an Orientalist: "A Letter to Major-General John Briggs, Honorary Secretary to the Royal Asiatic Society on the Discovery of Part of the Second Volume of the Jámi Al Tawáríkh of Rashíd Al Dín." By William Morley, Esq., of the Middle Temple, Barrister at Law (London 1839) concerned a discovery that caused a considerable stir and is cited in both the Society's obituary for Morley and in the Middle Temple bench registry as one of his most important Orientalist contributions. The formal publication of the twenty-four page letter followed its inclusion in the Annual Proceedings: "Art. II—Letters to the Secretary of the Royal Asiatic Society, by W. Morley, Esq., and Professor Duncan Forbes, on the Discovery of part of the Second Volume of the *'The Jámi Al Tawár'kh,'* supposed to be lost." The letter was read by Morley on June 15, 1839. It was then included in the Society's journal, and then published separately as a pamphlet, but not before further discoveries were made. Morley then transcribed and published the incomplete manuscript, which was in its original Persian, for the Society for the Publication of Oriental Texts. He was then invited to publish an English translation of the work for the Oriental Translation Committee (for which he borrowed a recently acquired Arabic version of this second volume from the librarian at India House). Rashíd Al Dín's masterpiece was precisely calculated to rouse all of Morley's scholarly and imaginative desire; indeed, in his notebooks he laboriously copied out descriptions and detailed tables of contents of several eastern universal histories with similar frameworks and comprehensive coverage.[37] It is a four-volume work of immensely exacting universal history told from the perspective of the Mongol khans who for whom Rashíd Al Dín (born c. 1247 CE) had worked as an eminently capable administrator, physician, and renaissance man. Morley discovered a partial manuscript of the second volume in Arabic in the Society library while preparing its catalog (the work exists in both the original Persian and Arabic, as Rashíd Al Dín had it copied and circulated in both languages for his bilingual countrymen). He corresponded with the archaeologist Quatremère de Quincy in Paris who was at the time translating a portion of the same work, but when no scholarly aid was forthcoming Morley undertook the work himself.

It becomes clear why Morley found Rashíd al Dín so fascinating: "Fadhl Allah Rashíd, or Rashíd al Dín Ibn Imád al Daulah Abu al Khair Ibn Mowaflik al Daulah" was first a physician, and then under the Mongol Sultans of Persia, Vazír, politician, polyglot, and linguist, and man of letters who additionally studied agriculture, architecture, metaphysics, and Islamic theology, and was fluent in Persian, Arabic, Mongolian, Turkish, Hebrew, and probably Chinese. He wrote "with extreme facility; this is attested by the voluminousness of his works, and by a passage in one of his writings, in which he asserts that he composed three of his greatest works, viz.: —the Kitáb al Tawdhihát, the Miftah al Tafásír, and the Risálat al Sultáníat, in the short space of eleven months . . . in the midst of the cares of government, and without reckoning numerous other treatises on various intricate subjects, which were written by him during the same period."[38] Like Morley's own notebooks, the four volumes of The Jámi Al Tawár'kh provide the historiography of an empire: it contains the history of the ancestors and descendants of Changíz Khán up to Oljáítú Sultán, as well as containing the accounts of the prophet Muhammad, various religious journeys of prophets, expeditions, revelations, and commencement of rituals; the empire's dynasties, revolutions, and deposed kings; the histories of the Hind and Sind (part of his history of India in the university history); a description of Kashmir; the history of the Brahman kings of Hind and of the Hind prophets and their religions and sects; the biography of the prophet Shákmúní ("and his various perfections"); an account of "the Four Cycles, according to the words of Shákmúní and the wise men and Brahmans of Hind"; "the history of the Israelites according to the Muhammadan traditions"; and "an account of the creation of the world, and the history of Adam and his descendants to the time of Nuh"; an account of the deluge, and of the Hebrew prophets according to Muslim tradition, giving them Persian names. The copies were usually accompanied by painted illustrations; this volume alone had twelve.

Three months later a colonial officer purchased a partial manuscript of this same volume, also in Arabic, which contained different portions from Morley's. Finally, in 1843 Morley writes another letter, published in the Society's journal as "Art. XXIX.—A Letter to Richard Clarke, Esq., &c., &c., &c., Honorary Secretary to the RAS, on a MS. of the The Jámi Al Tawár'kh of Rashíd al Dín, preserved in the Library of the Honourable East India Company." Morley writes with humility how the task of translation is now his: "to complete this curious chain of discovery which has rescued from oblivion one of the most valuable of the Oriental histories, lost for upwards of five centuries, Professor Falconer found a MS. of the The Jámi Al Tawár'kh in the library of the East India House, in Persian, apparently containing the entire work." But he discovers after examination that it is incomplete as well, and the ordering of its contents unclear. "[T]his MS. was placed in the hands of Professor Forbes, who undertook to prepare an account of it for the Journal of the Society, but his other occupations not allowing him leisure, he deputed to me the task of describing the precious volume. The MS. accordingly has, by the kindness of Professor Wilson, been confined to my care, and the following remarks are the result of my examination." The subsequent publications in the original language and England translation, both done at the invitation of high-ranked administrators in the Society, reveal two things: Morley's zeal to be recognized as an Orientalist in his own right; and that his approach to the medieval manuscript is of a piece with his fascination with Ancient Egyptian scripts. It is the written document that transmits the spirit of both what can be known and of unknowability: Morley is still seduced by the Romantic fulcrum between these two ways of approaching terrestrial and cosmic wisdom, and what entry that fulcrum can provide to universal knowledge and the absolute. Though he is historicist rather than poetical, Morley's researches move beyond the pragmatic into the realm of imagination via unknowability.

A different work that excited Morley's imagination even more appears at first glance to be no more than historical research: it is his contribution to the work of famed Orientalist and colonial administrator Sir Henry Miers Elliot, K.C.B. (1808–1853), foreign secretary to the Government of India. Sir Elliot devoted much of his correspondence to collecting materials for his multivolume *History of India, as Told by its Own Historians*, completed and published posthumously by John Dowson, a university professor. It takes some searching to discover Morley's contribution, which is mentioned but never detailed in his biographical notices, but it was to the original one-volume version of the work, now volume three: "The Muhammadan Period." Morley's C 46–49 notebooks, the fair copy manuscript of his edition of the collection of romance tales, the *Jámi ul Hikáyát*, was his own preparation of what is described in Dowson's table of contents as "IV. *Jámi u-l Hikáyát* of Muhammad 'Úfí" and alternately as "IV.—Jámi'u-l Hikáyát—[by] A munshi,[39] whose style had been improved by an Englishman, but the translation needed a thorough revision by the Editor." Morley was that Englishman.

Morley's astounding command of Persian and Arabic, necessary for his transcription, and then translation of *The Jámi Al Tawár'kh*, Rashíd al Dín's universal history, allowed him to begin a more playful approach with the *Jámi ul Hikáyát* (preface written in 1838, but finalized in 1840). The thirteenth-century polymath Rashíd al Dín was fluent in multiple languages including Hebrew and Chinese, and his linguistic speculation about the origins of language as originating in India (considered the oldest culture, as Morley mentions in his introduction to the *Jámi ul Hikáyát*) and China, would have given credence to Morley's idea that the study of languages facilitates the understanding of human history and cultural development along scientific fault lines.

His English title for the *Jámi ul Hikáyát* is "Pearls from the Sea of Tradition, A Collection of Tales translated from a Persian Manuscript preserved in the Library of the Oriental Translation Committee of Great Britain & Ireland"[40] (dated 1840 in ms). For this selected edition of the works' tales, Morley wrote a lengthy, scholarly introductory essay intended as a brief version of the erudite cultural context Edward William Lane had been preparing for his earlier translation of the *Arabian Nights* (to which he draws several comparisons with the text he himself presents to the reader).[41] When Morley's legal mind intrudes on his essay, as opposed to a broader philosophical mindset, is in his vituperations against Mohamed, who he casts as a political rather than spiritual man eager for control over men's minds rather than their enlightenment. This moral judgment stands in an untenable tension with his extolling of the high quality of Oriental literatures, particularly from Persia. His disgust at Islam would certainly make him a poor judicial appointment in India, where Arabic is one of the dominant languages of the populace. Equally in tension is Morley's pedantry, which leads him to rail against the English reader whose insularity, laziness in learning other languages, and lack of curiosity about other cultures stand in curious relation to what he considers to be the odious ignorance of followers of Mohammed.

If Morley seems at odds with his English readers, damning them even as he prepares to translate for them, this is secondary to his moral outrage at the entity he holds responsible for the incomprehensible attributes of the west's historical oriental enemy, the Ottoman Empire. Like his fellow countrymen (although unlike the philosopher and scientist striving for objectivity), Morley clearly holds a distinction between the mainstays of Islamic power and those lands he considers victimized by them such as India (and its neighbors) and Egypt. Like ancient Persia, India and Egypt are lands caught in a between-space, enmeshed in the political aggression of alien others to such an extent that their cultures are palimpsests, layers of cultures past and present all vying to be witnessed and translated by the west. Language as written records best exemplifies the vividly interrelated cultural strata of these two between-spaces. Therefore, the *Jámi ul Hikáyát*, which Morley believes to be the product of multiple taletellers rather than one man (an error corrected in Dowson's revision of Morley's work for Elliot's *History of India*) is, like the *Arabian Nights*, for him exemplary of the palimpsestic nature of such cultures. Its precise origin is a curiosity for him rather than an obstacle in his presentation of this work to the British public; yet his selective edition erases the frame narrative of the original work so that the tales are provided as if a collection of short stories. By obviating the framework, Morley's own introductory essay supplants it, orienting the reader to the unconnected and unsequential tales that follow. In so doing, Morley has reconstructed the archaeological experience in which strict chronology, a master narrative, and interconnections must be supplied by the scholar who translates artifacts and evidence into a convincing rendering of past life and its imaginative power. Morley believes in his own archaeological powers and the tools at his command, writing in his introduction,

> I have rendered my version as literal as possible as it is my wish to Orientalise the minds of my readers as much as I can . . . as I am convinced that the ideas of the Eastern nations can never be expressed so well as in their own words—With the single exception of the Latin, our language is perhaps more adapted than others for this species of conversion which is especially instanced in the sublimity of our version of the Old Testament compared with those in the other languages of Europe[.]

Despite Morley's stated ambition to be literal, linguistically and therefore ethnographically accurate, his goal is ultimately metaphysical. That is, by remaining firmly seated in his London law office he will know the true nature of "the Eastern nations," and moreover his command of Latin and English are the tools he needs to convey this knowledge; they are his philosopher's stone.

It must have seemed perfectly logical that he, too, should enter into the race to decipher the hieroglyphs, for which linguistic acumen and antiquarian fervor together with a propensity for imaginative speculation such as he possessed, were clearly requisite. These were the principal properties, after all, of Athanasius Kircher, but where he was impeded by the important lack of enough evidentiary material, nineteenth-century linguists knew they had the real key in their hands: the Rosetta Stone. But Morley was no philosopher; unlike Hegel he did not view understanding the hieroglyphs as a step in comprehending the disclosure of Spirit. Rather, entering the race for him was a quest, one taken up by the keenest minds in England and France, and because various factors—that it was due to Napoleon that the Rosetta Stone was discovered, or that Britain even possessed it, and that Champollion increased the stakes by refusing to admit Thomas Young's contributions to his initial discovery—these minds could be construed as knights of their two realms. Morley dearly wanted to join in as such a knight himself and followed the developments closely as one of the most exciting linguistic and antiquarian races for knowledge unfolded.

But there is additional evidence of Morley's thirst for romance beyond his translation of the *Jámi ul Hikáyát*. On the front page of his fair copy of his work for the printer, he has written on two lines "William Morley—June 5. 1840—"; in pencil someone else has written "Vol I," and also in pencil, quite possibly by Morley who was given to occasionally doodling in the margins of his notebooks, are two head portraits of women with classic Victorian hair styles.[42] Such sketches, the products of daydreaming, in a work of romance indicate the capacity for reverie, for engaging with otherness and sameness at the same time, for this is the only notebook containing drawings from life. Morley was no mere barrister, and no mere amateur scholar but a romancer whose work on Egyptian writing systems puts him in the tradition of Renaissance Hermeticists such as Ficino and, as much as he would hate to admit it, Athanasius Kircher.

VI. HIEROGLYPHIC FEVER

If Morley's amateur scholarship appears merely a Romantic Orientalism, his overweening interest in linguistics should disillusion us on that point.[43] Morley's scholarly endeavors work at this transformation into the modern predicated on the ancient past. He titled his notebook now labeled as *D273* "Oriental Collections Volume 3—containing Notes on the History, Religions, Languages and Literature of the East—With some remarks on Hieroglyphics—Collected between the months of March and September 1837—Wm Morley[.]" His earlier notebook, now labeled *E115*, was written between 1834 and 1835 and appears to be the fair copy of a book he is writing but abandons on the language and writing system of Egyptian hieroglyphs. Each page of *E115* is folded, with his manuscript in the right column and commentary, citations, or bibliographic information in the left; for his plates and inserted illustrations he either uses facsimiles or his own tracings on lighter paper from books or periodicals, as well as his own pencil and color drawings, including a drawing entitled "Nilometer of Elephantine." Intriguingly, for this notebook there is no title or working title, although on page 9 is what may be a working title: "On the Different Kinds of Egyptian Writing—." The "remarks on Hieroglyphics" in *D273* are mostly extracts from Thomas Young's periodical publications concerning his discoveries and may well be a retracing of important steps in the deciphering process that were missing in *E115*. But if in *E115* Morley had somehow gotten off course in his survey of the field and practical application of the deciphering process, it is nevertheless the most imaginative of his notebooks.

Indeed, Morley has undertaken to illustrate the volume himself, and the first page of each chapter is given a beautifully rendered drawing in color mostly likely taken from tomb paintings. He may have seen such paintings at the British Museum: at least now one can. For chapter two[44] he has made a pencil sketch of a tomb painting, very like ones in the British Museum from the tomb of the nobleman Nebamun (c. 1350 BC), with married couples sitting on stools and chairs side by side at a feast; it most clearly resembles the top register of EA37984, but Morley's drawing depicts damage to the heads of the female servant and one male guest. However, Morley has penciled in a line drawn to a circled citation "p. 78," indicating he has copied it from a publication. Given the lines of circulation between himself, Horace Hayman Wilson, and Samuel Birch, the British Museum's first Egyptologist, or given the Anglo-French struggle over dominance in Egyptian scholarship (as well as Napoleon's looting of artifacts that constituted the mainstay of the museum's Egyptian objects), he most probably ventured over to the nearby museum to view its collection of Egyptian artifacts. But to Egypt itself he most certainly did not. The romance is worth more than factuality, and yet as he makes clear at the end of a chapter surveying the scholarship on hieroglyphics and demotic writing, he himself is given to a certain kind of scientific romance in which he imagines himself the valiant British hero of the decoding race with the French.

Morley begins the notebook with a chapter surveying the history of western thought on the hieroglyphs beginning with Herodotus, which then transitions to an explanation of the three main writing systems used in Ancient Egypt: hieroglyphs for religious purposes, hieratic (a cursive version of the hieroglyphs) for scribes engaged in political or religious affairs, and demotic for everyday records, letters, and commercial documents. Morley's Romanticism should not be emphasized over his scholarly nature however, for his explanation of these three writing systems is unduly legalistic:

> Now those who are educated among the Egyptians, learn first of all, the method of Egyptian writing called *Epistolographic*; secondly the *Hieratic*, which the Hierogrammatists employ; and lastly, the complete kind, the *Hieroglyphic*; of which one sort is the *Kuriologic* [or curiologic, expressive of objects in a proper, not figurative or metaphorical, manner] by means of the first elements of words [that is plainly and directly expressive of words, by means of hieroglyphs employed as letters] and the other *Symbolic*; (these two sorts are the Phonetic and Ideagra[phi]c [*sic*] species of the moderns)[.][45]

However, it is this explanation expanded into sections for each system that then returns to the survey of modern linguistic accomplishment in the field.

Chapter two is devoted to the "enchorial" or demotic system, which Morley has termed "Epistolographic" in the quoted passage above but rarely uses afterward. To discuss the demotic both in terms of its derivation and western scholarship, thus far Morley draws on his note-taking for other scripts and writing systems of eastern cultures, particularly Chinese which he feels shares originary terrain with Egyptian hieroglyphs. Chapter three is entitled "The Pillar of Rosetta"; chapter four "On Enchorial Papyri and the Nature of

Egyptian Deeds"; chapter five "The Berlin Manuscript of Kosegarten and the Syngraph of Casali"; chapter eight "Grey's Enchorial Agreements"; chapter eleven "Enchorial Preambles to various [sic] Deeds—Enchorial Fragments." Chapters six, seven, nine, and ten are left blank, but the conclusion is beautifully decorated with a tracing of a demotic text with complex linear drawings above each of three columns depicting sacred symbols or deities with humans. The same page also contains a tracing of a fragment of large demotic writing with a citation note in Italian to the Vatican Library's collection, from which this papyrus was presumably taken. Although the name "C.F. Champollion" (incorrectly) is noted at the bottom, on the backside is a citation tp Bachmann in German, also on this Vatican papyrus, indicating Morley may have double-checked Bachmann's work against Champollion's. Again, the resistance to trusting French territorialism (if not in this case, French scholarship) raises its head.

As the chapter titles reveal, for Morley the key lies in the "enchorial" or demotic writing rather than the hieroglyphic, for this was the language of the people, the living language that both in its application and appearance most closely resembles Arabic and Persian scripts. In this, his thinking might appear quite progressive. Morley appears more at ease tackling the demotic, and it is also the linguistic puzzle better attuned to his own scholarship, whereas the hieroglyphic system—which his book portends to survey and explain—remains a code rather than a language to him. Yet the hieroglyphs have not lost their luster, for the contest between Champollion and Young to decipher the demotic register of the Rosetta Stone through comparison with the Greek register was based on the hope that success here would lead to decoding the hieroglyphic register. This connects to Morley's other linguistic interests in that the prevalence of papyri containing deeds and other documents that were increasingly but serendipitously finding their way to western markets, just as the Persian and Arabic manuscripts that made Morley's fame had been chance discoveries, and felicitously fleshed out by related manuscripts or different fragments of the same work. Moreover, the legalistic language and nature of the demotic deeds and other documents would have been thrillingly familiar given Morley's own career as a barrister. Certainly, notebook *D273* contains multiple transcriptions of deeds and other legal transactions from papyri recently translated from the demotic, and he was clearly intrigued by these records of everyday life.

It would have been this very life that would have stirred interest because the papyri being brought back to England were from the Alexandrian period; this is the Egypt of Classical historiography, of Roman imperial history in the making, of Shakespeare's tragedy of Cleopatra VII Philopator, last pharaoh of Egypt. Ptolemaic Egypt must have seemed not only more familiar, but more recoverable than the dynastic Egypt of the hieroglyphic record. The transcriptions of Morley copies are those provided by Young for papyri bought at Thebes in 1820 by George Francis Grey, Esq. of University College Oxford during his travels in the east. A reviewer in the *Edinburgh Review* retraces the contribution these papyri made to linguistic research: both Champollion and Young had been working on sixteen papyri brought to Paris by a M. Casati, one of which Champollion discovered had an enchorial [demotic] text very close to that of the Rosetta enchorial text.[46] A note in the *European Magazine and London Review* explains that two of the papyri, also purchased at Thebes by Casati, "a traveller recently returned from Egypt," were entirely in Greek, one in both Greek and Egyptian, and the rest in "hieroglyphics or hierotiques, accompanied by symbolical figures."[47] This confusion between the different writing styles is only increased by the reviewer's assumption that the majority of these documents were in the priestly hieroglypic rather than demotic script.[48] Young had made considerable progress in translating the one document among the Casati papyri that both Champollion and he had recognized as more valuable than those in Greek alone possessed by Boekh, Salt, and Drouetti (which scholars had been studying prior to Casati's cache) when Grey delivered his papyri to Young. "Fortunately for the cause of Egyptian Literature," as the patriotic *Edinburgh* reviewer notes, two of Grey's papyri were extremely well preserved, and although also only in Greek, Young quickly realized "to his inexpressible surprise and delight . . . that it was a Translation of the Enchorial Manuscript of Casati."[49] Again, chance discoveries of fragile documents made translative progress possible. Young had embarked on further study of several of Grey's papyri that had proved to be deeds in demotic with Greek registries (it is these which Morley transcribes in his notebook; Young published his translations with illustrations by Horne Took), and was making great progress when Amedeus Peyron, professor of Oriental Languages at Turin, published a translation of a demotic text belonging to the Royal Library at Turin, also from the Ptolemaic period. And so it went. Young published *An Account of Some Recent Discoveries in Hieroglyphical Literature* with John Murray in 1823, including his translations of the Grey papyri, and Champollion published his translation of the Rosetta hieroglyphic register in 1822, publishing his decisive work on the hieroglyphs in 1824: his *Précis du système hiéroglyphique* enabled the field of Egyptology to finally take off, particularly after he published his findings on the Turin King List, proving it to record the Egyptian dynasties chronologically, as well as his dating of the Dendera zodiac as belonging to the Roman period. Perhaps as a final touch to his victory over Young, who had been working on the task since the discovery at Rosetta, as well as German linguists, Champollion was made Professor of Egyptology at the Collège de France as a consequence.

This was the state of affairs when Morley was a young man training for the law. By the time he undertook his book on Egyptian writing, the antagonism between French and British linguists was well established after an initial period of collaborative consultation, an antagonism reflecting the Anglo attitude of the Wart with France and subsequently of the Napoleonic period, and its aftermath coloring his version of the story. Moreover, the decided Alexandrian slant on Egyptian life beginning with Classical authors had hardly been corrected, since western traders through the ages into the nineteenth century worked primarily from the great port of Alexandria, where western political consulates were also for the most part stationed. For much of the nineteenth century all Egyptian time continued to be condensed into that of the Ptolemies and translated via that lens. This started to change when William John Bankes, second son of Henry Bankes, discovered and removed the King's List from a wall in the Temple of Ramesses II at Abydos, cult center of Osiris. Both the city and temple had a strong candidacy for recording history for posterity, however slanted toward Ramesses's ideological requirements (the list ignores the kings of doubtful authority of the First and Second Intermediate Periods, and those of the Amarna Period; it was acquired by the British Museum in 1837). This list could be combined with the only list readily at hand, that compiled by Manetho at the behest of Ptolemy (Ptolemy I Soter, 323–283 BC) as part of his endeavor to incorporate himself and his reign into the dynastic lineage of the Egyptian pharaohs. Manetho's magnificent *Aegyptiaca* (*History of Egypt*) was a three-volume work providing an Egyptian-oriented, chronologically organized history to counter Herodotus's account of Egypt in his *Histories*. The urgency of the king's list was probably less to do with historical accuracy in the early nineteenth century, when a metaphysical rather than Egyptological ardor was still regnant, than with politics. The most recently discovered king's list was written on papyrus and found by Bernardino Drovetti in 1820 at Thebes (acquired by the Turin Museum in 1824). Because the papyrus had disintegrated during transport, it was in such small fragments that when Champollion examined it he could only decipher a number of royal names. (Subsequent lists were discovered in 1843 [the Karnak Tablet, which Richard Burton had described in 1825 but not excavated or recorded], 1861, 1866, and 1923).

The romance of this race to decipher the demotic and hieroglyphic writing systems is evident in Morley's first line of his introductory essay:

> "Amit ignotum pro magnifico est"—never has this maxim been more fully exemplified than in the subject before us; the Picture writing of Egypt has been for ages the fancied depository of the mysteries of Theology, and the secrets of the occult sciences, it has been venerated by the metaphysicians and the alchymist of bygone days as the sealed book which contained the full developement [*sic*] of those imaginary truths in the search after which they vainly expended both their lives and their substance, each enthusiast in his turn conceiving that

his favourite pursuit, would naturally be the one chosen to be recorded in the writings of the most learned class of the most learned nation that ever existed—

By the influence of these extravagant opinions the Egyptian hieroglyphs have been for several centuries the object of deep investigation and laborious research, but, till within the last few years, they have resisted every attempt made to decipher them.[50]

The recent advance is the Rosetta Stone; with its help Morley will explicate how the two contrasting systems, hieroglyphic and demotic, function. (He is presuming the third system, hieratic, to be self-explanatory as a journeyman's version of hieroglyphics.) Even if the decoding of the stone does not lead up to the fabled expectations of prior ages "to convert stones into gold, or to procure fire which should burn for ever [sic] without aliment," nevertheless, "we have already separated much of the pure gold of historical truth from the overwhelming dross of fable, and the lamp of history even now shines clearer through the mist of tradition, and enables us to distinguish with certainty things which for a thousand years have been obscured by the clouds of ignorance and superstition—."[51] As proof of how far the empirical research of the current day has come, Morley contrasts recent accomplishments to that of Kircher:

> The works of the worthiest of former times merit some attention on account of the originality of invention and great powers of imagination which they unquestionably display—Amongst these the magnum opus of the learned Father Kircher decidedly claims the preeminence both from its size and celebrity—The Jesuit has filled six immense volumes with his speculations, and professed to explain every inscription which came under his notice; rendering them all into barbarous latin [sic], almost as unintelligible as the hieroglyphs themselves, and expressive of various fanciful doctrines of religion and metaphysics of so extravagant a nature, that we may safely pronounce, that they could have arisen nowhere but in the heated imagination of the learned Father himself—[.][52]

Similarly misguided have been the Abbé Pluche, and more recently, the Chevalier Palin, who "made an astounding discovery that many of the Egyptian mss. are neither more nor less than the originals of the psalms of David expressed in an Deagraphic character similar to the ancient Chinese, and that we have only to write the inspired songs of the Psalmist in that character, in order to possess duplicates of the Egyptian papyri—."[53] However, like empirical science itself—of which linguistics is a branch—"The Pillar of Rosetta like the spear of Ithuriel quickly put to fight the dreams of these learned visionaries." Despite this, the labors of Young and Champollion have left "much to be done."[54] Indeed, Morley likens the quest to that of a Masonic ritual or excavation of a pyramid: "the entrance to the labyrinth has as yet only been discovered, and the inner recesses are unexplored." Recounting briefly the history of Champollion's *Lettre à M. Dacier* and Young's *Account of some recent discoveries in Hieroglyphical Literature*,[55] Morley then, rather self-blindly, proclaims his own allegiance to scientific fair-mindedness:

> This quarrel was afterward taken up with some virulence by writers of the respective nations to which the parties belonged, and poor Champollion who has been both admired and abused far beyond his deserts, was much bespattered by our English critics—Now the matter seems to me to rest thus; that Young first imagined and discovered the system of representing sounds, but failed in the application of it, whilst the Frenchman succeeded—They may therefore jointly claim the honour of having found the road to the intrepretation [sic] of hieroglyphics, since it is probably that neither would have succeeded in their operations but for the assistance of the other—[.][56]

And whereas the famed French linguist Silvestre de Sacy pointed out that Young had followed an incorrect hypothesis concerning the phonetic system employed in hieroglyphic representation, allowing Champollion the victory, nevertheless "De Sacy assigns the discovery to Champollion without laying a sufficient stress on 'les idées fondamentales' the credit of which evidently and by his own acknowledgement belongs to our countryman—Dr Young suggested the first ideas without having been sufficiently clear on the point to put them into practice—Champollion reduced these ideas to practical form and verified the analytical process employed by Young—The latter discovered the phonetic nature of the hieroglyphs, and the former the phonetic system of the Ancient Egyptians."[57] Indeed, de Sacy himself had originally sided with Young in the phonetic theory of hieroglyphics. Therefore, Britain can indeed claim the true victory, for in Morley's view Young had been the more brilliant of the two men; moreover, he had been the innovator, he was prior and so aligned with origin. However, it is true that "The honour of having taken the first steps on Enchorial discovery is due to the venerable Silvestre de Sacy." Still, he could go no further than identifying the names of "Alexander, Alexandria Ptolemy, and some few others," and "gave up the task," leaving it to the Danish Johan David Åkerblad ("formerly the Swedish Counsul at Alexandria," and a student of de Sacy), by Morley's account, to assign phonetic values to several characters in the demotic alphabet.[58] In fact, Young, de Sacy, and Åkerblad had all followed the hypothesis that the hieroglyphs, and therefore the demotic signs as well, were symbols; but Morley in arguing how Young's theory had mainly held the day, claims for Young "the invention of the grand secret of interpretation, namely the Phonetic system (that is the representation of sounds and not merely ideas by pictural [sic] and other marks)."⁵⁹ Still, Champollion realized that hieroglyphs are a mix of phonetic symbols, syllabic signs, and determinatives (ideograms standing for an idea, such as a divinity, a person, an abstract idea). Cleopatra VII's various royal names contained this mix, and Champollion was eventually able to decipher 111 signs, including 23 alphabetic letters.

Quoting Young's own words, Morley then reveals why Young is in his eyes a knight, indeed a knight errant whose quest did not begin as a self-promoting endeavor for fame (as, presumably, Champollion's was): "I had been induced by motives both of private friendship and professional obligation to offer to the Editors of a periodical publication an article . . . containing an abstract of Adelung's Mithridates a work then recently received from the continent." Johann Christoph Adelung was also a linguist; his *Mithridates, 1806–1817* was the first comprehensive analysis of the American Indian languages known to date. Clearly what would turn out to be Young's inspiration for translating hieroglyphics would be as romantic as Robert Southey's Celtic myth in *Medoc* or Joseph Smith's in *The Book of Mormon* in connecting the ancient world with the new one:

> In reading this elaborate compilation my curiosity was excited by a note of the Editor, Professor Vater, in which he asserted that the unknown language of the Pillar of Rosetta and of the bandages often found with the mummies was capable of being analysed into an alphabet of little more than thirty letters; but having merely retained a general impression, I thought no more of these inscriptions until they were recalled to my attention by the examination of some garments of papyrus which had been brought home from Egypt by my friend Sir William Rouse Boughton then lately returned from his travels in the East; with this accidental occurrence my Egyptian researches began.⁶⁰

Like the knight errant, but also like the antiquarian and linguist, a chance discovery is required before the task can be assailed. As for the alchemists of old, something magical is required, something like Morley's own chance discoveries of Arabic and Persian texts on material objects and in manuscripts. And even Champollion had begun on a wrong trail, first assuming that Egyptian hieroglyphs could be deciphered via the Coptic language, as many scholars beside himself held it to be the language of Ancient Egypt. Yet despite Champollion's clear victory in the field—and the fact that in 1828 he led an archaeological expedition to Egypt whereas Young never visited Egypt—Morley still concludes this section in 1834 with "The result of these researches [by Young] as is well known was a complete translation of the Inscription of Rosetta, and of several other Enchorial texts and dates of the highest importance in Egyptian Archæology—His researches as well as those of De Sacy and Akerblad and other writers with the inferences to be drawn from them will be fully considered in the following pages—."[61] It is as if Champollion has dropped out of the picture and only the romance of the knight Young will now be narrated. Indeed, Champollion's success was still only partial, and many hieratic and demotic characters remained to be deciphered, although by 1814 Young had successfully translated eighty-six demotic words; following Young, Morley would enter the contest himself and declaratively solve the Egyptian puzzle, or at least the demotic—and in his eyes most important—piece of it. The quest for the knowable, Morley's defense shows, is at war with the Romantic passion for unknowability, and despite Morley's romancing of this storied linguistic race, here there is no overt demonstration of his earlier quest for the unknown. Yet Morley remains a late Romantic; he displays no affinity for Victorian principles or ideologies.

Fittingly then, the page following this declaration is decorated with a careful design of the wings of Horus, the outline inked in and the wings painted a golden or light sepia wash. Wisdom and the all-seeing eye will preside over this version of the story. It might seem from this and the introductory essay that the logic of science, and not of superstition, alchemical trickery or intellectual theft—terms that have replaced and demoted the mysteries of cosmic knowledge—are the patrons of Morley's endeavor. Nevertheless, the all-seeing eye of Horus designates not empirical facts but Ra's cosmic wisdom. Without noticing the discrepancy between the image and his verbal intent, he begins chapter one with an excoriating dismissal of Classical scholarship:

> The knowledge of the Greeks and Romans of the nature of hieroglyphics appears to have been very scanty; the Greeks fancied that they [the Egyptians] were both invented and employed for the purpose of concealing the secrets of religion and philosophy, and that their use an study was confined to the priesthood; this applies equally to the Romans, and the story of a reward having been offered by one of the Caesars to him who should give an interpretation of the inscription on the obelisk which had been brought to Rome, as this reward was never claimed, leads us to conclude that the knowledge of the Romans on the subject amounted to nothing—[.][62]

Despite this easy dismissal of Classical erudition, Morley's supposed scientific endeavor illustrates how dependent scholars still were on Classical sources like Herodotus, Diodorus Siculus, and Clemens Alexandrinus (or as he calls him, "Clement, the Alexandrian Presbyter"). These sources provided information about hieroglyphics in particular, but also provided the only known information about Ancient Egypt. So for instance, after the dismissive opening to the chapter Morley notes that Herodotus ("the father of history") explains that the Egyptians used both sacred and demotic characters, and

Diodorus "repeats this statement almost in the same words," but then explains "that the popular characters were taught to all, but that the knowledge of the sacred characters was confined exclusively to the priests." (That both historians based their knowledge of Ancient Egypt on Alexandrian culture reveals why Diodorus might have thought writing was "taught to all" rather than to the elite only, a point not questioned during the nineteenth century.) Morley then comments: "This is all new information afforded by these two authors both of whom visited Egypt, it is in perfect accordance with the inscription of Rosetta which makes mention of only two kinds of writing[,] the one called 'sacred' & the other 'enchorial' . . . evidently identical with the Demotic of Herodotus and Diodorus," adding in a sidebar note "(insert this—Pliny also mentions two kinds of writing amongst the Egyptians [^ the one hieroglyphic + the other alphabetic – XXXVI – 8 – VI – 50]."[63] To this overly pedantic explanation, Morley adds information garnered from Athanasius Kircher and other antiquarians who he includes as authorities despite his earlier dismissals.

To shore up his survey of the field thus far, Morley inserts as much as possible corroborating scholarship both Classical and scholastic, as well as present day to prove his own credentials for elucidating the history of the linguistic quest. Quotations and citations from Herodotus, Stromata, Pliny, Diodorus Siculus, and Clement (but almost never Kircher) are seconded by scholars such as William Warburton (whose "Essay on Hieroglyphics" in the *Divine Legation of Moses Demonstrated* was absent from the introductory essay), Julius Klaproth, M. Letromie, Charles Wall, de Sacy, and even Champollion. Some of these points, Morley contends were significant: Clement, for instance, had already noted that "The Egyptian method of writing was Epistolographic, Sacerdotal, and Hieroglyphical, of this method, the Epistolographic and Sacerdotal were by letters of an alphabet; the hieroglyphical, by symbols; symbols were of three kinds, curiologic, tropical and allegoral [*sic*]—" Note (II) pp. 401–2—."[64]

However, even access to what he considers important contributions requires some jousting, for Warburton—who cites this identical passage—has incorrectly translated it from the Greek, thus rendering its information misleading and useless. Morley not only destroys Warburton here, but provides what he contends is the correct translation himself ("This version of Warburton's is decidedly incorrect—There is no such remote antecedent in the Greek as that adduced by the Bishop; there is not any reference to the general method of the Egyptians; but the first method mentioned is the Epistolographic").[65]

Finally at the end of the survey chapter, Morley explains his true intent: "In the following chapter I shall examine these different opinions and bring forward some arguments in favour of my own view of the subject, which I trust I shall demonstrate to be not far from the truth—."[66] Despite the modesty of the "I trust," the intent is declarative; the gauntlet has been thrown down. It is the demotic that he intends to succeed in reading rather than the hieroglyphic, which Champollion has already done so much to decipher. The "different opinions" referred to in his declaration are to the preceding sentence: "There has been much difference of opinion as to the nature of this writing, some maintaining that it is entirely ideagraphic [sic] to the total exclusion of phonetic and alphabetic powers, others that it partakes of both these properties, and other again who look upon it as purely alphabetic—."[67] If the aim seems less grand than Champollion's success, however incomplete, with hieroglyphics, it is certainly more in line with Morley's sense that the everyday language of documents, deeds, and romance is where the real metaphysical struggle takes place. Priestly language is for the superstitious and the ritualistic; the demotic language, to which English is the equivalent for him, is the stuff of hypothesis, debate, and adventure. It is the translative medium, it is what linguistics is all about. And it can provide knowability.

Yet oddly, the drawing that follows his vaunt is a finely executed ink drawing of the Great Sphinx, fully exposed (unlike the half-buried Sphinx of the frontispiece), and imagined as intact with a royal beard, its front paws surrounding a temple complex. Two figures, clearly Ancient Egyptians, discursively gesture toward it, one standing on the left paw. This prototype for the printer's engraver gives lie to the modesty of the vaunt, for he is clearly drawing on both the Greek riddle of the sphinx as representing all wisdom, and the Egyptian association of the sphinx with the pharaoh's protective spirit as well as the necromancy of their grandest pyramidal complex. Although the sphinx signals for the Romantics the very essence of unknowability, here it captures the sense that Morley's intended project requires the same herculean efforts he had attributed to Young, the high quality of mind, and the determination to achieve knowledge. The missing chapters are evidence that his theory was not working out quite as he had hoped, and to remedy this he returned to Notebook D273 to take long and careful notes on Young's published letters. Indeed, the transcribed excerpts are almost entirely from Young, with only a few interpolated comments revealing his own thoughts or dismissals of others' scholarship or theories. Perhaps the sphinx was an apt symbol after all for his unfinished project, for Egypt remained unknowable. And despite Morley's efforts to appear scientific in his research, the introduction to his unwritten book displays not only unscientific prejudices and romance, but also a real passion for the hieroglyphs. In these elements Morley displays, despite his seeming disregard for unknowability, the legacy of Romanticism's fascination with the unknowable as a form of knowledge and as a way to access the absolute.

VII. HIEROGLYPHICA

Hieroglyphic fever, like "the Chinese prejudice," is a metaphysical disease. The desire to read the signs and symbols of ancient wisdom, royal ritual, priestly rites, and even magic was already present in Ptolemaic Egypt, a period when even the priests no longer had a command of the hieroglyphic code and travelers like Herodotus were reduced to recording superstitions concerning the hieroglyphs' power. Hermeticism did nothing to quell the sense of archaic knowledge now lost, and alchemists attempted to reconstruct this knowledge, which was presumed to concern the boundaries between life and death, between animate and inanimate matter, and life and matter. Once contracted, the disease becomes symptomatic, recurrent in the channels of normal life.

So even when Morley settles down to a rather more staid attempt to understand Ancient Egyptian writing systems subsequent to his 1834–1835 notebook on the subject, his research is single-mindedly focused on proving Young's theories correct so that he might himself decipher the demotic code. There has been no reduction of the fever. But before beginning the lengthy section of Notebook D273 entitled "Hieroglyphics," he orients the notebook with prolonged notes on Sanskrit as an ancient language now fairly well understood, due to the efforts of Sir William Jones and the Royal Asiatic Society of Bengal. He also includes biblical scholarship, which he also understands to be scientifically accurate in terms of empirical knowledge about the ancient world. These focus largely on linguistic matters, although elsewhere he has copied excerpts concerning other matters: "Table of Scripture Measures," genealogies of the Hebrew kings and high priests, as well as those languages relative to biblical history including "Aramæan, Chaldee [biblical Aramaic], and Syriac," and "Versions of the Scriptures in the modern Oriental Languages."[68] He also copies information on the "Targums," or versions of the Old Testament "which have been composed in the Chaldee [*sic*] dialect—Ten of these have been preserved to our times—viz—[.]"[69] And he prefaces the "Hieroglyphics" section with the following excerpts on the loss of such linguistic knowledge, entitled "Destruction of Libraries," the second more or less translating the first:

—Si l'Occident a accusé nou sans raison le Khalife Omar de L'incendie de la bibliothè d'Alexandrie, l'Orient peut répondre a cette accusation en citant l'incendie de la bibliothéqe de Tripoli par les croisés, ou fureut consumes des millions de livres arabes –(Memoires geographiques et historiques sur l'Egypte par Quatremère—t.ii-p.505 [emphasis his])[.] La bibliothèques d'alexandrie fut incendiée par les Musulmans, parce que d'après les orders d'Omar, le Koran seul devait être considéré comme le livre des livres, et tout ce qui n'y était point contenu regardé comme inutile—La bibliothèque de Tripoli fut détruite par les chrétiens, parce qu'elle ne se composait que de Korans et d'autres livres d'interprétation religieuse—Von Hammer—

Omar destroyed the library of Alexandria, and threw the books contained in the Library of Medayín into the Tigris, within the space of two years, thus at once destroying the accumulated knowledge of the Greeks and the Persians, which had been carefully collected and preserved for centuries by the Ptolemies and the Sassamides—.[70]

His focus here is on the destruction of Persian and Arabic manuscripts, the two languages Morley can read; the widespread knowledge that the third and final destruction of the Library of Alexandria by the Moslem invaders is here recited as a disastrous interruption in the transmission of the invaluable accumulated knowledge of the ancient world. These sobering thoughts are followed by excerpts and notes on the "Origin of Alphabetic Writing," proving that scientific methods cannot be thwarted by such outright intellectual carnage. Here he reverts again to the hieroglyphic by way of discussion of the writing system of Ancient Egypt's contemporary and competitor in both magic and empirical knowledge acquisition, Chaldea. Using Nimrod's wife, Semiramis, as an entrée he writes: "—The most ancient monument of alphabetic writing which history has transmitted to us is of the date of the reign of Semiramis—Diodorus Siculus speaks of this queen having cut Syrian or Chaldæan letters in the rock of Bagistan in India," followed by "Aristotle on the credit of the most ancient records, speaks of the Chaldæan magi as prior to the Egyptian priests who nevertheless cultivated learning before the time of Moses—(Laertius lib.I.c.8)," and "Pliny says (lib. 7.c.56) that the Babylonians kept their astrominical observat^n engraved on bricks & Clemens Alexandrius (Stromata l.) says that Democritus transcribed his moral discourses from a Babylonian pillar; & Sanchoniathon, Plato, Berosus the Chaldæan, & others, seem to acknowledge the priority of the Chaldæans to the Egyptians, the Egypt^n Priests themselves acknowledged it, & Moses leaves no doubt on the subject—[.]" The authority of Moses cannot be doubted here, the comment shoring up Morley's belief in the literalness of the Bible. Earlier he had recorded that "According to our researches the Syrian alphabet used by the primitive Chaldæans is the most ancient of all, & the square letters used by the Hebrews since the Babylonish [*sic*] captivity, the Arabic, the present abysinian [*sic*], as well as the angular characters, Sanscrit (!!!) [*sic*] Pahli Calmuc [*sic*] &c were derived from it—."[71] And elsewhere one learns the "Origin of the word Adam."[72]

But on page 145 v. information more decisively in line with his Egyptological interests appears, copied from M. le Chev. Louis Demeni de Rienzi: "The ancient Greek Alphab^t, the ancient Phœnician, the Punic (!) [*sic*]

+ the Samaritan, which was the ancient character of the Hebrews, sprang from the Demotic characters of Egypt." However, Morley notes in one of his increasingly present comments, "There are some curious facts to be gathered from Rienzi's fragments, though his opinions are very extravagant, + frequently very ridiculous.

He seems to have been a man of laborious but misguided research—[.]" This thought is followed by a large flourish, revealing that Morley is not only feeling intellectually superior here, but that he believes he has found the key to the mystery.

When the "Hieroglyphics" section begins, which largely takes over the notebook and all but concludes it, Morley is secure that in copying Young's *Letters* as published in various periodicals (primarily *The Quarterly Journal of Science, Literature and the Arts*, but also *Hieroglyphics* and *The Classical Journal*), he will arrive at the theoretical and evidentiary materials he needs to explicate and prove his own theory of the demotic. That this feat was never accomplished may have more to do with Morley's own failing health as he entered his forties, and the increasing demands of the Royal Asiatic Society that he focus on Arabic and Persian texts. He therefore copies verbatim what was easily available in bound volumes by 1837 (and in fact, many of his extracts are taken from the 1827 edition). Quotes such as the following appear as decisive: "The tablet represented in Plate 51 is remarkable for the confirmat^n which its date affords of the accuracy of our chronology of the Ptolemies—It has no pure hieroglyphics—It begins immediately with"

> "The year 19, otherwise 4, of Cleopatra [Neotera] + Ptolemy surnamed Caesar"; that is, The year 34 B.C. + the same date is repeated in a form somewhat more distinct four times, in the 10th, 11th, 12th + 15th lines—In the lat it is followed by "The Queen gave to the high priests" .... then Ptolemy [Auletes?] ... Queen Cleopatra + King Ptolemy surnamed Cæsar" —.[73]

Young's confidence rubs off on Morley's own asides and interpolated exclamation marks as he laughs at other linguists' continued efforts to show one ancient language or another the antecedent of Egyptian, or as Champollion had originally done with Coptic, as the language spoken by the Egyptians. At times Young's voice nearly becomes Morley's own, as in quotations such as "I had lately been look[in]g over the Enchorial deeds of Mr. Grey with the hopes of advanc[in]g a few steps in the study of the language."[74] This might be a paraphrase of Morley's own claims in his manuscript on Egyptian writing systems—to advance a few steps, which is the same in this contest as winning the field.

The section on hieroglyphics shifts to a focus on the demotic (or as Morley consistently terms it, the enchorial) with a full eighty-six pages of closely written extracts (146 recto to 183 recto) interpolated by his own occasional brief comments. It is difficult to know precisely what he is thinking in terms of his own theory, except that he is confident he will arrive at a full understanding in order to complete his manuscript on the topic. That it is this notebook, however, and not the one devoted to Sanskrit grammar, and the geography and culture of Bengal (notebook D278), which concludes with the advertisements for the East India civil service and language lessons, providing perhaps the best clue as to why the quest was abortive. It may not have been the difficulty with Young's hypothesis and system, nor even the need to make a grander mark than he had done thus far with his Arabic and Persian research, but the need to try again for a colonial post.

VIII. CONCLUSION

However we understand Morley's aborted quest, it is clear that his metaphysical disease of hieroglyphica is none other than his version of Egyptian Romanticism, for Ancient Egypt tropes for him the otherness of Ancient Egyptian ways of thinking through decipherment of its language. It appears to stand in for the place from which he was perpetually excluded in his failed attempts to obtain a post with the East India Company as well as. In not understanding demotic, Morley's metaphysical disease was very much that of not being able to choose between the unknowable and the knowable, between the speculative and the empiricism of Aristotelian science. In short, he could not Egyptianize himself. This inability to choose is indeed the fulcrum or pyramidal point—the occultating moment—on which Morley, like so many others before him, teetered. His late Romantic response to Egypt, lacking as it was in a fully Romantic embrace of Egyptianization, would soon be replaced by nineteenth-century Egyptology with its sharp division between word and thing, as well as and a more fully developed science of linguistics, but resonances of the Alexandrian Dream and of Hermetic thinking that are clearly still present in his notebooks have continued to appear and weave into the thinking and imaginative projects of the Modern era. It may be that the twentieth century's continued fascination with Egyptian artifacts, monuments, and culture is not nostalgia for the ancient world so much as a reflection of a more distinctly traumatic understanding of what has been irrevocably lost. The longing for the originary place of western culture, and for what can't be known, has caused Egypt to be the ground of that longing, both its archaic ground and its *Ungrund*. For the west Ancient Egypt has remained the unknowable place *par excellence*.

Chapter 5

NOTES

1. Novalis, *Logical Fragments II*, no. 15, 70.
2. Derrida, *Of Grammatology*, 80.
3. Monstrosities and anomalies only proved infinite variability within the taxonomic system for a particular genus or species for Classical (seventeenth- and eighteenth-century) scientists. Foucault, *The Order of Things*, 150–157.
4. See particularly Hans Aarsleff's introductory to Humboldt's *On Language* for the role Humboldt attributes to hieroglyphs in language development.
5. Ibid, 89.
6. Ibid, 131.
7. Ibid, 27.
8. Ibid, 26, 173.
9. Ibid, 32.
10. See Derrida's lengthy endnote concerning the Thoth-Hermes association with the origination of writing. Derrida, *Of Grammatology*, note 31, 328–329.
11. Plotkin, "Scribble," 116.
12. "Scribble (Writing Power)," 118.
13. Quoted in Derrida, "Scribble (Writing Power)," 124–125.
14. Warburton, *The Divine Legation of Moses*, Vol. I, 133.
15. Derrida's commentary on this clarifies Warburton's critique of Kircher: "Warburton will not claim that the priests never wanted to 'hide their knowledge' by veiling it. But by demonstrating that neither this veil not this intention was originary, he wants to 'unveil' the error that had made concealment the (secret) mainspring of writing. Kircher's mistake is itself the effect of a (real but secondary) veil: by lifting the veil and returning to the natural origin, one will unveil the error" ("Scribble (Writing Power)," 125).
16. Derrida, "Scribble (Writing Power)," 126:

> [Hieroglyphic writing] is the sought-after "internal proof": hieroglyphic writing does not surround knowledge like the detachable form of a container or signifier. It structures the content of knowledge. This explains why, according to Warburton, when other peoples were reaching toward a more manageable and economical system of writing (the alphabet), the Egyptians should have wished to preserve, with their writing, the very treasure-house of their knowledge-a premise indispensable to the author's theses on the religion and politics of the Hebrews and the condition for a revival of Biblical studies as well, a major concern of Warburton's in his struggle against "freethinking."

17. Foucault, *Order of Things*, 110–111. See Derrida's critique of Foucault's analysis of power in "Scribble (Writing Power)."
18. Ibid, 111.
19. Derrida, *Of Grammatology*, 15.
20. Ibid, 17.
21. Quoted from Madeleine V.-David's *Le président de Brosses et les cultes de l'ancienne Égypte* (1969) in Derrida, *Of Grammatology*, 80. (The quote is unattributed except by an abbreviation of David's name.)

22. Ibid, 81; emphasis Derrida's.
23. Ibid, 80.
24. See Johnson, *System and Writing in the Philosophy of Jacques Derrida*, 88–91.
25. A Resident Member resides in Great Britain or Ireland; a Non-Resident Member resides abroad. Although Morley was not elected a member until he is thirty-two, he may well have been affiliated with the RAS since its inception however, as his Orientalist notebooks begin when he is fifteen.
26. Hutchinson, *A Catalogue of Notable Middle Templars*. Morley is also listed in Martin and Hutchinson's *Middle Temple Records*; clearly he remains 'notable,' although again, not as a barrister.
27. Notebooks *C 46-49* in the British Library, India Office Records and Private Papers. Morley's other notebooks in this collection I will reference are D273, D278, and E115.
28. Champollion's first published discovery was his 1822 *Lettre á M. Dacier relative á l'Alphabet des hieroglypics phonetiques employès* . . . .
29. "For this Presidency a study of the three languages in England is strongly recommended, though an intimate acquaintance with all, as devolving too heavy a task upon many students, is not imperatively enjoined."
30. Morley, Notebook D273.
31. Letters Received by Horace Hayman Wilson (1786–1860), British Library, India Office Records and Private Papers Archive, Mss Eur E301, vol 8 folio 1–2.
32. Morley, Notebook D273, 146v.; emphasis added.
33. *Report of Annual Proceedings of the Royal Asiatic Society of Great Britain and Ireland*, vol 1, 1824, viii.
34. Ibid, i–ii. However, this solution was not viable: "This proposal was, however, pronounced to be, for the present, impracticable, by reason of the temporary nature of the arrangements made for the reception of the museum and library of the East India Company" (ii), and Sir Charles Wood suggested "That perhaps the East India museum and that of the Society might, advantageously for the public, be transferred to the new museum at South Kensington; while the three libraries of the East India House, Haileybury, and Board of Control, now belonging to the India Office, together with that of the Society, might, perhaps, be amalgamated in some manner to be determined upon by mutual agreement, and either accommodated together in the new building projected, or in the Society's house, or, under conditions to be specially negotiated, transferred together to the library of the British Museum." Ibid, iii.
35. He was awarded by the Royal Asiatic Society of Bengal for his scholarly publications, his correspondence contains many letters from members of the London society, and by 1849 his letters are addressed to him with the honorific for a Fellow of the Royal Asiatic Society.
36. Morley, Notebook D273.
37. One, by Abú Suleiman Dáúd surnamed Al Fakhr Al Benágiti, is an abridgement of a much longer work, and is divided into nine parts which are then divided into books, chapters, or sections, all of which Morley records in notebook D273.

38. Morley, "Letter to Major-General John Briggs," 15.

39. "Munshi" is a Persian word used in both the Mughal and British empires to denote native language teachers and secretaries.

40. Morley, Notebooks C 46–49. Introduction, I. 4 recto, "The collection of Stories here presented to the public are selected from a Ms. in four volumes preserved in the Library of the Oriental Translation Committee by whose kindness it has been lent to me for the purpose of translation—."

41. "This I am also encouraged by the example of Mr Lane by whose learning + taste the charming tales of the Thousand + one nights which have so long delighted the English reader though transmitted through the flimsy medium of the French tongue." Ibid, 9 recto).

42. One is of a young lady with a top knot and ringlets at her temples; the other of an older woman with a larger nose and the hair folded low on the neck back into a bun. Both are simple hairstyles done without aid of a maid, and so were possibly of his wife and either mother or mother-in-law.

43. As Foucault notes, "the isolation of the Indo-European languages, the constitution of a comparative grammar, the study of inflections, the formulation of the laws of vowel gradation and consonantal changes—in short, the whole body of philological work accomplished by Grimm, Schlegel, Rask, and Bopp, has remained on the fringes of our historical awareness, as though it had merely provided the basis for a somewhat lateral and esoteric discipline—as though, in fact, it was not the whole mode of being of language (and of our own language) that had been modified through it." Foucault, *Order of Things*, 281.

44. Morley, Notebook E155, page 43 recto.

45. Ibid, 13 verso. From here on, "v." will stand for verso, and "r." for recto.

46. Anonymous review, *Edinburgh Review*, 528–539.

47. *The European Magazine and London Review* (1823), 178:

Casati, a traveller recently returned from Egypt, has brought from thai country, amongst other antiquities), sixteen rolls of *papyrus*, two of which are in the Greek. . . . The Casati papyrus in the Bibliotheque Nationale is facsimiled in Young's *Hieroglyphics*, Pl. 31–32. (cf. Revillout, Chrestomathie Dent., 62; Br., Thes., 880)

48. The reviewer also assumes that Casati's other papyri, which he had obtained on "the island of Elephant" (the Elephantine, at Aswan), were in such poor condition because "torn and injured by the awkwardness of a priest" (178).

49. Anonymous review, *Edinburgh Review*, 535.

50. Morley, Notebook E115, 1 v.

51. Ibid, 2 r.

52. Ibid, 2 v.

53. Ibid, 3 v.–4 r.

54. Ibid, 4 v.–5 r.

55. Young, *An Account of some recent Discoveries in Hieroglyphical Literature and Egyptian Antiquities including the Author's original alphabet as extendd by Mr Champollion with a translation of five Greek and Egyptian Mss. By Thomas Young*

M.D. F.R.I. Fellow of the Royal College of Physicians (London: John Murray, 1823). Reprinted with abbreviated title in 2010 by Cambridge University Press.

56. Morley, Notebook E115, 5 v.–6 r.
57. Ibid, 6 v.
58. Ibid, 6 v.–7 r.
59. Ibid, 5 r.
60. Ibid, 7 v.–8 r.
61. Ibid.
62. Ibid, 8 r.–9 v.
63. Ibid, 10 r.–10 v.
64. Ibid, 17 v.–18 r.
65. Ibid, 17 v.
66. Ibid, 42 v.
67. Ibid, 41 r.–42 v.
68. Morley, Notebook D273, 123 v., 131r.
69. Ibid, 123 r.
70. Ibid, 82 r.–82 v. The excerpt continues:

Five centuries later the Mongols destroyed the libraries of Alahamút and Baghdád—Ata Malik Jowaïní obtained permission from Hulakú to save works which were worthy of the attention of the Khán—Unfortunately he selected only the Korans and the whole of the remainder of this precious collection consisting not only of works relating to the mysteries and doctrine of the Ismaïlís, but also of numberless valuable treatises on philosophy, mathematics, and astronomy, were delivered over to the flames—This auto da fé was held in imitation of that by the Sultán Yakúb of Fez, who a hundred years before the destruction of the Order of Assassins had burnt all their theological works—The conflagration of the Library of Baghdád is still more to be lamented than that of Alahamút; here were destroyed the treasures of Arabic Literature which had been accumulating for nearly 600 years, and all the Persian manuscripts which had escaped destruction at Medayín—In the same century in which happened the destruction of the Libraries of Alahamút and Baghdád, those of Tripoli, Nishapin and Káhirah were also burnt—The Library of Tripoli, destroyed by the Crusaders contained the enormous number of three millions of Arabic works—[Makrizi; Ibn Khaldín, Ibn Forat; Abú Al Faraj].

71. Ibid, 44 r.–45 v.
72. Ibid, 56 v.
73. Ibid, 149 v.
74. Ibid, 151 r.

Appendix
Further Reading

Aravamudan, Srinivas. *Enlightenment Orientalism: Resisting the Rise of the Novel.* Chicago: Chicago University Press, 2012.
Armitage, David. *The Ideological Origins of the British Empire.* Cambridge: Cambridge University Press, 2000.
Aristotle. *Fragments.* Trans. by Jonathan Barnes and Gavin Lawrence. In *The Complete Works of Aristotle.* Vol. 2. Ed. by Jonathan Barnes. Princeton: Princeton University Press, 1984. 2384–2462.
Ashton, John. *English Caricature and Satire on Napoleon I.* 2 vols. London: Chatto & Windus, 1884.
Athenaeus, *The Deipnosophists*, 6 Vols. Trans. by C. B. Gulick. Cambridge, MA: Harvard University Press, 1927.
Barnes, Jonathan. *The Presocratic Philosophers.* London: Routledge, 1982.
Bennett, Tony. *Pasts Beyond Memory: Evolution, Museums, Colonialism.* London: Routledge, 2004.
Benz, Ernst. *The Mystical Sources of German Romantic Philosophy.* Trans. by Blair R. Reynolds and Eunice M. Paul. Allison Park, PA: Pickwick Publications, 1983.
Bopp, Franz. *Analytical Comparison of the Sanskrit, Greek, Latin and Teutonic Languages, Shewing the Original Identity of their Grammatical Structure.* Intro. by F. Techmer, ed. by E. F. K. Koerner. Rpt. ed. Amsterdam: Benjamins, 1974.
Croce, Benedetto. *What is Living and What Is Dead of the Philosophy of Hegel.* Trans. by Douglas Ainslie. 1915; Kitchener, Ontario: Batoche Books, 2001.
Curran, Brian and Anthony Graftan. *Obelisk: A History.* Cambridge, MA: The MIT Press, 2009.
Darwin, Erasmus. *The Temple of Nature, or, The Origin of Society.* London: J. Johnson, 1803.
Dieckmann, Lisolette. *Hieroglyphics: The History of a Literary Symbol.* St. Louis: Washington University Press, 1970.
Goethe, Johann Wolfgang von. *Iphigenie Auf Tauris.* Ed. with Introduction and Notes by Philip Schuyler Allen. Boston: Ginn & Co., 1906.

Hegel, Georg Wilhelm Friedrich. *Phenomenology of Mind*. Trans. by J.B. Baillie. 1807; rpt. Mineola, NY: Dover Publications, 2003.

Heidegger, Martin. *Schelling's Treatise on the Essence of Human Freedom*. Trans. by Joan Stambaugh. Athens: The Ohio University Press, 1985.

Hornung, Erik. *The Secret Lore of Egypt: Its Impact on the West*. Trans. by David Lorton. Ithaca: Cornell University Press, 2001.

James, George G.M. *Stolen Legacy: The Egyptian Origins of Western Philosophy*. New York: Philosophical Library, 1954.

Kelly, Jason M. *The Society of the Dilettanti: Archaeology and Identity in the British Enlightenment*. New Haven: Yale University Press, 2010.

Kuzniar, Alice A. *Melancholia's Dog: Reflections on Our Animal Kinship*. Chicago: Chicago University Press, 2006.

Krell, David Farrell. *Contagion: Sexuality, Disease, and Death in German Idealism and Romanticism*. Bloomington: Indiana University Press, 1998.

Lane-Pool, Stanley. *A History of Egypt in the Middle Ages*. New York: Scribner & Son, 1901.

———. *Life of Edward William Lane*. s.l.: Williams and Norgate, 1877.

Lane, Edward William. *Manners and Customs of the Modern Egyptians*. 1836; 5th ed. London: John Murray, 1860.

Makdisi, Saree. *Making England Western: Occidentalism, Race, and Imperial Culture*. Chicago: Chicago University Press, 2014.

———. *William Blake and the Impossible History of the 1790s*. Chicago: Chicago University Press, 2002.

Manassa, Colleen. *The Late Egyptian Underworld: Sarcophagi and Related Texts from the Nectanebid Period*. Wiesbaden: Harrassowitz Verlag, 2008.

Martin, Charles Trice and John Hutchinson. *Middle Temple Records*. London, 1923.

Mayer, Paola. *Jean Romanticism and Its appropriation of Jacob Böhme*. Montreal: McGill-Queen's University Press, 1999.

Mesmer, F.A. *Mesmerism: A Translation of the Original Scientific and Medical Writings of F.A. Mesmer*. Trans. and compiled by George Bloch. Los Altos: William Kaufmann, Inc. 1980.

Morton, A.L. *The Everlasting Gospel: A Study in the Sources of William Blake*. London: Lawrence and Wishart, 1958.

Pearce, Susan. "Belzoni's Collecting and the Egyptian Taste." In *The Lustrous Trade: Material Culture and the History of Sculpture in England and Italy, c.1700–c.1860*. Ed. by Cinzia Maria Sicca and Alison Yarrington. London: Continuum, 2000. 191–210.

Pessin, Sarah. "Khoric Apophasis: Matter and Messianicity in Islamo-Judao-Greek Neoplatonism." In *Negative Theology and Jewish Modernity*. Ed. by Michael Fagenblat. 180–197.

Poovey, Mary. *A History of the Modern Fact: Problems of Knowledge in the Sciences of Wealth and Society*. Chicago: Chicago University Press, 1998.

Pope, Maurice. *The Story of Decipherment*. London: Thames and Hudson, 1975. Piranesi, Luigi Feracci. *Piranesi: The Complete Etchings*. Cologne: Taschen, 2016.

Stoudt, John Yost *Jacob Boehme: His Life and Thought*. Eugene: Wipf and Stock, 2004.
Thompson, E.P. *Witness against the Beast: William Blake and the Moral Law*. New York: New Press, 1993.
Thompson, Jason. *Wonderful Things: A History of Egyptology. Vol. I From Antiquity to 1881*. Cairo: The American University in Cairo, 2015.
Weeks, Andrew. *Boehme: An Intellectual Biography of the Seventeenth-Century Philosopher and Mystic*. Albany: The State University of New York Press, 1991.
Rene Wellek, ed. *William Warburton 1698–1779*. New York: Garland Publisher, 1978.
Wigley, Mark. "Postmortem Architecture: The Taste of Derrida." *Perspecta* 23 (1987): 156–179.
Wilson, David M. *The British Museum: A History*. London: British Museum Press, 2002.
Thomson, James. *The Works of James Thomson*. London: Printed for A. Millar and sold by T. Cadell, 1768.
Verbrugghe, Gerald P. and John Moore Wickersham. *Berossos and Manetho, Introduced and Translated: Native Traditions in Ancient Mesopotamia and Egypt*. Ann Arbor: University of Michigan Press, 1996.
Wolosky, Sira. "Two Types of Negative Theology; Or, What Does Negative Theology Negate?" In *Negative Theology and Jewish Modernity*, ed. by Michael Fagenblat. 161–179.
Wood, David and Robert Bernasconi, eds. *Derrida and Différance*. Evanston: Northwestern University Press, 1985.
Wortham, John David. *The Genesis of British Egyptology, 1549–1906*. Norman: University of Oklahoma Press, 1971.
Yates, Francis A. *The Rosicrucian Enlightenment*. New York: Barnes & Noble Books 1972.

Works Cited

Aarsleff, Hans. "Introduction." In Humboldt, *On Language: The Diversity of Human Language-Structure*. Trans. by Peter Heath. Cambridge: Cambridge University Press, 1988, vii–xxxiv.

Abu-Lughod, Janet L. *Before European Hegemony: The World System A.D. 1250–1350*. New York: Oxford University Press, 1989.

Al-Jabarti, *Napoleon in Egypt: Al-Jabarti's Chronicle of the French Occupation, 1798*, edited by Jane Hathaway. Princeton: Markus Wiener Publishers, 2006.

———. *Al-Jabarti's History of Egypt*. Ed. by Jane Hathaway. Princeton: Markus Wiener Publishers, 2009.

al-Qifti, Ali Ibn Yusuf. *Ta'rikh al-hukama' (History of Learned Men)*. Excerpt, trans. by Emily Cottrell. The Blog of Coptic Literature, Culture & Politics. https://copticl iterature.wordpress.com/2017/10/05/the-account-of-the-arab-historian-al-qifti-on -the-destruction-of-the-library-of-alexandria/.

Anonymous review, *Edinburgh Review*, 45, 528–539.

Apuleius. *The Golden Ass*. Trans. by Sarah Ruden. New Haven: Yale University Press, 2011.

Aristotle. *The Basic Works of Aristotle*. Ed. by Richard McKeon. New York: The Modern Library, 2001.

Assmann, Jan. *The Mind of Egypt: History and Meaning in the Time of the Pharaohs*. Trans. by Andrew Jenkins. Cambridge, MA: Harvard University Press, 2003.

———. *Moses The Egyptian: The Memory of Egypt in Western Monotheism*. Cambridge, MA: Harvard University Press, 1997.

Atwood, Roger. *Stealing History: Tomb Raiders, Smugglers, and the Looting of the Ancient World*. New York: St. Martin's Press, 2004.

Baldwin, George. *Political Recollections Relative to Egypt; Containing Observations on Its Government under the Mamluks;—Its Geographical Position;—Its Intrinsic and Extrinsic Resources;—Its Relative Importance to England and France; and Its Dangers to England in the Possession of France: with A Narrative of the Ever-Memorable British Campaign in the Spring of 1801*. London, Printed by H.

Baldwin and Son, New Bridge-street; For T. Cadell, Jun., and W. Davies, in the Strand, 1801.

Barkan, Leonard. *Unearthing the Past: Archaeology and Aesthetics in the Making of Renaissance Culture.* New Haven: Yale University Press, 2001.

Barthes, Roland. *Image/Music/Text.* Trans. by Stephen Heath. New York: Farrar, Straus and Giroux, 1977.

Beiser, Frederick. *Hegel.* New York: Routledge, 2005.

Belzoni, Giovanni Battista. *Travels in Egypt and Nubia.* 1822; rpt. Vercelli, Italy: White Star, s.p.a., 2007.

Benz, Ernst. *The Theology of Electricity: On the Encounter and Explanation of Theology and Science in the 17th and 18th Centuries.* Princeton: Princeton University Press, 1989.

Bernal, Martin. *Black Athena: The Afroasiatic Roots of Classical Civilization.* Vol. I. Rutland, England: Rutland Local History & Record Society, 1987.

Bewell, Alan. "The Political Implication of Keats's Classicist Aesthetics." *Studies in Romanticism* 25 (1986): 220–229.

Blake, William. *The Complete Poetry and Prose of William Blake.* Ed. by David V. Erdman. New York: Random House, 1988.

Boehme, Jakob. *De Signatura Rerum* (The Signature of All Things). London: Forgotten Books, 2008.

———. *Mysterium Magnum, An Exposition of The First Book of Moses Called Genesis,* Vol. I. Trans. by John Sparrow. San Rafael: Hermetica, 2007.

Bonnet, Charles. *The Black Kingdom of the Nile.* Cambridge, MA: Harvard University Press, 2019.

The Book of Fate, [The Oraculum] *formerly in the possession of and used by Napoleon, rendered into the English language by H. Kirchenhoffer, from a German translation of an ancient Egyptian manuscript found in the year 1801 by M. Sonnini in one of the royal tombs near Mount Libycus in Upper Egypt.* New York: H.S. Nichols, 1823.

Bowden, Hugh. *Mystery Cults of the Ancient World.* Princeton: Princeton University Press, 2010.

Bowie, Andrew. *Schelling and Modern European Philosophy, An Introduction.* London: Routledge, 1993.

Brouzas, Christopher G. "Libraries in Ancient Athens." *The Classical Outlook* 29.2 (1951): 13–15.

Brown, Robert. *The Later Philosophy of Schelling: The Influence of Boehme on the Works of 1809–1815.* Lewisburg: Bucknell University Press, 1977.

Bruno, Giordano. *Cause, Principle and Unity, and Essays on Magic.* Trans. and ed. by Richard J. Blackwell and Robert de Lucca. Cambridge: Cambridge University Press, 1998.

Budge, E.A. Wallis. *Egyptian Magic.* 1901; rpt. Mineola, NY: Dover Pubs., 1971.

———. *The Nile: Notes for Travellers in Egypt.* London: Thomas Cook & Son, 1890.

Canfora, Luciano. *The Vanished Library: A Wonder of the Ancient World.* Berkeley and Los Angeles: The University of California Press, 1989.

Casson, Lionel. *Libraries in the Ancient World.* New Haven: Yale University Press, 2001.
Celadon. *The Golden Age, or The Future Glory of North America, Discovered by an Angel to Celadon in Several Entertaining Visions.* s.l., s.n., 1785.
Champollion, Jean-François. *Lettre à M. Dacier . . . relative à l'alphabet des hiéroglyphes phonétiques employés par les égyptiens pour inscrire sur leurs monuments les titres, les noms et les surnoms des souverains grecs et romains.* Paris: Didot, 1822.
Chauveau, Michel. *Egypt in the Age of Cleopatra: History and Society under the Ptolemies.* Trans. by David Lorton. Ithaca, NY: Cornell University Press, 2000.
Clark, David L. "Lost and Found in Translation." *Studies in Romanticism* (Summer–Fall 2007): 161–182.
———. "'The Necessary Heritage of Darkness': Tropics of Negativity in Schelling, Derrida, and de Man." In *Intersections, Nineteenth-Century Philosophy and Contemporary Theory.* Ed. by Tilottama Rajan and David L. Clark. Albany: State University of New York Press, 1995. 79–146.
Clayton, Peter A. *The Rediscovery of Ancient Egypt: Artists and Travellers in the 19th Century.* London: Thames and Hudson, 1982.
Cole, Juan. *Napoleon's Egypt: Invading the Middle East.* New York: Palgrave Macmillan, 2007.
Coleridge, S.T. *The Collected Works of Samuel Taylor Coleridge*: Vol. 16. Poetical Works: Part 2. 2 vols. Ed. by J.C.C. Mays. Princeton: Princeton University Press, 2001.
Colla, Elliott. *Conflicted Antiquities: Egyptology, Egyptomania, Egyptian Modernity.* Durham: Duke University Press, 2008.
Cooper, Basil. "Egyptology and the Two Exodes, A rare original article from the *British Quarterly Review*." Rpt. London: Jackson, Walford & Hodder, 1860.
De Quincey, Thomas. *Confessions of an English Opium-Eater and Other Writings.* Ed. by Robert Morrison. Oxford: Oxford University Press, 2013.
Déotte, Jean-Louis. "Rome, the Archetypal Museum, and the Louvre, the Negation of Division." In *Art in Museums.* Ed. by Susan Pearce. London: Athlone, 1995. 215–232.
Derrida, Jacques. *The Animal That Therefore I Am.* Ed. by Marie-Louise Mallet. Trans. by David Wills. New York: Fordham University Press, 2008.
———. *Archive Fever: A Freudian Impression.* Trans. by Eric Prenowitz. Chicago: University of Chicago Press, 1996.
———. "Différance." In *Margins of Philosophy.* Trans. by Alan Bass. Chicago: University of Chicago Press, 1982. 1–27.
———. *Glas.* Trans. by John P. Leavey, Jr. and Paul Rand. Lincoln: University of Nebraska Press, 1986.
———. *Khōra*, in *On the Name.* Trans. by David Wood, John P. Leavey, and Ian McLeod. Stanford: Stanford University Press, 1995. 89–127.
———. *Of Grammatology.* Trans. by Gayatri Chakravorty Spivak. Baltimore: The Johns Hopkins University Press, 1998.

———. *On Spirit: Heidegger and the Question.* Trans. by Geoffrey Bennington and Rachel Bowlby. Chicago: University of Chicago Press, 1989.

———. "The Original Discussion of Différance." Trans. by David Wood, Sarah Richmond, and Malcolm Bernard. In *Derrida and Différance.* Ed. by David Wood and Robert Bernasconi. Evanston: Northwestern University Press, 1985.

———. "The Pit and the Pyramid: Introduction to Hegel's Semiology." In *Margins of Philosophy.* Trans. by Alan Bass. Chicago: University of Chicago Press, 1982. 69–108.

———. "Post-Scriptum: Aporias, Ways and Voices." Trans. by John P. Leaey, Jr. In *Negative Theology.* Ed. by Harold Coward and Toby Foshay. New York: State University of New York Press, 1992. 283–323.

———. "Sauf le nom (Post-Scriptum)." In *On the Name.* Trans. by David Wood, John P. Leavey, Jr., and Ian McLeod. Stanford: Stanford University Press, 1995. 35–85.

———. "Scribble (Writing-Power)." *Yale French Studies,* In Memory of Jacques Ehrmann: Inside Play Outside Game 58 (1979): 117–147.

———. *Writing and Difference.* Trans. by Alan Bass. Chicago: University of Chicago Press, 1993.

Diderot, Denis. "Letter on the Deaf and Dumb." In *Diderot's Early Philosophical Works.* Trans. and ed. by Margaret Jourdain. Chicago: The Open Court Publishing Company, 1916. 158–218.

Diodorus Siculus, *The Library of History.* 12 vols. Loeb Classical Library. Cambridge, MA: Harvard University Press, 1933.

Diogenes Laertius, *Lives of Eminent Philosophers.* Trans. by R. D. Hicks. Cambridge, MA: Harvard University Press, 1925.

Doyle, Laura. *Freedom's Empire: Race and the Rise of the Novel in Atlantic Modernity, 1640–1940.* Durham: Duke University Press, 2008.

The Egyptian Book of the Dead: The Papyrus of Ani in the British Museum. Trans. by E.A. Wallis Budge. London: British Museum, 1895.

El Kadi, Galila and Alain Bonnamy, *Architecture for the Dead: Cairo's Medieval Necropolis.* Cairo: The American University in Cairo Press, 2007.

The English Standard Version Bible: Containing the Old and New Testaments with Apocrypha. Oxford: Oxford University Press, 2009.

The European Magazine and London Review. London, 1823.

Fadlan, Ibn. *Ibn Fadlan and the Land of Darkness: Arab Travellers in the Far North.* Trans. by Paul Lunde and Caroline Stone. New York: Penguin, 2012.

Fagan, Brian. *The Rape of the Nile: Tomb Robbers, Tourists, and Archaeologies in Egypt.* New York: Charles Scribner's Sons, 1975.

Fagenblat, Michael, editor. *Negative Theology as Jewish Modernity.* Bloomington: Indiana University Press, 2017.

Fay, Elizabeth. *Becoming Wordsworthian, A Performative Aesthetics.* Amherst: University of Massachusetts Press, 1995.

Foshay, Raphael. "'Tarrying with the Negative': Bataille and Derrida's Reading of Negation in Hegel's Phenomenology." *Heythrop Journal* XLIII (2002): 295–310.

Foucault, Michel. *Archaeology of Knowledge.* New York: Vintage Books, 1982.

———. *The Order of Things: An Archaeology of the Human Sciences.* New York: Random House, 1994.
Freud, Sigmund. *Moses and Monotheism.* New York: Vintage, 1955.
Furstenberg, François. *When the United States Spoke French: Five Refugees Who Shaped a Nation.* New York: Penguin, 2015.
Gasché, Rodophe. *The Tain of the Mirror: Derrida and the Philosophy of Reflection.* Cambridge, MA: Harvard University Press, 1986.
Gittings, Robert, ed. *Letters of John Keats.* Oxford: Oxford University Press, 1970.
Godwin, William. *Lives of the Necromancers.* London: Frederick J. Mason, 1834.
Gray, Ronald. *Goethe the Alchemist: A Study of Alchemical Symbolism in Goethe's Literary and Scientific Works.* Cambridge: Cambridge University Press, 1952.
Guyer, Paul. *Kant and the Claims of Taste.* Cambridge: Cambridge University Press, 1997.
Hadot, Pierre. *The Veil of Isis: An Essay on the History of the Idea of Nature.* Trans. by Michael Chase. Cambridge, MA: Belknap Press, 2006.
Halim, Hala. *Alexandrian Cosmopolitanism.* New York: Fordham University Press, 2013.
Hegel, Georg Wilhelm Friedrich. *Aesthetics: Lectures on Fine Art.* 2 vols. Trans. by T.M. Knox. Oxford: Clarendon Press, 1975.
———. *Between Fichte's and Schelling's System of Philosophy.* Albany: The State University of New York Press, 1977.
———. *Phenomenology of Spirit.* Trans. by A.V. Miller. Oxford: Oxford University Press, 1977.
———. *The Philosophy of Fine Art.* Trans. by F.P. B. Osmaston. 4 vols. London: Bell, 1920.
———. *Philosophy of History.* Trans. by J. Sibree. 1899; rpt. Mineola, NY: Dover Publications, 1956.
Hermetica: The Greek Corpus Hermeticum and the Latin Asclepius in a New English Translation. Notes and Introduction by Brian P. Copenhaver. Cambridge: Cambridge University Press, 1995.
Herodotus. *The Histories.* Trans. by Robin Waterfield. Oxford: Oxford University Press, 1998.
Herold, J. Christopher. *The Age of Napoleon.* Boston: Houghton Mifflin, 1987.
Hessayon, Ariel and Sarah Apetrei, eds. *An Introduction to Jacob Boehme: Four Centuries of Thought and Reception.* New York: Routledge, 2013.
Humboldt, Wilhelm Freiherr von. *On Language: The Diversity of Human Language-Structure.* Trans. by Peter Heath, intro. by Hans Aarsleff. Cambridge: Cambridge University Press, 1988.
Hutchinson, John. *A Catalogue of Notable Middle Templars, with Brief Biographical Notices.* London, 1902.
Jenkins, Ian. *Archaeologists and Aesthetes in the Sculpture Galleries of the British Museum 1800–1939.* London: British Museum Publications, 1995.
Johnson, Christopher. *System and Writing in the Philosophy of Jacques Derrida.* Cambridge: Cambridge University Press, 1993.

Journal of the Royal Asiatic Society of Great Britain and Ireland. Vol. 1 (January 1, 1834). Cambridge University Press for the Royal Asiatic Society.

Kant, Immanuel. *Critique of the Power of Judgment.* Trans. Paul Guyer. Rev. Ed. Cambridge: Cambridge University Press, 2000.

Kahn, Charles H. *Pythagoras and The Pythagoreans, A Brief History.* Indianapolis: Hackett Publishing, 2001.

Keats, John. "Hyperion." In *Keats's Poetry and Prose.* Ed. by Jeffrey N. Cox. New York: W.W. Norton, 2009. 475–496.

———. *Keats's Poetry and Prose.* Ed. by Jeffrey N. Cox. New York: W.W. Norton, 2009.

Kelley, Theresa. "Keats, Ekphrasis, and History." In *Keats and History.* Ed. by Nicholas Roe. Cambridge: Cambridge University Press, 1995. 212–237.

Krell, David Farrell. *The Tragic Absolute; German Idealism and the Languishing of God.* Bloomington: Indiana University Press, 2005.

Kristeva, Julia. *Desire in Language: A Semiotic Approach to Literature and Art.* Trans. by Thomas Gora, Alice Jardine, and Leon S. Roudiez. New York: Columbia University Press, 1980.

———. *Powers of Horror, An Essay on Abjection.* Trans. by Leon S. Roudiez. New York: Columbia University Press, 1982.

———. *Revolution in Poetic Language.* Trans. by Margaret Waller. New York: Columbia University Press, 1984.

Kuzniar, Alice. *Delayed Endings: Nonclosure in Novalis and Hölderlin.* Athens: University of Georgia Press, 1987.

Landor, Walter Savage. *Gebir: A Poem in Seven Books.* London: Cassell & Co, 1887.

Letters Received by Horace Hayman Wilson (1786 – 1860), British Library, India Office Records and Private Papers Archive, Mss Eur E301, vol 8 folio 1–2.

Levinas, Emmanuel. *Totality and Infinity: An Essay on Exteriority.* Trans. by Alphonso Lingis. Pittsburgh: Duquesne University Press, 1969.

Loris, Seth. *The Virtue of Sympathy: Magic, Philosophy, and Literature in Seventeenth-Century England.* New Haven: Yale University Press, 2015.

MacLeod, Roy, ed. *The Library of Alexandria.* London: I.B. Tauris, 2004.

Magee, Glenn Alexander. *Hegel and the Hermetic Tradition.* Ithaca: Cornell University Press, 2008.

Magnuson, Paul. *Reading Public Romanticism.* Princeton: Princeton University Press, 2014.

Manetho, *History of Egypt and Other Works.* Loeb Classical Library. Cambridge, MA: Harvard University Press, 1940.

de Manoncourt, Charles Nicolas Sigisbert Sonnini. *Travels in Upper and Lower Egypt, Undertaken by Order of The Old Government of France.* Trans. by Henry Hunter. New Edition. London: John Stockdale, 1807.

Mbembe, Achille. "Necropolitics." Trans. by Libby Meintjes. *Public Culture* 15.1 (2003): 11–40.

Mee, John. *Dangerous Enthusiasm: William Blake and the Culture of Radicalism in the 1790s.* Oxford: Oxford University Press, 1994.

———. "Is There an Antinomian in the House?" In *Historicizing Blake*. Ed. by Steve Clarke and David Worrall. Macmillan, 1994. 43–58.
Merleau-Ponty, Maurice. *Phenomenology of Perception*. New York: Routledge, 2012.
Mignolo, Walter D. *Local Histories/Global Designs: Coloniality, Subaltern Knowledges, and Border Thinking*. Princeton: Princeton University Press, 2012.
Montet, Pierre. *La Vie Quotidienne en Égypte au Temps des Ramsès*. Paris: Librairie Hachette, 1946.
The Monthly Review, Or, Literary Journal. Vol. 74. London, 1814.
Morgan, Diane. *Kant Trouble: The Obscurities of the Enlightened*. London: Routledge, 2000.
Morley, William Hook. *A Descriptive Catalogue of the Historical Manuscripts in the Arabic and Persian Languages Preserved in the Library of the Royal Asiatic Society of Great Britain and Ireland*. London: John W. Parker & Son, 1854.
———. "Letter to Major-General John Briggs, Honorary Secretary to the Royal Asiatic Society on the Discovery of Part of the Second Volume of The Jámi Al Tawár'kh of Rashíd al Dín." London, 1839.
———. The Morley Notebooks *C 46–49*, D 273, D 278, and E115. British Library, India Office Records and Private Papers, n.d.
Napoleon's Oraculum and Dreambook. New York: S.N., 1839.
Néret, Gilles, ed. *Description de l'Egypte: publiée par les orders de Napoléon Bonaparte*. Cologne: Taschen, 2007.
Nietzsche, Friedrich. *Nietzsche: Thus Spoke Zarathustra*. Ed. by Robert Pippin, trans. by Adrian Del Caro. Cambridge: Cambridge University Press, 2011.
———. *Twilight of the Idols and The Anti-Christ*. Trans. by R. J. Hollingdale. Harmondsworth: Penguin, 1968.
von Hardenberg (Novalis), Friedrich. "Logical Fragments I and II." In *Philosophical Writings*, Trans. by Margaret Mahony Stoljar. Albany: The State University of New York Press, 1997. 47–82.
———. *Notes for a Romantic Encyclopaedia*. Trans. by David W. Wood. Albany: The State University of New York Press, 2011.
———. *The Novices of Saïs*. Trans. by Ralph Manheim. Brooklyn: Archipelago Books, 2005.
Paracelsus. *Paracelsus, Essential Readings*. Trans. by Nicholas Goodrick-Clarke. Berkeley: North Atlantic Books, 1999.
Plato. *The Collected Dialogues of Plato, Including the Letters*. Ed. by Edith Hamilton and Huntington Cairns. Princeton: Princeton University Press, 1973.
Plutarch. *Moralia, Volume V, Isis and Osiris. The E at Delphi [sic]. The Oracles at Delphi No Longer Given in Verse. The Obsolescence of Oracles*. Loeb Classical Library. Cambridge, MA: Harvard University Press, 1936.
———. "On Isis and Osiris." In *Plutarch's Morals: Theosophical Essays* (1908). Trans. by Charles William King. 1908; rpt. Whitefish: Kessinger Publishing, 2006.
Pococke, Richard. *A Description of the East and some other Countries*. 2 vols. London: W. Boyer, 1743.

Pollard, Justin and Howard Reid. *The Rise and Fall of Alexandria, Birthplace of the Modern World*. New York: Viking Penguin, 2006.

Polwhele, Richard. *The Idyllia, Epigrams and Fragments of Theocritus, Bion, and Moscus; and the Elegies of Tyrtaeus*. Translated from the Greek, with dissertations and notes. In *The British Poets, Including Translations*. Chiswick: C. Whittingham, 1822.

Potts, D.T. "Before Alexandria: Ancient Libraries of the Ancient Near East." In *The Library of Alexandria*. Ed. by Roy MacLeod. London: I.B. Tauris, 2004. 19–33.

Quatremère de Quincy. *Considérations morales sur la destination des ouvrages de l'art. (1815)*. Paris: Fayard, 1989.

Raine, Kathleen. *Blake and Antiquity*. Abington, Oxon: Routledge & Kegan Paul, 1979.

Rancière, Jacques. *Mute Speech: Literature, Critical Theory, and Politics*. Trans. by James Swenson. New York: Columbia University Press, 1998.

Reeve, Clara. "The History of Charoba, Queen of Aegypt." In Reeve, *The Progress of Romance*. London: J. and J. Robinson, 1785.

Report of Annual Proceedings of the Royal Asiatic Society of Great Britain and Ireland, 1824–1834. London, 1834.

Roemer, Nils. *Jewish Scholarship and Culture in Nineteenth-Century Germany: Between History and Faith*. Madison: University of Wisconsin Press, 2005.

Rousseau, Jean-Jacques. *The First and Second Discourses together with the Replies to Critics and Essay on the Origin of Languages*. Ed. and trans. by Victor Gourevitch. New York: Harper and Row, 1986.

Russo, Lucio. *The Forgotten Revolution: How Science Was Born in 300 BC and Why It Had to Be Reborn*. Berlin: Springer-Verlag, 2004.

Salt, Henry. *Essay on Dr. Young's and M. Champollion's Phonetic System of Hieroglyphics: With Some Additional Discoveries*. Cambridge: Cambridge University Press, 2014.

Sanders, Paula. *Creating Medieval Cairo: Empire, Religion, and Architectural Preservation in Nineteenth-Century Egypt*. Cairo and New York: The American University in Cairo Press, 2008.

Schelling, Friedrich Wilhelm Joseph Von. *The Ages of the World*. Trans. by Jason M. Wirth. Albany: State University Press of New York, 2000.

———. *Bruno or On the Natural and the Divine Principle of Things*. Trans. by Michael G. Vater. Albany: State University of New York Press, 1984.

———. *Historical-critical Introduction to the Philosophy of Mythology*. Preface by Jason M. Wirth. Trans. by Mason Richey and Markus Zisselsberger. Albany: State University of New York Press, 2007.

———. *Philosophical Investigations into the Essence of Human Freedom*. Trans. by Jeff Love and Johannes Schmidt. Albany: State University of New York Press, 2006.

———. *System of Transcendental Idealism* (1800). Trans. by Peter Heath, and Introduction by Michael Vater. Charlotte: University of Virginia Press, 1993.

Schiff, Stacy. *Cleopatra: A Life*. New York: Little, Brown and Co., 2010.

Scott, C. Rochfort. *Rambles in Egypt and Candia, with Details of the Military Power and Resources of Those Countries, and Observations on the Government, Policy, and Commercial System of Mohammed Ali*. 2 vols. London: Henry Colburn, 1837.

Shelley, Mary. *The Last Man.* Ed. by Anne McWhir. Peterborough, Ontario: Broadview Press, 2014.

Shelley, Percy Bysshe. *Shelley's Poetry and Prose*, 2nd edition. Ed. by Neil Fraistat and Donald Reiman. New York: W.W. Norton, 2003.

Simmel, Georg. "The Ruin." In *Essays on Sociology, Philosophy and Aesthetics.* Ed. by Kurt H. Wolff. New York: Harper and Row, 1965. 259–266.

Sloterdjik, Peter. *Derrida, An Egyptian.* Cambridge: Polity Press, 2009.

St. Clair, William. *Lord Elgin and the Marbles*, 2nd edition. Oxford: Oxford University Press, 1983.

Starkey, Paul and Janet Starkey, eds. *Travellers in Egypt.* London: I.B. Tauris, 2001.

Steegmuller, Francis, trans. and ed. *Flaubert in Egypt: A Sensibility on Tour.* Chicago: Academy Chicago Press, 1987.

Steigerwald, Joan. "Epistemologies of Rupture: The Problem of Nature in Schelling's Philosophy." *Studies in Romanticism* 41.4 (2002): 545–584.

Strathern, Paul. *Napoleon in Egypt.* New York: Bantam/Random House, 2008.

Sweeney, Emmet, ed. *Ages in Alignment.* 4 vols. New York: Algora Publishing, 2006–2008.

Tang, Chenxi. *The Geographica Imagination of Modernity: Geography, Literature, and Philosophy in German Romanticism.* Stanford: Stanford University Press, 2008.

Terrada, Rei. "Looking at the Stars Forever." *Studies in Romanticism* 50.2 (2011): 275–309.

Thomson, James. *The Works of James Thomson, with his Last Corrections and Improvements.* 4 vols. Farmington Hills, MI: Gale Ecco Print Editions, 2010.

Volney, Constantin Francois. *The Ruins, or Meditation on the Revolutions of Empires.* Trans. by Joel Barlow. Paris: Levrault, 1802; Rpt. with additions, Boston: Josiah P. Mendum, 1869.

———. *Travels Through Syria and Egypt, in the years 1783, 1784, and 1785.* 2 vols. London: G.G.J. and J. Robinson, 1787.

Voltaire, François Marie Arouet de. *The Philosophy of History.* New York: Philosophical Library, 2007.

Warburton, William. *The Divine Legation of Moses Demonstrated on the Principles of a Religious Deist.* 2 vols. London: Printed for Thomas Tegg, 1738, 1741.

Warburton, William. *The Divine Legation of Moses Demonstrated.* 4 vols. New York: Garland Publishers, 1978.

Wasserman, Earl R. and Betty T. Bennett, Stuart Curran, eds. *Shelley: A Critical Reading.* Baltimore: Johns Hopkins University Press, 1977.

Wendorf, Richard. *The Elements of Life: Biography and Portrait-Painting in Stuart and Georgian England.* Oxford: Clarendon Press, 1990.

Williams, Frederick Lake. *Letter I. of a Series, on a Fragment of the . . . Statue of Amniphosis . . . or Memnon . . . Being the substance of a Letter to the Royal Antiquarian Society of London.* London: printed for the author and published by E. Wilson, 1815.

Wilson, N. G., ed. *Historical Miscellany.* Cambridge, MA: Harvard University Press, 1997.

Winkelmann, Johann Joachim. *Reflections on the Painting and Sculpture of The Greeks: with Instructions for the Connoisseur, and An Essay on Grace in Works of Art. Translated from the German Original of Abbé Winkelmann, Librarian of the Vatican, F.R.S., &c.&c.&c.* by Henry Fusseli, A.M. London: Printed for the translator, and sold by A. Millar, in the Strand, 1765.

Wirth, Jason M. Foreword to *Historical-critical Introduction to the Philosophy of Mythology.* Trans. by Mason Richey and Markus Zisselsberger. Albany: State University of New York Press, 2007. vii–xiii.

Witt, Reginald Eldred. *Isis in the Ancient World.* Baltimore: The Johns Hopkins University Press, 1997.

Wordsworth, William. *The Prelude: 1799, 1805, 1850.* Ed. by M.H. Abrams. New York: W.W. Norton, 1979.

Yates, Frances. *Gordano Bruno and the Hermetic Tradition.* Chicago: University of Chicago Press, 1964.

Young, Thomas. *An Account of Some Recent Discoveries in Hieroglyphical Literature and Egyptian Antiquities: Including the Author's Original Alphabet, as Extended by Mr. Champollion, with a Translation of Five Unpublished Greek and Egyptian Manuscripts.* London: John Murray, 1823.

Young, Thomas. *Hieroglyphics Collected by the Egyptian Society*, 2 vols. London: The Egyptian Society (Vol. I), and The Royal Society of Literature (Vol. 2), 1823.

Žižek, Slavoj. "The Abyss of Freedom." In *The Abyss of Freedom/Ages of the World* by F.W.J. Von Schelling. Ed. by Žižek. Ann Arbor: University of Michigan Press, 1997. 1–104.

———. *Tarrying with the Negative: Kant, Hegel, and the Critique of Ideology.* Durham: Duke University Press, 1993.

Index

aesthetics, xiii, 23–25, 29. *See also* Hegel, *Aesthetics*
Agrippa, Cornelius, 8, 11–12
Åkerblad, Johan David, 182, 201–2
alchemy, 1, 8, 10, 12–13, 43, 47, 53, 59, 67, 105–7, 132, 175–76
Alexander the Great, xii, xiv, xvi–xvii, xx, 3, 6, 11, 15, 18–20, 44–45, 47, 51–53, 55–58, 71, 78, 117, 126n8, 156–57, 165, 201
Alexandria, xii, xviii–xix, 3–4, 6–9, 11, 13–15, 20–21, 27–28, 30, 33, 36, 37n7, 37n16, 40n62, 41–45, 47–59, 75, 90, 112, 117, 125, 136, 156, 175, 199; Alexandrian Library, 3–5, 7–8, 14, 27, 36, 44–46, 49–50, 55, 58–60, 76, 83nn21–22, 84n25, 186, 188, 207; Alexandrian Museum, xvii, 3–4, 55
Al Dín, Rashíd, 190–92
Al-Jabartai, xviii, xix, xxi; *Chronicle of the French Occupation 1798*, xxi
Al-Qifti, Ali Ibn Yusuf, xx, 45–46, 82, 83n14; *History of Learned Men*, xx, 45, 83n14
Amenhotep III, 5, 37n14, 99–100, 102, 126, 127nn10–11
Ammon, 56
Amun-Re, 61, 84n30

Apis bull, xi, 4, 8, 56–57, 69, 124–25, 154; Serapium, 37n14
Apuleïus, 8, 12, 65
Aristotle, xvi, 3, 11, 14, 50, 55, 57, 79, 157, 207
Assmann, Jan, xxiin9, 68, 84n30, 146, 162, 171n100
Assurbanipal, library of, 58, 84n22
Assyria, 6, 15, 19–20, 29–30, 71–72, 131
astrology, 1, 3, 52–53

Bhagavad Gita, 66
Bankes, William John, 97, 199
Banks, Sir Joseph, 32, 40n63
Battle of the Nile, 33, 40n62, 96
Belzoni, Giovanni, 5, 35, 88–89, 99, 101, 124, 126n10
Bernal, Martin, *Black Athena*, x
Bewell, Alan, 30, 39n54
Bible, 51, 69, 126n2, 138, 187, 207; New Testament, 27, 66; Old Testament, 7, 117, 128n55, 158, 194, 206
Birch, Samuel, 189, 196
Blake, William, xx, 17, 43–44, 47, 59, 61–62, 67–68, 72–80, 83n9, 85n61; *Milton: A Poem in Two Books*, 73–75

Boehme, Jacob (Jakob Böhme), 47, 60, 62–63, 66–69, 71, 73, 82n3, 85n55, 85nn61–62, 90, 93, 133, 138–39, 141, 144–48, 150, 154, 162–63, 170n59; Behemism, 47, 60, 90; *On Generation and the Logos*, 62; *Mysterium Magnum*, 145, 170n59

Book of the Dead, 5, 13, 23, 38n25, 54, 105, 123, 157

Boswell, James, 87–88

Bracciolini, Poggio, 11

British Museum, 5–6, 29–30, 32–36, 38n25, 48, 88–89, 100–101, 126n10, 185, 188–89, 195–96, 199, 211n35

Bruno, Giordano, x–xi, xxi, 1, 9–15, 37nn20–21, 44, 47, 60, 68, 134, 144–45, 147–55, 157, 162–64; *Heroic Frenzies*, 13, 15, 152–53, 155, 163; *Spaccio della bestia trionfante*, 14–15, 145

Budge, Wallis, xi, 6, 38n25, 48, 171n84, 171n92

Burke, Edmund, 24, 92

Byron, Lord, 31–32, 35, 97, 113

Caesar, Julius, 46, 50, 78. *See also* Ptolemy XV

Cairo, xii, xix, 30, 33, 50, 90, 104, 113–14, 116, 128n42, 156, 171n91; City of the Dead, 112–18

Cambyses II, xiv, 4, 48, 117

Canfora, Lucian, 45–46, 50

Celadon, 17

Chaldea, 1, 3, 43, 52–55, 58–59, 69, 136, 177, 207

Champollion, Jean-François, xxi, 5, 33, 82, 97–98, 174–75, 178–79, 182, 194, 197–205, 208, 211n29

China, xv, 90, 92, 112, 126, 184, 193

Chinese, 38n41, 176, 179, 181, 184–85, 191–92, 196, 200, 206

Chinoiserie, 14

chora, xix, xxi, 133–35, 137–46, 150, 152–54, 157–59, 163, 165, 167, 169n39

Clark, David L., xxiin6, 11, 86n76, 145–48, 170n69

Cleopatra VII Philopator, 4, 37n14, 40n68, 46, 51–52

Coleridge, Samuel Taylor, 47, 62–63, 68, 87–89, 91, 126n2, 182

colossi, xiii, xvii, xxi, 1, 6, 25–26, 36, 52, 87, 97–103, 126, 127n12

Commission des Sciences et Arts d'Égypte, xiii, 5, 32–34, 53, 84n30, 90–91, 106

Coptic, 46, 82n7, 175–76, 202, 208

cosmology, xvi, 1, 8, 12–14, 44, 61, 74, 103, 141, 148, 155, 168n13, 170n54, 176

Darwin, Erasmus, 153, 175

Dee, John (London Hermetic circle), 14

Democritus, 42, 207

Denon, Baron Dominique Vivant, 33, 90

De Quincey, Thomas, 32, 35–36, 69, 182; *Confessions of an English Opium-Eater*, 28–29

De Quincy, Quatremère, 75–76, 191

Derrida, Jacques, xxiin5, 22, 37n22, 38n24, 57–58, 60, 79, 84n25, 89, 100, 102, 122, 126n3, 129n76, 134–35, 138–45, 150–54, 157–58, 163–64; *Glas*, 22, 100–102, 144, 171n84, 173–74, 177, 179, 210n11, 210nn16–18; *Of Grammatology*, xvi, xxiin5, 210n11; "Pit and the Pyramid," 79–80

De Sacy, Silvestre, 201–2, 204

Descriptions de l'Égypte, xiii

Diderot, Denis, 174

Dilettanti Society, 31

Diodorus Siculus, 2, 49–51, 98–100, 126nn8–9, 127n12, 203–4, 207; *Bibliotheca Historica*, 50, 98

Djoser, xii, 72, 112

Drovetti, Bernardino, 199

East India Company, xiv, 126, 181–82, 184–87, 191, 208–9; East India House, 192, 211n35

Eckhart, Meister, 60, 150, 154
Egypt: History of, xii, xix, xxiin9, 2, 7, 20, 49–50, 81, 126n8, 142, 156; Lower Egypt, 2, 17, 19, 21, 56, 112, 117; Upper Egypt, 2, 17, 19, 21, 56, 84n30
Egyptian Campaign. *See* Napoleon
Egyptian deities: Ammon, 56; Amun-Re, 61, 84n30; Horus, 16–19, 43, 48, 132, 138, 140, 153–54, 164, 167–68; Isis, xiv, xvii, 6, 8, 12–16, 36, 43, 57, 59, 65–71, 74–75, 104, 126n8, 131–32, 138–39, 142, 145, 149–58, 161–68; Osiris, 8, 16, 36, 43, 57, 124–25, 126n8, 131, 138, 142, 153, 162, 164–65, 167–68, 199; Ptah, 56, 57, 125; Ra, Rā, 16, 36, 132, 152–57, 164; Seshat, 5; Set, 131, 152–53, 164, 166–67; Thoth, x, 5–6, 8–9, 14, 36, 122–24, 135, 153, 177; Thoth-Hermes, 165, 210n11
Egyptian Hall, 29
Egyptianism, x–xi, xiv, xx–xxi, xxiin3, 2, 9–10, 13–15, 41, 44, 57, 60, 78, 149, 151, 157, 174, 186
Elgin Marbles, 28, 30–31, 39n54
Enlightenment, ix, xiii, xv–xvi, 12, 52, 91, 173, 175
Epicurus, 14–15, 43, 47
Euclid, xvi, 54, 75, 137
European Magazine and London Review, 198, 212n48
Eusebius, 64

Ficino, Marsilio, 7–9, 11–12, 37n11, 37n13, 133, 195; Florentine Academy, 7; *The Pimander*, 8
Foucault, Michel, 44, 102, 126, 177–78, 212n44
Freemasonry, 4, 21–22, 42, 47, 59, 75, 162
French Revolution, 34, 161; French Republic, xiv, 156
Freud, Sigmund, 13, 60, 148, 152, 164, 179; *Moses and Monotheism*, 13, 152

German Idealism, 10, 36, 133
Godwin, William, 11, 12, 73; *Lives of the Necromancers*, 11–12
Goethe, Johann Wolfgang von, 10, 47, 59, 66, 145, 175
gnostic, 8–9, 36, 91, 150
Greece, x, xii, xiv, 19–21, 42, 46, 47, 59, 76, 163, 171n91

Harpocrates, 43, 154
Haydon, Robert Benjamin, 30, 31, 39n54
Hebrew, 12, 29, 37n21, 121, 149, 174–76, 181, 182, 184, 191–92, 206–8, 210n17
Hecataeus of Abdera, 2, 4–5, 48, 50–51; *Aegyptiaca* (*History of Egypt*), 2, 49, 199
Hecataeus of Miletus, 48, 51
Hegel, G.W., xi–xiii, xv–xvi, 2, 4, 10, 15–16, 22–25, 29, 31–36, 37n6, 38n41, 43–44, 47, 61–63, 67, 69, 72, 75–82, 85n55, 88–90, 93, 96–97, 100–103, 118–25, 127n15, 132–33, 138, 143–45, 158–60, 164, 176, 194; *Aesthetics*, xx, 44, 72, 77, 78, 85n55, 89, 101, 120–22, 125, 143–44; *Phenomenology of Spirit*, 37n6, 89, 118, 129n67, 144, 158; *Philosophy of Fine Art*, 29; *Philosophy of History*, 64, 77
Heliopolis, 19, 28, 49
Hemans, Felicia, 33, 36
Hen kai pan (One in All), 67–68, 74, 85n46, 162
Hermes Trismegistus, xviii, 8, 43. *See also* Ficino, *The Pimander*
Hermeticism, xi, xvi, xviii, xx–xxi, 1–2, 4, 6, 8–9, 12–15, 23, 36, 43–44, 47, 49–50, 53, 59–61, 65–66, 69, 71, 73, 75, 77–81, 104, 120, 132–34, 138–39, 141, 148, 153, 155, 157, 162–64, 175–76, 183, 195, 206, 209; *Corpus Hermetica*, xviii, 8–9, 14, 37n10, 37n13, 43, 163
Herodotus, x, xviii–xix, 4–5, 7, 21, 27, 41, 48–49, 51, 64, 77, 88, 98–99,

102, 116–17, 121, 124, 126n8, 128n55, 142, 176, 196, 199, 203–4, 206
hieroglyphs, xii, xiv, xviii, xvi, xx–xxi, 4, 6–7, 10, 13–14, 24, 27, 40n63, 44, 49, 51, 54, 64–65, 69, 79–82, 90–91, 96–98, 102–8, 113, 117, 121–23, 126n6, 149, 168, 169n21, 173–79, 181–83, 185, 188, 194–206, 210n5, 210n17; demotic, xxi, 123, 175, 182, 196–209; hieratic, 33, 179, 196, 200, 203
Hölderlin, Friedrich, xvi, 59, 67, 119, 133, 143, 155, 158, 160–61, 163; *Hyperion*, 143, 163, 170n57
Horus. *See* Egyptian deities, Horus
hypocephalus, 48

India, xii, xiv–xv, 17, 26, 29, 33, 38n37, 38n41, 52, 70, 90, 92, 96, 112, 121, 156–57, 180–81, 183–84, 188, 191–93, 207
Institut d'Egypte, 33, 91
Isis: veil of Isis, 59, 68–69, 131, 162, 173. *See also* Egyptian deities, Isis
Island of Philoe, 116–17

Jefferson, Thomas, 41–42, 59, 82n2
Jones, Sir William, 161, 181, 206
Judeism, 2, 7–8, 13–14, 27, 152; Egypto-Judeo, 13

ka, 8, 21, 123, 143
Kabbalism, 1, 8, 13
Kant, Immanuel, 3, 20–26, 29, 38n41, 39n41, 47, 62, 66, 77, 82n6, 92, 148, 155, 159; *Critique of Judgment*, xx, 22, 77; *Dreams of a Spirit-Seer*, 23
Keats, John, xvi, xx–xxi, 17, 27–28, 30–31, 35–36, 47, 78, 80–82, 86n89, 96, 127, 158, 164–65; *Hyperion*, xvi, xx, 30–31, 86n89, 39n54; *Lamia*, xxi, 158, 164–67
Khufu (Cheops), xi, 25, 72, 114–15

Kircher, Athanasius, xiii, 9–12, 14, 16, 48, 54, 133, 173–74, 178–80, 194, 196, 200, 204, 120n16
Kristeva, Julia, 91, 139–40, 147, 153–54, 165, 169n39

Landor, Walter Savage, 40n68
Leibniz, Gottfried, xi, xiii, 24, 47, 108–11
Levinas, Emmanuel, 92, 94, 107
Linnaeus, Carl, 175–76
Llull, Raymond, 12, 47
Lucretius, 11–12, 42, 60–61; *De Rerum Natura*, 11, 14, 42–43, 60, 175
Luxor, xii, 104, 106, 114, 118

magic, xvii, xxi, 1, 3, 5–6, 8, 10, 12–13, 43, 46, 48, 53, 68–69, 75, 109, 124–25, 133, 138, 151, 153–58, 161–62, 164–66, 170n59, 174, 176, 206–7
Magnus, Albertus, 12
Mamluks, 115–16, 156, 171n91, 180, 189–90
Manetho, xviii, 37n9, 49, 56, 124, 128n55, 199; *Aegyptiaca* (*History of Egypt*), 33, 56, 199
Martin, John, 27–28
Memnon, 5, 29–31, 36, 87–88, 98–102, 126n10, 127n12
Memphis, xii, xix–xx, 2, 19, 51, 56–57, 65, 104, 112, 117, 124–25, 128n55
metaphysics, xvi–xvii, xx, 3, 23–24, 53, 58, 159, 174, 191, 194, 199–200, 205–6, 209
Middle Temple, 180–82, 185, 188, 190
Mignolo, Walter, 105, 127n32
Mirandola, Pico della, 12
Mohammed Ali, Viceroy of Egypt, 113
Monthly Review, 57
Morley, William Hook, xxi, 174, 179–209, 211nn26–28; *Jámi ul Hikáyát*, 182, 190–94
Moses, xi, xiii, xvii, 2, 6–8, 13, 65–66, 69, 88, 134, 152, 170n59, 177, 204, 207

mummies, xiii, xiv, 32–33, 65, 78, 80, 112, 115, 118, 121, 202
Muslim, xviii, 46, 90, 113, 115, 156, 191

Napoleon, Bonaparte, x, xiii–xiv, 5–6, 17, 28, 30–35, 52–53, 62, 76, 78, 83n16, 84n30, 90, 101, 156–57, 161, 194, 196, 199; Egyptian Campaign, x, xiv, 8, 28, 53, 83n16, 96, 104, 106, 129n55, 156
Naturphilosophie, xxi, 43–44, 155
Near East, 19, 26, 59, 92, 94, 96, 112, 180–81
necropolis, xii, xxi, 42, 69, 104–7, 109–14, 117, 120
necropolitics, xxi, 105, 112–13, 116
negative theology, 60, 62, 66, 85n32, 150, 152–53, 159
Neo-Egyptianism, 111, 174
Neoplatonism, 1, 7–8, 43, 59, 141, 150
Nietzsche, 28, 78; *Thus Spoke Zarathustra*, 28
Nineveh, xv, 128n55
Novalis, (Georg Philipp Friedrich Freiherr von Hardenberg), xvi, 1, 4, 10, 12, 23, 131, 136, 158, 164, 161, 164, 167–68; *Logical Fragments*, 173; *Novices of Saïs*, xxi, 72, 138, 152, 158, 162–63, 172n106
Nubia, 20, 71–72, 104, 160

obelisk, x–xii, xvii, 1, 6, 25–28, 31, 52, 54, 101–2, 104, 106, 114, 119, 149, 153, 178, 203
Oraculum, 6, 156–57
Osiris. *See* Egyptian deities, Osiris
Ottoman Empire, xiv, 16, 19, 20, 30, 33, 42, 116, 193; Ottoman Egypt, xiv, xvii–xx, 32, 44–46, 50, 93, 156, 171n91

Paracelsus, 11–12, 47, 62, 73, 85n61, 132, 135

Persia, xii, xiv, xix, 4, 19–20, 45, 48, 52, 56, 59, 72, 83n21, 112, 117, 177, 180, 188, 191, 193; Persian, 181–87, 190–92, 197, 202, 207–9, 212n40, 213n71
Philoponus, John, 45, 50
Plato, x, xxiin3, 3, 8, 11, 37n10, 43, 52, 55, 57, 59–61, 65, 86n69, 108, 132–36, 143, 147–51, 155, 159, 207; *Republic*, 74, 77; *Symposium*, 3; *Timaeus*, x, xxi, xxiin3, 4, 39n53, 55, 60, 73, 119, 133–46, 152–53, 155–56, 158, 161, 163–66, 169n51
Plutarch, x, 65, 69, 131, 153, 164; "Isis and Osiris," 69, 71, 132–36, 139, 153
Pococke, Richard, xi–xii, 32, 98
Polwhele, Rev. Richard, 51
potencies, 22, 66, 80, 90, 95, 119
Ptah. *See* Egyptian deities, Ptah
Ptolemy, Claudius, 52, 54
Ptolemy I (Ptolemy Soter), xvi, 2, 6–7, 20, 33, 45, 47, 49, 51, 55–58, 117, 199, 201
Ptolemy IV Philopator, 54
Ptolemy XV Caesar (Caesarion), 208
Ptolemy XVI Philadelphius, 45, 208
pyramid, xi–xii, 1, 22–23, 26–27, 32, 72, 75, 79–80, 87, 90, 101–4, 106, 112–14, 117–21, 127n15, 143–45, 153, 201; Giza pyramids, xi–xii, 25, 45, 72, 104, 112–13, 116, 136; Khufu, xi, 25, 72, 114; Saqqara, xi–xii, 37n14, 50, 56, 72, 112, 117–18, 124
Pythagoras, 3, 8, 12, 37n11, 43, 54–55, 65, 74, 83n17, 86n69, 133, 135, 137, 149, 168n13, 169n21, 177; Pythagorean cult, 8, 43, 134

Q'uran, 45

Rā. *See* Egyptian deities, Rā
Ramesses II (Gr. Ozymandias), 4–6, 30–31, 35, 37n14, 72, 88, 97–100
Ramesseum, 4–5, 58, 98–99, 127n11

Reeve, Clara, 40n68, 180
Rosetta Stone, 10, 33, 40n63, 96, 194, 196–98, 200, 202, 204; Rosetta, 115, 198
Rousseau, Jean-Jacques, ix, 177, 179
Royal Asiatic Society of Great Britain and Ireland, xxi, 181–82, 185–90, 206, 208, 211n36

Säis, 36, 55, 70–71, 131, 142–43, 161, 170n54
Salt, Henry, xiv, 32, 35–36, 198
Sanskrit, 68, 161–62, 183, 187, 206, 209
Schelling, F.W. J., xi, 10, 13, 15, 23, 38n29, 43–44, 47, 59–73, 77–78, 87–88, 94–95, 119, 132–33, 137–41, 145–49, 151–52, 154–55, 158–60, 167, 172n129; *Ages of the World (Die Weltalter)*, xx–xxi, 13, 44, 60–63, 66, 68, 72–73, 82, 85n55, 87, 90, 140, 145, 148–49, 152–53, 155, 157–59, 161, 163–64; *Bruno, or On the Natural and Divine Principle of Things*, xx–xxi, 14–15, 38n29, 151, 155; *Deities of Samothrace*, 158; *Treatise on the Essence of Human Freedom*, xxi, 145, 147–48, 157, 167
Scott, C. Rochefort, xxi, 113–18, 128n55; *Rambles in Egypt and Candia*, xxi, 113–18
Seleucus, 45, 58
Serapis, 8, 43, 56–57, 59, 65, 125, 154
Set. *See* Egyptian deities, Set
Seti I, 89, 91, 100
Shakespeare, *Antony and Cleopatra*, xii, 52, 197
Shelley, Mary, xx, 17, 27, 35–36, 43–44, 69–76, 80, 82, 93, 113; *The Last Man*, xx, 27, 35, 45, 69–72, 74, 93, 104, 183
Shelley, Percy Bysshe, xvi, 5, 59, 64, 70, 96; *Alastor*, xxi, 103–11, 118, 127nn26–27, 128n38, 183; "Ozymandias," xxi, 5, 96–103
Silk Route, xii, xiv
Simmel, Georg, 106, 109–10
Sloane, Sir Hans, 163
Sloterdijk, Peter, 2, 37n22
Soane, Sir John, 35–36, 89, 91
sphinx, 25–30, 35, 72, 79, 96, 104, 106, 118, 122, 205; Great Sphinx, 25–26, 45–46, 72, 106, 154
Spinoza, xvi, 13, 68, 162
Strato of Lampsacus, 57
sublime, xii, 14–15, 22, 26, 92, 94, 102–3, 121
Swedenborg, Emanuel, 23, 73, 85n61

Tacitus, 102, 121
Thebes, xii, xx, 2, 4, 17, 19, 28, 30, 48, 50–51, 56, 84n30, 104, 129n55, 131, 198–99
Thoth. *See* Egyptian deities, Thoth
Thucydides, 77
Thutmose III, 36, 37n14
translation, xii, xv–xviii, 5, 7–10, 12–13, 17–18, 54, 78, 82n2, 82n7, 95, 110–11, 115, 119, 128n38, 138, 150–52, 166, 183, 185–88, 190–94, 198, 202, 204, 212n41, 212n56
Travels of Mirza Abu Taleb Khan, xix
Turin Museum, 36, 153, 199

Ungrund, 13, 20, 22, 41, 62, 89, 93, 95, 141, 145, 147–48, 157–58, 167–68, 209

Valley of the Kings, 5, 39n59, 105, 112, 124
Volney, Comte de, 16–17, 19, 28, 41–42, 53, 62–63, 82, 83n16, 92, 160; *Ruins of Empire*, xv–xvi, xx–xxi, 6, 9, 16–20, 28, 41–42, 53, 63, 83n16, 116, 155–56, 160; *Voyage en Egypte et en Syrie*, 41

Voltaire, 64–66; *Philosophy of History*, 64

Warburton, Rev. William, 177–78, 204, 210nn16–17
Wedgwood, 35, 40n67
Wilkinson, John Gardner, 35
Wincklemann, Johann Joachim, 29, 39n53, 75–78, 144, 160; *History of Art in Antiquity*, 144
Wordsworth, William, xv, 17, 34–36, 93–94, 118, 127n26, 180; lyric poems, 94, 118; *The Prelude*, 93, 137
writing systems, xvi–xvii, xxi, 174, 176–78, 195–96, 199, 206, 208

Young, Thomas, 97, 182, 185, 194–95, 197–98, 200–203, 205–6, 208–9, 212n43, 212n48

Zizek, Slavoj, 119, 163–66
Zoroaster, 8, 12; Zoroastrianism, 12, 53, 68

About the Author

Elizabeth A. Fay is professor of English at the University of Massachusetts Boston. She specializes in British Romantic literature and has published four previous monographs on British Romantic topics, including *Fashioning Faces: The Portraitive Mode in British Romanticism* (2010), *Romantic Medievalism: History and the Romantic Literary Ideal* (2002), *A Feminist Introduction to Romanticism* (1998), and *Becoming Wordsworthian: A Performative Aesthetics* (1995). She has also published a monograph on feminist rhetoric, and has coedited two volumes of essays, including *Urban Identity and the Atlantic World* (2013). She has also coedited a scholarly edition, *Felicia Hemans's Siege of Valencia: A Parallel Text* (2002).

www.ingramcontent.com/pod-product-compliance
Lightning Source LLC
Chambersburg PA
CBHW020114010526
44115CB00008B/830